DEATH AND TRAUMA

THE SERIES IN TRAUMA AND LOSS

CONSULTING EDITORS
Charles R. Figley and Therese A. Rando

Figley, Bride, and Mazza   *Death and Trauma: The Traumatology of Grieving*

ISSN 1090-9575

DEATH AND TRAUMA
The Traumatology of Grieving

edited by

Charles R. Figley
Psychological Stress Research and Development Program
Florida State University
Tallahassee, Florida

Brian E. Bride
St. Jude's Recovery Center, Inc.
Atlanta, Georgia

Nicholas Mazza
School of Social Work
Florida State University
Tallahassee, Florida

Taylor & Francis
Publishers since 1798

USA	Publishing Office:	Taylor & Francis 1101 Vermont Avenue, NW, Suite 200 Washington, DC 20005-3521 Tel: (202) 289-2174 Fax: (202) 289-3665
	Distribution Center:	Taylor & Francis 1900 Frost Road, Suite 101 Bristol, PA 19007-1598 Tel: (215) 785-5800 Fax: (215) 785-5515
UK		Taylor & Francis Ltd. 1 Gunpowder Square London EC4A 3DE Tel: 171 583 0490 Fax: 171 583 0581

DEATH AND TRAUMA: The Traumatology of Grieving

1 2 3 4 5 6 7 8 9 0   B R B R   9 8 7

This book was set in Times Roman. The editors were Catherine Simon and Caroline Schweiter. Cover design by Ed Atkeson, Berg Design.

A CIP catalog record for this book is available from the British Library.

⊚The paper in this publication meets the requirements of the ANSI Standard Z39.48-1984 (Permanence of Paper)

Library of Congress Cataloging-in-Publication Data

Death and trauma: the traumatology of grieving/edited by Charles R.
  Figley, Brian E. Bride, and Nicholas Mazza.
    p. cm.—(The series in trauma and loss)
  Includes bibliographical references.
  1. Bereavement—Psychological aspects. 2. Post-traumatic stress
disorder. 3. Sudden death—Psychological aspects. 4. Grief
therapy. 5. Post-traumatic stress disorder—Treatment. I. Figley,
Charles R. II. Bride, Brian E. III. Mazza, Nicholas.
IV. Series
RC455.4.L67D43   1997
155.9'37—dc21   96-47172
                                             CIP

ISBN 1-56032-525-9 (case)
ISBN 1-56032-526-7 (paper)
ISSN 1090-9575

For my father, John David Figley (1923–1980)—C.R.F.
For my grandparents, Allan Francis Bride (1915–1996)
and Ida Frohman Bride (1922–   )—B.E.B.
For my mother, Catherine Giordano Mazza (1914–1995)—N.M.

Contents

PART I: CONCEPTUAL SYNTHESIS

PART III: GENERIC TREATMENT APPROACHES

Contributors

JOHN E. BAKER, Ph.D.
Clinical Instructor in Psychology
  (Psychiatry)
Harvard Medical School
  at the Cambridge Hospital
Cambridge, Massachusetts
Consulting Psychologist
Family Service Clinic at Middlesex
  Probate Court
Cambridge, Massachusetts
Private Practice
Belmont, Massachusetts

JOANNE CALLAHAN
Thought Field™ Therapy Training Center
Indian Wells, California

ROGER J. CALLAHAN, Ph.D.
Thought Field™ Therapy Training Center
Indian Wells, California

KATHLEEN R. GILBERT, Ph.D.
Department of Applied Health Science
Indiana University
Bloomington, Indiana

SUSAN H. HORWITZ, M.S.
Division of Family Programs
Department of Psychiatry
University of Rochester Medical Center
Rochester, New York

KATHLEEN O. NADER, DSW
Private Practice, Consultation,
  and Training
Laguna Hills, California

LASSE A. NURMI, M.A.
Senior Lecturer and Psychologist
Police Academy
Espoo, Finland

FRANCINE SHAPIRO, Ph.D.
Mental Research Institute
Palo Alto, California

MICHAEL A. SIMPSON, M.D.,
  M.R.C.Psych.
Center for Psychosocial and Traumatic
  Stress
Medical University of South Africa
Pretoria, South Africa

ROGER M. SOLOMON, Ph.D.
On Site Academy
Gardner, Massachusetts

ANNE SPECKHARD, Ph.D.
Family Systems Center
Alexandria, Virginia

ARLENE STEINBERG, Psy.D.
(Adjunct) Assistant Professor
Teachers College
Columbia University
New York, New York
Private Practice
New York, New York

MARY BETH WILLIAMS, Ph.D.
Trauma Recovery, Education,
  and Counseling Center
Warrenton, Virginia

Foreword

The woman in the audience was nodding her head vigorously. It was one of those agreements with my words as a speaker that I long ago learned signals the person's having "been there, done that." On this occasion, I was talking about what tends to get lost when a traumatic death is approached either exclusively as a trauma or solely as a loss. At the midmorning break in the conference, she approached me with her personal story. When she was 6 years old, she had discovered her father's body hanging in their garage after a successful suicide attempt. Concerned about the impact upon the little girl, her family immediately brought her for psychological assistance. For the next half century, the woman saw a succession of therapists who, in varying degrees and fashions, addressed with her the psychological impacts of growing up fatherless. However, it would be fully 50 years after her father's death before one therapist finally asked her the crucial question to start her on the road to healing: "Exactly what did you see when you found your father?" At long last, someone had begun to tap into her experience of the horrific event that had stimulated the unresolved post-traumatic stress preventing her from achieving closure on the loss.

While, in this case, those specializing in bereavement had missed the boat in overlooking the trauma brought about by the circumstances of the death, it might just as easily have been a trauma expert who failed to recognize the loss issues. In fact, it's not too much of a stretch, if any, to state that in general traumatologists know little to nothing about loss and, conversely, thanatologists know about the same amount regarding trauma. This is quite alarming given that, by definition, in all trauma there is loss and in the majority of losses there is significant trauma. Unfortunately, the fields of traumatology and thanatology —although conceptually, clinically, and often empirically associated—have remained relatively independent, with scenarios such as that described above among the regrettable consequences.

The curious separation between the two dovetailing fields is kept in force by significant misconceptions in both camps. Traumatology, with its tenets much more clearly embedded in psychiatry than are thanatology's, suffers from the adoption of that discipline's narrow vision with regard to loss, bereavement, grief, and mourning. Currently, there exists no diagnostic category for complicated bereavement in the DSM-IV (*Diagnostic and Statistical Manual of Mental Disorders*, American Psychiatric Association, 1994). Attempts had been made to rectify the serious conceptual and clinical errors and omissions regarding uncomplicated, as well as complicated, bereavement in the DSM. However, it essentially was suggested that thanatologists content themselves with locating complicated bereavement under the existing diagnostic subcategory of depressive disorders. Such an uncritical acceptance of the general myth that depression is the primary symptom revealing problems after loss is an indication of a general lack of understanding about the issue. If complicated bereavement had to be placed under only one of the current diagnostic categories, on the basis of current empirical and clinical data it would more correctly be located under the anxiety disorders. Given that traumatology draws so significantly from an area that in general sustains somewhat indifferent attitudes toward loss and its aftermath, it is not surprising that the traumatologists have paid so little attention to loss and the phenomena of grief and mourning.

From the thanatological side, there are also important errors and oversights. Chief among these is the overutilization of models and expectations of bereavement originally generated from White, middle-class women who had lost their husbands within the previous year. Depending upon the particular constellation of factors circumscribing a given death, these models—and the treatment implications associated with them—may be quite inappropriate for a traumatic death, hurting, rather than merely not helping, the bereaved survivors. Coinciding with this is thanatology's propensity to focus on bereavement as a "loss" experience solely, and thus to disregard or completely dismiss the post-traumatic sequelae that eventuate when the death involves traumatic characteristics.

Essentially, what occurs is that each field addresses the issues it has been trained to identify and treat. Consequently, after a death under traumatic circumstances, the traumatologists focus on trauma mastery and the thanatologists focus on accommodation of loss. Unfortunately, what the traumatically bereaved individual requires is assistance with both. While a few authors in each field have recognized this important reality—for example, Eth and Pynoos (1985) and Lindy (1986) in traumatology and Raphael (1986) and Redmond (1989) in thanatology—the vast majority of authors, researchers, and practitioners in both fields have insufficiently integrated treatment of post-traumatic stress and loss when working with such survivors.

The reality is that traumatically bereaved individuals need therapists who understand post-traumatic stress, comprehend loss (physical, psychosocial, and secondary) and its consequent grief and mourning, and know how to intervene in both areas separately and in conjunction. These therapists must remain cognizant of four very important points:

1   Uncomplicated acute grief, in and of itself, is a form of post-traumatic stress disorder (PTSD). Similarity of PTSD and grief is found in three

broad areas: their manifest symptomatology, their alternating modes of denial/inhibition and intrusion/facilitation experienced during the working-through process, and their ultimate treatment requirements for cognitive completion with affective release. This necessitates the working through of related affects, integration of conscious and dissociated aspects, mourning of relevant secondary physical and psychosocial losses, acquisition of new ways of being to move adaptively into the new world, development of a comprehensive perspective on the event and one's level of control therein, emotional relocation of what was lost, acceptance of fitting responsibility and relinquishment of inappropriate guilt, revisions of the assumptive world demanded by the event and its repercussions, creation of meaning out of the experience, integration of the event into the totality of one's life, formation of a new identity reflecting survival of the event, and appropriate reinvestment in life (Rando, 1994).

2   There are six factors that make any death circumstance traumatic, and that alone or in combination generate post-traumatic stress above and beyond that found in uncomplicated acute grief. The six factors making any death circumstance traumatic include suddenness and lack of anticipation; violence, mutilation, and destruction; preventability and/or randomness; loss of a child; multiple death; and the survivor's personal encounter with death secondary to either a significant threat to survival or a massive and/or shocking confrontation with the death and mutilation of others (Rando, 1994).

3   A death that is traumatic constitutes a high risk factor for the development of complicated mourning on the part of the survivor. Therefore, traumatically bereaved individuals tend to require intervention that is more than mere grief facilitation.

4   After a traumatic death, the particular configuration of post-traumatic stress in relation to grief points to specific treatment implications. Where there is an overlay of significant post-traumatic symptomatology blanketing mourning, full-scale intervention for post-traumatic stress must precede work on loss-related aspects of grief and mourning. When post-traumatic elements are interspersed within the grief and mourning, selected techniques for working through post-traumatic symptomatology can be incorporated into overall interventions for grief and mourning, and both issues can be addressed simultaneously or intermittently (Rando, 1993).

Finally, there is a book that incorporates these crucial points and begins to detail for the reader the pivotal theoretical and clinical issues present when trauma and loss intersect. *Death and Trauma: The Traumatology of Grieving* is the first volume devoted entirely to a conceptual and phenomenological exploration of traumatic bereavement—or, as termed on occasion herein, death-related PTSD. The book is the first with a purpose to delineate effective coping strategies for mourners within specific contexts of traumatic death, along with generic treatment approaches applicable to survivors of all types of traumatic death. Thus, this important book defines for the therapist both the precise methods of coping that have proven therapeutic for a variety of traumatically bereaved individuals and the precise types of intervention that can enable these to occur.

The editors of this book, Charles R. Figley, Brian E. Bride, and Nicholas Mazza, have begun officially to bridge the gap that has existed between traumatology and thanatology. Commencing to rectify the previously identified problems resulting from the inadequate integration of trauma and loss, they have provided a compendium of theoretical and practical resources for those committed to intervening in traumatic bereavement.

Of special note for front line clinicians reading this book is the matrix from which the chapters spring. The Preface and the first three chapters, which provide such specific conceptual syntheses, anchor the clinical chapters. This volume gives the reader both the abstract protocols and the discrete information necessary to be able in any context to identify and appreciate the similarities, differences, and combinations of trauma and loss in terms of their experiences, sequelae, and treatment demands. Specific clinical data regarding coping mechanisms and intervention, provided in the nine subsequent chapters, facilitate the application of this knowledge in a variety of contexts and via a variety of treatment approaches. Thus, both process and content are supplied for treatment of traumatic bereavement.

The particular contexts addressed in this volume yield investigations into areas of traumatic bereavement that traditionally have been underappreciated. Traumatic pregnancy loss, the death of a child, children experiencing parental loss, elementary school children encountering the deaths of peers in catastrophic events, the death of a co-worker—all provide valuable and relevant areas of inquiry as unique scenarios embodying significant areas of trauma and loss. Successful coping strategies for the bereaved are delineated, along with effective intervention methods and guidelines for their therapists. These potent chapters are unusually effective in portraying the experience of traumatic bereavement and then highlighting specifics to enable the successful working through of it.

The chapters on generic treatment approaches offer interventions and models that are applicable across a variety of traumatic loss situations. Starting from the perspective of traumatized parents struggling to function in the family following the death of one of their loved ones, proceeding to a model for family therapy following the death of a family member, and concluding with two bizarre-appearing, but impressively effective, methods for treating trauma-induced distress, this section provides the reader with well-defined clinical tools to add to the armamentarium brought to bear in working with the traumatically bereaved. Like the rest of the book, the integration of theory, experience, and intervention of a combined trauma and loss experience undergirds these chapters.

Because of a number of contemporary sociocultural and technological trends, the proportion of natural deaths occurring in Western society is decreasing while the proportion of traumatic deaths is increasing (Rando, 1992–93). This translates to the clinician's seeing escalating numbers of cases involving traumatic loss. For this reason, the therapeutic guidelines and intervention strategies proposed in this book—either for specific contexts or for generic treatment protocols—will become increasingly relevant to all therapists, whether they are identified with traumatology, thanatology, or neither one. The reality is that traumatic bereavement will become—if it has not already—a significant focus of attention in the consulting room of the contemporary psychotherapist. This book will be a mainstay in his or her professional library.

Whenever there is a fundamental shift in the nature of things, it should be noted. *Death and Trauma: The Traumatology of Grieving* signals the arrival of a long overdue change in our thinking about and practice of intervention in loss occurring in traumatic circumstances. The editors and contributors are to be congratulated in breaking through the previous boundaries and misconceptions that have artificially dichotomized traumatology and thanatology, and for providing us therapeutic paradigms and skills to understand and treat the experiences entailing both trauma and loss.

Therese A. Rando, Ph.D.
Institute for the Study and Treatment of Loss
Warwick, Rhode Island

REFERENCES

American Psychiatric Association. (1994). *Diagnostic and statistical manual of mental disorders* (4th ed.). Washington, DC: Author.

Eth, S., & Pynoos, R. (Eds.). (1985). *Post-traumatic stress disorder in children.* Washington, DC: American Psychiatric Press.

Lindy, J. (1986). An outline for the psychoanalytic psychotherapy of post-traumatic stress disorder. In C. Figley (Ed.), *Trauma and its wake: Traumatic stress theory, research, and intervention* (Vol. 2, pp. 195–212). New York: Brunner/Mazel.

Rando, T. (1992–93). The increasing prevalence of complicated mourning: The onslaught is just beginning. *Omega: Journal of Death and Dying, 26*(1), 43–59.

Rando, T. (1993). *Treatment of complicated mourning.* Champaign, IL: Research Press.

Rando, T. (1994). Complications in mourning traumatic death. In I. Corless, B. Germino, & M. Pittman (Eds.), *Death, dying, and bereavement: Theoretical perspectives and other ways of knowing* (pp. 253–271). Boston: Jones and Bartlett.

Raphael, B. (1986). *When disaster strikes: How individuals and communities cope with catastrophe.* New York: Basic Books.

Redmond, L. (1989). *Surviving: When someone you love was murdered.* Clearwater, FL: Psychological Consultation and Education Services.

Preface

Perhaps my interest in the traumatizing nature of death started on the battlefield. Although it was my misfortune to end up as a Marine in Vietnam in the mid-1960s, I was fortunate enough not only to survive, but to witness how large numbers of men coped with the traumatic death of close friends. I was fresh out of high school, and my observations were both spontaneous and unsystematic. It was not until I was completing my master's thesis at Penn State University in 1972 that I began to interview Vietnam combat veterans about their war experience and the long-term impact it had on them.

For the next 5 years I interviewed nearly 600 war veterans. Throughout this program of research, those I interviewed continually mentioned the pain of living with the loss of friends and comrades, in addition to the loss of their own innocence as boys and young men and the loss of their sense of invulnerability.

However, my primary research focus was—then and always—on the "so what?" question. I was concerned about the research implications for helping in the recovery process. And most often this involved the interpersonal and support networks of these men: their families.

Those few of us in the 1970s interested in traumatic stress were drawn together by our interest in the impact of death and dying on the human functioning of the survivors. Lifton's (1969) "death imprint" (the radical intrusion of a memory of an image or feeling) and death anxiety occur across traumatic events. Yet, unfortunately, when the diagnosis of post-traumatic stress disorder (PTSD) emerged from the third revision of the *Diagnostic and Statistical Manual of Mental Disorders* (DSM-III; American Psychiatric Association, 1980), death, grief, bereavement, and the like were missing from any discussion of what constitutes a traumatic event. Despite this, traumatology quickly evolved into a field of its own (Donovan, 1991; Figley, 1988) and now claims an impressive body of literature, several journals, and various international associations. Yet, the gulf that separates traumatology from the field of thanatology is largely artificial.

In the 1980s, an appreciation for wide variations in the grief process emerged. Thanks largely to the innovative work of Rando (1983, 1984, 1988, 1993) and

Raphael (1983, 1986) building upon the innovation of Lehrman (1956), Parkes and Brown (1972), and Parkes and Weiss (1983), a much more complicated view of bereavement that is informed by the traumatic nature of the circumstances of death emerged. Parkes and Weiss (1983) called this "conflicted mourning." Raphael (1983) called it "distorted mourning."

According to Rando (1993), in complicated mourning, "given the amount of time since the death, there is some compromise, distortion, or failure of one or more of the six 'R' processes of mourning" (p. 149). These processes are (a) recognize the loss, (b) react to the separation, (c) recollect and reexperience the deceased and the relationship, (d) relinquish old attachments to the deceased and the old assumptive world, (e) readjust to move adaptively into the new world without forgetting the old, and (f) reinvest. The experience of bereavement and mourning is especially subjective, and what is a "normal" death of a loved one to one person may be extremely abnormal and consequently extremely stressful to another.

Other than some isolated efforts (Redmond, 1989), no model has emerged to treat traumatic bereavement within a systemic context: to treat the entire family that is traumatized simultaneously as a result of the death of someone valued by a family.

GRIEF COUNSELING

The specialization of grief counseling includes bereavement and death studies. This literature has always focused on traumatic stress, though the term is rarely used. More importantly for this book, the field of thanatology has always been concerned with family and other systems and how they cope with death. Although they rarely use systems or family social science concepts, grief specialists have always been concerned about the consequences of survivorship among members of a family or system that has lost a member through death.

TRAUMA COUNSELING

Surprisingly, the traumatology literature rarely notes the traumatic nature of surviving the death of a loved one. Thus, neither literature references the other in spite of the fact that bereavement so closely parallels traumatic stress reactions, and various forms of dysfunctional/abnormal bereavement parallel PTSD.

The diagnosis of PTSD applied to death and bereavement may be discouraged by the very document that helped begin the field of traumatology: the DSM. It has been argued that because nearly everyone experiences the death of a family member, friend, or acquaintance, the inclusion of death as a stressor for survivors would trivialize PTSD. But after a decade of use, that argument seems erroneous at best and irresponsible at worst.

PURPOSE OF THIS BOOK

This book attempts to link the parallel fields of thanatology and traumatology. Specifically, the purpose of the book is fourfold: First, the book is to provide a theoretical bridge between the two fields by providing the conceptual terminology, such as defining "normal" versus "dysfunctional" bereavement and defining the meaning and range of death-related PTSD.

Second, the book is to confirm and illustrate the identical patterns of reactions between those who survive the death of a loved one and those who survive other types of traumatic events. This effort is part of the natural development of a field, or in this case fields, of study.

The third purpose of this book is to apply the most useful theoretical models to the bereavement experience and, in turn, acknowledge the utility of generalizing bereavement models to other traumatic experiences. By doing so, both fields can enrich each other.

Similarly, the fourth purpose of the book is to identify and apply the most useful, effective approaches in the traumatology literature to the study, diagnosis, and treatment of bereavement. And, in turn, to acknowledge the utility of applying the most effective approaches in the bereavement literature to the study, diagnosis, and treatment of traumatic stressors other than the death of others.

CONTENT

The book is organized into three parts: Conceptual Synthesis, Effective Coping with Specific Contexts, and Generic Treatment Approaches.

Part I: Conceptual Synthesis

Given the paucity of efforts to integrate traumatology and thanatology, these chapters attempt to begin this process. Chapter 1, "Traumatic Bereavements and Death-Related PTSD," is written by South African psychiatrist Michael A. Simpson, who is recognized as a pioneer in the conceptualization, study, and treatment of grief and bereavement. Simpson traces the development of the fields of thanatology and traumatology and critiques the treatment of death and bereavement of the World Health Organization's *International Codes for Diagnosis* and the American Psychiatric Association's DSM. Evidence of the extraordinary impact of the death of a loved one is provided to support his assertions.

The other chapters in Part I take the reader to a more complex level of analysis in attempting to understand the complex, overlapping nature of grief and traumatic stress. Chapter 2, "Childhood Traumatic Loss: The Interaction of Trauma and Grief," is written by Kathleen O. Nader, who is in private practice, consultation, and training in Aliso Viejo, California. Nader provides a model that identifies the differences and similarities of loss and traumatic experiences and of trauma and bereavement, including the interaction of the two. The symptoms of traumatic stress and bereavement are intensified when both are present, and they can significantly impair grief dream work, relationship to the deceased, issues of identification, and the processing of anger and rage. This often leads to a sense of estrangement from others who could enable the grieved to recover more quickly.

Chapter 3, "Death of a Co-Worker: Conceptual Overview," is written by Lasse A. Nurmi, a police psychologist, and Mary Beth Williams, a frequent author and lecturer. They first focus on how death is handled in businesses and other work settings. After noting the typical impact of types of death on fellow employees, including case materials, the authors emphasize the importance of personal beliefs and other factors in accounting for both grief and traumatic stress reactions. They conclude with a model of the development of post-traumatic stress reactions connected with the death of a co-worker.

Part II: Effective Coping with Specific Contexts

Despite the fact that only recently have professionals begun to link the concepts, models, and assessment of thanatology and traumatology, humans have, somehow, coped with the death of loved ones all along. The chapters in this section attempt to investigate one or more contexts to discuss how individuals and families cope with the death of those they care about. Chapter 4, "Traumatic Death in Pregnancy: The Significance of Meaning and Attachment," is written by Anne Speckhard, the leading American expert on postabortion grief and traumatic stress. Pregnancy loss is one of the most frequent losses to death experienced by human beings. Pregnancy loss is almost always traumatic for the mother and frequently is equally so for the father, especially late in the pregnancy. A useful model for helping others recover from this loss as quickly and painlessly as possible is provided.

Chapter 5, "Couple Coping with the Death of a Child," is written by Kathleen R. Gilbert, an Indiana University professor of family health studies. After noting the grief process, drawing from common terms in traumatology, Gilbert discusses the complexities of "dyadic grief." The chapter includes examples of couples who adopted many of the principles of positive couple coping and effectively worked through to resolve their grief.

Chapter 6, "Death as Trauma for Children: A Relational Treatment Approach," is written by Arlene Steinberg, a clinical psychologist in private practice in New York. Following a discussion of developmental issues regarding grief reactions, she examines the traumatic impact on children, reviewing class theories and research studies. Effective therapeutic methods for grieving children that can be adopted by either a parent or a professional, beginning with a discussion of assessment, are also included.

Chapter 7, "Minimizing the Impact of Parental Grief on Children: Parent and Family Interventions," by John E. Baker, a clinical psychologist at a family service clinic, focuses on how the traumatized parent functions in light of surviving children. In the first section, Baker notes how children's grief—especially over the death of a sibling—interacts with parental grief; he then contrasts that grief with other types of traumatic stress experienced within the family. The bulk of the chapter focuses on intervention into the family system to help all members cope with the death of a child.

In Chapter 8, "Treating Traumatic Grief in Systems," Kathleen O. Nader shares her insights as an experienced clinician in applying the models she presented in Chapter 2. Nader covers several traumatic death situations in schools: a shooting incident, the death of a family in a plane crash, and a tornado. In each context Nader shows the sources of stress and the various ways children, staff, and parents reacted.

The last chapter in this section, Chapter 9, "Death of a Co-Worker: Facilitating the Healing," is written by Mary Beth Williams and Lasse A. Nurmi. Here they apply their models to intervening with traumatized systems, beginning with a case example. The importance of encouraging and facilitating the grieving process for the family, closest friends, and co-workers of the deceased is discussed. The role of social support, the use of debriefing sessions, and the long-term development of peer support and peer intervention are noted, and the importance of training and psychoeducation that draws on thanatology and traumatology, in addition to critical incident stress principles, is emphasized.

Part III: Generic Treatment Approaches

This final section includes some promising treatment approaches that have been perfected only in the last several years. They are promising because they not only draw from and are equally effective in both traumatology and thanatology work, but are also powerful and efficient methods of treatment.

Chapter 10, "Treating Families with Traumatic Loss: Transitional Family Therapy," is written by Susan H. Horwitz, a member of the University of Rochester Medical Center's Family and Marriage Clinic for many years. Transitional Family Therapy is described following a discussion of several cases and a discussion of the powerful impact of death in families. The role of symptomatology as a systemic reaction to grief is noted.

Chapter 11, "Eye Movement Desensitization and Reprocessing: A Therapeutic Tool for Trauma and Grief," is written by nationally known clinical psychologists Roger M. Solomon and Francine Shapiro. Eye Movement Desensitization and Reprocessing (EMDR), like Transitional Family Therapy, is proving to be effective with a wide variety of problems, including traumatic grief/bereavement. The major features of EMDR and the emerging research proving its effectiveness are described. Solomon and Shapiro emphasize that EMDR, which is extremely powerful and efficient in uncovering and resolving trauma-induced anxiety, should be used within the context of an effective treatment plan.

Chapter 12, "Thought Field Therapy: Aiding the Bereavement Process," is written by Roger J. and Joanne Callahan, both of the nationally recognized Callahan Training Center in Indian Wells, California. Described in this chapter are several of Roger Callahan's inventions: Thought Field Therapy, Psychological Reversal, and Perturbations. Although the Thought Field Therapy approach is far from conventional, it is proving to be at least as powerful and effective as EMDR.

Together these chapters represent a subtle shift in the mental health research and services landscape. Buffeted by the winds of managed health care and influenced by many emerging journals, Internet special interest groups, and the associations that interest them, professionals identified exclusively with thanatology or traumatology are dwindling quickly in number.

The trauma experienced by survivors is inescapable. The challenge of the millennium for professionals who care about survivors is to work collectively toward a common goal: to gather together the most efficient and effective tools of our collective trade to ease the pain of grief and promote the natural process of bereavement. The extraordinary powerful and efficient treatment methods described in the latter section of this book are illustrations of the byproducts of cooperation.

Charles R. Figley, Ph.D.

REFERENCES

American Psychiatric Association. (1980). *Diagnostic and statistical manual of mental disorders* (3rd ed.). Washington, DC: Author.

Donovan, D. (1991). Traumatology: A field whose time has come. *Journal of Traumatic Stress, 4*(3), 433–436.

Figley, C. R. (1988). Toward a field of traumatic stress studies. *Journal of Traumatic Stress, 1*(1), 3–11.

Lehrman, S. (1956). Reactions to untimely death. *Psychiatric Quarterly, 30,* 564–578.

Lifton, R. J. (1969). *Death in life.* New York: Vintage Books.

Parkes, C. M., & Brown, R. J. (1972). Health after bereavement: A controlled study of young Boston widows and widowers. *Psychosomatic Medicine, 34,* 449–461.

Parkes, C. M., & Weiss, R. S. (1983). *Recovery from bereavement.* New York: Basic Books.

Rando, T. A. (1983). An investigation of grief and adaptation in parents whose children have died from cancer. *Journal of Pediatric Psychology, 8*(1), 3–20.

Rando, T. A. (1984). *Grief, dying, and death: Clinical interventions for caregivers.* Champaign, IL: Research Press.

Rando, T. A. (1988). *Grieving: How to go on living when someone you love dies.* Lexington, MA: Lexington.

Rando, T. A. (1993). *Treatment of complicated mourning.* Champaign, IL: Research Press.

Raphael, B. (1983). *The anatomy of bereavement.* New York: Basic Books.

Raphael, B. (1986). *When disaster strikes: How individuals and communities cope with catastrophe.* New York: Basic Books.

Redmond, L. (1989). *Surviving: When someone you love was murdered.* Clearwater, FL: Psychological Consultation and Education Services.

Acknowledgments

We would like to thank a number of people for their help and support in completing this book. First and foremost, we would like to thank the authors of the chapters in this volume for their hard work, dedication, and patience during the years it took to bring this project to fruition. We owe a great debt to Kathy VanLandingham and Peggy McDowell for their administrative support, which made this book possible. We are especially grateful to the following persons for their thoughtful comments and criticisms as reviewers of manuscripts: Morton Bard, Sharon Bauer, Laura Boyd, Ann Burgess, Don Catherall, Scott Cohen, Alicia Skinner Cook, Sheila Eaton, Daniel Fasko, Kathleen Gilbert, Evelyn Goslin, Isabelito Guiao, Chrys Harris, Are Holen, John Jordan, Sally Karioth, Jacob Lindy, Janice Lord, Dennis Peck, Lu Redmond, James Reese, Laura Smart, Beth Stamm, Arlene Steinberg, M. Elizabeth Stevens-Guille, Harold Widdison, and Mary Beth Williams. We also appreciate the support and encouragement of Dianne Montgomery, Dean of the School of Social Work, and Penny Ralston, Dean of the Interdivisional Program in Marriage and Family. Finally, we thank our families and loved ones for their unfailing support.

Part One

Conceptual Synthesis

Chapter 1

Traumatic Bereavements and Death-Related PTSD

Michael A. Simpson

This book can play a notable part in bringing together the cognate, but too often independent, fields of thanatology and traumatology, thus promoting the useful view of grief as a traumatic stress response. In the book, notable pioneers in the discipline of traumatology join current workers in both fields to explore aspects of the overlapping territory. They help to develop an understanding of the relationship between the demands of resolution of grief and mastery of trauma and between the modes of processing experiences and reexperiencing in trauma and grief, and they give useable accounts of practical treatment.

The editors and contributors make a valuable contribution to the development of these very significant areas of inquiry and service by formally bridging the gap between them and encouraging further exploration of issues of death and trauma.

Writing this chapter stirred a sense of nostalgia, as I looked back at personal experiences within the historical development of the fields represented here. But nostalgia isn't what it used to be. It may be a sign of more rapid cycles of social movements and of academic and intellectual currents that one can look back, from mid-life, and recognize that one has been privileged to play an early and formative role in the development and maturation of several separate academic, practical, and social movements. There is much to learn from examining the dynamics and characteristics of such trends, and there's no need to wait until all the histories of this era have been written before learning from experience.

THE EMERGENCE OF MODERN THANATOLOGY

The late 1960s saw the development of modern thanatology and what came to be called the Death Movement and the Hospice Movement (Simpson, 1989a).

3

Who or what they were moving, and where they were moving to, was not always clear. It was a lively group in the early days, oddly compatible, often charismatic, cheerful, and creative, as well as practical: John Bowlby, Herman Feifel, Bob Fulton, Dick Kalish, Bob Kastenbaum, Robert Lifton, Colin Murray Parkes, Lily Pincus, Beverly Raphael, Cicely Saunders, Ed Shneidman, Michael Simpson, David Sudnow, Avery Weisman, and others were among the initial group, later joined by other early notables such as Philippe Aries, Earl Grollman, Sylvia Lack, Bal Mount, Robert Twycross, Mary Vachon, Bill Worden, and eventually, Dora Black, Therese Rando, and others.

There were also many other devoted workers who were too busy doing what needed to be done to spend time writing or telling others of their work, but who contributed substantially to the considerable progress that was achieved. Then there were a few, often greatly feted at the time, energetic speakers who assiduously milked the tearstained lecture circuit until there wasn't a dry seat in the house, and who were so busy telling others what to do that there was very little time for them to do it themselves (see Simpson, 1979a, 1987). A few early figures in thanatology encompassed trauma themes in their work and were also notable in early traumatology, Lifton, Parkes, Rando, Raphael, and Simpson, for instance. But perhaps the field of thanatology, and especially clinical thanatology, has settled into a comfortable middle-age, for the relative lack of collaboration, let alone integration, with the developing field of traumatology is curious and is to the detriment of both. The conceptual and practical relationship between these spheres of interest is clear, and continued exploration of their borderlands, as exemplified in this book, will be fruitful.

THE EMERGENCE OF MODERN TRAUMATOLOGY

Traumatology, which emerged as a coherent field about a decade later than thanatology, also had a cohort of unusually effective early leaders; both intellectually acute and organizationally effective, they outnumbered the thanatology pioneers and were able to network more effectively from the early days. Apart from very early notables like Leo Eitinger, Calvin Frederick, and E. T. Quarantelli, and in addition to those mentioned in the last paragraph, were figures such as Ofra Ayalon, Art Blank, Joel Brende, Ann Burgess, Yael Danieli, Atle Dyregrov, Spencer Eth, Charles Figley, Bonnie Green, Sarah Haley, Mardi Horowitz, Terence Keane, Henry Krystal, Bob Laufer, Jack Lindy, Richard Mollica, Bob Pynoos, Raymond Scurfield, Chaim Shatan, Susan Solomon, Bessel van der Kolk, Lars Weisaeth, Mary Beth Williams, and John Wilson.

EVOLUTION AND DEVELOPMENT OF THE DISCIPLINES

Both disciplines developed in relation to the evolving impact of death and trauma in modern society, and to the failures of modern technologically oriented services to show adequate comprehension or compassion in regard to these common challenges. In *The Facts of Death* (Simpson, 1979b), the changing meanings of these phenomena are discussed:

> We have lost, to a significant extent, the sort of shared public beliefs that convinced generations that war could be a noble, clean, and heroic enterprise that created a better world. . . . Each death diminishes us more grossly. We used to have a large extended family, and lived embedded in an active and communicating community. . . . You can no longer say that "no man is an island." These days many men are indeed islands, and each of us belongs to a smaller archipelago. (pp. 2, 8)

With the rise of terrorist actions as sources of trauma, it was commented that

> It has become substantially less practical to live for a cause these days, though much easier to die for someone else's cause. One thing you can say for modern democracy; it has brought the privilege of political assassination within reach of the man in the street. (p. 3)

In the first part of the twentieth century, during an era of unprecedented carnage, and when sexual expression had become widely denied and officially restricted, increasing effort was expended on diligently overturning the preceding era's taboos regarding sex. In a later part of the century, amid relatively unbridled expression of sex but while the realities of death were widely denied and the dying greatly restricted by repressively insensitive terminal care, we saw analogous efforts to demystify and come to terms with the twin taboo of death (Simpson, 1977). In the era of AIDS (Simpson, 1989b) when death became so explicitly sexualized and sex so acutely linked to death, we saw the emergence of serious popular and professional attention to trauma. The previous era of comparably major concern with the art and craft of dying, the Ars Moriendi, followed the Black Death and extensive warfare and social turmoil (Simpson, 1979b).

The importance of these twin fields goes beyond individual therapy and extends to larger sociopolitical significances. The relationship between death, trauma, and ideologies and the field of political thanatology deserves further study (Simpson, 1985, 1995a). The impact of responses to death and trauma, ignored in political settlements of social violence, can cause further damage to survivors and prejudice lasting peace (Simpson, 1992). Expert knowledge of trauma and grief responses, and even of published studies in these areas, can be perversely used by repressive systems to improve the efficiency of means of oppression (Simpson, 1993a, 1993c). And inhabitants of regions suffering warfare and disaster are growing resentful of being expected, without their informed consent, to serve as experimental subjects for eager researchers and intervention-mongers from other and safer lands (Simpson, 1993b). It will be fruitful, as a younger "movement," for traumatologists to contemplate some of the lessons learned in the course of the history of thanatology, when Terminal Chic replaced Radical Chic, because similar problems may emerge as traumatology becomes more broadly accepted and popularized.

The problems of "death education" have not yet fully developed in these early days of trauma education, though one can note some similar problems in research methodology and interpretation (Simpson, 1979c, 1979d). Other even more currently pertinent problems have been reviewed in detail (Simpson, 1980a, 1980b, 1982), and these deserve our attention lest they become features of traumatology as well. These problems included issues of competition and rivalry, of personal empire-building (although there is always enough death and mayhem to go around; everyone gets their share, personally and professionally), and of lack of humility, as unexamined and inbred beliefs became dogma. There was a tendency to insist on doing too much for too many: "Has dying become a toll-bridge? Should nobody die or grieve without benefit of hospice?" To insist on providing care for those who will do well anyway can make even ineffective treatments seem useful.

There were problems with excessive incredulity, and the overeager acceptance of concepts that were emotionally appealing but not supported by data, like the KR5, the Kubler-Ross 5-stage model of adjustment to the prospect of death. In its place, I proposed the more valid 2-stage model: a stage in which you believe there must be 5 stages, and the stage when you realize there are not. The KR5 are no longer professionally or uncritically accepted, except in some college textbooks, those elephant's graveyards of formerly fashionable concepts. Traumatologists are currently dealing with some analogous banal premature certainties, such as some of the excesses of MPD (Simpson, 1995b) and satanic cult and UFO abduction claims, which are often more fiercely believed in the less objective proof there is.

We grew concerned, as is also appropriate in some modes of response to trauma, with therapeutic interventions that foster dependency on the caregiver and that fail to empower the autonomy of the survivor, and with busybodies who believe that self-help is so important that they must do it for you. There was concern about the shift from ostensibly descriptive models to oppressively prescriptive models, from enabling people to talk about the unspeakable to the tendency of some to insist on incessant communication—amounting to the denial of denial and the repression of repression.

GRIEF COMPONENT

Writing this chapter has also provoked thoughts about likely future developments at this interface. A relation between traumatology and thanatology may seem so obvious as to be a tautology, for almost all traumatic stressors encompass death or the threat of death. You may have grief without much trauma, but you can never have much trauma without grief. Ignoring the trauma component of grief, or the grief component of trauma, is surely negligent.

Bereavement and the effects of experiencing the death of others have been ambivalently and oddly treated within psychiatric nosology. Karam (1994) recently published a very important and challenging study of bereavement-related depression; the relationship to post-traumatic stress syndromes has been less competently considered.

DSM SYSTEM

The DSM system (American Psychiatric Association [APA], 1987, 1994a), and now the World Health Organization's (1992) ICD-10, strive to be "etiologically neutral," to allow reliable diagnoses independent of the theoretical allegiances of the observer, but these systems persistently either ignore bereavement and grief or treat it with unique peculiarity.

First, rapidly reject a canard that confuses some; it is said by some that DSM should strive to avoid positing etiological factors, and that this principle makes post-traumatic stress disorder (PTSD) anomalous. Surely the only logically defensible principle would be to avoid constructing diagnoses dependent upon unproven (and, especially, unprovable) etiological theories. What would be the sense of rigorously excluding diagnostic recognition of known and established etiologies (see also Simpson, 1993b)? Apart from PTSD, the DSM system contains more than 100 diagnoses that would be meaningless and useless except for their integral recognition of etiological factors: delirium; dementias; disorders induced by various drugs and substances, including alcohol; and others.

But DSM resolutely insists on treating bereavement, alone of all stressors known to mankind, as excluded from significant diagnoses. Even if a patient meets all the criteria for depression, DSM discourages us from making that diagnosis if the person has been bereaved. Like so many of DSM's rules with far-reaching effects, this one was based on no competent ongoing research nor could it have been based on any sensible review of existing research. The ICD-10 classification system does not mention bereavement as an exclusionary factor in diagnosing depression, or PTSD, and almost totally ignores grief.

As Karam (1994) wisely emphasizes, a critical question exists: Is there any significant difference between the cluster of symptoms otherwise called depression when they follow shortly after a bereavement and when they do not? The answer, according to most competent research, is no. Why, uniquely in the case of bereavement, must depressive symptoms cross a special and higher threshold of greater severity evidenced by unusual intensity or duration, before the diagnosis of major depression can be made?

It is an absolutely typical feature in practice that depressed patients often relate the onset of their depression to any of a range of distressing life events: loss of a love affair, financial and work problems, interpersonal conflicts, etc. In every case, we can diagnose depression, unless the onset was preceded by the death of a loved one. Why? Even more oddly, a relationship between depression and earlier bereavements is often accepted, but the diagnosis is withheld if the grief was recent or current.

The regular presence of depressive symptoms in bereavement has been repeatedly confirmed (Jacobs & Kim, 1990; Karam, 1994; Zisook & Schuster,

1991). Jacobs and colleagues (1989) found that 32% of bereaved subjects met the DSM-III criteria for major depression 6 months after their bereavement, and 27% did so a year afterwards. Bornstein, Clayton, Halikas, Maurice, and Robins (1973) using the earlier Feighner criteria, found that 35% of widows suffered from depression at 1 month after their bereavement, 25% at 4 months, and 17% after 1 year. Some 45% of the widows met the criteria at some time during that first year, and 13% met the criteria for depression for the entire year. Other relevant studies include those of Clayton and Maurice (1974) and Clayton et al. (1974). These studies found no grounds on which to distinguish bereavement-related depressions from other depressions, for research purposes. More recently, using DSM-III-R criteria, Zisook and Schuster (1991) found 24% of widows matched a diagnosis of depression at 2 months, and 16% at 13 months.

Karam's 1994 study, based on a competent epidemiological study of psychiatric disorders within the community, was methodologically sound. He found the overall lifetime prevalence of major depression to be 27.8% rising to 32.3% if the exclusion criterion for bereavement was not applied. Of those who had at least once in their life suffered from depression, 34% had experienced at least once depression related to bereavement; 25.7% of episodes of depression were so related. When Karam compared bereavement-related depressions with other depressions, he found no difference in the mean duration of depression, mean age at onset of first episode, risk of recurrence, frequency of dysfunction, or proportion of sufferers seeking or receiving therapy.

On what grounds, then, can one justify the exclusion of any depression that meets the symptom criteria of the DSM from the diagnosis of major depression? What obscure and undeclared theory does the supposedly atheoretical DSM use to justify exclusion?

Stroebe and Stroebe (1987) emphasized "the absence of a clear boundary separating normal grief from clinical depression" (p. 25), but they did not see grief and depression as the same syndrome, mainly because there are symptoms characteristic of grief but not depression (such as yearning and preoccupation with memories) and because they saw depression as one form of pathological grief response, along with other syndromes that do not necessarily feature depression.

DSM-III-R (APA, 1987) states as a specific exclusion for depression that "the disturbance is not a normal reaction to the death of a loved one (Uncomplicated bereavement)" (e.g., p. 223). The nosological unease may stem from a reluctance to pathologize "normal" reactions, but DSM never properly faces the matter of normalcy. Adjustment reactions may in various circumstances be "normal" in the sense of predictable, expectable, and frequent, but they are still classified. And a response to losses in love or business, whether "normal," expectable, or excessive, readily qualifies for a diagnosis of depression, as long as no bereavement has occurred. Also, the Note in DSM suggests that with extremes of severity or duration, the diagnosis would then perhaps be "bereavement complicated by Major Depression" (p. 222). Within the V Codes ("conditions not attributable to a mental disorder that are a focus of attention or treatment") uncomplicated bereavement is listed, and it is stated that "a full depressive syndrome frequently is a normal reaction to such a loss" (p. 361).

DSM-IV (APA, 1994a, 1994b) introduces a slight variant: the exclusion clause in the depression criteria requiring that "the symptoms are not better accounted for by Bereavement," which is ambiguous, and that "the symptoms last longer than 2 months" (p. 299) or show other features of particular severity. This is curious. The duration required to allow diagnosis of depression rather than bereavement is now "longer than 2 months," rather than the "prolonged duration" of DSM-III-R. Although this period is longer than the 2 weeks' duration required to diagnose depression in the absence of bereavement, it hardly represents the usual meaning of "prolonged." The origins of this choice of a demarcation point of 2 months are not clear.

Osterweis, Solomon, and Green (1984) found that after a year of bereavement, "10–20 percent still have persistent symptoms of depression" (p. 4). Worden (1983), in his very wise and practical grief work, comments that various estimates have been made of the duration of mourning and grief: "In the loss of a close relationship I would be suspicious of any full resolution that takes under a year and, for many, two years is not too long" (p. 16). He cites studies that found less than half of widows had returned to their normal selves at the end of the first year, and that even 3 or 4 years could be needed to achieve stability— and these were not studies of people considered to show pathological grief. Worden describes some distinctions between grief and depression, but, like most authors who have even considered the topic, fails to clarify that people may grieve, or be depressed, or both. It should also be emphasized that while some features are fairly specific to grief, they are often present *along with* depressive symptoms, rather than replacing them.

In the V-Code section of DSM-IV, bereavement (no longer specified as "uncomplicated") is rather better described. "As part of their reaction to loss," it remarks, "some grieving individuals present with symptoms characteristic of a Major Depressive Episode" (APA, 1994b, p. 299), suggesting that this diagnosis "is generally not given unless the symptoms are still present 2 months after the loss" (p. 299).

Zisook, Schuchter, and Lyons (1987), in their elegant studies of symptoms and problems in the recovery from bereavement, found no sign of any discernable dysfunction at 2 months; certainly not with regard to depressive features, which did not decrease as rapidly as other affects, and were relatively enduring, as other studies they cited there confirmed. Rando (1984) comments that "it was once thought that the symptoms of grief lasted only 6 months; it is now known that some symptoms may take up to 3 years to be resolved. Most of the more intense reactions of grief subside within 6 to 12 months."

Jacobs (1993) also emphasizes the difficulty in clearly distinguishing bereavement and depression, and, very relevantly, the existence of depressive syndromes in up to 45% of the bereaved. He comments that about 80% of these syndromes are "transient and benign," that is, "they resolve spontaneously in 6 months or less." Where does the DSM 2-month definition come from?

One aspect that also complicates the issue, and adds to the reluctance to recognize bereavements as potential depressions, is the strong view taken by many clinical thanatologists that antidepressant medication is inappropriate and ineffective in managing the bereaved. Yet there is no strong basis for what amounts almost to unanimity on this point.

GRIEF AND PTSD

The relationship between grief and PTSD is even more important and more often neglected. In Davidson and Foa (1993), the distinction between PTSD and simple phobia is discussed, but the relations between PTSD and grief, and grief and depression, are overlooked.

Jacobs (1993) reviews some of the studies showing that intrusion and avoidance (as measured by the Impact of Events Scale) is just as intense in bereavement by long-term illness as in traumatic bereavement. As Jacobs affirms, such findings imply that the exclusion of "normal bereavement" in the DSM criteria for PTSD may need revision. This exclusion was not included within the abbreviated structure of the criteria, but in the full version of the text. In DSM-III-R (APA, 1987, p. 247), for example, the definition of a psychologically disturbing event that is "outside the range of usual human experience" is specified as "(i.e. outside the range of such common experiences as simple bereavement, chronic illness, business losses, and marital conflict)." Yet, within the scale offered for rating the severity of psychosocial stressors (p. 11), marital conflict and business problems are rated as "moderate," and chronic illness and death of spouse are rated as "extreme"—only one coding term short of "catastrophic"—whereas death of both parents is rated at the "extreme" level. This makes the definition on page 247 contradictory and inconsistent.

March (1993), discussing the "criterion A" issue, remarks that "all [stressors] involve the potential for physical injury or death." Burstein (1985) and others summarized in March (1993, pp. 42–44) describe the occurrence of all the phenomena of PTSD, in the absence of stressors meeting the A criterion, and the difficulty of demonstrating a real and consistently substantial difference between the effects of "catastrophic" and "everyday" stressors.

Jacobs (1993, pp. 179–181) discusses the neglected topic of the potential relationship between PTSD and pathologic grief, but his discussion is often muddled and unclear. He sees the most obvious similarity as between PTSD and delayed grief, and he speculates what the relationship might be between these states. Without intrusive symptoms, delayed grief "may be a forme fruste" of PTSD. Severe grief, according to him, has intrusive symptoms that coexist with numbing and avoidant phenomena, which would surely seem still more like PTSD.

The similarities between typical features of normal grief and PTSD are striking, and their differences need to be more carefully delineated. Jacobs (1993) usefully includes (pp. 363–369) proposed criteria for normal and pathologic grief, as proposed in 1989 by Beverly Raphael, which merit more attention and discussion than they have received.

SYMPTOMATIC CRITERIA FOR PTSD

A comparison of the symptomatic criteria for PTSD as in DSM-IV with authoritative descriptions of normal grief from major authorities is now provided. In this section, the DSM criteria are followed by symptoms of bereavement as listed by Worden, 1983 (W); Parkes, 1982 (P); Rando, 1984 (Rn); Raphael, 1983 (Rp); and Stroebe and Stroebe, 1987 (S). It is accepted that in grief, the stimuli and recollections relate both to the actual circumstances of the loss and to the lost individual, that is, to the substance of what has been lost as well as to the manner of that loss.

Criterion B

1 *Recurrent and intrusive distressing recollections . . . including images, thoughts, or perceptions*: preoccupation (W, p. 24), preoccupation with thoughts of the lost person (P, p. 46), painful repetitious recollection (P, p. 77), intense preoccupation with the image of the deceased, recurring thoughts and reminiscences (Rn, p. 24), grief attacks . . . waves of . . . painful emotional and physical sensations (Rn, p. 34), preoccupation with the image of the lost individual, recurring memories (Rp, pp. 363, 364), preoccupation with the image of the deceased, often vivid, hallucinatory (S, pp. 9, 11).

2 *Recurrent distressing dreams*: distressing dreams or nightmares (W, p. 26), dreaming of the lost individual as if still alive (W, p. 364), dreams (P, p. 61), dreaming about the deceased (Rn, p. 33).

3 *Acting or feeling as if the traumatic event were recurring (including a sense of reliving the experience, illusions, hallucinations, and dissociative flashback episodes)*: sense of presence, hallucinations (W, p. 24), memories remarkable for their clarity, which may have a horrific quality (P, p. 48), illusions (P, pp. 59, 103–104), hallucinations (P, pp. 59, 164), thinking the loved one has been seen (Rn, p. 33), visual and auditory hallucinations of the deceased . . . an intuitive, overwhelming sense of . . . presence (Rn, p. 34), acting as though the lost individual were still alive, hallucinatory experiences (Rp, p. 363), firm conviction of having seen/heard [the deceased] (S, p. 11).

4 *Intense psychological distress at exposure to internal or external cues resembling an aspect of the trauma*: anxiety (W, p. 21), a relatively minor event triggering major grief responses (W), pangs . . . when something occurs that brings the loss to mind (P, p. 39), distress at reminders of the loss (Rp, p. 364), reminders evoke feelings of sadness (Rn, p. 26), heightened emotional arousal (Rn, p. 30), depression precipitated by reminders (S, p. 10).

5 *Physiological reactivity on such exposure*: anxiety (W, p. 21), physical sensations (W, p. 23), indications of autonomic activity . . . on exposure to reminders (P, p. 39), somatic distress (Rn, p. 24), a sense of panic or generalized anxiety

. . . intermittently . . . distress associated with memories of earlier losses, height-ened physical arousal (Rn, p. 30), upsurges of grief . . . in the presence of certain stimuli (Rn, p. 115), bodily complaints (S, p. 12).

Criterion C

1 *Efforts to avoid thoughts, feelings, or conversations associated with the trauma*: numbness (W, p. 23), to avoid all thoughts of the lost person (P, p. 67), numbness, unable to comprehend what has happened (Rn, p. 29), numbness, dis-belief (Rp, p. 363).

2 *Efforts to avoid activities, places, or people*: avoiding reminders of the deceased (W, p. 26), attempts to avoid painful reminders (P, p. 52), avoiding people and situations that will act as reminders (P, p. 67), withdrawing from the pain of seeing others with their loved ones (Rn, p. 36), avoiding grief work (Rn, p. 63).

3 *Inability to recall an important aspect*: denial of the facts of the loss (W, p. 11), absentmindedness (W, p. 25), disbelief in the fact of loss (P, pp. 62, 63), selective forgetting (P, pp. 62–69), denial of the fact of the loss (Rn, p. 35).

4 *Markedly diminished interest or participation in activities*: social with-drawal (W, pp. 25, 26), loss of interest in . . . matters that normally occupy atten-tion (P, pp. 46, 50), cessation of interest in the outside world, inhibition of activity by withdrawal (Rn, p. 24), anhedonia, apathy (Rn, p. 32), loss of enjoyment of hobbies, social and family events, and other activities (S, p. 10).

5 *Feeling of detachment or estrangement from others*: depersonalization, de-realization (W, p. 23), withdrawal, shuts herself up at home (P, p. 71), loss of capacity to love (Rn, p. 24), withdrawal (Rn, pp. 29, 32), social withdrawal be-havior (Rn, p. 36), problems in social interaction (S, p. 9), difficulty maintaining social relationships, rejection of friendship, withdrawal from social functions (S, p. 11).

6 *Restricted range of affect*: loss of capacity to love (Rn, p. 24), the emo-tional response . . . is denied (Rn, p. 29), apathy (Rn, p. 32), detachment (Rn, p. 38), absent grief, inhibited grief (Rn, p. 59), a lack of feelings (W, p. 23).

7 *Sense of foreshortened future*: a heightened sense of personal death aware-ness, heightened sense of one's own mortality (W, p. 21), a disinclination to look to the future or to see any purpose in life (Rn, p. 25), fears of dying (S, p. 10).

Criterion D

1 *Difficulty in falling or staying asleep*: sleep disturbances (W, p. 25), diffi-culty in sleeping at night (P, p. 34), insomnia (Rn, p. 24), inability to sleep (Rn, p. 36), sleep disturbances (S, p. 12).

2 *Irritability or outbursts of anger*: anger (W, p. 21), irritable (P, p. 34), anger (Rp, p. 364), anger (Rn, pp. 25, 30, 31), irritability (Rn, p. 33), hostile reactions to others (S, p. 9), irritability, anger (S, p. 10).

3 *Difficulty concentrating*: confusion, difficulty concentrating (W, p. 24), con-fusion, unable to comprehend, disorganization (Rn, p. 29), lack of concentration (Rn, p. 32), retardation of thought and concentration (S, p. 11).

4 *Hypervigilance*: anxiety, sense of insecurity (W, p. 21), jumpy, "all tuned

up," "on edge" (P, p. 34), heightened physiological arousal (Rn, p. 33), restlessness (S, p. 9), foreboding and fears, agitation, jitteryness, searching behavior (S, p. 10), suspiciousness (S, p. 11).

   5 *Exaggerated startle response*: oversensitivity to noise (W, p. 23), tenseness, jitteryness, overactivity (S, p. 10), heightened physical arousal (Rn, p. 30).

Clinically significant distress and impairment in functioning are common to both states, and they are of similar duration. Other common features seen in both PTSD and grief include guilt and shame, self-destructive impulses, hostility to others, lasting changes in value systems and beliefs, and a lasting search for meaning.

CONCLUSION

PTSD usually arises in situations in which grief, either normal or pathological, is a very likely outcome indeed, in which the absence of grief would be odd. The risk factors for the development and exacerbation of PTSD are similar to those associated with grief and pathological grief. Why, then, exclude grief? Because it has a clear cause? So has PTSD. Because it can be self-limiting? So is PTSD. Rothbaum and Foa (1993) showed that in PTSD "a high rate of spontaneous remission is noted, most of which takes place in the early months after trauma" (p. 23).

   The domination of DSM, coupled with a lack of operational criteria for grief, may have led to failure to recognize grief as a primary, secondary, or comorbid diagnosis. Grief is omitted from many of the popular screening instruments and interview schedules, so it is underreported.

   We need to pay more attention to seeking to understand the similarities and differences between these modes of response to tragedy. It would appear that before the recent rapid rise in recognition of the PTSD paradigm, many responses to awful events may have been dismissed as "merely" grief; our more recent preoccupation with PTSD may have led to underrecognition and undermanagement of the grief component of such reactions.

   Although more serious study is needed, a number of experts have noted the relevance of this relationship, especially in recent reviews. The classic publications of Shatan (1973, 1974) valuably emphasized the role of grief and "impacted grief" in the experience of Vietnam combat veterans. Horowitz (1993) recognized the similarities between bereavement and responses to trauma and elegantly described the "pathological intensifications of grief" (p. 54). He specifically addressed the ambiguity of the DSM definition of the stressor criterion as involving events "beyond the usual range of experience," saying

> Of course, the death of a loved one, especially a shocking or unexpected death, is well beyond the ordinary range of experience for that individual! But because all persons experience the death of loved ones . . . there is a tendency for some clinicians to regard a bereavement as "an ordinary life experience."

Lifton (e.g., 1993) has repeatedly emphasized the elements of loss, bereavement, and grief within the traumatic stress syndromes, and suggests that "many of the symptoms in the traumatic syndrome have precisely to do with impaired mourning" (p. 17), where grief has been too overwhelming to be resolved.

Brende (1993) described a 12-step program for victims of trauma, in which step 8 explicitly deals with grief and "completing the grief process" (p. 875). Scurfield (1993) stated his belief that "there are rage dynamics intrinsic to trauma exposure and separate from the grief reaction" (p. 290), but does not sufficiently explain the differences or explore the substantial rage component in normal, let alone pathological, grief. Williams (1993) considered emotional responses to trauma, including PTSD, grief reactions, trauma-specific elements, and individual differences, as "interacting factors" (p. 926), with a common overlap of symptoms; Johnson (1993) saw PTSD and grief reactions as "two inextricably intertwined strands . . . ultimately inseparable" (p. 482), because the experience of loss is itself part of the trauma. Simpson (1993c), working with victims of torture and repression, described "survival work" as analogous to grief work, and adapted principles of grief counseling to working with such survivors.

Fitting to close this chapter is a very early example of a pathological response to a traumatic bereavement responding to an Existentialist therapeutic response, from the teachings of Buddha (*The Teaching of Buddha*, 1984).

> Once there was a young woman named Kisagotami, the wife of a wealthy man, who lost her mind because of the death of her child. She took the dead child in her arms and went from house to house begging people to heal the child. They could do nothing for her, and finally a follower of Buddha advised her to see the Blessed One, who was then staying at Jetavana, and so she carried the dead child to Buddha.
>
> The Blessed One looked upon her with sympathy and said: "To heal the child I need some poppy seeds. Go and beg four or five poppy seeds from some home where death has never entered."
>
> So the demented woman went out and sought a house where death had never entered, but in vain. At last, she was obliged to return to Buddha. In his quiet presence her mind cleared and she understood the meaning of his words. She took the body away and buried it, and then returned to Buddha and became one of his disciples.

REFERENCES

American Psychiatric Association. (1987). *Diagnostic and statistical manual of mental disorders* (3rd ed., rev.). Washington, DC: Author.

American Psychiatric Association. (1994a). *Diagnostic and statistical manual of mental disorders* (4th ed.). Washington, DC: Author.

American Psychiatric Association. (1994b). *Quick reference to the diagnostic criteria from DSM-IV*. Washington, DC: Author.

Bornstein, P. E., Clayton, P. J., Halikas, J. A., Maurice, W. L., & Robins, E. (1973). The depression of widowhood after thirteen months. *British Journal of Psychiatry, 122,* 561–566.

Brende, J. O. (1993). A 12-step recovery program for victims of traumatic events. In J. P. Wilson & B. Raphael (Eds.), *International handbook of traumatic stress syndromes* (pp. 867–878). New York: Plenum.

Burstein, A. (1985). Posttraumatic stress disorder. *Journal of Clinical Psychiatry, 46,* 554.

Clayton, P., Herjanic, M., Murphy, G. E., et al. (1974). Mourning and depression: their similarities and differences. *Canadian Psychiatric Association Journal, 19,* 309–312.

Clayton, P., & Maurice, W. L. (1974). Mortality and morbidity in the first year of widowhood. *Archives of General Psychiatry, 30,* 747–750.

Davidson, J. R. T., & Foa, E. R. (Eds.) (1993). *Posttraumatic stress disorder: DSM-IV and beyond.* Washington, DC: American Psychiatric Press.

Horowitz, M. J. (1993). Stress-response syndromes: A review of posttraumatic stress and adjustment disorders. In J. P. Wilson & B. Raphael (Eds.), *International handbook of traumatic stress syndromes* (pp. 49–66). New York: Plenum.

Jacobs, S. (1993). *Pathologic grief: Maladaptation to loss.* Washington, DC: American Psychiatric Press.

Jacobs, S. C., Hansen, F. F., Berman, L., et al. (1989). Depression of bereavement. *Comprehensive Psychiatry, 30,* 215–224.

Jacobs, S. C., & Kim, K. (1990). Psychiatric complications of bereavement. *Psychiatric Annals, 20,* 314–317.

Johnson, S. J. (1993). Traumatic stress reactions in the crew of the Herald of Free Enterprise. In J. P. Wilson & B. Raphael (Eds.), *International handbook of traumatic stress syndromes* (pp. 479–485). New York: Plenum.

Karam, E. G. (1994). The nosological status of bereavement-related depressions. *British Journal of Psychiatry, 165*(7), 48–52.

Lifton, R. J. (1993). From Hiroshima to the Nazi doctors: The evolution of psychoformative approaches to understanding traumatic stress syndromes. In J. P. Wilson & B. Raphael (Eds.), *International handbook of traumatic stress syndromes* (pp. 11–23). New York: Plenum.

March, J. S. (1993). What constitutes a stressor? The "Criterion A" issue. In J. R. T. Davidson & E. R. Foa (Eds.), *Posttraumatic stress disorder: DSM-IV and beyond* (pp. 37–54. Washington, DC: American Psychiatric Press.

Osterweis, M., Solomon, F., & Green, M. (Eds.). (1984). *Bereavement: Reactions, consequences, and care.* Washington, DC: National Academy Press.

Parkes, C. M. (1982). *Bereavement: Studies of grief in adult life.* London: Tavistock.

Raphael, B. (1983). *The anatomy of bereavement.* New York: Basic Books.

Rando, T. A. (1984). *Grief, dying, and death: Clinical interventions for caregivers.* Champaign, IL: Research Press.

Rothbaum B. O., & Foa, E. B. (1993). Subtypes of posttraumatic stress disorder and duration of symptoms. In J. R. T. Davidson & E. B. Foa (Eds.), *Posttraumatic stress disorder: DSM-IV and beyond* (pp. 23–26). Washington, DC: American Psychiatric Press.

Scurfield, R. R. (1993). Post-traumatic stress disorder in Vietnam veterans. In J. P. Wilson & B. Raphael (Eds.), *International handbook of traumatic stress syndromes* (pp. 255–295). New York: Plenum.

Shatan, C. F. (1973). The grief of soldiers: Vietnam combat veterans' self-help movement. *American Journal of Orthopsychiatry, 43*(4), 640–653.

Shatan, C. F. (1974). Through the membrane of reality: Impacted grief and perceptual dissonance in Vietnam combat veterans. *Psychiatric Opinion, 11*(6), 6–15.

Simpson, M. A. (1977). Death and modern poetry. In H. Feifel (Ed.), *New meanings of death* (pp. 313–333). New York: McGraw-Hill.

Simpson, M. A. (1979a). *Dying, death and grief: A critically annotated bibliography and source book of thanatology and terminal care.* New York: Plenum.

Simpson, M. A. (1979b). *The facts of death.* Englewood Cliffs, NJ: Prentice-Hall.

Simpson, M. A. (1979c). Death education: Where is thy sting? *Death Education, 3,* 165–173.

Simpson, M. A. (1979d). The psychology and sociology of death. In H. Wass (Ed.), *Death: Facing the facts* (pp. 108–136). Washington, DC: Hemisphere.

Simpson, M. A. (1980a). The future of death–exploration or exploitation? *Thanatology Today, 2*(5),1–2; *2*(7), 3–4.

Simpson, M. A. (1980b). Research in thanatology: Problems of methodology. *Death Education, 108*(4), 139–150.

Simpson, M. A. (1982, January–February). *Care of the dying in the developed and developing worlds: Where have we come from? Where are we? Where are we going?* Keynote address presented at a conference on Care of the Dying in Australia and the Third World: Whose Responsibility? Perth, Western Australia, Australia.

Simpson, M. A. (1985). Death and ideology: Political thanatology and the "femme fatale" syndrome. *Seminars in Contemporary Cultural Studies Series* (Monograph No. 6).

Simpson, M. A. (1987). *Dying, death and grief: A critical bibliography.* Pittsburgh, PA: University of Pittsburgh Press.

Simpson, M. A. (1989a). Hospice: A historical perspective. *Pallicom (Australia), 5*(7), 5–11.

Simpson, M. A. (1989b). The malignant metaphor: A political thanatology of AIDS. In I. B. Corless & M. Pittman-Lindeman (Eds.), *AIDS: Principles, practices and politics* (ref. ed.; pp. 397–410). Washington, DC: Hemisphere.

Simpson, M. A. (1992, December). Amnesty means never having to say you're sorry: Amnesty and its potential to damage survivors of trauma. *Critical Health, 41,* 23–26.

Simpson, M. A. (1993a). Bitter waters: The effects on children of the stresses of unrest and oppression. In J. Wilson & B. Raphael (Eds.), *International handbook of traumatic stress syndromes* (pp. 601–624). New York: Plenum.

Simpson, M. A. (1993b, June). *Change as trauma: Challenges in the transition to democracy in South Africa.* Final Plenary Address to the Third European Conference on Traumatic Stress, Bergen, Norway.

Simpson, M. A. (1993c). Traumatic stress and the bruising of the soul: The effects of torture and coercive interrogation. In J. Wilson & B. Raphael (Eds.), *International handbook of traumatic stress syndromes* (pp. 667–684). New York: Plenum.

Simpson, M. A. (1995a). What went wrong? Diagnostic and ethical problems in dealing with the effects of torture and repression in South Africa. In R. J. Kleber, C. R. Figley, & B. Gersons (Eds.), *Beyond trauma: Selected papers from the First World Conference on Traumatic Stress* (pp. 187–212). New York: Plenum.

Simpson, M. A. (1995b). Gullible's travels; or, the importance of being multiple. In J. Berzoff, M. Elin, & L. Cohen (Eds.), *Multiple personality disorder: Controversies and critical issues* (pp. 87–134). New York: Jason Aronson.

Stroebe, W., & Stroebe, M. S. (1987). *Bereavement and health: The psychological and physical consequences of partner loss.* Cambridge, UK: Cambridge University Press.

The teaching of Buddha (461st ed.). (1984). Tokyo: Bukkyo Dendo Kyokai.

World Health Organization. (1992). *The ICD-10 classification of mental and behavioural disorders: Clinical descriptions and diagnostic guidelines.* Geneva, Switzerland: Author.

Williams, T. (1993). Trauma in the workplace. In J. P. Wilson & B. Raphael (Eds.), *International handbook of traumatic stress syndromes* (pp. 925–933). New York: Plenum.

Worden, J. W. (1983). *Grief counselling and grief therapy.* London: Tavistock.

Zisook, S., & Schuster, S. (1991). Depression through the first year after the death of a spouse. *American Journal of Psychiatry, 148,* 1346–1352.

Zisook, S., Schuchter, S. R., & Lyons, L. E. (1987). Adjustment to widowhood. In S. Zisook (Ed.), *Biopsychosocial aspects of bereavement* (pp. 51–74). Washington, DC: American Psychiatric Press.

Chapter 2

Childhood Traumatic Loss: The Interaction of Trauma and Grief

Kathleen O. Nader

Studies of children's traumatic responses have provided evidence of both an independence of and an interaction between trauma and grief reactions (Eth & Pynoos, 1985; Nader, Pynoos, Fairbanks, & Frederick, 1990; Pynoos et al., 1987). The fourth edition of the *Diagnostic and Statistical Manual of Mental Disorders* (DSM-IV; American Psychiatric Association [APA], 1994) describes a traumatic event as one in which (a) the child experiences, witnesses, or is confronted with an event(s) that involves actual or threatened death or serious injury, or a threat to physical integrity of oneself or others, and (b) the child's response involves intense fear, helplessness, horror, or disorganized or agitated behavior. A traumatic death, as described in this chapter, is one that is or occurs within such an event (e.g., deaths during disasters, war, other violence, suicide, or severe accidents).

When there is traumatic death, the child must contend with the symptoms of trauma, of grief, and of an amalgam of the two. Lack of attention to the interaction of trauma and grief may undermine individual treatment as well as derail aspects of large-scale intervention programs following traumatic deaths (Nader & Pynoos, 1993b). Normal grief resolution may be impeded without first attending to the traumatic nature of the death(s). After a tornado, Penny, a second-grader, was unable to focus upon issues of grief until she reenacted her experience of a wall collapsing and her dead sister's inaction before her death (see Chapter 8). Penny's affect remained flat until she was assisted to express her anger at her sister for not running to safety. Afterward, Penny became animated, completed the story of her experience, and began to enact elements of her grief experience. Similarly, 13-year-old Angelica, who found her father shot to death after a robbery, was unable to actually grieve until she first attended to traumatic aspects of the experience. Angie was the only daughter and believed that she was her father's favorite. When she found his bloody body, she shook him and called repeatedly to him in hopes he would revive in response to his favorite child's call. Her continued focus upon the loss of her father after the robbery may have been confusing to a clinician who was prepared to begin grief interventions and was unaware of the necessity of focusing first upon traumatic issues. When Angie elaborated how much her father meant to her, she was in fact listing the reasons that she needed him to respond to her traumatically helpless call. She was able to begin grieving after reworking this portion of her experience, recognizing her desperate wish for his response and accepting that he could not be called back to life.

When grief treatment leaves traumatic aspects of responses unaddressed, the results may be antitherapeutic to the school community as well as to grieving and/or traumatized individuals. Dissention between community groups (e.g., families of survivors vs. families of deceased) may hinder efforts toward recovery. After one disaster, a school district accepted the services of a grief counselor for the families of the deceased children in addition to the services of a trauma consultant and intervention team for the rest of the school. For the bereaved, issues of traumatic rage and horror were not adequately addressed. The community divided over the number and placement of memorials as well as over issues of accountability for the injuries and deaths. The mother of one of the deceased became unavailable to her surviving children as a result of her engrossment with the dead child, with the manner of his death, and with issues of accountability. Some of her angry or insistent behaviors were upsetting to school staff and students. A surviving brother, who was not exposed to the actual danger, nevertheless experienced repeated traumatic images of his brother's smashed body. He began to express suicidal thoughts that were relieved only after his referral to the trauma team.

Both trauma and grief concerns must be addressed as they become appropriate for the child or adolescent. Each child or adolescent has his or her own rhythm in processing aspects or memory segments of the traumatic experience. The rhythm of treatment must match the child's rhythm and ability to address components of the traumatic event and the traumatic death (Nader, 1994). Some children spend one or two sessions on trauma and then a session on grief issues. Others may need several trauma sessions and perhaps sessions on the secondary impact of the traumatic event between grief-work sessions. Moreover, treatment sessions may allot time both to trauma and to grief issues (see the case example in Chapter 8).

The combination of trauma and grief may affect the bereavement process in a number of ways (Figure 2.1): (a) the interplay of grief and trauma may intensify symptoms common to both, (b) thoughts of the deceased may lead to traumatic recollections, (c) traumatic aspects of the death may hinder or complicate issues of bereavement such as grief dream work, relationship with the deceased, issues of identification, and processing of anger and rage, and (d) a

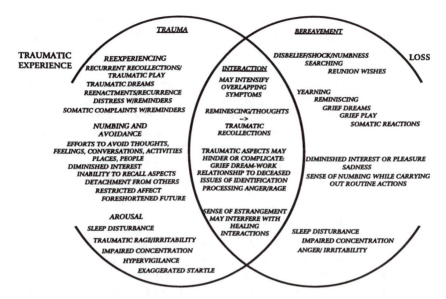

Figure 2.1   Interaction of grief and trauma. Other overlapping symptoms include anxiety, agitation, helplessness, emotional pain, loss of energy, depression, and guilt.

sense of post-traumatic estrangement or aloneness may interfere with healing interactions. These issues are discussed as they apply to the reexperiencing, avoidance/numbing, and arousal symptoms as well as to associated features of post-traumatic stress disorder (PTSD).

STUDIES OF CHILDHOOD BEREAVEMENT

Studies of childhood bereavement most often focus upon death of a parent or death of a sibling (Raphael, 1983; Rosen, 1986). Rosen (1986) summarizes the possible symptoms in children following the death of a parent: guilt, anger, grief, abandonment, denial, hopelessness, fears that the surviving parent will die or abandon them, intellectual problems, phobic reactions, regression, depression, insomnia, eating disturbances, loss of trust, separation anxiety, idealization of the dead, disturbances in behavior, predisposition to adolescent suicide, and developmental interference. Regression and restlessness are also common (Krupnick, 1984). Loss of a sibling, on the other hand, does not pose survival issues or the same kind of developmental interference for the child (Rosen, 1986). Among the reactions to loss of a sibling are guilt (for survival, health, past actions, or jealousy), sadness, hurt feelings, loneliness, anger, confusion, fear, difficulty sharing feelings, disbelief, apathy, and numbness. The long-term results of sibling loss may be affected by the nature of the child's relationship with the sibling and the manner in which the family handles the loss (Bank & Kahn, 1982; see also Chapter 10).

A number of variables affect the grieving process, including the age and emotional stability of the child, the sex of the deceased and of the bereaved, and the nature of social supports following the death (Krupnick, 1984). Pathological bereavement has been associated with several factors, including the preexisting marital relationship, and with sudden unexpected or traumatic death (Raphael, 1983). Parkes and Weiss (1983) observed three circumstances that especially affected the difficulty of recovering from bereavement: the suddenness and un-expectedness of the loss, ambivalence toward the lost relationship, and over-dependence on the relationship suggesting an underlying insecurity about attachments. Traumatic loss is sudden and unexpected and may engender am-bivalence toward the lost relationship as well as complicate response to the loss.

TRAUMATIC LOSS

Studies of childhood bereavement, heretofore, have not separated children's reactions to traumatic deaths from reactions to deaths of a less catastrophic nature. In this chapter, case examples and clinical experience are presented that provide preliminary observations about the differences in and the interaction between the two reactions.

Traumatic Versus Grief Reexperiencing

Bereavement	Trauma
Yearning and/or searching	"Why?"
Reminiscing	Intrusive distressing recollections
Grief dreams	Traumatic or bad dreams
Grief play	Traumatic play or reenactment
Somatic reactions	Somatic reactions
Distress with thoughts	Intense distress with thoughts, symbols, and reminders

Although, after noncatastrophic loss, children may not repetitively relive or reexperience the event itself, specific moments with the deceased (e.g., during the ailment or injury, happier times, or moments regretted) may be reviewed. Preoccupations with the loss may take the form of yearning or searching for the dead in early stages of bereavement and, subsequently, in reminiscing about the deceased (Raphael, 1983; Rosen, 1986). In contrast to these thoughts that are aimed at reprocessing regretted moments or at recapturing the dead person and memories or aspects of him or her, traumatic reexperiencing includes intru-sive distressing thoughts and images, dreams that recall the fear or horror of the experience, intense psychological distress in response to symbols or reminders of the event, and reenactments or play of frightening or upsetting aspects of the event as well as those recalling better times (APA, 1994; Pynoos & Nader,

1988). In normal bereavement, remembering the deceased is a part of the course of adaptation, reorganization, and recovery. It may engender pleasurable as well as sad thoughts and generate play that assists the child in working through, accepting, and redefining the relationship with the deceased (Raphael, 1983). Traumatic memories, on the other hand, may be overwhelming. These memories may be sufficiently stressful that they cannot be integrated into existing representations of the world without assistance (Horowitz, 1976). Play may be unrewarding, dangerous, or distressing, as well as providing temporary relief (Nader & Pynoos, 1991; Terr, 1979). Moreover, in addition to age-appropriate yearning and searching (Raphael, 1983), after a traumatic death children may have a greater preoccupation with why the tragic death occurred (cause or life purpose) and concern with who is responsible for the death (Pynoos et al., 1987; Stuber, Nader, Housekamp, & Pynoos, 1996). (The issue of responsibility as it relates to guilt will be discussed later.)

Intrusive Distressing Recollections   Traumatic reexperiencing may interfere with the processes of grieving in a number of ways. Thoughts of the deceased are ongoing in the process of grief resolution. For example, reminiscing about the deceased and longing for his or her return are normal components of the grieving process. If aspects of the traumatic event are not addressed, attempts at remembering the deceased may lead to traumatic recollections such as thoughts of the manner in which the death occurred or thoughts of the disfigurement. Every time Angelica thought of her father, she saw, in her mind, the image of the bullet in his head, the blood on him and on the wall of her room where he was shot, and the limpness of his body. She recalled the horrifying silence after she called to him.

Even in the absence of direct viewing of the injuries or the body, traumatic reexperiencing may replace grief-associated thoughts of the deceased. When a significant other is known to be undergoing or has undergone actual life threat or traumatic death, children may produce their own imagery or be obsessed with thoughts about the manner of the death (Nader & Pynoos, 1993a, 1993b). For example, the brother of one of the children who died in a tornado was away from the school on a field trip during the tornado. He was not expected by his family to have a traumatic response. Thoughts of his brother, however, led to repetitive imagery, thoughts, and dreams depicting the horrible, bloody smashing of his brother (as he imagined it) under parts of the school wall. Similarly, every time a 17-year-old Kuwaiti girl thought of her dead cousin, who had been like a big brother to her, she imagined his body riddled with bullets after a battle with the Iraqis. She thought of him lying in a makeshift hospital and of the Iraqi commander telling physicians to let him die because he was not worth saving. She had not directly witnessed but had only heard the story of his death. She repetitively reexperienced his violent death in her thoughts, images, and distress when reminded of him.

After traumatic or noncatastrophic loss, children may engage in repetitive retelling of the incident (Pynoos & Nader, 1988). For both trauma and grief this may be the child's way of seeking support, gauging the responses of others in determining how to feel (Krupnick, 1984), or making sense out of the experience. Preoccupations with aspects of a traumatic event, however, may prevent or delay grieving. These preoccupations include engrossment with specific episodes of the traumatic event (e.g., the moment of endangerment, of calling for help, or of injury), concerns about the cause (e.g., whose fault, the perpetrator's reasons, or issues of guilt), personal impact of the manner of the death (e.g., proximity, location, or continued threat), and threat from the angry spirit of the victimized dead. Mary was standing next to a very close friend when the friend was killed by a sniper unknown to either of them. Thinking that the bullet had actually been meant for her, Mary became beset with her own endangerment and survival. She reluctantly voiced an additional fear that the spirit of the dead girl might come to harm her in retaliation for being wrongly killed. Her affect remained flat, and there were no signs of grieving in the first several months following the event. Interventions regarding the traumatic aspects of her experience were necessary to facilitate normal grieving and recovery.

Recurrent Distressing Dreams   Traumatic and grief phenomena may occur separately within the same period of time. Grief dreams of the deceased as he or she was prior to the death, for example, may be of reunion with the deceased, of restoration of the previous relationship with the deceased, of reassurance that the deceased is now "okay," or of reminiscences of times past. Traumatic dreams incorporate aspects of the trauma, such as the action, the witnessing, the injury, the sense of threat, and/or the fear of loss (Bilu, 1989; Nader, 1996; Terr, 1979). Resolution of specific traumatic issues may necessarily precede the dream work of bereavement. A 16-year-old girl was taken hostage with her family and then the rest of her family was killed. During the course of her treatment, her brother and mother appeared to her in a dream reassuring her that they were now okay and telling her good-bye. There was an obvious omission of her father from this dream. The kidnapper had reassured her that her father was fine, despite the bloodstain on the floor where she had last seen him tied and gagged. Before addressing these matters in treatment, she was unable to accept reassurance in her dreams that her father was okay (Nader, 1996). With obvious longing for reunion, one Croatian boy described a dream of his father who had been killed in the war. In the dream, his father told him that he would come home and not to worry. The boy described with obvious distaste how the appreciated dream was then disrupted by war scenes and horrible deaths. Traumatic preoccupations may disrupt grief work in dreams.

Intense Psychological Distress or Physiological Reactivity in Response to Reminders or Symbols of the Event   Traumatic reminders elicit a variety of traumatic symptoms characterized by psychological and/or physiological distress (Armsworth & Holaday, 1993; Newman, 1976; Saylor, Swenson, & Powell,

1992). Items or events that symbolize the trauma may be particularly difficult for those who are both traumatized and grieving. They may then elicit both traumatic memories and memories of the person whose presence, interactions, relationship, support, and other qualities are lost to the bereaved. Moreover, the needs of one group (e.g., those without direct traumatic exposure who are grieving) may clash with the needs of others (e.g., those with direct traumatic exposure). The former group may desire multiple visible reminders to ensure that others will remember the deceased. In contrast, the latter group may require periods without reminders (Nader & Pynoos, 1993b).

Both trauma and grief may result in somatic reactions and in increased illness. Reminders of the deceased or confirmations of his or her absence may result in waves of somatic distress including palpitations, deep inner pain, sighing respirations, or a choking feeling (Raphael, 1983). Although studies on the long-term medical effects of loss on children are limited, a few investigators have linked specific diseases (e.g., thyrotoxicosis, rheumatoid arthritis, and diabetes) with loss in adults (Krupnick, 1984). Increased somatic complaints and vulnerability to illness have been documented for both traumatized adults and children (Nader & Fairbanks, 1994; van der Kolk & Saporta, 1991; Van Eerderwegh, Bieri, Parilla, & Clayton, 1982).

Trauma symptoms may become interlinked, thus complicating response and recovery. It may take a number of trials to teach a dog to associate food with the sound of a bell and therefore to salivate in response to the bell, or take a number of times holding the stomach a certain way in association with a particular emotion to have the one automatically produce the other. The intensity of a traumatic experience, perhaps in combination with the biochemistry of traumatic response, may produce the association in one trial. For example, the child or adolescent may have tightened his or her stomach when seeing or hearing about the traumatic death. Subsequently, whenever the child tightens the stomach (with or without awareness of doing so), the associated set of traumatic symptoms may occur. At other times, thoughts of the deceased may elicit the tightened stomach and the other symptoms. These associations have been observed clinically in children following a variety of traumatic events.

Impact of Adult Reexperiencing upon Children   The traumatic reactions of parents and children who have experienced the same traumatic event often correlate (Pynoos & Nader, 1989). Parental disagreement about action to take during the event, parental distress, and changes in parenting function following disasters influence children's reactions and recovery (Bloch, Silber, & Perry, 1956; Handford et al., 1986). Moreover, the overall traumatic reactions of adult caretakers affect their abilities to assist children's and adolescents' recovery and affect the postevent atmosphere, possibly resulting in secondary consequences for children and adolescents. Traumatic reexperiencing reactions of adult caretakers (parents, teachers, school administrators, health care providers) may affect children's recovery from traumatic grief in specific ways. For example, preoccupations with the nature of the loss may result in overprotective behaviors (Bloch et al., 1956; Nader & Pynoos, 1993b). Post-trauma parental overprotectiveness is among the factors found to be associated with persistent symptoms in children (McFarlane, 1987). After a natural disaster, a traumatized assistant teacher's overprotectiveness of children interfered with restoring a sense of normalcy in the classroom. Additionally, adults' intolerance of traumatic reminders may result in irritable or restrictive behaviors that interfere with working through aspects of the traumatic death in play. For example, after a school shooting, one school administrator began to send children home if they brought toy guns to school or wore a T-shirt with the image of a gun on it.

Just as children depict traumatic imagery in drawings, adults may concretize their traumatic imagery in memorials to the dead following catastrophic events (Nader & Pynoos, 1993b). For example, a tornado knocked down a school wall, killing nine children. After the tornado, a memorial was designed primarily by the parents of the deceased with a school administrator. The memorial was made of black marble, and it resembled a tombstone. The image engraved upon the marble was a spiral staircase (which resembled a tornado) with two children walking up toward a light. When parents of survivors complained that it looked like a tombstone, the compromise reached was to lean the marble at an angle backward. School staff then began to comment on how much it resembled the falling wall. In another case, after the 1988 Armenian earthquake, a memorial to the dead placed in one of the affected towns was an arch with a hand and a head emerging from the main design. This was likened to the body parts that had been visible from under collapsed buildings (Pynoos et al., 1993). These traumatic images may serve as constant reminders of the tragedy and may be distressing to children.

Issues of Numbing and Avoidance

Bereavement	Trauma
Shock, disbelief, numbness	Avoidance of thoughts, feelings, conversations
Sadness	Restricted affect
Diminished interest or pleasure	Diminished interest or participation
Numbness in carrying out activities	Avoidance of people, places, activities
	Inability to recall aspects of the event
	Detachment/estrangement from others
	Sense of foreshortened future

Symptoms of numbing and avoidance are common in the early phases of bereavement (Raphael, 1983) and are associated with continuing phases of both trauma and grief. In uncomplicated bereavement, shock and disbelief often appear soon after the death and are relinquished as the child moves to other phases of grieving. A sense of numbness in carrying out activities may persist for traumatized or nontraumatized bereaved children but may alternate or coexist with periods of play or excessive activity (Raphael, 1983). After trauma, numbing and reexperiencing may either alternate (Horowitz, 1976) or coexist as levels of numbing diminish over time and with the return of ego strength (Nader, 1994).

Diminished Interest in Activities and Avoidance   For both trauma and grief there may be a diminished interest in activities or a reduced ability to enjoy activities (APA, 1994; Pynoos & Nader, 1988). This reduction may be related to preoccupations, depressions, or disturbances in the ability to experience joy. After a traumatic experience, however, reduced activities may also be a form of avoidance of reminders of the event (e.g., places of play or noises of play may serve as reminders), avoidance of emotions (any emotion, happy or sad, may trigger overwhelming emotional release), or a response to fears (e.g., of danger outside or of recurrence). Aspects of traumatic avoidance may hinder grief resolution. Avoidance of reminders of the event and its traumatic circumstances (e.g., of thoughts, conversations, feelings, activities, people, locations, or other items that arouse recollections of the trauma) may interfere with expressing sadness, reminiscing, and discussing/playing in order to work through the loss.

Detachment or Estrangement   Supportive behaviors by others have proved to be therapeutic both for grief (Marris, 1991) and for trauma resolution (Nader et al., 1990). Traumatic detachment, estrangement, a sense of aloneness, or the complications of the post-traumatic situation may thwart or prevent therapeutic supportive interactions (see Chapter 8). For example, a boy whose schoolmate was murdered by her father in their church parking lot said that he felt as close as before to his family and friends. A little while later he stated that he felt that his family did not love him as much anymore because when he was feeling bad about what happened they did not come to talk to him. This sense of suffering alone with his experience made it harder for him to approach family members with his traumatic or grief reactions. The family had always openly discussed what delighted or bothered them. The family's behaviors had not actually changed. The boy's sense of aloneness had increased, while his support seeking had diminished.

An inability to benefit from the support of others may be a part of post-event decision making and/or of age variables. For example, a 16-year-old girl's father died in a boating accident during a storm; he was struck in the head by a flying object, the boat capsized, and he drowned. She had been close to her father, and she was jolted by the sudden and traumatic nature of the loss. Thereafter, she maintained an emotional distance from others in order to avert the threat of loss or intense helplessness. As a result she was unable to fully allow anyone to support her through her grieving process, which subsequently remained unresolved. Clinical experience suggests that a resistance to support that might obstruct intervention is more common in adolescents than in young children, who have not yet fully lost their trust of adults. Adolescents may resist a post-traumatic tendency toward regression (including an increased need for dependence) by more urgently insisting upon independence. This is complicated by peer pressure, which demeans an increased need for adult assistance. Children with a damaged sense of trust (e.g., after ongoing abuse or molestation) may also have difficulty accepting intervention, support, or comfort.

A sense of emotional isolation is common both following traumatic experience and following the death of a significant other. Consequently, the sense of isolation may be more pronounced when there is both trauma and loss, as in the case of one fifth-grade girl who began to express suicidal wishes. She had difficulty enduring her sense of aloneness with thoughts of bullets going through her friend and her intense related sadness over the loss.

The increased sense of aloneness may be a result of the reactions of others to the traumatic loss. Adults may wish to reinstate themselves as a protective barrier between the children and the outside world (Pynoos & Nader, 1988). A sniper attack occurred in a community somewhat wary of outsiders. One teacher made efforts to isolate her classroom from outside intrusions, including those from helping professionals, following the death of one of her students. Despite classroom activities to honor the dead child, classmates appeared to endure their grief and traumatic reactions alone. The efforts of the teacher to provide a protective shield for the children only further isolated them. A brief grief group with a trauma specialist provided relief for these children. Other children may also add to the sense of isolation. For example, elementary school–aged children hold varying degrees of fear of the contagion of death or of victimization. After one disaster, children rejected the sibling of one of the children who died, as though rejecting her would also push away the danger.

Children very affected by the loss of a peer have reported that after a few weeks or months they think others are no longer grieving and, therefore, hide their own sorrow from others. A few weeks after a drowning, a friend of the boy who died described feeling very alone with his grief feelings. He tried not to express grief because he thought that everyone else was already over it. Similarly, classmates of a boy who died in a plane crash began to engage in traumatic and grief play together in the schoolyard. Over time, one child began to have multiple accidents. He finally admitted to the school nurse that he fell down because he was sad about his dead friend and needed an excuse to cry. He was afraid that the other children were no longer sad and would think him silly for crying.

Effects of Adult Avoidance upon Children   Avoidance of traumatic emotions by adult caretakers may hinder the development of an atmosphere conducive to recovery for children. Adults' expectations of the future, avoidance (e.g., of reminders of the event, of traumatic emotions, or of discussions of the event), restricted affect, and/or increased interpersonal distance are significant to the post-trauma environment. For example, a school staff member who was responsible for restoring order to a school after a disaster would not allow her husband or her administrator to comfort her in the immediate aftermath of the event. She feared that she would completely break down and be unable to continue restoration efforts. This intense resistance to being supported continued following the trauma and became a severe hindrance to trauma resolution. She continued to be unable to let down her guard lest overwhelming traumatic anxiety should occur. The intensity of her avoidance affected her ability to reinstate a sense of safety and an atmosphere of support for the children.

Arousal Phenomena

Bereavement	Trauma
Sleep disturbance	Sleep disturbance
Impaired concentration	Impaired concentration
Anger/irritability	Anger/irritability
	Hypervigilance
	Exaggerated startle response

The overlap of trauma- and grief-related arousal symptoms, such as disturbed sleep, impaired concentration, and increased anger or irritability, may intensify the symptoms. In addition to these symptoms, traumatic events may also engender hypervigilance and/or exaggerated startle response. Anger may take the form of traumatic rage. These symptoms may disrupt normal development and interfere with learning and school performance; both have been found for traumatized and for grieving children (Dawes, Tredoux, & Ferstein, 1989; Jesse, Strickland, & Ladewig, 1992; Terr, 1981, 1983; see also Krupnick, 1984). Disruption to a child's or adolescent's developmental path may be increased by the dual nature of the experience.

Sleep Disturbance   Sleep disturbance is common both to traumatic and to grief reactions (Richters & Martinez, 1991; Rosen, 1986). Following traumatic events, children have described disturbed, restless sleep; nightmares; and early awakenings. They have described difficulties getting to sleep related to repetitive intrusive thoughts of the traumatic experience, to thoughts of the deceased, or to fear of dreaming (of the deceased or of the trauma). After his mother was murdered, a young boy would spend the time before going to sleep reviewing what had happened. His grandmother said that she could see his eyes begin to move back and forth like he was seeing it all again and then he would begin to speak of what he had witnessed.

Fears or Hypervigilance   Children describe new fears and increases in old fears following traumatic events (Famularo, Kinscherff, & Fenton, 1990). Some of these fears are related to the deceased. Children who have already learned the permanence of death become frightened of the return of the dead following traumatic events. After the sniper attack, several of the fifth-grade children were frightened because the dead girl's grandmother said her spirit was among them. Usually after dark, they thought they saw the girl beckoning to them or saw her eyes in the closet. They feared what she might do to them. In another example, a woman who had been a babysitter in a suburb of Chicago shot children in their classroom, killing one child and injuring others. An 8-year-old boy who had witnessed the shootings and had been a close friend of the dead and injured began to become frightened when sitting alone in a room. He feared that the now-dead woman would jump up out of the floor at him and shoot him too.

Blood and injury serve both as traumatic reminders and as something to be feared. Children may respond with increased anxiety or other post-traumatic symptoms when they see blood or injury following traumatic experiences. There is often an increase in injury on the playground following catastrophic events due to post-trauma increases in aggression or clumsiness. Moreover, post-traumatic symptoms, misconceptions, and fears of the deceased may become linked to each other. For example, a child who died in one disaster had had a broken arm. In their attempts to understand why individuals died, children exposed to the disaster began to say that someone with an injury such as a broken arm was more likely to die. The increases in injury on the playground became more frightening than previously perceived. Children ran to the school nurse for minor scrapes they might have ignored in the past.

Anger and Impulse Control   Disturbances in impulse control following bereavement have been observed more prominently in males after the age of 8 (Krupnick, 1984; Raphael, 1983). This may be primarily a function of cultural expectations and a greater prohibition for males against direct emotional expression. Following trauma, loss of impulse control has been associated with biochemical changes in adults (van der Kolk & Saporta, 1991). For children, difficulties with impulse control, including increases in aggression or recklessness following children's traumatic experiences, have been attributed to the challenge to impulse control after seeing adults unable to control themselves; to irritability and anger resulting in reduced tolerance of behaviors, demands, and slights of others; to revenge fantasies and the desire for retaliation; and to the inhibition of reexperiencing phenomena (Doherty & Rosenthal, 1988; Dreman & Cohen, 1990; Nader & Fairbanks, 1994; Pynoos & Nader, 1988). Anger at the deceased as well as the assailant, a sense of the unfairness of the death, and/or the helplessness associated with both trauma and grief may complicate resolution of factors associated with decreased impulse control (see the case example at the end of the chapter). The increase or loss in impulse control is among the factors demanding the child's energy and attention and may leave the child feeling over-whelmed following the traumatic experience. There may be a lack of energy in general to contend with both trauma and grief issues.

Anger commonly appears in the course of bereavement. Following trauma, it may be murderous rage. In the face of intense helplessness or threat, anger is a mobilizer. Specific biochemical reactions spur the person to flee or fight for his or her life. The intensity of the traumatic helplessness and/or of the offense to rightness may be a predictor of the intensity of the resulting rage. The intensity may be frightening to children and adolescents as well as to adult caretakers. The result may be impairment of impulse control or, conversely, inhibition of the expression of anger. The intensity, multiple levels, and complicated nature of the anger/rage may complicate recovery. Although the rage may be murderous following a traumatic experience, it does not commonly result in severe physical harm to others. Certainly, no amount of rage justifies harming another. The increase in reckless, aggressive, or inhibited behaviors in children and adolescents following traumatic exposure, however, suggests the need for early intervention in order to counteract a cycle of aggression or violence (Nader & Fairbanks,1994).

Outrage following a traumatic experience may be directed toward multiple individuals for multiple reasons: for example, at the perpetrator for doing harm or for not valuing the physical and emotional lives of the victims; at the victim(s) for being victimized, for endangering themselves, for not protecting themselves, or for dying and thus leaving the survivors behind; at adults for not protecting children; and at the self for lack of self-protection, for not helping someone else, or for not preventing harm. Thus relationships, identifications, self-esteem, and other issues affecting development may be disrupted. Experiences before, during, and after the traumatic event may affect the relationship with the deceased and others (see the sections "Guilt or Increased Sense of Responsibility" and "Issues of Identification").

Effects of Adult Traumatic Arousal

Adults may be plagued by any or all of the arousal symptoms common to trauma and/or grief. Sleep disturbance, irritability, and poor concentration may affect work performance and interpersonal relationships, thereby both indirectly and directly affecting children. Despite multiple traumatic symptoms from all three DSM-IV main symptom groups, with the appropriate interventions parents and teachers can be helped to assist children following traumatic events. Children may become anxiously attached to adults, as well as to children, with whom they experience a trauma. Clinicians have successfully treated these adults and facilitated their part in the children's recovery process (Nader & Pynoos, 1993b).

After a sudden catastrophic event the search for "why" may include concerns about "whose fault." There may be a need to blame someone for the loss and/or injury of the child(ren). Facilitating anger associated with loss without addressing issues of traumatic rage, desires for revenge, and other trauma issues may have deleterious consequences. Grief treatment that does not properly address traumatic issues may result in vindictive actions toward those deemed in a position to protect children. For example, after a disaster, one of the parents became enraged at the school principal, who had in fact been heroic in his efforts to usher the children out of the danger area and to pull away debris afterwards in order to rescue children. She claimed that the principal had always been a poor administrator and blamed him for the death of her child. She insisted upon having a memorial placed outside his office window to continually "remind him of what he had done." The grief therapist, who was not a part of the trauma team and was apparently unaware of the interaction of traumatic and grief symptoms, encouraged the expression of anger and this placement of a specific memorial.

Suddenly losing a child in a tragic way can leave parents feeling cheated and as though the child has been stolen from them. They may feel that someone or some agency should make restitution for this horrible loss. Litigation may be one method to do this. The number and placement of memorials to the child may become an issue; to parents of children who die suddenly and tragically, there may never be enough memorials. After a disaster at one school, numerous plaques, a playground (dedicated to the deceased), two paintings, and a constructed memorial for the front of the school were donated. There was community dissention over the number, nature, and location of memorials placed in the school. Children may become involved in the "battle" or "caught in the middle," which may undermine therapeutic relationships with a variety of caretakers and disrupt repair and support. Correspondence and discussions with principals of schools in which a child has died suggests that none, one, or two memorials are common. Many schools honor the child in an assembly (e.g., with readings, music, or poetry) or through an activity (e.g., classroom storywriting or drawings, a dedicated play or puppet show, or making something for the family).

Associated Features

Guilt or Increased Sense of Responsibility   Guilt feelings have been associated with prolonged or complicated grieving (Raphael, 1983) and with increased traumatic symptoms (Nader, Pynoos, Fairbanks, Al-Ajeel, Al-Asfour, 1993; Pynoos et al., 1987). Moreover, guilt may complicate post-trauma recovery (see Nader, 1994). Guilt, an increased sense of responsibility for the outcome of some aspect of the event, or compassion for the deceased perpetrator may alter the relationship with the deceased and thus interfere with both grieving and trauma resolution. Sonya accidently hit a girl with a ball on the playground. The girl became angry at Sonya and would not believe it was an accident. Later the girl was killed in the sniper attack. Sonya became preoccupied with not having been able to convince the girl that it was an accident. Although she had not been close to the girl, she felt a sense of connection with her that had not existed before the event. Sonya had increased traumatic and grief reactions as a result of her sense of guilt over not having repaired the bad interaction with the deceased before her death.

The sense of responsibility to prevent or repair harm often becomes intensified under threatening circumstances. Issues of responsibility may consequently become traumatic preoccupations. During the tornado and wall collapse, a very small boy who was not near the wall turned to see what was happening. He saw a little girl who had been hit by falling concrete blocks lying motionless on a table. Although glass and debris continued to fly through the room, he stood frozen, asking himself if he should carry her to safety or run for his life. As glass came toward him, he ran for his life. The girl was among the deceased. Afterward, he remained preoccupied with whether or not he could or should have assisted the little girl. Adults and adolescents who engage in rescue efforts following a catastrophe are affected by this intensified sense of responsibility and by a drive to undo the harm. For example, immediately after one disaster, school personnel and rescue workers attempted to revive a dead child long beyond a reasonable amount of time. The possible consequences of this phenomenon (i.e., the rush and intensity and the extreme sense of responsibility to revive and repair an endangered person) has been recognized in hospital intensive care units (ICUs). In some ICUs, when there is life endangerment one person is charged with standing back to remain an "objective observer" to keep time, give information, and make recommendations (e.g., when to cease resuscitation efforts).

One consequence of this kind of experience can be an attachment or connectedness to the deceased without a prior relationship. Compassion for a deceased perpetrator may affect children's ability to process the event and the resultant anger. Staff members who attempted to revive a woman who held children hostage and then shot herself to death in front of them felt guilty at their inability to assist. They and the children who witnessed the death felt close to this woman who was, until the incident, a stranger to them. One staff member collected information about the woman's life, spoke of her as though she were a close friend, and remained preoccupied with her for years following the incident. The children who were held hostage at gunpoint by the woman had been directed to ask her not to kill herself and to let her know that they cared about her and wanted her to live. Although she was unknown to the children before that day, the children were saddened by her death and had difficulty expressing their anger in response to being frightened by the guns and the horror of her death.

An adult or adolescent may be able to identify the point at which a sense of responsibility took over and objectivity toward the unknown deceased was lost. Doing so is sometimes of assistance in reworking this aspect of traumatic response. In contrast, children may not recognize this point and therefore must be assisted in other ways to deal with the duality of their reactions. In the preceding example, the staff member who collected information about the deceased intruder was able to recognize that the loss of emotional distance from the woman occurred after looking directly at her bleeding face, seeing her helpless and alone, and feeling an intense responsibility, even need, to do something to help. Because the woman was bleeding from every bodily opening, there was nothing that could be done. Therefore, the staff member was immobilized, like the soldiers in the foxhole who fared more poorly than those who were able to take action. The children were assisted to address their feelings toward the woman, first from the part of themselves that felt compassion toward her, and then from the part of themselves that felt angry toward her.

Suicidal Ideation   Suicidal ideation, especially as a desire for reunion with the deceased, is not uncommon following death. Actual suicide attempts are less common for uncomplicated bereavement. Traumatic death, however, may increase the likelihood of suicide risk. With uncomplicated bereavement, thoughts of death are usually limited to thoughts that the person should have died with the deceased or that the person would be better off dead (APA, 1994). Following traumatic death, some children express the wish to be dead because they cannot stand living with their thoughts and emotions. After the sniper attack a girl sat in class, unable to pay attention, and began to think of enacting her own death. She drew pictures of her dead friend, of flowers, of crosses, and of caskets. Children have expressed a sense of being overwhelmed by thoughts of the traumatic nature of a death and by the sudden unexpected loss. The adolescent Kuwaiti girl, who after the Gulf Crisis could not think of her beloved cousin without thinking of him riddled with bullets and dying without aid, also wished to be dead. After the tornado, the brother of the deceased described earlier could not think of his brother without picturing the horrible nature of his death. He also experienced the emotional loss of his mother. He wished to die. These particular children posed an actual suicide risk before their treatment.

Previous Loss

A previous loss may affect the child's ability to process the current trauma and/ or the traumatic loss. It may be necessary to work through unresolved issues from a previous loss or a previous trauma before or while current issues related to the traumatic death are addressed. A fifth-grade classmate of the deceased girl had been under gunfire on the playground during the sniper attack and had witnessed the killing of her friend. The classmate had lost a sister 2 years earlier in a drowning, and she had worried that prompter resuscitation might have saved her sister. In her initial recall of the sniper attack, she focused upon the arrival of the paramedics, shortening the period of time so that there was more likelihood of a successful rescue. She then discussed at length the fact that it was already too late and her schoolmate probably died right away (Pynoos & Nader, 1989). Only then could she focus on the horrible sight of her schoolmate's bloody injuries and work through both trauma and grief issues.

In addition, the reactions and coping methods used following a loss may become patterns of behavior that affect the response to a traumatic experience and/or a subsequent traumatic loss. Janis's father had died tragically in a boating accident when she was an adolescent. When faced with an unknown woman who was bleeding from a fatal gunshot wound to the head, she became overwhelmed by the need to intervene successfully. She had been unable to do anything to prevent her father's death. Her coping response to her father's death was to become totally in charge and in control, never allowing things to fall apart as they had after her father's death. Following her traumatic exposure to the shooting, the continued need to be in control interfered with her ability to allow others, including friends and assisting professionals, to help her recover.

Issues of Identification

Identification with the deceased has been described as more dramatic and more common in children than in adults (Birtchnell, 1970). In moderation, such identifications can be enriching. There may be adaptive internalizations of positive aspects of the personality or interests of the lost person (Raphael, 1983). Taken to an extreme, however, identifications can become frightening, for example, when they imply adoption of symptoms and death or result in peer rejection or criticism (Krupnick, 1984). After traumatic or noncatastrophic loss, children may attempt to replace a deceased parent, sibling, or friend and thus compromise their own identity development. The tendency to idealize the dead may lend to this overidentification or may interfere with processing anger toward the deceased (Krupnick, 1984; see also Chapter 8).

After the traumatic death of a significant other(s), issues of identification become complex. In addition to identification with a deceased relative or friend, children and adolescents commonly identify with several roles or individuals following traumatic events, for example, with rescuer, victim, perpetrator, or witness. The child may change his or her identification in the course of treatment and recovery. Taking on one role or another may be linked to wishes or fantasies of action during the traumatic event (see the case example at the end of the chapter).

Identification is complicated when the object of identification has suffered traumatic death. Children may fear being like someone who is killed or who kills. Children, adolescents, and adults may look for ways in which they are like the victim; for example, they may identify with the victim after a suicide (see Nader, 1994). When the perpetrator or the victim of a traumatic event is a primary caretaker, concerns about being like him or her may affect both child/adolescent and current caretakers, for example, when father kills mother and then kills himself (Pynoos & Nader, 1990). Some children fear identifying in any way with the deceased. After the tornado, when children were asked if they wanted to be like the close friend who had died, they usually said, "No," and often answered "No way!" thinking that to be like him would mean to die or be vulnerable to death. One of the children killed in the tornado had had a broken arm. Other children decided that if you were injured you were more likely to be killed. They became frightened of having a broken arm or other injury. The sister of a first-grader who had been in the danger zone thought that when she was in first grade she too would be in a disaster or other life-endangering situation at school.

Issues of identification may become apparent in the choice of friends following trauma or traumatic death. Traumatized children may gravitate toward others who are traumatized or become attached to those who went through the trauma with them. Ten years after bone marrow transplantation, 10 adolescents were asked to bring a classmate with them to also be interviewed. All 10 brought with them another adolescent who had had an extremely stressful prior life experience (Stuber & Nader, 1995). This tendency to either choose friends who are also traumatized or cling to friends who went through the trauma with you has also been observed in otherwise traumatized children; for example, the children who were held hostage and witnessed a suicide clung to one another, and children who were in the area of death and damage during a tornado also became very attached to one another. Similarly, children and adolescents may use a deceased friend like an invisible friend who is altered to validate traumatic changes in their own behavior (see the case example at the end of the chapter).

Multiple Losses

Traumatic experiences may result in multiple losses including loss of a significant other killed in the event, loss of preexisting relationships, loss of one's own expected life course, and loss of previous aspects of the self (e.g., happiness, confidence, innocence, humor, and courage). These multiple losses may increase post-traumatic senses of helplessness and hopelessness.

Emotional Loss of Parents　　After a catastrophic death, parents may, in their grief and traumatic rage, become preoccupied with the deceased and may become emotionally unavailable to their surviving children. Furthermore, children may feel the need to protect parents from emotions or thoughts that may make the parents feel worse. Thus children and adolescents may lose the ability to seek support from parents. Following a disaster, one parent became obsessed with having her child's classmates remember her dead child. She began to spend excessive time at the dead child's school seeking mementos of her child from his classmates, pushing to install multiple memorials in the school, and looking for ways to make certain that the school administrators were reminded that they had not properly protected her child. She became emotionally unavailable to her surviving children, who subsequently appeared to become increasingly depressed.

Loss of Friends　　Children and adolescents (and adults) can lose friends over time following a traumatic experience. Changes in the traumatized children's or adolescents' attitudes or behaviors may be a factor. For example, after the sniper attack a previously popular girl became irritable and bullying, and the other children complained to her mother or simply stopped playing with her. After the tornado, one little girl who used to comfort and reassure other children was too distraught to continue doing so. Other children seemed confused when they sought comfort from her, and they reduced their interactions with her.

The child or adolescent may see the world differently from other children following trauma. Pessimistic attitudes or fears about the future may develop. These changed views become apparent in children's or adolescents' play/ activities, art, and behavior. A teacher asked the class to draw a picture of what they would bring up from the bottom of the ocean. The children drew treasures and shells and beautiful fish. One boy badly injured in the sniper attack drew a shark. The other children thought him strange.

The traumatized child or adolescent may withdraw because of the changes in his or her own attitudes. There may be changes in what seems meaningful and valuable as well as in expectations and fears. For example, an adolescent girl complained that her best friend now seemed superficial to her and was not respectful of her family. The girl had lost all of her own family members in a kidnapping and murder experience. Her friend had not changed and, in fact, was engaging in fairly typical adolescent complaining about her parents and siblings. The survivor of the kidnapping and murder, however, now felt strongly that everyone should value their families.

In general, untraumatized friends may withdraw because the ongoing traumatic affects and preoccupations become fatiguing. Friends may themselves experience a helplessness to assist and may withdraw or become avoidant. For example, there may be a need for the traumatized person to repetitively retell the story, as in Kuwait, where elementary school children repeatedly listed all of the horrors of the occupation in front of each other to an interviewer. Although children's reasons for retelling may include other variables (e.g., seeking reassurance of safety or a need for others to know and understand what the victim went through), adults and adolescents have reported that friends do not always understand the incremental changes or the repeated attempts to reprocess through retelling aspects of an experience.

Loss of Self or Self-Concept   After uncomplicated bereavement, changes in the child's or adolescent's environment may necessitate reevaluation of roles in the family or standing in the world (e.g., after changes in economic status or loss of a primary caretaker) (Raphael, 1983). A child or adolescent (or adult) experiences a variety of losses related to his or her own life and self-image following a traumatic experience. In addition to losses of the preexisting sense of self, an injured child, even without actual losses in physical functioning or body parts, may experience a loss of wholeness and a sense of being damaged. For both the physically injured and uninjured, patterns, relationships, career plans, and the normal flow of life may be disrupted by post-trauma changes. For example, before a shooting, an 11-year-old girl had been fairly independent. After the shooting, she became frightened of being alone and afraid that anyone with hands in their pockets might have a gun. This completely altered her functioning. In another instance, a popular adolescent girl had had a happy family life with mature parents, a stable family income, lots of friends, and plans for law school. After her family was murdered, she had to leave her friends behind and move in with younger, less mature relatives with less stable circumstances and a troubled marriage. With an intense desire to restore a stable and loving home life, she quickly became involved with a young man who was as dear to her as her father had been. She began to discuss early marriage without college. Although, after several treatment sessions, she made plans for college and delayed the idea of marriage, she was unable to consider a law degree after the emotional pain she experienced during the court process when testifying against her family's murderer.

Competence may actually diminish, with decreased self-confidence, impaired memory and concentration, changed outlook, and increased fears. For example, after the Gulf Crisis, Kuwaiti adolescents expressed concern that they would not be able to concentrate in school in the coming year. After the sniper attack, a fifth-grade girl who had been well liked and a good student became irritable and unable to concentrate or study well. She lost friends and her class standing. The girl whose family was murdered had been a straight A student. For 1 year after the murders, she had a C average.

Performance during the event may affect subsequent confidence and sense of worth. One Kuwaiti adolescent boy had watched and loudly protested while a known animal- and human-killing Iraqi soldier beat a man almost to death. He was ashamed that he had been frozen with fear when the soldier had pointed a gun at him. After the war, he walked and sat with a lowered head and was unable to experience pleasure. He had frequent thoughts of the gun pointed at him, which caused him to shake in fear. Recognizing that he had probably saved the other man's life helped only a little until he recognized how well his mind had worked during the time the gun was pointed at him—his mind had not been frozen—he had also saved his own life by actively deciding not to move.

A mental health professional who worked with families of individuals who died traumatically once said that it was part of his job to help people to accept that they would never be the same after their traumatic loss. On the contrary, it is essential for the clinician to recognize that the parts of the person that have taken a back seat to traumatic sequelae still exist and can be recovered or, if damaged, can be repaired or even positively transformed. After thorough and effective treatment, parents and friends (or adolescents in treatment themselves) have commented that children or adolescents were functioning better than before the event.

CASE EXAMPLE

Ralph was a happy 12-year-old boy, who enjoyed activities with his best friend John and John's family. He had no history of behavior problems. During a violent rampage by a sniper through a crowded restaurant, Ralph was shot twice, once in each arm. The sniper had entered the restaurant and for 72 minutes walked around the room shooting people. John and John's mother were among those who were killed. John's father was shot multiple times but survived. Ralph witnessed the death, mutilation, and injury of many other individuals. He lay under the table thinking how much he wanted to get up and beat up the sniper. After the sniper was shot and killed, the SWAT team, who were dressed in the same army fatigues as the assailant, entered the restaurant kicking over bodies. Ralph thought they were more snipers. When one SWAT member reached down to pull him up from under the table, Ralph tried to punch him. Then Ralph tried to awaken his best friend by poking him in the thigh, shaking him and calling to him.

His grieving process began in a somewhat predictable fashion (denial, then a sense of the presence of his dead friend) despite traumatic symptomatology and a delay in aspects of grieving. Ralph had felt that John was trying to communicate with him through the snowy screen of the television set when he was in the hospital following the shootings. He experienced this presence again the first time he reentered a restaurant of the same chain where the massacre had occurred. After leaving the hospital, Ralph began to behave violently and self-destructively and to take drugs, using them to anaesthetize himself from the emotional pain. Urged on by his traumatic rage, he provoked fights or carried weapons into areas known to be frequented by aggressive, weapon-carrying adolescents. Later it was recognized that Ralph became violent in response to specific traumatic reminders, for example, whenever he wore boots like the sniper, whenever anyone poked him in the thigh (as he had poked his friend), or whenever anyone grabbed him on the arm (as the SWAT member had).

It was 2 years and some hospitalizations before Ralph's mother found trauma specialists. In the beginning of his treatment, Ralph moved between the roles of perpetrator and helpless victim. Intermittently, especially whenever he felt helpless, he would sink down to the floor and take the position that he had taken under the table in the restaurant (Nader & Pynoos, 1991). When he did this outside of session, people became angry with him (e.g., teachers in class or group therapy members at the hospital). In other treatment sessions, Ralph became the attacker, for example, the soldier sneaking up on unsuspecting enemy and shooting them, the sniper shooting at ants outside the therapy room, the medieval soldiers attacking the fort. This aggression expressed itself in his continuing to provoke fights at school or in areas where adolescents gathered. In one or two sessions, he was both attacker and attacked, dressing a doll like himself and attacking it brutally. This and self-mutilation behaviors were methods by which Ralph expressed his rage at his own helplessness and ineffectuality. At one point he entered a phase of fascination with blood and gore, watching bloody movies and reading books about Charles Manson and other bloody murderers. He appeared to be desensitizing himself to the horror he felt in response to all of the blood he had witnessed.

Grief work was only possible between every several trauma sessions. Early grief work was difficult for Ralph. After talking about John and becoming quite sad, he was overwhelmed by his emotions and then he again became enraged. Once Ralph was able to discuss his dead friend, however, John became an intermittent companion in the sessions. Throughout the treatment, Ralph carried John with him like a supplemental part of himself, editing John as Ralph's own life unfolded. He used John to affirm his own decision making: "If John were alive now, he would be [learning to skateboard/getting a tattoo/liking punk rock/smoking dope] like me." It was over a year before Ralph was able to return to the site of the massacre. The restaurant had been torn down after the event, and was supposed to have been replaced by a memorial park. What Ralph found was a dusty, empty block with a handmade wooden plaque to the many who died in the massacre. Despite his disappointment, he ceremoniously placed flowers in memory of John. Months later, another indicator of progress in his traumatic grief work was a visit to the gravesite and a private conversation with John.

Ralph was the child of divorced parents. During the course of his treatment, he spent several sessions exhibiting regressive and symbolic behaviors that indicated a need to make up developmental tasks abandoned during the breakup of his family and a need to censor traumatic emotions. For example, he entered the session, sat on the floor and worked his way up from the 3-year-old size Lego building blocks to the 7-year-old size Legos week by week; he played with little toy knights defending a progressively more elaborate fort. During this phase, he began each session by building a door out of Legos. The first door was impenetrable. Over the weeks, he signaled his increased readiness to let the clinician in on his secret fear, pain, and rage by making the door more accessible. Initially, true to his traumatic fears and pessimism, the bad knights were stronger than the good knights. Eventually, "the good guys" won.

In response to peer pressure, Ralph stopped his treatment prematurely after 2 years. He was doing well, however. His fight-provoking and violent behaviors had ceased. His blatant self-mutilation was replaced by a few tattoos. His obsession with blood and mutilation had ceased. He walked into the last few sessions and lay down as though he were again under the table in the restaurant. He announced that he was finished with therapy. He was able to explain that his friends told him that he did not need it. In these sessions, he gradually worked his way up to a sitting position and showed increased strength and determination. He was prepared, in session, for the possible emotional and behavioral consequences of the unfinished portions of his treatment and welcomed to return when needed. A few months later, he moved away with his parents. Subsequent contact with them revealed that he had moved into the rescuer role. In the early months after his traumatic experience, he began to associate with others who had had troubling life experiences. He was now (after high school) regularly rescuing his friends from danger. The only time he became a part of a fight was to prevent harm to one of his friends. He was stabbed protecting his friend and reentered therapy following the stabbing.

CONCLUSION

Early bereavement greatly increases a child's susceptibility over time to school dysfunction, depression, and delinquency. The latter or other symptoms of grief may interfere with normal ego development and psychological growth (Krupnick, 1984). There is disagreement regarding the long-term effects of childhood bereavement and the role of these effects in subsequent psychopathology. Some possible long-term consequences of childhood bereavement (traumatic or uncomplicated) are increased ill health, mental disturbances such as depressive disorders, disturbances in identity and intimacy, troubles with the law, and difficulties parenting (Krupnick, 1984; Terr, 1991). Sudden unexpected or traumatic loss has more commonly been associated with pathological grief and the negative results of loss (Raphael, 1983). Bereavement may become pathological when trauma issues and symptoms are inadequately addressed.

Treating traumatic grief requires an understanding of trauma, grief, and the interaction of the two. Trauma work usually precedes grief work; the two must occur in a child's or adolescent's own rhythm. Reexperiencing, avoidant/ numbing, and arousal symptoms common to both trauma and grief may be intensified following traumatic events. Consequently, recovery may be complicated and adverse effects on development may be increased.

Thoughts of the deceased are an essential part of the bereavement process. After traumatic death, however, thoughts of the deceased may lead to traumatic reexperiencing and/or arousal symptoms. Processing traumatic intrusive thoughts and images may necessarily precede the normal grief tasks of effective yearning, reminiscing, grief play, and grief dream work. Addressing issues of traumatic rage, desires for revenge, and other trauma issues is necessary in order to prevent the escalation of harmful behaviors that might in fact perpetuate or increase the anger.

Following a traumatic experience, children and adolescents may need assistance in sorting out issues of identification for many reasons: (a) to value realistically and use the good modeling of deceased individuals, (b) to relinquish a sense of inheriting poor modeling, (c) to process the roles that become relevant to trauma recovery (e.g., victim, witness, rescuer, or perpetrator), and (d) to be free to develop their individual identities. Moreover, issues of guilt or responsibility common to traumatic experience may affect the child's or adolescent's relationship to the deceased and thereby affect resolution of traumatic grief issues.

Traumatic experiences may include multiple losses. In addition to the loss due to death(s) or changed circumstances, children and adolescents may be contending with emotional loss of parents, loss of friends, loss of self-concept, and loss of specific competencies. All of a child's or adolescent's primary and secondary losses due to a traumatic death must be addressed in treatment. Clinical evidence of the complicated nature of traumatic death strongly suggests that an understanding of trauma, grief, and the interaction of the two is essential to recovery.

REFERENCES

American Psychiatric Association. (1994). *Diagnostic and statistical manual of mental disorders* (4th ed.). Washington, DC: Author.

Armsworth, M. W., & Holaday, M. (1993). The effects of psychological trauma on children and adolescents. *Journal of Counseling & Development, 72*(1), 49–56.

Bank, S. P., & Kahn, M. D. (1982). *The sibling bond.* New York: Basic Books.

Bilu, Y. (1989). The other as a nightmare: The Israeli-Arab encounter as reflected in children's dreams in Israel and the West Bank. *Political Psychology, 10*(3), 365–387.

Birtchnell, J. (1970). Depression in relation to early and recent parent death. *British Journal of Psychiatry, 116,* 299–306.

Bloch, D., Silber, E., & Perry, S. (1956). Some factors in the emotional reaction of children to disaster. *American Journal of Psychiatry, 113,* 416–422.

Dawes, A., Tredoux, C., & Feinstein, A. (1989). Political violence in South Africa: Some effects on children of the violent destruction of their community. *International Journal of Mental Health, 18*(2), 16–43.

Doherty, M. B., & Rosenthal, P. A. (1988). Depressive states in 11 psychiatrically hospitalized preschoolers: Investigation and review. *Child Psychiatry and Human Development, 19*(1), 60–73.

Dreman, S., & Cohen, E. (1990). Children of victims of terrorism revisited: Integrating individual and family treatment approaches. *American Journal of Orthopsychiatry, 60*(2), 204–209.

Eth, S., & Pynoos, R. (1985). Interaction of trauma and grief in childhood. In S. Eth & R. Pynoos (Eds.), *Post-traumatic stress disorder in children* (pp. 169–186). Washington, DC: American Psychiatric Press.

Famularo, R., Kinscherff, R., & Fenton, T. (1991). Posttraumatic stress disorder among children clinically diagnosed as borderline personality disorder. *The Journal of Nervous and Mental Disease, 179,* 428–431.

Handford, H. A., Mayes, S., Mattison, R., Humphrey, F., Bagnato, S., Bixler, E., & Kales, J. (1986). Child and parent reaction to the Three Mile Island nuclear accident. *Journal of the American Academy of Child and Adolescent Psychiatry, 25,* 346–356.

Horowitz, M. (1976). *Stress response syndromes.* New York: Jason Aronson.

Jesse, P. O., Strickland, M. P., & Ladewig, B. H. (1992). The after-effects of a hostage situation on children's behavior. *American Journal of Orthopsychiatry, 62*(2), 309–324.

Krupnick, J. L. (1984). Bereavement during childhood and adolescence. In M. Osterweis, F. Solomon, & M. Green (Eds.), *Bereavement, reactions, consequences and care* (pp. 99–141). Washington, DC: National Academy Press.

Marris, P. (1991). The social construction of uncertainty. In C. M. Parkes, J. Stevenson-Hinde, & P. Marris (Eds.), *Attachment across the life cycle* (pp. 82–84). New York: Routledge.

McFarlane, A. C. (1987). Posttraumatic phenomena in a longitudinal study of children following a natural disaster. *Journal of the American Academy of Child and Adolescent Psychiatry, 26,* 764–769.

Nader, K. (1994). Countertransference in treating trauma and victimization in childhood. In J. Wilson & J. Lindy (Eds.), *Countertransference in the treatment of post-traumatic stress disorder* (pp. 179–205). New York: Guilford.

Nader, K. (1996). Children's traumatic dreams. In D. Barrett (Ed.), *Trauma and dreams* (pp. 9–24). Cambridge, MA: Harvard University Press.

Nader, K., & Fairbanks, L. (1994). The suppression of reexperiencing: Impulse control and somatic symptoms in children following traumatic exposure. *Anxiety, Stress and Coping: An International Journal, 7,* 229–239.

Nader, K., & Pynoos, R. (1991). Play and drawing as tools for interviewing traumatized children. In C. Schaeffer, K. Gitlan, & A. Sandgrund (Eds.), *Play, diagnosis and assessment* (pp. 375–389). New York: Wiley.

Nader, K., & Pynoos, R. S. (1993a). The children of Kuwait following the Gulf Crisis. In L. Lewis & N. Fox (Eds.), *Effects of war and violence in children* (pp. 181–195). Hillsdale, NJ: Laurence Erlbaum.

Nader, K., & Pynoos, R. (1993b). School disaster: Planning and initial interventions. *Journal of Social Behavior and Personality, 8*(5), 299–320.

Nader, K., Pynoos, R., Fairbanks, L., Al-Ajeel, M., & Al-Asfour, A. (1993). Acute post-traumatic stress reactions among Kuwait children following the Gulf Crisis. *British Journal of Clinical Psychology, 32,* 407–416.

Nader, K., Pynoos, R., Fairbanks, L., & Frederick, C. (1990). Children's PTSD reactions one year after a sniper attack at their school. *American Journal of Psychiatry, 147,* 1526–1530.

Newman, C. F. (1976). Children of disaster: Clinical observations at Buffalo Creek. *American Journal of Psychiatry, 133*, 312–316.

Parkes, C. M., & Weiss, R. S. (1983). *Recovery from bereavement.* New York: Basic Books.

Pynoos, R., Frederick, C., Nader, K., Arroyo, W., Eth, S., Nunez, W., Steinberg, A., & Fairbanks, L. (1987). Life threat and posttraumatic stress in school age children. *Archives of General Psychiatry, 44*, 1057–1063.

Pynoos, R. S., Goenjian, A., Tashjian, M., Karakashian, M., Manjikian, R., Manoukian, G., Steinberg, A., & Fairbanks, L. A. (1993). Post-traumatic stress reactions in children after the 1988 Armenian earthquake. *British Journal of Psychiatry, 163*, 239–247.

Pynoos, R. S., & Nader, K. (1989). Children's memory and proximity to violence. *Journal of the American Academy of Child and Adolescent Psychiatry, 28*(2), 236–241.

Pynoos, R., & Nader, K. (1988). Psychological first aid and treatment approach for children exposed to community violence: Research implications. *Journal of Traumatic Stress, 1*(4), 445–473.

Pynoos, R. S., & Nader, K. (1990). Children's exposure to violence and traumatic death. *Annals of Psychiatry, 20*(6), 334–344.

Raphael, B. (1983). *The anatomy of bereavement.* New York: Basic Books.

Richters, J. E., & Martinez, P. (1991). Community violence project: I. Children as victims or witnesses to violence. *Psychiatry, 56*, 7–21.

Rosen, H. (1986). *Unspoken grief: Coping with childhood sibling loss.* Lexington, MA: Lexington Books.

Saylor, C. F., Swenson, C. C., & Powell, P. (1992). Hurricane Hugo blows down the broccoli: Preschoolers' post-disaster play and adjustment. *Child Psychiatry and Human Development, 22*(3), 139–149.

Stuber, M., & Nader, K. (1995). Psychiatric sequelae in adolescent bone marrow transplant survivors: Implications for psychotherapy. *Journal of Psychotherapy Practice and Research, 4*(1), 30–42.

Stuber, M., Nader, K., Housekamp, B., & Pynoos, R. (1996). Appraisal of life threat and acute trauma responses in pediatric bone marrow transplant patients. *Journal of Traumatic Stress, 9*(4), 673–686.

Terr, L. (1979). Children of Chowchilla: Study of psychic trauma. *Psychoanalytic Study of the Child, 34*, 547–623.

Terr, L. (1981). Psychic trauma in children: Observations following the Chowchilla schoolbus kidnapping. *American Journal of Psychiatry, 138*, 14–19.

Terr, L. (1983). Chowchilla revisited: The effects of psychic trauma four years after a school-bus kidnapping. *American Journal of Psychiatry, 140*, 1542–1550.

Terr, L. C. (1991). Childhood traumas: An outline and overview. *American Journal of Psychiatry, 148*(1), 10–20.

van der Kolk, B., & Saporta, J. (1991). The biological response to psychic trauma: Mechanisms and treatment of intrusion and numbing. *Anxiety Research, 4*, 199–212.

Van Eerdewegh, M., Bieri, M., Parilla, R., & Clayton, P. (1982). The bereaved child. *British Journal of Psychiatry, 140*, 23–29.

Chapter 3

Death of a Co-Worker: Conceptual Overview

Lasse A. Nurmi and Mary Beth Williams

The death of a co-worker has an enormous impact on persons with whom that individual spent the majority of time. If the death was job-related (through duty or location), its reality is even more immediate and its impact can be even more widespread. Secondary victims in work-related deaths are onlookers, fellow workers who were indirectly exposed, and the companies or institutions themselves, as well as rescue workers, police, mental health personnel, and debriefers who intervened after the death (Otto, 1986).

Thomas Mann wrote that "a man's dying is more the survivor's affair than his own" (Stillman, 1986, p. 145). The death of a co-worker, no matter what the cause or circumstances, is always premature; it reminds those in good health that life is not forever and that mortality is fleeting and forces them to consider the impending reality of their own deaths.

The objectives of this chapter are as follows: to review the literature examining the impact of various types of deaths on fellow personnel and the organization as a whole; to present cases that support the conclusions of the literature review; and to stress the need for critical incident debriefings as soon as possible after an event, illustrating this process through debriefings of police officers. Although the case examples are from the experiences of a police psychologist and a school social worker/private practitioner, the conclusions that may be drawn from them are generalizable to a multitude of work settings.

HOW DOES A BUSINESS ORGANIZATION HANDLE DEATH?

The culture of a business organization provides an unwritten set of informal norms that guide the actions and behavior of employees and includes values and traditions, formal and informal practices, long-term purpose, and institutional philosophy guiding daily routines (Burrello & Reitzug, 1993; Kuh, 1993). The values and assumptions of the organization form its unquestioned reality; help define roles, relationships, and acceptable behaviors; and organize ways members perceive, think, feel, and behave about events that occur (Rockwood, 1993).

Work settings, as systems with interdependent parts and relationships, vary in complexity of size and organizational structure. When one part of the system changes, for example by virtue of the death of a worker, the impact may be wide-ranging both within the physical work setting itself as well as outside the immediate environment. The organizational impact of the death of a worker depends, to a great degree, upon the culture of that organization (i.e., the organization's assumptions concerning the value of the individual worker, and the definition that the workplace gives to human relationships and human nature) (Fuqua & Kurpius, 1993). It is often not until a crisis develops or a death occurs that those assumptions and values become overt and visible. Some occupations and work settings are inherently more stressful and dangerous than others. The exposure to life-threat in these settings may differ with the employee's position in the organizational hierarchy, the relationship he or she has with others, or the job conditions (Spielberger, 1979). In some organizations, although never planned for or expected at the time it occurs, death must be considered as possible because of the nature of the work. Police officers, rescue workers, fire fighters, military personnel, and now even educators are constantly facing dangerous situations that might result in injury or even death. In fact, one major area of concern for educators is what to do about students who are violent to teachers.

The death of an employee is handled in a variety of ways by an organization, depending upon its culture. Employees may be given leave with or without pay to attend funeral services or to spend time with family members of the deceased. Public recognition of the death may occur; a flag may be flown at half mast, arm bands may be worn on uniforms by employees, or a wreath may be placed on the front door of the office. How the employee is honored, ignored, eulogized, or denigrated also varies. Persons may be assigned to assist the family of the deceased to provide physical and emotional support or to give information to the press. Letters of appreciation and condolence or flowers may be sent from the leadership or from individual members, and top management may attend services or make condolence calls. In addition, debriefings of fellow employees may occur.

IMPACT OF TYPES OF DEATH ON TRAUMATIC STRESS REACTIONS OF FELLOW EMPLOYEES

The death of an employee may occur from a variety of causes or circumstances. What makes the death of one employee more traumatic than the death of another? Research has shown that several factors increase the impact of the event upon those involved. The following section of this chapter describes some of those factors related to the type of death and the resulting traumatic effect: death-related factors of location, degree of threat, exposure to the death, duration, and symbolic meaning; relationship between the deceased and his or her co-workers; and other personal factors.

Human-Made Versus Naturally Occurring Deaths

Deaths that are the result of the malevolent actions of one person toward another are harder to understand and are more likely to shatter basic assumptions that life is good, fair, and predictable (Creamer, Burgess, Buckingham, & Pattison, 1993; Janoff-Bulman, 1992). An unexpected, untimely death caused by another human being (e.g., by murder or suicide) often produces a numbed response of disbelief and destroys assumptions about the world. Deaths caused by God rather than a person appear to be easier to accept. For example, deaths that occur when a tornado destroys a business may be less shocking than deaths from a terrorist attack on that business or deaths that are the result of a hostage situation, even if the death was the suicide of the perpetrator, as was the recent case in Lahti, Finland. In this case, the three hostages escaped, and the captor killed himself by placing two pistols to his head. The psychologists who were working with him, directly and in consultative roles, were shocked by the end to the almost 3-day-long siege. Technologically caused incidents, whether through machine or human error, also may have more long-term consequences than naturally caused incidents (Baum, Fleming, & Singer, 1983). Families and friends of three young fire fighters, killed when their engine crossed a train track that did not have a working signal to indicate the oncoming Metroliner that hit them, continue, 3 years after the accident, to display post-traumatic stress disorder (PTSD) symptoms and condemn the rail system for not preventing the accident through proper safety measures.

Prolonged Duration of a Death

When a co-worker dies from a long, protracted illness, fellow workers have time to process, adjust to, and even accept the impending loss. There is less of a chance that they will develop post-traumatic stress reactions (PTSRs), irrespective of the cause of death, than if that death were due to a sudden medical emergency. For example, two psychologists were recently overheard discussing their continued shock at the death of a colleague who had a fatal heart attack 2 years earlier while attending a conference in another country. The individual had been buried before many colleagues had even heard of his death and therefore they had no chance to say good-bye. As a consequence, they were still mourning his passing. The institutional response to death after a prolonged illness frequently tends to be less dramatic as well, although employees still may be given time off to attend the funeral and organizational representatives may be assigned to assist the family. This is particularly true if the employee had a position of power and influence or had been highly loved or respected. The following case example illustrates this aspect of the stressor event.

> Prior to Christmas vacation, a high school teacher had looked exceptionally tired and gaunt. He had recently completed his doctoral dissertation and fellow staff believed that the process had exhausted him. In fact, a fellow teacher told him "you look like hell and really need to see a doctor" as he left the building. After vacation, the principal announced to fellow personnel that the teacher would not be returning; he had advanced AIDS and was so susceptible to infection that he would have no contact with persons outside a small circle of friends. The school response was one of shock and grief after the principal, in an assembly, announced that the teacher was dying; for many students and faculty, it was their first encounter with an AIDS victim. A box was placed in the office for cards and letters. Teachers donated sick leave so that he would continue to be paid through the remainder of the school year. They also contributed money for a video cassette recorder. The school paper ran a story, written by a student, that described the teacher as "a man who taught her the power of learning" (Singletary, 1992, p. 1). The teacher died 6 months later. A memorial service was held and many students, staff, and parents attended. The grief was measured; the reactions, appropriate and, generally, less intense. Students, parents, and staff had the opportunity to prepare for the death. They did not need any extraordinary intervention or debriefings after the service.

Suddenness of the Death

Death may also be accidental and sudden. In these instances, the death is frequently due to an act of violence (e.g., a robbery that eventuated in murder or domestic violence) or an accidental circumstance (e.g., a car wreck). An unexpected death, because it is a surprise, may lead to overreaction and less feelings of control by survivors, as well as to a higher degree of maladjustment (Carey, 1977; Danto, 1975; Weisman, 1973). Jacobs (1993) noted that the "form and meaning of unnatural dying strongly shapes the bereavement of the survivor . . . by introducing themes of violence, victimization, and volition" (p. 82). These deaths may cause reactions that vary from denial and numbing to intense emotional outbursts. If the death involves more than one member of the organization or, in some cases, many members (e.g., through a corporate plane crash or mass shooting), the loss can be extreme and the reactions could be "so devastating that organizational programs lose their ability to function effectively" (Williams, 1993, p. 930). In these instances, more immediate intervention through defusing and debriefing is needed. The following case illustrates this aspect of death.

> A fourth-grade teacher, transporting a student home from college for Christmas vacation, was asleep in the passenger seat when the student lost control of the car on a slippery road and crashed into a tree. The teacher was killed instantly. By that Sunday afternoon, all personnel and most students had been notified, through a

telephone tree, of the death. A debriefing/planning meeting for staff was set for 7:30 a.m. the next morning. During this meeting, the teacher's teammate and best friend was given sick leave with pay to be with her friend's family and to help plan the funeral. Two school psychologists, the school social worker, the principal, and the guidance counselor were assigned to the fourth-grade classrooms to help teachers with debriefings. After a classroom debriefing, these support staff members, as needed, counseled small groups and individuals. They remained on call during the next few days, and even negotiated with parents to permit children to attend the funeral. The funeral was held after school so staff, children, and parents could attend. The teacher had a far-reaching impact and had been a surrogate mother to many students. Therefore, debriefings for small groups of students were also needed at junior high and high school levels. These older students were even more upset than present fourth-graders; many had personal, individual relationships with the teacher. A substitute teacher was assigned to the class until a permanent replacement was found. The teacher's belongings were quietly taken from her locker and her classroom by fellow staff. Three and a half years later, her best friend continues to teach in the classroom across the hall. She says that there is "not a day that she doesn't look across and mourn the loss" of her friend.

Self-Inflicted Death

Suicide generally takes longer to grieve and is often difficult to process. The reaction to a suicide death is generally even more dramatic if the dead worker gave no signals of his or her impending action or if signals were misinterpreted or ignored. Anger toward the deceased who committed suicide may be greater because he or she "cut out" and abandoned fellow employees (Staudacher, 1987). Suicide can be perceived by others as a hostile rejection, particularly if relationship problems existed between co-workers (O'Conner, 1984).

Suicide is often the manifestation of a desire to escape. In police officers contemplating suicide, their mood generally improves once they have made the decision and fellow officers generally do not suspect or expect the attempt (Allen, 1986). Institutions vary in willingness to assume responsibility for a suicide (e.g., if the individual's action was reaction to job-related stress rather than family problems) and willingness to respond to the death itself.

A law-enforcement officer, aged 38, with 15 years of service had been having family problems and was depressed. His colleagues recognized this depression because his work was affected. However, he did not share what was happening in his private life even with his partner, although the partner had offered assistance. One day, in the dressing room after his shift while his partner and others were in the sauna, he took his service revolver, put it in his mouth, and pulled the trigger. His fellow officers heard the shot, ran to the dressing room, and found him beyond help. The shot had splattered his brains over the walls. The shocked fellow officers went to get their lieutenant, and his defensive reaction horrified them. "The wall will be cleaned; the open position will be advertised, and the officer will be replaced"; in other words, "clean up the mess and let's go on as if nothing happened!" Ten years later, these officers continue to discuss the reaction with anger and disgust. Because their fellow officer committed suicide, he was not given a formal police funeral, the flag was not lowered to half mast, his name was not placed on the front wall of the police academy honoring deceased officers, there was no debriefing, and his family was left alone to deal with the grief.

Other-Inflicted Death

Suicide as a personal solution to a downward spiraling of interpersonal difficulties is easier to be explained away, though, than is the meaningless, random murder of a police officer or the unnecessary killing of a spouse as an outcome of a domestic dispute.

A couple with two children (a boy, aged 7, and a girl, aged 5) were living in a violent common-law marriage. The wife, aged 27, had found another man, wanted to move out, and had left the house. When she came back to get her belongings, her unemployed husband, aged 31, who had been drinking and taking antidepressants, threatened her with his shotgun. The wife called the police and two young officers came to talk to him. The man assured them that he was "only joking" and would permit her to get her belongings. The next morning, for protection, she requested a police escort. The escort assigned consisted of two officers: an experienced law enforcement sergeant and a plainclothes criminal investigator. As the escort approached the house, the wife got into their car and assured them that there was no danger. They drove to the house and found the man standing by the front door, the 7-year-old peering under his arm. The officers and the wife left the car and approached the man. The wife shouted that they were coming to get her things and the man responded "okay." The uniformed officer then said to his friend, "Look, the headlights are on in the car; go turn them off." As the plainclothes officer bent down to turn off the lights, he heard a shot.

The uniformed officer had been shot through the top of his head and died instantly. The plainclothes officer raised his head and saw the shotgun pointing at him. He had no time to get to his own weapon under his sweater and started to run in a zig-zag pattern. The man fired at his back and the officer, with 120 shot pellets in his lungs, ran until he lost consciousness. The shooter followed his petrified wife into a neighbor's house and shot her. She ran outside, yelling "don't shoot"; he reloaded his gun, shot her in the back, and then, as she continued to yell, shot her in the head. He then reloaded and shot himself in the mouth. The 7-year-old later described the death of the uniformed officer to police; he had not witnessed the deaths of his parents, because a neighbor had taken him and his sister into a nearby forest. The ambulance arrived quickly and took the wounded officer to a local health center and then to the university hospital.

Later that day, the psychologist from the local health center called the sheriff and said that three debriefings would be given: the first, for the wife's family and three of the neighbors, including the children's babysitter, who had protected them from seeing their mother's murder and father's suicide; the second, for the shooter's family; and the third, for the families of the dead and wounded officers and for the staff of the department. She requested that two officers come to the first session to not include the deceased. Worden (1991) noted that these tasks ⋯ting the reality of the loss, experiencing the pain of grief, adjusting ⋯onment without the deceased, and withdrawing emotional energy ⋯ationship.

z (1986) was among the first to incorporate traumatic distress and ⋯ the emotional response to death. Jacobs (1993) wrote that this ⋯n integrated emotional trauma and separation distress. Not all losses ⋯h are traumatic. Persons who exhibit prolonged emotional distress, ⋯e more at risk for a PTSR (Jacobs, 1993).

⋯h (1986) observed that anxiety, loss and grief, shock, and reactiva-⋯ical components of a PTSR. Williams (1993) recognized that, fol-⋯death of a co-worker, fellow employees may experience a PTSR ⋯ntrusive thoughts; depression and crying; feelings of perpetual fa-⋯leeping, or poor sleep habits including sleeplessness and nightmares; ⋯or gain; withdrawal and reduced activity levels for work or eating; ⋯irritability; and an inability to focus thoughts. Manolias and Hyatt-⋯1993) noted that the development of a PTSR is generally due to a ⋯n of individual and situational factors related to the co-worker's per-⋯what happened in the event, his or her own state of mental and ⋯ulnerability, and what coping mechanisms he or she uses.

⋯iety of factors complicate grieving and put persons at risk for devel-⋯TSR. Among these factors are having a history of family dysfunction ⋯le prior losses, psychosomatic illness and psychological problems, or ⋯e/addictions; having a stance on life that is one of suffering and pain; ⋯n adequate support system; experiencing a controversial loss (e.g., a ⋯to AIDS) or an ambiguous loss (the body is never recovered); having ⋯iatic relationship with the dead (e.g., unresolved professional jealousy ⋯confrontations); being extremely emotionally distraught over the death; ⋯ncurrent losses or stressor; or minimizing/denying the grief response ⋯& Burnell, 1989; Rando, 1993; Stearns, 1984; Wolfelt, 1988).

⋯S CONTRIBUTING TO THE DEVELOPMENT ⋯TSR

⋯risk factors that have been previously described in this chapter include ⋯pectedness of the death and the intensity and proximity of exposure to ⋯. The severity of the threat to one's own life is also important, and a ⋯hreat frequently leads to a more serious reaction (Raphael, 1991). Pre-⋯psychological vulnerability and a feeling of powerlessness and helpless-⋯ring the death also can lead to more serious reactions. However, as ⋯z (1986) noted, persons who develop PTSRs are not necessarily more ⋯ impaired prior to the death than those who do not. The following ⋯have been found to be important in mediating the PTSRs of employees ⋯eath of a co-worker.

explain the facts. The sheriff, trained by a police psychologist instructor, understood the process of debriefing and agreed. He also closed the station and requested that the highway patrol take over so that his entire staff (37 persons) could attend their debriefing. The sheriff did the death notification and then went to the wounded officer's family. He also contacted two officers to help organize the funeral and do money collections on a national level.

Within 5 hours, information was sent to every possible police organization throughout the country by computer network and the incident was reported on television less than 2 hours later. The police psychologist instructor learned of the incident while conducting an extended training. He was unable to fly to the scene immediately but arrived within a few days to meet with the sheriff, other officers, the wounded officer (who received an individual debriefing), and with a young officer who felt especially guilty over the death since she had not passed on a note stating that the shooter was dangerous to her fellow officers. Four weeks later an additional debriefing for police officers was held; during this debriefing, the officers were able to display their emotions and mourn the death of their co-worker.

Other Death-Related Factors

Death occurring in the line of duty has a major impact on an organization. It hurts all members of the working unit or organization and is a threat to the remaining personnel. This is particularly true if the deceased individual was following all the rules and doing his or her job properly, yet was killed anyway. Superstitious thoughts and rituals may develop after these deaths, particularly in occupations in which the work involves risk and exposure to potentially fatal situations on a regular basis. Military personnel during wartime, police officers, rescue workers, pilots, and others may wear talismans to protect themselves against a specific cause of death met by a co-worker.

Green (1982) found that exposure to a greater degree of grotesqueness of death leads to a significantly more intense reaction to a stressor event. Geographic proximity to the death scene also may interfere with and slow healing (Stillman, 1986). If the event occurred at or near the work site, employees are constantly reminded of the incident. If the event occurred in another city or at the individual's home, it remains more distant and avoidable. For example, Michigan social workers employed in settings in which two of their colleagues were murdered by clients expressed job-related fears and requested more preparation against violence as well as debriefings (National Association of Social Workers, 1993). Co-workers who might have been harmed, particularly if they had been in the same location at the time of a violent death, are affected when they realize their own potential for injury or death (Feuer, 1994). Creamer et al. (1993) observed that working near, with, or by a person who has died is more traumatic even if the co-worker was not present at the time of death.

Green, Lindy, and Grace (1985) found that the nature and intensity of the threat of death was related to its impact. Latane and Darley (1970) noted that PTSD is more likely to develop when the event causing the reaction is unforeseen and unusual or rare, and involves threat or harm to self or property. Standing next to someone who is murdered during a robbery or watching one's partner get shot and then being shot oneself, for example, may lead to long-lasting PTSRs, if not a chronic PTSD.

The threat to one's own life frequently combines with the degree of exposure to the event to compound the reaction. Even if an individual is not in danger (when, for example, a co-worker is murdered by an angry spouse), that co-worker has been exposed to the brutality and violence of the event.

Personal Beliefs

A variety of individually held beliefs concerning the stressor event (the death) can affect later reactions to the death. If remaining employees believe that the event may recur (e.g., an industrial accident caused by negligence of the employer) or if employees believe that the event was the result of betrayal by the employer (e.g., security measures were not taken), their later reactions may be more intense. For many employees, it is easier to believe that the event was caused by an uncaring outsider than by the employer or job situation itself (Lawson, 1987; Silver & Wortman, 1980).

Symbolic losses accompanying the physical death of a co-worker also affect reactions. Although obvious, it is important to note that the loss is even greater to a fellow employee if the dead individual was to be the godparent of an unborn child, the co-author of a proposed book, or the future mate or lover. If those who remain at the job are unable to find meaning or purpose in the death, they may be more affected (Hannaford & Popkin, 1992).

Other Factors

Factors other than the type and manner of death and personal beliefs of survivors play important roles in reactions. The function and status of the dead employee in the organization, the emotional bonds of the employee to others and the intensity of those relationships (particularly as they affected management), and the age and length of service of the employee (newly hired vs. about to retire after 30 years of service) also affect the reactions of individuals and the organization as a whole to the death.

Grief Reactions and PTSRs

The most common reaction to the death of a co-worker is grief, a normal process of experiencing the psychological, social, and physical reactions to a perception of loss (Rando, 1988). Grief is a universal response to death, usually recognized through its phenomenology and psychological manifestations of sadness, intrusive images, crying, insomnia, disbelief, emotional numbness, nightmares, fatigue, loss of interest in activities, disorganization, anxiety, and despair

(Jacobs, 1993). These symptoms are highl for acute post-traumatic stress.

The grieving process follows a fairly bargaining, depression, guilt, and accepta 1984). Grieving may begin at the moment delayed onset. For example, if the surviving high job-related demands placed on him or may first have to address those tasks and surviving employee may be angry at the dec that has been thrust upon him or her. Gri review events leading to the death, and often potential guilt.

In past years, mourning that acknowledg of the mourner's capacity to grieve, and depr mechanism of denial, evidence of an incap important to help the depressed person mou acknowledging loss and pain (Smith, 1975). natural part of the grieving process and berea eral state of existence. Bereavement is a "gen experiencing a significant loss" whereas grie regaining equilibrium after the loss" (Cook &

O'Conner (1984) noted that the grieving p readjustment to occur. Stage I (death–8 weeks sion, protest, shock, and denial. It is a time for let go of familiar, habitual patterns of doing bus a member; new patterns of organizational respo vised until the position is filled or a successor i changes as does, perhaps, the organizational cul

Stage II (8 weeks–12 months) is a time of i of the organization again becomes more automa by the death now experience depressive episod times (e.g., an office celebration, the birthday of sary of the death) may be especially difficult.

During Stage III (12–24 months), life return nization. New employees are fully integrated i those who were extremely close to the deceased, teacher's best friend, continue to mourn. For the been completed after the second year. This proce organization has a frequent turnover of employees that has new teachers every fall).

The normal tasks of grief and bereavement, then & Mordock, 1990). Co-workers must accept the pai review their positive and negative relationships with tions related to the loss, verbalize any guilt, and cc

ships that include acce to the envi from the re

Horow a PTSR in incorporati through de however, a

Weisa tion are ty lowing the involving tigue, over weight los lethargy o Williams combinati ception o physical

A va oping a and mult drug abu lacking a death du a proble or angry having c (Burnell

FACTO OF A

Specifi the une the dea greater existing ness d Horow menta factors to the

Role of the Organization and Social Support

The institutional culture, in the form of policies and procedures surrounding death, can lessen, modify, or even exacerbate a traumatic stress reaction in surviving employees. How the death is announced (how one "gets the news") is important (Staudacher, 1987). Family, friends, and co-workers should hear of the death through established phone trees, word of mouth, or direct announcement from organizational superiors rather than from the media or not at all. It is a greater shock to walk into work in the morning and learn that one's office mate suffered a stroke and died the night before than it is to receive a phone call at home and thus have time to process the loss.

The institutional response to the deceased varies with the proscribed and ascribed role of the individual in that organization. The unexpected death of five of the top management personnel in a plane crash frequently has more of an impact than does the death of a newly hired mail clerk. When death disrupts work practices greatly and when the welfare of a greater number of persons is involved, persons are more likely to develop a PTSR (Creamer et al., 1993; Manolias & Hyatt-Williams, 1993).

Survivor's Guilt

If a co-worker was in close proximity to the deceased at the time of death or was working directly with the deceased and the death was not a natural event, the immediate reaction of the survivor often is joy to be alive, yet sadness at the death of the co-worker. These conflicting feelings, according to Jacobs (1993), are associated with a higher risk of complications after the loss. Shortly thereafter, feelings of survivor's guilt may intrude as the individual asks "Why not me?" or "What might I have done to prevent the death?" More removed survivors, in the same unit or team, may also ask what they could have done in a preventive fashion. For example, they may say, "I should have been the one to be killed, but the shift just changed and [the deceased] took my place" or, "I should have recognized the symptoms of depression that led to my partner's suicide." These "what if's"—"what if I had, what if I hadn't"—are normal; however, the stronger the feelings of guilt, the more intense may be the traumatic reaction. Lippert (1991) found that the suicide death of a police officer frequently produces guilt reactions in fellow officers.

Two months after the death of the officer at the hand of the depressed husband in the case examined earlier, the young officer who did not pass on the note that the man was potentially dangerous continued to have serious guilt feelings that led to a PTSR. In another instance, an officer who interrogated a suspected car thief followed procedure and let him go. He immediately stole another car and, thinking a road block for a bank robbery was for him, ran down and killed the patrol officer assigned to the block. The young officer who had released the suspect felt guilty and was also unjustly blamed by fellow officers.

Feelings of guilt may also occur if co-workers have regrets or remorse concerning unfinished business with the deceased. They may have had a verbal altercation with the deceased shortly before the death. Guilt is greater when nasty words have been said and resolution of anger did not occur (O'Conner, 1984). Also, if a co-worker was either actively or passively responsible for the death through negligence, carelessness, or ignorance, feelings of guilt contribute to more serious PTSRs. Hearing and ignoring suicidal threats, failing to follow prescribed procedure when entering a burning building, and not covering one's partner as he or she enters a hazardous situation are examples. Survivor guilt may be existential ("Why did I live when my partner died?") or content related ("I did not act during the event; I responded badly or did not act responsibly") (Williams, 1988, 1993). Thus, if a co-worker is to blame for the death, guilt and the subsequent traumatic reaction are greater.

Closeness of the Relationship to the Deceased

Although a general assumption that the closer the attachment to the deceased, the more serious the traumatic reaction has generally been held, Jacobs (1993) noted that there are few systematic studies of this observation. However, disruption of close attachments through death can be devastating and have long-reaching effects. Closeness includes the degree of emotional bonding between individuals and is a component of the meaning of the lost relationship. The elementary school teacher killed in the car wreck was part of a team of four teachers. One of those four was her best friend. This survivor was closely bonded to her dead friend's children and parents and was called upon to assist in making funeral arrangements. She continues to have severe anniversary reactions and post-traumatic symptoms years after the accident.

Personality Characteristics and Coping Patterns

Personality characteristics, including genetic and constitutional predispositions, are major factors influencing and modifying recovery and, according to Breslau and Davis (1987, p. 261), "affect the ways in which people appraise stressors, the range of learned responses available to them, the amount of effort they expend in dealing with them." Furthermore, a variety of personality characteristics affect grieving patterns, including religious beliefs and training, family models dealing with death, established patterns of reactivity, personal approach to death, health attitudes, and health history.

Coping is an attempt to lessen the psychological and physical pain associated with the death of a co-worker, and it can be an active or passive process. In some instances, survivors attempt to deny the death or its impact on the organization, wanting things to remain as they were. In other instances, survivors become angry and aggressive, yet dangerously detached. A third group of survivors may turn to substances and activities to help them escape the death or avoid responsibility. As O'Conner (1984) noted, the ideal coping style is one of transcendence, an openness to the loss and its accompanying changes, a willingness to commit to the present, and a desire to reorganize following the death.

Coping strategies may be covert and not directly observable (e.g., reducing negative feelings through cognitive avoidance or escape), or may be overt and action oriented (Houston, 1987). Typical overt, action-oriented strategies include working extra hours, engaging in strenuous physical activity, using substances or participating in addictive behaviors, and thrill seeking.

Coping patterns established over the lifespan also can help to exacerbate or mitigate a traumatic reaction. Eating to extremes, using addictive substances, or isolating oneself (as examples of the avoidance phase of a PTSR) can delay healing, as can overwork or overdisplay of emotions, especially rage (intrusive coping mechanisms). Persons who do not develop positive coping skills and are not given training and support from an organization through peer support, debriefings, counseling, or therapy may develop or continue unhealthy, destructive coping patterns that lead to a PTSR or PTSD.

A combination freight boat/barge carrying metal raw materials capsized when the freight shifted and caused an imbalance. Two of the 10 crew members survived. The chief machinist of the boat had planned ahead, just in case such an accident might happen. He had emergency clothes, food, lamps, batteries, and other supplies available and had identified how he might be evacuated through the thinnest part of the hull. He had his own level to measure the sway and rocking of the boat and was mentally prepared when the accident happened. The second officer of the ship, known as a "real seaman," was working on the bridge when the boat capsized. He was pushed down a flight of spiral stairs into the hull, where he was rescued by the chief machinist. Although both seamen were debriefed after the event, only the machinist has been able to return to his position. He was physically and mentally prepared for disaster and his recovery has been excellent. The second officer has been unable to return to work and has been medically retired. He had not prepared for such an event.

Battin, Arkin, Gerber, and Wiener (1975) found that these individuals often exhibited complainer, manipulator, pseudo-dependent, or dependent coping patterns. Complainers note that fate is against them and utilize negative behavioral responses (whining, frequent absences, anger outbursts) to seek attention and sympathy or provoke guilt. The response of peers to these individuals is negative. Manipulators constantly seek help from others, praise them for that help, and then indirectly criticize those helping interventions. They tend to become overinvolved in the plans of others by offering to help themselves and then express feelings of helplessness when their efforts fail. Pseudo-dependents deny any need for assistance or their own need to grieve and refuse offers of help. They are insistent on showing how well functioning and strong they are. They talk about the dead without emotion and are extremely suspicious of others. Dependents exhibit a lack of independent resourcefulness and a lack of capacity to do things on their own, to adjust to the death of the co-worker. They are suspicious of the efforts of others and fear loneliness.

If a co-worker has healthy mechanisms of coping in place (expressing grief appropriately, physical exercising, practicing religion, talking with peers to get support, journaling or using other creative means of expression, developing positive rituals, reminiscing about the deceased, joining support groups), the chances of developing a PTSR and later PTSD are lessened (Hannaford & Popkin, 1992). The most effective coping strategies include the following: learning to accept one's personal shortcomings and lack of control over what ultimately happened (the death), recognizing the positive contribution one made in a critical incident; learning that happiness is a by-product of other activities and is not achieved directly, developing a sense of humor, accepting the reality that life's struggles never end and life is unfair, and finding a purpose in life (Woolfolk & Richardson, 1978). Persons affected by a traumatic incident need to talk about it (emotional release) to understand their own reactions and need to make use of multiple sources of support—peers, family members, or spiritual/religious practices. In addition, co-workers need to avoid destructive responses and close the incident by making peace, getting a final report, attending a trial, or performing other activities. Persons who demonstrate an independent style of coping learn to express feelings in a positive manner and recover sooner from the death of the co-worker, accepting and becoming resigned to the loss and its accompanying changes (Battin et al., 1975; Hoyt, 1993).

Persons with emotional tension, dysphoria, and a history of multiple family losses are more likely to develop depression and pathological outcomes to loss. Having a greater amount of fear during an event, as well as a history of prior psychological treatment and psychological problems, may make a co-worker more sensitive and more likely to develop a PTSR. The occurrence of other stressors during the first 4 months following a death also can lead to a greater likelihood of developing a traumatic reaction. The subjective experience of trauma is more significant than objective characteristics of the stressor (death) are. Persons who perceive themselves to be in threatening situations or who perceive themselves to be guilty have more significant reactions to the death (Creamer et al., 1993; Sanders, 1989).

Although it is difficult to assess vulnerability to the development of a PTSD, past history of coping and reactions to stress may give some indication as to how much grief an individual can bear before developing maladaptive response patterns. If an employee has a familial and personal history of psychiatric disorders, reflecting some type of genetic vulnerability (e.g., a familial, cross-generational history of bipolar disorder), he or she may be at risk for developing a PTSD. The loss of a significant nurturing individual during childhood can also put an individual at risk for a later reaction, particularly if the co-worker lost was close and nurturing to the survivor (Lloyd, 1980). In addition, persons who work in the emergency field over long periods of time eventually develop secondary traumatic stress reactions and/or disorders (vicarious traumatization) as an inevitable component of that work (Danieli, 1994).

Gender and Age

It appears that females are more likely to develop a greater level of distress and a greater likelihood of a PTSR than are males (Creamer et al., 1993). However, in a more recent study, Barnett found that positive and negative job experiences are not gender relative and have similar impacts on the mental health of men and women (Adler, 1993b). Recent studies have examined how the immune systems of men and women differ in response to stress. In a new study by Kiecolt-Glaser et al., it appears that women become more physically aroused to a stressful, hostile situation (e.g., marital conflict) (Adler, 1993a). Women are more likely to develop complications of bereavement as well as major depressions, anxiety disorders, and somatization disorders. Age is also a factor. Younger adults appear to be at a greater risk for development of a post-traumatic bereavement reaction than are the elderly, although the reasons for this are still unknown (Jacobs, 1993).

Cultural Factors

Cultural patterns and customs can also affect grieving patterns and the development of PTSRs. If the expression of grief is culturally supported, mandated, or encouraged, persons may have an easier time of adjusting to a loss through these ritualistic expressions. The organization needs to recognize the cultural customs and traditions of the deceased. Although viewed by the prevailing American culture as highly undesirable, self-mutilation and outward expression of anger toward death are encouraged in some cultures. Others have customs that dictate how to adjust to a death through composed or emotionless mourning (Rosenblatt, 1975). Cultures vary in their concepts of locus of control and whether or not the death can be assigned to an act of fate. Funeral practices vary among cultures as well. For example, in the United States, funerals typically occur within a few days of the death. In Finland, the funeral often takes place between 2 and 3 weeks after the death. Wakes and public viewing of the body by persons other than family members are not the norm, nor is embalming. The coffin may be opened for immediate family members and other relatives shortly before the service to take a "last look." The lock is then put back in place and the service is held with a closed coffin. In the United States, streams of persons file past the coffin to pay last respects and note "how good he [or she] looks." The coffin may remain opened until the close of the service when funeral home staff ceremoniously shut and lock it forever. In Finland, cemeteries are honored places of great beauty that are meticulously maintained; frequent pilgrimages are made to place candles on the graves of the dead at prescribed times of the year. In the United States, while many cemeteries are maintained by paid staff, others are in disarray; family members often do not make regular visits to the grave sites and, in many instances, are not even aware where grandparents or other relatives are buried.

The cultural background of the organization also affects recovery. In some institutions employees openly express grief by placing wreaths on doors, wearing arm bands, or flying flags at half mast. In others the expression of grief is minimized and business goes on as usual. The formal and informal norms of the organization therefore affect death-related roles, behaviors, and perceptions. In some instances, employees may be given leave to attend funerals, but that leave, called bereavement leave, must be taken as sick leave and the number of days allowed varies with the organization.

Response of the Media

A positive, supportive media response to a death may improve opportunities for healing (Stillman, 1986). However, in many instances, if the death has been the result of a sensational action (terrorist bomb, revenge murder by a disgruntled employee, hostage situation, death in the line of duty), the media intrude into the event. This intrusion may be persistent questioning and interviewing of survivors and/or repeated bombardment through visual and auditory images of what occurred as they are presented on television or radio. If the death directly involved an organization, it is important for one person to be designated as the media contact. This person monitors access to information and individuals, plans for appropriate press releases that are factual and avoid sensationalism, grants interviews, and highlights the positives of an organization's coping strategies. If a legal response to the event is also involved, media coverage again occurs and frequently opens old wounds and rekindles a PTSR. For this reason the National Organization of Victim Assistance has developed ethical guidelines for the media that may be obtained from that organization. It is also important that, as part of their ongoing crisis intervention plans, organizations develop protocols for media involvement. Having a plan in place in the event of a crisis can allow an organization to restrict media access without appearing to "cover up" the facts.

PTSD: PATHOLOGICAL GRIEF RESOLUTION

Grief may become pathological and unresolved, resulting in a chronic PTSD with its cycle of intrusion and avoidance. The following case example illustrates how such a disorder may develop.

> After being shot during a drug bust, a narcotics officer's drinking intensified from weekend maintenance to constant use of alcohol to alleviate his pain. He eventually went to the police psychiatrist who hospitalized him and, as he noted, "loaded him up with seconal and librium." Finally, after the officer experienced many drug-

induced blackouts, his wife destroyed the pills. He was medically retired after 13 years of service, pulled even further into himself, and increased his substance use. His wife became paranoid and "changed the channel if a cop show was on." Eventually, they divorced.

Now, 15 years later, the interviewee has had approximately 1 year of post-traumatic-oriented therapy and 1 year of sobriety from alcohol. He recently went on a journey, an almost spiritual quest, to find himself for several months and did not keep his wife informed of his whereabouts. He has had surgery to repair shooting-related adhesions and hernias. He still tends to abuse prescription medications and is taking a variety of drugs. His flashbacks occur less regularly and are less intense. Yet he still has anniversary reactions and is triggered by violence, police shows, and "news of other cops being shot." Counseling has helped him deal with his anger and has "taught him to stay out of confrontations with people" because confrontations trigger him "to the point of blind rage." He still asks many "what ifs": "What if I had done something differently? What if we hadn't been assigned to narcotics for 7 years and perhaps hadn't been sloppy?" When asked what could have prevented or lessened his PTSD, he says "debriefing and intense therapy at the time; treatment that was trauma oriented."

Most persons successfully resolve a PTSR before it becomes chronic PTSD. However, some individuals undergo significant personality changes and a personality decline and eventually develop a chronic PTSD. Treatment outcomes for chronic sufferers, according to Solursh (1988), are generally poor. If the decline continues, the individual may also develop extraordinary defensiveness, extensive psychic impairment, growing hypochondria, severe reexperiencing of the death, predominance of psychic numbing, extensive use of substances to self-medicate, damaged object relations, and a high resistance to therapeutic change (Gersons & Carlier, 1994; Titchener, 1982). Parkes (1965) and Parkes and Weiss (1983) described these reactions in terms of pathological grief, differentiating among unanticipated grief, conflicted grief (if a relationship was ambivalent), and chronic grief. A major symptom of pathologic grief is fear of losing control, as is a morbid disturbance of self-esteem. Many losses do not lead to PTSD. However, in many instances, loss and trauma are intimately related.

Gersons and Carlier (1994) view PTSD as a consequence of stagnated coping that arises from the "incomprehensibility of a traumatic experience which cannot be 'pinned down' or given an appropriate place in the total picture of life" (p. 13). Employees with PTSD may begin to exhibit chronic lateness, overuse of sick leave, or excessive absenteeism (Williams, 1993).

If symptoms of post-traumatic stress exist 4 months postevent, it is likely that the individual will have them at 14 months postevent (Creamer et al., 1993). It is also likely that a PTSD has developed. High levels of initial symptoms, therefore, are strong predictors of later symptom levels. Persons who do not reduce the extent of intruding memories, dreams, and images of the death within a short period of time are more likely to have other symptoms that remain, including anxiety, depression, concentration and relationship difficulties, attempts to avoid triggers of the death, and physiological symptoms. Other evidence of PTSD includes the hardening of emotion, feelings of homicidal desire, and depression anxiety that recurs for years.

Fire fighters who have lost co-workers frequently find that the experience of loss is life changing. The intensity of their PTSD is a sign that they are responsible and conscientious about their jobs because PTSD "tends to affect quality personnel" (Holt, 1985, p. 26). Police officers who are severely affected by deaths of fellow officers, construction workers who have observed cave-in deaths of fellow employees, or Department of Transportation workers on busy highways who observe or even hear of the deaths of fellow employees from care-less drivers experience a variety of fears. One is fear of loss of control over one's own life, which contributes to feelings of vulnerability and lack of control (Sheehan, 1991, 1994; Solomon, 1988). Such individuals may withdraw from others and, as a PTSD develops, may feel as if they are "going crazy." They may fear being seen by others in the organization as weak, inadequate, and incompetent or may fear loss of their job. These feelings of invulnerability may lead to hypervigilance and suspiciousness, directly affecting intimacy. Anger may lead to doubts of self-control or explosions of rage and can be a substitute for feelings of fear and helplessness (Sheehan, 1989; Solomon & Horn, 1984).

Thus, the impact of the death of a co-worker on an individual's sense of vulnerability appears to be related to the development of a PTSD (Roberts, 1982). If an individual has come face to face with personal vulnerability through proximity to the death, involvement in the death (as witness, co-victim), or exposure to the grotesqueness of the death, and if he or she has limited or impaired coping abilities, that individual is more likely to develop a more reactive pattern of emotionality, a heightened sense of danger, nightmares, rage at the causal agent, withdrawal, and other components of the PTSD reaction. In these situations, usual coping techniques do not work and a sense of danger threatens to overwhelm the surviving co-worker (Ainsworth & Pease, 1987).

If the individual who develops PTSD was not directly involved in the event or even had no direct contact with the deceased, the PTSD is known as secondary traumatization. Little is known about the effect of quality of the relationship between co-workers, social and cultural climate of the organization, and degree of empathy of the organization and co-workers to those affected by the death on the development of a secondary reaction.

CONCLUSION

On the basis of numerous debriefings and treatment of numerous traumatized individuals, several conclusions can be made. No matter what the cause of death of an employee, the organization needs to have a plan to help survivors deal with that death. The plan may or may not include debriefing (e.g., if the death is after a protracted, expected illness, debriefing may not be necessary), but it should specify leave policies for co-workers (bereavement leave, sick leave, leave with pay, or leave without pay), organizational responses, and organizationally encouraged rituals. Death after a long illness needs to have an official acknowledgment (e.g., a moment of silence to honor the deceased). The plan should have established rituals by which information is delivered (as to reason for death, funeral plan, and needs of the family). The plan should also recognize that although suicide is not to be glorified, the life of a person who has killed him- or herself needs to be honored and the impact of that need needs to be recognized and processed. Organizations need to be encouraged to give leave with pay to fellow workers to attend funerals or help the families of the deceased, to provide transportation to funerals if necessary, and to acknowledge the contribution of the deceased to the organization publicly. In essence, a range of service/treatment options should be set in place. In Chapter 9, organizational and individual therapeutic interventions are examined.

REFERENCES

Adler, T. (1993a). Men and women affected by stress, but differently. *The APA Monitor, 24*(7), 8–9.

Adler, T. (1993b). Stress from work, home hits men, women equally. *The APA Monitor, 24*(7), 10–11.

Ainsworth, F. B., & Pease, K. (1987). *Police work.* Leicester, UK: British Psychological Society.

Allen, S. W. (1986). Suicide and indirect self-destruction behavior among police. In J. T. Reese & H. A. Goldstein (Eds.), *Psychological services for law enforcement* (pp. 413–418). Washington, DC: U.S. Government Printing Office.

Battin, D., Arkin, A. M., Gerber, I., & Wiener, A. (1975). Coping and vulnerability among the aged bereaved. In B. Schoenberg, I. Gerber, A. Wiener, A. H. Kutscher, D. Peretz, & A. C. Carr (Eds.), *Bereavement: Its psychosocial aspects* (pp. 294–309). New York: Columbia University Press.

Baum, A., Fleming, R., & Singer, J. E. (1983). Coping with victimization by technology disaster. *Journal of Social Issues, 39*(2), 117–138.

Breslau, N., & Davis, G. C. (1987). Post-traumatic stress disorder: The stressor criterion. *The Journal of Nervous and Mental Disease, 175*(5), 255–264.

Burnell, G. M., & Burnell, A. L. (1989). *Clinical management of bereavement.* New York: Human Sciences Press.

Burrello, L. C., & Reitzug, U. C. (1993, July/August). Transforming context and developing culture in schools. *Journal of Counseling and Development, 71*(6), 669–677.

Carey, R. G. (1977). The widowed: A year later. *Journal of Counseling Psychology, 24,* 125–131.

Cook, A. S., & Dworkin, D. S. (1992). *Helping the bereaved: Therapeutic interventions for children, adolescents, and adults.* New York: HarperCollins.

Creamer, M., Burgess, P. Y., Buckingham, W., & Pattison, P. (1993). Posttrauma reactions following a multiple shooting: A retrospective study and methodological inquiry. In J. P. Wilson & B. Raphael (Eds.), *International handbook of traumatic stress syndromes* (pp. 201–212). New York: Plenum.

Danieli, Y. (1994). Countertransference and trauma: Self-healing and training issues. In M. B. Williams & J. F. Sommer, Jr. (Eds.), *Handbook of post-traumatic therapy* (pp. 540–550). Westport, CT: Greenwood Press.

Danto, B. L. (1975). Bereavement and the widows of slain police officers. In B. Schoenberg,

I. Gerber, A. Wiener, A. H. Kutscher, D. Peretz, and A. C. Carr (Eds.), *Bereavement: Its psychosocial aspects* (pp. 150–163). New York: Columbia University Press.

Feuer, B. (1994). The association of flight attendants employee assistance program responds to workplace trauma: A dynamic model. In M. B. Williams & J. F. Sommer, Jr. (Eds.), *Handbook of post-traumatic therapy*. Westport, CT: Greenwood Press.

Fuqua, D. E., & Kurpius, D. J. (1993, July/August). Conceptual models in organizational consultation. *Journal of Counseling and Development, 71*(6), 607–618.

Gersons, B. P. R., & Carlier, I. V. E. (1994). Treatment of work related trauma in police officers: Post-traumatic stress disorder and post-traumatic decline. In M. B. Williams & J. F. Sommer, Jr. (Eds.), *Handbook of post-traumatic therapy* (pp. 325–333). Westport, CT: Greenwood Press.

Green, B. L. (1982). Assessing levels of psychological impairment following disaster: Consideration of actual and methodological dimensions. *Journal of Nervous and Mental Disease, 170*, 544–552.

Green, B. L., Lindy, J. D., & Grace, M. C. (1985). Posttraumatic stress disorder: Toward DSM-IV. *Journal of Nervous and Mental Disease, 173*, 406–411.

Hannaford, M. J., & Popkin, M. (1992). *Windows: Healing and helping through loss.* Atlanta, GA: Active Parenting.

Holt, F. (1985, November). Post-traumatic stress disorder and the firefighter. *Fire Engineering*, 24–26.

Horowitz, M. J. (1986). *Stress response syndromes.* New York: Jason Aronson.

Houston, R. K. (1987). Stress and coping. In C. R. Snyder & C. E. Ford (Eds.), *Coping with negative life events* (pp. 373–399). New York: Plenum.

Hoyt, D. P. (1993, February). *The effects of traumatic stress on public safety personnel.* Paper presented at the IATC Conference, San Diego, CA.

Jacobs, S. (1993). *Pathologic grief: Maladaptation to loss.* Washington, DC: American Psychiatric Press.

Janoff-Bulman, R. (1992). *Shattered assumptions: Towards a new psychology of trauma.* New York: Free Press.

Kubler-Ross, E. (1969). *On death and dying.* New York: Macmillan.

Kuh, G. D. (1993). Appraising the character of a college. *Journal of Counseling and Development, 71*(6), 661–668.

Latane, B., & Darley, J. M. (1970). *The unresponsive bystander: Why doesn't he help?* New York: Appleton Century-Crofts.

Lawson, B. Z. (1987). Work-related post-traumatic stress reactions: The hidden dimension. *Health and Social Work, 12*(4), 250–258.

Lippert, W. W. (1991). Police officer suicide or homicide: Treating the affected department. In J. T. Reese, J. M. Horn, & C. Dunning (Eds.), *Critical incidents in policing, revised* (pp. 171–190). Washington, DC: U.S. Government Printing Office.

Lloyd, C. (1980). Life events and depressive disorders reviewed. *Archives of General Psychiatry, 17*, 529–535.

Manolias, M. B., & Hyatt-Williams, A. (1993). Effects of postshooting experiences on police-authorized firearms officers in the United Kingdom. In J. P. Wilson & B. Raphael (Eds.), *International handbook of traumatic stress syndromes* (pp. 385–394). New York: Plenum.

National Association of Social Workers (1993, June). Slayings stir on-job fears. *NASW News, 38*(6), 3.

O'Conner, N. (1984). *Letting go with love: The grieving process.* Apache Junction, AZ: Mariposa Press.

Otto, U. (Ed.) (1986). *Katastrof-och forsvarspsykiatri.* Lund, Sweden: Studentlitteratur.

Parkes, C. (1965). Bereavement and mental illness, part 2: A classification of bereavement reactions. *British Journal of Medical Psychology, 38*, 13–26.

Parkes, C. W., & Weiss, R. S. (1983). *Recovery from bereavement.* New York: Basic Books.

Rando, T. A. (1988). *How to go on living when someone you love dies.* New York: Bantam Books.

Rando, T. A. (1993). *Treatment of complicated mourning.* Champaign, IL: Research Press.

Raphael, B. (1991, June). *Critical appraisal of post trauma mental health services and critical incident stress debriefing.* Paper presented at the Harvard University Conference on Trauma, Boston, MA.

Roberts, M. (1982, April). *Post-shooting trauma presentation.* San Francisco, CA: San Francisco Police Department.

Rockwood, G. F. (1993, July/August). Edgar Schein's process vs. content consultation. *Journal of Counseling and Development, 71*(6), 636–638.

Rosenblatt, P. C. (1975). Uses of ethnography in understanding grief and mourning. In B. Schoenberg, I. Gerber, A. Wiener, A. H. Kutscher, D. Peretz, & A. C. Carr (Eds.), *Bereavement: Its psychosocial aspects* (pp. 41–49). New York: Columbia University Press.

Sanders, C. M. (1989). *Grief: The mourning after.* New York: Wiley.

Sheehan, P. L. (1989). The relationships among combat trauma, fear of close personal relationships and intimacy. Doctoral dissertation, Indiana University. Submitted to *Dissertation Abstracts International.*

Sheehan, P. L. (1991). Critical incident trauma and intimacy. In J. T. Reese, J. M. Horn, & C. Dunning (Eds.), *Critical incidents in policing, revised* (pp. 331–334). Washington, DC: U.S. Government Printing Office.

Sheehan, P. L. (1994). Treatment of intimacy issues of traumatized people. In M. B. Williams & J. F. Sommer, Jr. (Eds.), *Handbook of post-traumatic therapy* (pp. 94–105). Westport, CT: Greenwood Press.

Silver, R. L., & Wortman, C. B. (1980). Coping with undesirable life events. In J. Garber & M. E. P. Seligman (Eds.), *Human helplessness.* New York: Academic Press.

Singletary, B. (1992, March 9). Appreciation: Dr. Hamlin is one of the stars in my hall of fame. *Lasso,* 5.

Smith, J. H. (1975). On the work of mourning. In B. Schoenberg, I. Gerber, A. Wiener, A. H. Kutscher, D. Peretz, & A. C. Carr (Eds.), *Bereavement: The psychosocial aspects* (pp. 18–25). New York: Columbia University Press.

Solomon, R. (October, 1988). Post-shooting trauma. *The Police Chief,* 40–46.

Solomon, R., & Horn, J. (1984). Post-shooting trauma reactions: A pilot study. In J. T. Reese & H. Goldstein (Eds.), *Psychological services for law enforcement* (pp. 383–393). Washington, DC: U.S. Government Printing Office.

Solursh, L. (1988). Combat addiction—post-traumatic stress disorder re-explored. *Psychiatric Journal of the University of Ottawa, II*(1), 17–20.

Spielberger, C. D. (1979). *Police selection and evaluation.* New York: Praeger.

Staudacher, C. (1987). *Beyond grief: A guide for recovering from the death of a loved one.* Oakland, CA: New Harbinger.

Stearns, A. K. (1984). *Living through personal crisis.* New York: Ballantine Books.

Stillman, F. (1986). The invisible victims: Myths and realities. In J. T. Reese & H. A. Goldstein (Eds.), *Psychological services for law enforcement* (pp. 143–146). Washington, DC: U.S. Government Printing Office.

Titchener, J. L. (1982). Post-traumatic decline: A consequence of unresolved destructive drives. In C. R. Figley (Ed.), *Trauma and its wake: Traumatic stress theory, research, and intervention* (Vol. 2, pp. 5–19). New York: Brunner/Mazel.

van Ornum, W., & Mordock, J. B. (1990). *Crisis counseling with children and adolescents: A guide for nonprofessional counselors.* New York: Continuum.

Weisaeth, L. (1986). Post-traumatic stress disorder after an industrial disaster. In P. Pichot, P. Berner, P. Wolf, & K. Thau (Eds.), *Psychiatry—The state of the art* (pp. 299–307). New York: Plenum.

Weisman, A. (1973). Coping with untimely death. *Psychiatry, 36,* 366–377.

Williams, T. (1988). Diagnosis and treatment of survivor guilt: The bad penny syndrome. In J. P. Wilson, Z. Harel, & B. Kahana (Eds.), *Human adaptation to extreme stress: From the Holocaust to Vietnam* (pp. 319–336). New York: Plenum.

Williams, T. (1993). Trauma and the workplace. In J. P. Wilson & B. Raphael (Eds.), *International handbook of traumatic stress syndromes* (pp. 925–933). New York: Plenum.

Wolfelt, A. D. (1988). *Death and grief: A guide for clergy.* Muncie, IN: Accelerated Development.

Woolfolk, R. I., & Richardson, F. C. (1978). *Stress, sanity, and survival.* New York: Monarch.

Worden, J. (1991). *Grief counseling and grief therapy: A handbook for the mental health practitioner* (2nd ed.) New York: Springer.

Part Two

Effective Coping
with Specific Contexts

Chapter 4

Traumatic Death in Pregnancy: The Significance of Meaning and Attachment

Anne Speckhard

Perhaps because of its unavoidably commonplace nature, the traumatic potential of pregnancy loss has long been overlooked by clinicians and researchers. Political struggles over the definition of developmental personhood have likewise clouded the issue. It is important to stress, from the outset, that the traumatic potential of such loss as experienced by the pregnant individual is in no way dependent upon consensual—or even legal—definitions of personhood. Although categorical definitions may be called upon by particular factions to support a given political stand on whether or not the decision to terminate a pregnancy should be considered a legal right sanctioned by law, such societal debates are not germane to the highly personal idiosyncratic experience of any particular individual nor to the field's understanding of the traumatic potential of such experience. Although meaning has long been recognized as an essential component of the traumatic experience (Hill, 1971), it was essentially taken for granted that meaning played a role only in obvious, consensually agreed upon traumatic situations—such as violent death, the ambiguity of missing-in-action status, or divorce. Recent theoretical and clinical developments in traumatology have highlighted the interpretative nature of the trauma response. Thus even "mundane" events can carry powerful traumatic potential, a potential comprehensible only within a uniquely individualistic developmental–contextual framework (Donovan, 1991; Donovan & McIntyre, 1990).

Clearly, not every pregnancy loss, or interruption of pregnancy, is experienced as a traumatic death. Indeed, for many women, such events may not even be considered losses. Obviously, this chapter is not about these individuals. This chapter focuses on the traumatic death response of women to the loss, or inter-ruption, of their pregnancies. However, although physiological reactions of reexperience and boundaries defining the traumatic event, among other things, often differ across the sexes, men may also experience the loss/interruption of pregnancy as traumatic (Shostak & Mclouth, 1984), as may other interested and disinterested parties (e.g., extended family, siblings of the fetus/embryo, and health care providers) (Hern & Corrigan, 1978). Because of the uniquely indi-vidual nature of traumatic experience, it is crucial for clinicians and researchers to bear in mind that one person's ease of experience does not logically negate the very real nature of the experiences of others. Thus, while this chapter, in keeping with the overall theme of the book, is about the experience of preg-nancy loss as a traumatic death event, the same experience can be lived in very different manners by different individuals. It goes against the grain of a genuine developmental–contextual approach to treat this subject categorically (Donovan & McIntyre, 1990).

IDIOSYNCRATIC MEANING AS CENTRAL
TO UNDERSTANDING PREGNANCY LOSS TRAUMA

By definition, psychological trauma is a highly individualistic, contextually interpretative response to experience, occurring on both a physiological and psychological level (Donovan, 1991, 1992). Studies of the complex nature of trauma-related vulnerability and resiliency have highlighted the fact that indi-viduals respond differently to potentially traumatic experiences depending upon previous experience, context, and expectations. In other words, the meaning of any given experience can vary greatly, not only from one individual to another, but significantly over the duration of a given individual's lifetime. Thus, given the appropriate context and the idiosyncratically necessary antecedent priming experience(s), virtually any experience can have traumatic impact, even retro-spectively as new experiences change the meanings that are assigned to previ-ously experienced events.[1]

This elemental understanding of trauma being "meaning driven" is often overlooked in the address of the role of normative events to potentially function in a traumatogenic capacity for an individual (or class of individuals) within any, or all, contexts. This oversight is a result of the fact that sophisticated

---

[1]This retrospective semiogenesis of trauma occurs particularly with respect to voluntary induced abortion. At the time of the abortion, the experience may not be considered a traumatic death event. However, years later, when assigning meanings that result in parental attachment to a pregnancy during the same stage of development as that in which the previous pregnancy(ies) was aborted, an individual may experience a cognitive dissonance, creating retrospective assign-ments of meaning that redefine the earlier pregnancy interruption(s) as a traumatic death event(s). This becomes particularly powerful for the individual who subsequently undergoes the loss of a "wanted" pregnancy, because such loss(es) can come to be redefined as a spiritual punishment for, or simply as a physical consequence of, earlier terminations, which may themselves also become redefined as currently "wanted" and as containing the traumatic death(s) of one's fetal child(ren).

trauma theory originated in, and (except in rare instances) continues to be defined from, studies relating to those events in regard to which there is a great deal of external and internal consensus regarding their potential traumatogenic nature (e.g., combat-related post-traumatic stress disorder [PTSD]; rape-, incest-, and child abuse–related trauma; and natural catastrophic trauma). The result is that far too much attention has been placed in the development of trauma theory on defining the nature of potentially traumatic events and the levels of expected trauma genesis, and far too little attention has been paid to the internal experiential meanings attached to these traumatogenic events and the subsequent psychological trauma that ensues.

Despite widespread nonrecognition it is, however, indisputable that individual meanings attached to events and circumstances, as they are experientially and physiologically mediated, are in fact the actual driving force behind the psychological trauma response and determine whether or not an event is experienced as traumatic. Likewise, because the events and circumstances that are experienced as trauma vary by individual, the potential for traumatization cannot ever be anticipated solely from an external perspective. In other words, trauma, apart from the meanings assigned within the experience of an individual, is an indifferent phenomenon. Trauma by itself is never preprogrammed in an a priori sense. Given the right set of present and antecedent circumstances and meanings, basically anything can, even retroactively, result in traumatogenesis. Trauma is always an unavoidably individualistic response to experience.

With regard to the potential traumatogenic nature of pregnancy loss/ interruption this fact has been greatly disregarded. Unfortunately, the fierce political–ideological debate surrounding the relative rights and humanity of the fetus/embryo has made it difficult for clinicians and researchers to objectively consider the possibility that a given individual pregnancy loss or interruption may be experienced as traumatic either at the time of the event itself or retrospectively as circumstances in the individual's life change. Obscured by the controversy over "right to life" versus "freedom of choice" arguments is the fact that psychological trauma is potentiated by the unique experiential meanings attached to events or circumstances as they are experienced within the distinctively idiosyncratic context of the individual. Hence, what is missed is recognition of the fact that any pregnancy loss or interruption of pregnancy has the potential for any given individual to be experienced traumatically depending upon that individual and his or her current and antecedent experiential–meaning contexts.

This chapter examines the many symbolic meanings that are frequently assigned to a pregnancy experience and its manner of termination. As the contextual and idiosyncratic meanings of the individual experiencing the event are understood as pivotal to the potential traumatogenic capacity of pregnancy loss or interruption, these assignments of meanings can also be understood as potential predictors of increased risk.

Clinical experience working with individuals traumatized by pregnancy loss/ interruption and a synthesis of the literature pertaining to theories of attachment, loss, grief, and trauma suggest a theory regarding the traumatogenic capacity of pregnancy loss/interruption. Its thesis is, simply stated, that the potential for psychological trauma to occur in response to pregnancy loss/interruption is greatly increased when the assignment of meanings, particularly those that promote parental attachment to the fetus/embryo, have occurred (even on an unconscious level), thereby creating an experiential–meaning context that renders the loss or interruption of pregnancy[2] as containing multilevel and complex losses.[3] Such losses frequently include, but are not limited to, defining the loss as a type of inescapable human death event and/or the death of one's fetal child.[4]

To support and examine this thesis, this chapter describes the normal unfolding (and withholding) of a parental attachment process that occurs during pregnancy; the types of traumatogenic assignment of meanings that may exist even when termination is the desired outcome, including projective identifications with the fetus/embryo; the behaviors that (as a result of a disrupted attachment) are often activated upon death of the fetus/embryo; and the complicated mourning processes that occur when death in pregnancy is experienced as the traumatic disruption of parental attachment and grieving is not adequately supported. Assessment and treatment strategies are presented as well as a theoretical basis for understanding and attending to traumatic pregnancy loss[5] experiences.

TRAUMATIC PREGNANCY LOSS DEFINED

Although there have been many studies documenting the experience of pregnancy loss as trauma (Barnard, 1990; Cavenar & Spaulding, 1978; DeVeber,

---

[2]Pregnancy loss in this context can even include the loss of a "wished-for," but not yet conceived, pregnancy, as when the losses involved with infertility become defined in such a manner that menses is experienced as signaling, yet again, the traumatic death of the "wished-for" conception and successfully delivered pregnancy. Thus even ideas can be experienced traumatically when their meanings are such that they render a normal experience such as menses as containing elements of death and inescapability.

[3]The losses involved in pregnancy loss/interruption are as varied as the meanings that are assigned to it, but can and often do include a perception of loss of, and/or threat to, relationship with the biological partner; loss of parental or spousal role assignment(s); loss of control and/or the belief in an orderly world; loss, or threat of loss, to subsequent fertility; loss of social status and/or independence as an adult parental member of society; loss of a family member; loss of a good self-concept based on one's fertility, role assignments, and/or one's nurturing and protective capacities; and loss of a sense of one's personal invulnerability based upon assumptions about oneself that are challenged by the loss.

[4]Throughout this chapter the scientific terms of fetus and embryo are used as appropriate to the stage of development to refer to the life that is lost when pregnancy fails or is terminated. Alternately, the term *fetal child* is used in referring to the bereaved's perception of that same loss when an attachment to the fetus/embryo has occurred in the bereaved. Although it is not a scientific description per se, the term *fetal child* serves the scientific purpose of providing a more accurate description of the bereaved's experience of the pregnancy loss and anguish over it.

[5]Although not all interruptions of pregnancy are experienced as involving a loss (e.g., an induced abortion where no loss is perceived), for the purpose of this work, and in the service of simplicity, the term *pregnancy loss* is used hereafter in referring to traumatogenic pregnancy terminations of any type (i.e., therapeutic and nontherapeutic abortion, miscarriage, and stillbirth) because these do generally involve a perception of loss.

Ajzenstat, & Chisholm, 1991; Erikson, 1989; Furlong & Black, 1984; Hanley, Piersma, King, Larson, & Foy, 1992; Magyari, Wedhase, Ifft, & Callahan, 1987; Ney, 1982; Ney & Wickett, 1989; Peppers, 1987, 1989; Rue, 1981; Rue & Speckhard, 1992; Selby, 1990; Speckhard, 1987a, 1987b; Speckhard & Rue, 1992, 1993), the proportion of women traumatized is unknown (Koop, 1989; Speckhard, 1989). However, the potential for trauma exists for all women undergoing a pregnancy loss, depending upon how the event is defined by the woman. When it is perceived by the woman as involving a human death event, particularly when parental attachment to the deceased has occurred, the experience very closely conforms to the DSM-IV criteria (American Psychiatric Association [APA], 1994) for defining a trauma.

Central to the DSM-IV criteria defining a stressor capable of causing trauma is that the event involves "actual or threatened death or serious injury, or other threat to one's physical integrity; or witnessing an event that involves death, injury, or the threat to the physical integrity of another person." Accordingly, the stressor capable of producing trauma is usually experienced with "intense fear, helplessness, or horror" (APA, 1994, p. 424).

Such emotions are common to many pregnancy loss experiences, especially if circumstances allow for the death event to be perceived, if parental attachment has occurred, and/or the woman is emotionally unsupported in dealing with the event. Seeing, touching, or holding the remains of a dead fetus/embryo is often experienced as the witnessing of a human death event. This experience of perceiving a human death, and the response of psychological trauma, is not limited to the woman herself, but at times extends to the health care professional as well (Kaltreider, Goldsmith, & Margolis, 1979) who may witness the delivery of a dead fetus or the dismemberment of fetal parts.

If parental attachment to the fetus/embryo has occurred, the trauma expands to including the perception of threat to, and death of, one's own fetal child, which in some cases occurs by physical violence and/or human volition (the volitional element often worsening the trauma for adults). The pregnancy loss event may also include the perception of a threat to one's own bodily integrity, including a threat of death to self, and the uterus may afterward be regarded as a death site (Speckhard, 1985, 1987b; Speckhard & Rue, 1992, 1993).

Prior to DSM-IV, the criteria for defining a traumatic event was that the experience be one that "would be markedly distressing to almost anyone," and "outside the range of usual human experience (i.e., outside the range of such common experiences as simple bereavement)" (APA, 1987, p. 247). No woman expects to miscarry, experience a stillbirth, or undergo an abortion[6,7] (voluntary

---

[6]*Abortion* in this chapter is used to refer to induced abortion only; the term *miscarriage* is used to refer to spontaneous abortion.

[7]Likewise, those who opt for abortion frequently have already lost a significant degree of control in having experienced a birth control failure or other means of having become "unintentionally pregnant"; thus not only was abortion an unexpected course of action, so also was the pregnancy itself.

or therapeutic), and the experience is likely to be "markedly distressing to almost anyone." However, it is both a common experience and one that may involve only simple bereavement, the degree of traumatization depending, for the most part, upon what sorts of assignments of meaning,[8] particularly those that define relationship, existed prior to the death event (Speckhard & Rue, 1992, 1993). The DSM-IV criteria demonstrate a recognition for the ubiquity of some traumatic events that are unfortunately not at all outside the "range of normal human experience."

When trauma does occur, simple bereavement usually does not. Impacted grief and complicated mourning are the more likely result (Speckhard & Rue, 1993). Likewise, the ubiquity of pregnancies that end in fetal/embryonic death is similar to the experience of disaster or war: Despite its ubiquity, a pregnancy loss experience falls outside the range of usual human experience in that the events that occur defy normal expectations.

Although perception of the event is central, the sudden physiological trauma to the body that occurs with pregnancy loss may also be emotionally overwhelming, requiring the employment of the dissociative defenses normally used to defend against psychic trauma.[9] Each of the factors listed above has separately, and in combination, the potential for engendering trauma responses that can overwhelm the psyche, requiring a dissociative response (Speckhard & Rue, 1992, 1993).

COMPLICATED MOURNING AND TRAUMATIC PREGNANCY LOSS

When attachment in pregnancy is disrupted by fetal/embryonic death, a grieving process ensues that often becomes what Rando (1991, 1993) labeled a *complicated mourning process*. Four factors interact to influence circumstances when grief over a pregnancy loss does not take a straightforward course, as in simple bereavement.

First, it is the thesis of this chapter that attachment in pregnancy is often not socially recognized and attachment behaviors that occur upon separation from an attachment figure are also not generally understood.

Second, if there is survivor guilt associated with how a pregnancy terminated or traumatic images (either perceived or imagined) of how the fetal/ embryonic death and exit/removal from the uterus occurred, these can often overwhelm the psyche with trauma that requires dissociation as a defense

---

[8]As already noted, such meanings are infinite in variety and may include reactions to having become pregnant in the first place, the pain involved in the loss, loss of control, etc.

[9]The normal physiological processes that are set in motion at birth to offset the bodily changes, hormonal shifts, and physical trauma occurring during pregnancy and at birth do not necessarily occur in the same healing fashion following miscarriage, abortion, or stillbirth (Kohn & Moffitt, 1992; Sears, 1982). The resultant physiological imbalances may as a result be more intensely experienced, of longer duration, and more difficult to recover from.

mechanism. When the traumatic material is dissociated in whole, or part, the bereaved often does not have access to all the feelings surrounding the traumatic death, thus blocking resolution (Speckhard & Rue, 1992, 1993).

Third, the fetal/embryonic death by any type of pregnancy loss may symbolically signify more than simply the death event at hand, contributing to the current level of stress and in many cases stirring up previously dissociated trauma. Because pregnancy is one of the primary means by which family ties are extended, loss in pregnancy can often strongly symbolize other role losses that may be actual or threatened. The virtual nonentity of the fetus/embryo makes possible the assignment of many symbolic meanings to the events of pregnancy and its termination, which allows for a number of differing losses[10] to potentially be perceived upon pregnancy termination (even by healthy birth) and the need for a grieving process to ensue. These losses may be even more strongly experienced than the death of relationship to the fetus/embryo per se. To an understanding of these three topics the remainder of this chapter is devoted.

Fourth, in our culture, the loss of a pregnancy itself, notwithstanding the many symbolic losses involved (which may or may not be consciously acknowledged), is often socially disenfranchised. Doka (1989) noted that when a loss cannot be openly acknowledged, publicly mourned, or socially supported, grief becomes disenfranchised. Because death in pregnancy and during the perinatal period is often not societally recognized as a significant loss, there are few rituals that are consistently available and offered as means for supporting the grief process of the bereaved, as are usually offered as grief support for other more recognized types of death experiences (e.g., viewing of the deceased, funeral, burial, obituary, and sending of cards and flowers). Likewise, the social sanctions, and even outright hostility, that exist for choosing to abort can often contribute to the difficulty of a woman trying to express, or work through, her grief over an induced termination of pregnancy (Speckhard, 1985, 1987b).

Writing on the subject of coping with infant and fetal loss, Gilbert and Smart (1992) pointed out that such losses constitute an assault upon the assumptive world of the individual(s) undergoing the loss(es), in terms of the meanings and emotions attached to the child (including those of parental attachment); upon the bereaved's sense of personal invulnerability and view of oneself and one's child as generally positive and as deserving of good; and/or upon one's belief in an orderly world. Differing assumptions regarding these same topics are also possible (i.e., a sense of personal vulnerability, a view of oneself and/or one's child as undeserving, and a belief in a less than orderly world) and are also affected by such losses, often in terms of reinforcing a negative view of oneself, one's fetal child, and/or of one's place as increasingly vulnerable in a negative world.

---

[10]Examples of such losses may include role losses such as that of parent-to-be or fertile person, the potential of sibling relationships, identifications with the fetus/embryo, and a deepening of commitment with one's partner.

ATTACHMENT AND LOSS IN PREGNANCY

Contrary to many popular beliefs, attachment between parent and child begins in pregnancy, not at birth.[11] That attachment on the part of the fetus begins in utero is a scientifically well established fact. While only sparse research exists on the subject of maternal attachment in pregnancy, Leifer (1980), who conducted a landmark study of the psychological processes undergone by pregnant women, wrote: "Pregnancy is hardly the picture of psychological passivity that many have painted in regard to the pregnant woman's psychological processes of relating to the developing fetus" (p. 185). In her study following women throughout pregnancy, Leifer concluded that "a major psychological task of pregnancy is the development of emotional attachment to the fetus; that this attachment develops in marked and discernable stages; and that the strength of the bond with the fetus established by the end of pregnancy is predictive of early maternal behavior and attitudes" (p. 185).

In describing the psychological process of emotional attachment to the developing fetus, Leifer wrote: "Women used pregnancy to identify and initiate a 'relationship' with the fetus" (Leifer, 1980, p. 185). Similarly, Rando (1993) wrote that in no other relationship are so many dreams, hopes, needs, thoughts, feelings, beliefs, meanings, and expectations projected onto the other as in the parent–child relationship. She stated: "This is because the parent begins the process of projection onto a fantasized child-to-be long before the birth of the child" (Rando, 1993, p. 614).

Leifer's research, as well as other clinical and small research studies of the psychological processes of parental attachment in pregnancy (Borg & Lasker, 1989; Condon, 1986; Gilbert & Smart, 1992; Klauss & Kennel, 1976; Peppers & Knapp, 1980b; Speckhard, 1985, 1987b), have consistently reported that for the pregnant woman, attachment often begins shortly after conception; but far before birth, when an image of *baby* is formed, projections of identity begin, and the emotions are engaged in decisions about nurturing and protecting the growing fetal life.

However, while many prominent theorists have long held the view that maternal relationship begins after conception, rather than at birth (Benedek, 1970; Bibring, 1961; Deutsch, 1945), and preliminary research efforts in the last two decades have in fact borne that out, few have understood the importance, in terms of potential traumatization to the individual, of the disruption of these bonds. Of the many meanings that may be assigned to a pregnancy, parental attachment is the strongest, in terms of creating a context for its loss, or interruption, to be experienced as the traumatic death of one's unborn child.

This recognition of the traumatogenic potential of disrupted attachments in pregnancy was highlighted by Speckhard (1985) and Speckhard and Rue (1992,

---

[11]For some, attachment on the part of the adult may even begin before conception, as when an attachment is formed to the idea of one's child, hence the very real experience of loss that occurs for those who attempt to conceive but find that they are infertile.

1993) in their clinical studies of women who experienced psychological trauma in response to induced abortion. On the basis of their clinical work and interviews with women traumatized by abortion, as well as other types of pregnancy loss, Speckhard and Rue (1992, 1993) asserted that the degree of attachment in pregnancy is very often predictive of the degree of traumatization that occurs when a pregnancy fails or is voluntarily terminated. In regard to abortion loss, these authors demonstrated that the bonds of attachment to the developing fetus/embryo are frequently established very early in pregnancy and the breaking of these bonds may be experienced traumatically, even when the termination of pregnancy has been the desired course of action, as in abortion. (Speckhard, 1985, 1987a, 1987b; Speckhard & Rue, 1992, 1993).

Likewise, Gilbert and Smart (1992) identified the need to remediate the disruption of the assumptive world of parents who were coping with infant or fetal loss occurring by stillbirth, miscarriage, or therapeutic abortion. In their listing of the assumptions that are assaulted in these types of losses, the authors highlighted the assignment of meanings to the fetal child, especially in terms of parental attachment to the fetal child and the parents' abilities to protect their unborn child.

Ambivalence in the Maternal Attachment Process

In her research, Leifer (1980) concluded that making bonds of attachment to the developing fetus was an important preparatory task for the parental role. However, she found that some mothers made conscious efforts to withhold themselves from the process of attaching to the developing fetus/embryo until late pregnancy or birth. Interestingly, those that avoided attachment gave reasons such as the fear of miscarriage, or of loss, for doing so. Thus the psychodynamics and previous loss experiences of the pregnant women determined, in part, the strength and timing of when the bonds of attachment occurred.

From clinical studies of women traumatized by their abortion experiences, Speckhard (1985, 1987b) found that maternal attachment was often extended in pregnancy even as the decisions to terminate the pregnancy were being made. Hence ambivalence in bonds of attachment extended during pregnancy also occurs where abortion is the decided upon outcome.

From his exploratory studies of parental attachment during pregnancy carried to term, Condon (1986) reported that ambivalence toward the fetus may arise when resentment, stemming from the losses and threats of pregnancy, coexists with feelings of attachment or affection. This ambivalence in meanings assigned to the pregnancy (i.e., of an undue burden coexisting with the view of the fetus/embryo as one's fetal child) explains how a woman can suffer traumatization over the loss of her fetal child even after having made the voluntary decision to abort it. In these cases the fact that attachment to the fetal child existed, but was not strong enough to mobilize forces in favor of carrying the pregnancy to term, can in itself retrospectively create a self-concept that assaults the individual's sense of self as good and nurturing, one's potential role as a good parent, and one's sense of personal invulnerability, as well as that of one's child.

Ambivalent feelings toward and projections of negative self-concept upon a child at any stage in the child's life may be viewed as potential precursors to child abuse. Indeed, researchers have documented that not only does attachment begin in pregnancy, but that child abuse often begins in utero as well. Condon (1986) documented cases in which parents attempted to hurt their developing fetuses by punching the mother's abdomen, ingesting an overdose (to the fetus) of stimulants or depressant drugs, and other such acts. Thus a fetal child can become the repository of negative feelings about the parental self, or others, and the subject of an ambivalent attachment, even of abuse.

Regarding parental attachment during pregnancy, Condon (1986) wrote that "some degree of ambivalence is probably ubiquitous" (p. 513). Clinical work with men and women who have suffered various types of pregnancy loss suggests that ambivalence toward the fetus/embryo (despite its probable ubiquity in all pregnancies) is often assigned highly symbolic retrospective meaning(s) following the loss, even when that loss had no volitional aspects. For instance, those who miscarry or who suffer a stillbirth often are plagued with guilt, wondering if their ambivalence was somehow responsible for the loss, especially if the loss coincided with a particular expression of that ambivalence.

> A 27-year-old woman traumatized by a recent miscarriage at 13 weeks for which no medical reason was found reported that she felt guilty for the miscarriage. When asked why she felt this way, she related how she and her husband had argued the day of the miscarriage, the argument ending with the woman stating to her husband, "I should never have gotten pregnant. This is the last thing we need right now." Within less than 24 hours her pregnancy miscarried, hence the retrospective genesis of guilt-inducing, traumatogenic meaning (i.e., her conclusion that her ambivalent feelings and thoughts of rejection "killed" the fetus).

Role Reversals and Projective Identification in the Attachment Process

Freud (1914/1957) stated that parental love for a child is an expression of the parents' own long-abandoned childish narcissism revisited. Although this is a pathologizing view of parental love, projections upon and role reversals with a child, beginning even with a fetal child, can and do occur. If "loved" in this manner, a child may often be expected by the parents to fill their unmet dreams and wishes (projected in fantasy as a means of meeting their needs). This seems to be particularly prevalent in (but is in no way limited to) emotionally impoverished adolescent girls who become pregnant hoping to create someone to love them.

Hence, while bonds of attachment form in pregnancy, not all attachments and assignments of meaning are healthy. For instance, the attachment experiences that a parent has had are often reenacted with a child. A parent who has not had a stable nurturing attachment figure often does not know how to provide one or does not feel emotionally equipped to invest in a child's nurture. Likewise, a parent who has not had a stable attachment figure in childhood may begin, even before birth, to reverse roles with the fetal child, expecting to find in the child a lost, or never fully provided, stable attachment figure. This projective identification of the fetal child with the childhood self of the parent(s) often feeds the parent's drive to provide the child with more than he or she had. Thus nurture of the fetal child, as with older children, often becomes invested with the need to overcome any failures in attachment that occurred in the parent's history, or may include a reenactment of those disruptions of attachment. Naturally this forebodes problems for both parent and child and greatly complicates the meanings assigned to either a loss or interruption of pregnancy.

A 33-year-old patient came to therapy for help overcoming trouble in relationships with men and feelings of depression and guilt that had haunted her since a college abortion. Upon detailed exploration of the pregnancy and abortion experience it became clear that the patient had used her pregnancy unconsciously in an attempt to (through a reenactment) come to terms with her childhood experience of her mother's alternately nurturing and rejecting behaviors. Her mother had been a heavy drinker and had on numerous occasions been abusive to the patient and had communicated to her a deep hatred of herself and of all the female sex. At times, however, her mother had been good and steady in her parenting, which created confusion and ambivalence in the patient, who both loved and hated her mother as she loved and hated herself.

This patient had used the conception and death of her pregnancy to give expression to the confusion she had felt from her mother, and felt for herself as well, over whether or not she wanted to be female and able to produce offspring, whether she wanted to and was able to nurture, and whether she would destroy what she had created, as her mother had through abuse, at least partially, destroyed her own children. The patient had attempted to gain symbolic mastery of her conflicts by allowing herself to become pregnant and recreating the very conflict she was trying to come to terms with by becoming parentally attached to the developing fetus, knowing that she would not carry it to term. "I loved that baby, but I didn't want to be a mother," the patient recounted.

In her description of the abortion she related how she had used it as a replaying of her own rejection at the hands of her mother, and described her guilt over having reenacted this rejection with her own fetal child. In describing her use of the abortion as a symbolic suicide, she described how she had projectively identified with her fetal child's death: "My mother never wanted a girl. . . . She never wanted me. I think I used the abortion as the closest thing I could do to killing myself. I didn't have the courage to commit suicide, so I killed my baby. I should have died instead."

The patient's extreme ambivalence toward herself and toward her mother, whom she both hated and revered, was reflected in her ambivalent attachment to the fetus. She referred to it as "my baby" and tearfully recounted her decision to abort and her failure to protect her "baby" from what she recalled experiencing during the abortion—violent images of "my baby being torn from my body." As the patient worked through the ambivalent attachment she had created, she began to discuss her horrifying and deeply troubled relationship with her mother as well. She began to grieve that troubled attachment and to understand how she had attempted to come to terms with it through replaying it in the subsequent ambivalent attachment she had made to the fetus whose life had been ended in abortion.

Characteristics of the Attachment to the Fetal Child

From the research and clinical data, it is clear that the fetus, because it is a metaphorical nonentity, or blank slate, can easily become a repository for projections of feelings about self or others. Moreover, these feelings projected onto the fetus are often the determinants of the strength, consistency, and valence (positive versus negative) of the bonds of attachment that form in regard to the developing fetus/embryo. Just as the bonds of attachment to the fetus/embryo may be strongly, consistently, and positively built, or by contrast, be ambivalently experienced, withheld, or terminated, the trauma that can occur upon pregnancy termination often reflects the dynamics of these bonds and must be understood in these terms in order to be adequately resolved.

To fully understand, predict, and/or remediate the level of psychological traumatization that can potentially ensue as a result of disrupting whatever parental bonds of attachment exist in reference to the fetal child, an understanding of the strength, consistency, and valence of these bonds must be elucidated, as well as the potential trauma responses that may be activated for the individual concerned when any disruption of a primary attachment (or triggered reexperience of such) occurs.

BOUNDARY AMBIGUITY, ATTACHMENT THEORY, AND TRAUMATIC DEATH IN PREGNANCY

Ambiguity in relationships has long been studied as a source of stress in families and individuals (Boss, 1985). In her research on the stress produced by ambiguous boundaries in family systems, Boss found that when a family member was physically absent but psychologically present (or vice versa) the degree of stress and dysfunction in the family system was the greatest. Likewise, when a family had resolved the boundary ambiguity and congruence between psychological and physical presence of its members through "grieving or closing out" a physically or psychologically absent member, or by other means of creating congruence, the family distress and dysfunction were greatly decreased.

Pregnancy is certainly a prime example of a situation in which boundary ambiguity exists: A potential family member is present but not yet present; potentially attached to, but not yet known; potentially nurtured, but also subject to choice and fate. Certainly when attachments and role transitions begin but are then stopped traumatically (e.g., a fetus is nurtured but fails to live; a healthy child is attached to in fantasy, but in reality a handicapped child is stillborn; attachments are begun, but abortion is chosen), the boundary ambiguity that arises in regard to bonds of attachment and roles in the potential or existing family unit can be excruciatingly stressful. Moreover, when the death of the fetus is experienced traumatically the boundary ambiguity existing in these individuals and systems is often not open to conscious resolution because so much of the emotional impact of the event (and in many cases, parts of the event itself) is dissociated due to its traumatic nature. As Speckhard (1985, 1987b) found with women traumatized by their abortions, ambiguous boundaries often increase, rather than decrease, with traumatic death in pregnancy; this is due to the fact that when separation by death occurs, the attachment to the developing fetus/embryo may persist despite its death. This psychological presence (and resultant boundary ambiguity) persists until a final and total acceptance of the death occurs (i.e., the boundaries are closed with recognition that reunion with the attachment figure is physically impossible because death has occurred).

When aspects of the death event have been dissociated from consciousness and the individual resolution has been delayed because of the unconscious urges to keep alive the psychological attachment to the fantasized fetal child, the resultant competing, dual thought process in which the death is recognized consciously, yet the bonds of attachment persist unconsciously, is one of high boundary ambiguity. When a pregnancy loss is not adequately mourned, the impacted grief and resultant ambiguity over family boundaries is often responsible for disrupting family bonds for years into the future, and is expressed in future family dynamics that bear the legacy of an unacknowledged and incompletely mourned traumatic death event. Thus treatment of traumatic death in pregnancy must have as one of its goals resolving ambiguous family boundaries through addressing the persistent attachment process, and the grief process it has impeded.

A 28-year-old married mother of two presented for therapy after her third miscarriage, which she stated had "unglued" her in a way the other two had not. Although she had experienced grief over her previous two miscarriages, they had occurred between two successful pregnancies and she had been able to move on as she became involved with parenting two active preschoolers. However, when the third miscarriage occurred, her husband had not bonded to the fetus, felt relatively little grief over its loss, and thus did not understand her grief and trauma reactions to the pregnancy loss. Likewise, her extended family responded with only minimal sympathy because they had witnessed her handling the two previous losses so well.

As the patient began to relate her story it became clear that she was dealing with a situation of extreme boundary ambiguity as strong feelings of attachment (i.e., psychological presence) persisted for not only the fetus/embryo under discussion but the others as well, despite their obvious physical absence. Moreover, her anxiety was greatly increased because no one else in her nuclear or extended family felt the way that she did. For them this was not an ambiguous situation; no persistent attachment remained. They did not understand her trauma and grief responses and stigmatized her for continuing to want to talk about her persisting attachments to her deceased fetal children (i.e., their persistent psychological presence in her mind). This situation of boundary ambiguity for the patient, which was very disparate from other family members' experience, created an environment in which she felt forced to keep her feelings and thoughts secret or risk being labeled *crazy*. Likewise, it had begun to disrupt the harmony between her and her husband, her extended family, and her daughters.

The miscarriage occured at home, with the delivery of the fetus in the toilet, followed the next day by delivery of the placenta. Inadequately prepared by her health care provider, who assumed she knew what to expect, the patient was surprised by the placenta, and was horrified when it was delivered. She became frantic with concerns over her bodily integrity. Likewise, she was very hurt that she had been left alone at home with her two children to experience this sort of trauma, which called into question whether or not she could rely upon her family and her doctor in times of crisis. Lastly, she was subsequently unable to get through to her husband and relatives how traumatized and abandoned she felt and, even though she had been through two miscarriages previously, how grieved she was over this one. Thus there was not only the persistent attachment that was bothering her, but aspects of abandonment and disrupted attachment from her circle of attachment figures (including her doctor) as well, which only made their subsequent stigmatization of her reactions worse.

As the patient hid a growing obsession with the fetal child, trying to bury her hurt and anger over the lack of recognition of its loss, she became severely depressed. When she came to therapy, she received the long-needed permission to name and discuss her experience in terms of grief and trauma, and finally she found a place where she could express what she had attempted to numb inside of her. In this regard, the therapist followed her lead and the fetus was referred to in the manner in which she chose to refer to it, as "her baby," which allowed the patient to let out a torrent of emotion that had been locked up inside. This simple reflection of her internal reality tapped into an outpouring of tears and gratitude coupled with anger that only in a therapist's office had she finally found another person who understood that, despite the fact that she was only two and half months pregnant, she had attached to her fetal child.

As with most trauma patients she took time to warm up to the process of therapy and only gradually revealed what she was sure were evidences of how *crazy* she had become. An example of her fears was that she worried over how obsessed she had become with her fetal child because almost daily she envisioned her. Interestingly, she envisioned her as 3 years old, which would have been the age of the first miscarried "child" had it been born. Pondering her obsessive thoughts she stated, "I'm the only one that remembers her, and maybe I made her older in my mind to remember the others as well. Maybe I feel guilty that I never really grieved for them since I got so busy with Sherry after she was born."

In part of her treatment the patient addressed some emotional abandonment issues in her own childhood that had been triggered by being abandoned in the experience of this miscarriage. In the present however, her past issues became intertwined with her present inability to move on from attachment to the deceased lest the deceased lose all identity as having ever existed. Because all three of the miscarriages had involved real attachment on her part, she could not let them go without someone validating their reality. To do so felt too much like the emotional abandonment she herself had endured in childhood and was presently enduring. To be able to grieve, and let them go, she needed someone to allow her to talk about how her fetal children had been real as well as how her attachment to them was real.

As she worked simultaneously through her issues surrounding abandonment and her attachment to her fetal children, she began to see that letting them go would not need to be an abandonment. Her grief found an outlet in memorializing them with a needlepoint giving them the names she used privately in referring to them in her mind, thus allowing them to be real, however deceased. Likewise, she solidified her beliefs about them being in heaven, which released her from further responsibilities to them and allowed her to feel comfortable with letting them go. As this patient worked through clarifying her family boundaries and making them congruent with how other members of her family defined the family's membership, she learned that she could share her feelings with others without demanding that they feel the same, and in receiving comfort from her spouse and extended family she was able to work through her own issues regarding abandonment.

Of significance in this case, and in others like it, is a point that Rando (1991, 1993) made regarding the mourning process: that often the bereaved will "grieve out" a family member while deciding to keep some level of attachment with the deceased. When this is done in a manner that does not deny that death has occurred (i.e., the attachment is recognized as being "other-worldly" and unlike attachments occurring "in this life"), it can signify a healthy closure of all boundaries occurring in "this life" (i.e., those relating to physical and psychological presence). Likewise, the revisiting of grief on anniversary dates, even years after the death, is normal and should not be pathologized as a persistent attachment.

Laing (1969) wrote that families unconsciously make agreements as to who is, and who is not, considered a part of the family system. Resolution of boundary ambiguity (Boss, 1985) within a family requires addressing on some level the members' collective agreement as to who is present, and not present, in the family. Similarly, it requires that the loss and continued attachment to the deceased be recognized and, in time, be relinquished via a process of grieving so that other attachments may no longer be overshadowed by a physically absent, but psychologically present, family member.

This often means coming to terms with what the pregnancy symbolized, the characteristics that were attributed to the fetal child, and the hopes and dreams that were harbored for birth and beyond, and finding ways in which these three can be put to rest. For some this means naming and grieving for a fetus/embryo that in imagination and emotion had become "my baby." In these cases death rituals that are culturally embraced can often be useful to mark the letting go of the fetal child. Such rituals might include holding a religious service in which the deceased is turned over to God; creating a gravesite, or a marker, despite the frequent absence (or prior disposal) of fetal remains; or having a wall plaque or special memento in the home to mark the fetal child's place in the bereaved's heart. There are many ways to facilitate grief, but most important with traumatic pregnancy loss is to end the persistent psychological attachment (and the resultant boundary ambiguity) and to address the meanings surrounding the event, which in terms of cognitive restructuring may continue to persist in the present. This occurs by creating a safe environment in which frightening and negative meanings and/or the persistent bonds of attachment to the fetus/embryo can be discussed.[12] If such admissions occur, the therapy then needs to provide an environment in which the traumatic assignments of meaning and of attachment that define the loss as a death event can be reviewed so that the death no longer needs to be denied either consciously or unconsciously, and grief may occur unimpeded.

When the dissociated aspects of the death event are recovered the patient has the opportunity to work through realization that an attachment has occurred as well as to finally sever the bonds of attachment. Normal aspects of grief and trauma resolution frequently include a desire to undo the loss or search for it. The therapy process must facilitate a final resolution by keeping these processes conscious until the bereaved realizes on all levels of consciousness that undoing the loss or finding the deceased still living are impossible tasks. When this conscious grief process occurs, psychic energy is freed to put into other bonds of attachment (frequently to repair relationships with subsequently born siblings or a spouse who was blamed for the loss, who may not have felt "in" the family since the loss occurred).

Search Process Following a Disrupted Primary Attachment

Writing on grief and loss, Bowlby (1979) described a set of behaviors typical of persons (at any stage of the life cycle) who had undergone separation from an important attachment figure. This behavioral set consists of expressions of protest and sadness, a search process for the lost attachment figure, and, in long-term separation or unresolved grief upon death, detachment. His theories give credence to the view of ambiguous boundaries occurring as a result of a psychological attachment persisting beyond the death of the attachment figure as a potentially normative, though unhealthy, adaptation to the death.

When there has been an attachment in pregnancy (especially one in which the attachment is defined in association with other lost relationships), these behavioral reactions to separation described by Bowlby can occur in reaction

---

[12]It is important to state here that the meanings and persistence of attachment that may or may not exist need to be assessed carefully, following the subtle clues given by the individual being treated. An iatrogenic situation can (and of course should never) be created if negative meanings and suggestions of attachment are attributed to the pregnancy that never before existed. There exists a fine line between listening carefully to what is being said and suggesting what is not being said, and this division is one that should be carefully respected in the therapy process.

to fetal/embryonic death as well. Indeed, if the fetal child had become symbolically important to the bereaved or had been internally formulated as an attachment figure for the parent, or as a means of symbolically resolving past attachment traumas, these attachment behaviors should be expected to occur.

They are, however, rarely anticipated or understood. Although the disruption of attachment in pregnancy is the central dynamic underlying trauma and grief reactions following pregnancy loss (Speckhard, 1985, 1987b; Speckhard & Rue, 1993), it is also the most completely overlooked and misunderstood. The loss of a fetus/embryo by death is already minimized in our culture. Even more overlooked, then, is the loss of attachment of meanings and relationship to a deceased fetal child. Hence it is rare for those bereaved by pregnancy loss to receive support for resolving what the attachment symbolized in terms of their own psychodynamic needs, and such losses are as a result often described as that from which many do not ever completely recover (Rando, 1986).

Search Process Following Death in Pregnancy

Bowlby (1979) stressed that when death occurs, the disruption in attachment is often not consciously accepted until after an exhaustive search process for the deceased attachment figure occurs, and this can create problems for the bereaved. According to Bowlby, if demands are made upon the bereaved to accept the death before the search process has proven the impossibility of reuniting with the deceased, a conscious acceptance of the death often coexists with an unconscious continuation of the search process for the deceased (i.e., similar to Boss's (1985) concept of boundary ambiguity). When this occurs, resolution of grief is impossible until the unconscious search is somehow concluded, and the death, and disrupted attachment brought about by the death, are accepted in their finality (i.e., the physical and psychological boundaries are congruent).

The search process in those bereaved by pregnancy loss is often evident in the following behaviors, all of which, according to Bowlby's (1979) theory, are aimed at reinstating the lost attachment figure: keeping the fetal child alive in memory (by remaining preoccupied with the characteristics of the deceased fetal child, gaining weight as though one were still pregnant, or experiencing waking daydreams or nighttime dreams about holding the baby and hallucinations of hearing an infant crying), and/or projecting feelings about the deceased fetal child onto another child or children (by becoming pregnant again soon after the loss; wanting to adopt, or actually adopting, a same-age child; and forming an attachment to other children similar to the deceased fetal child in terms of perceived characteristics and age).

Experience of those bereaved in pregnancy of a fetal attachment figure suggests that the fetal child is often kept alive in fantasy and preoccupation with who it could have been, and/or through projection of feelings for the deceased fetal child onto another child or children—each of these being an expression of the bereaved's inability to accept the finality of the loss.

Hence, in these persons, a search and reinstatement process coexists with conscious denial that grief persists. This type of competing dual thought process—on the one hand denying grief, but on the other unconsciously keeping alive a preoccupation with (i.e., search for) the deceased fetal child—was documented by Speckhard (1985, 1987b) in women who were psychologically traumatized by their abortions. Likewise, in this regard women undergoing various types of perinatal losses frequently make suicidal expressions that are often no more than expressions of wanting to rejoin the deceased (thereby creating congruent boundaries).

Speckhard and Rue (1993) wrote that women who have suffered a traumatic pregnancy loss will often only admit to the existence of a persistent psychological attachment and search behaviors after becoming secure in therapy.

A 28-year-old woman came in for therapy for help in "getting over" a relationship of the previous 2 years. As the patient described the relationship, she made light of an abortion that had occurred near its end. However, despite her wish to minimize the impact of the abortion, she kept bringing up material about it and her persisting ambivalent attachment to her fetal child. She explained, "I really wanted it, but I tried not to think of it as a baby, otherwise it would be too hard. Sometimes I would think about what it would look like and talk to it. . . . When the day came I asked the doctor to put me out, so I wouldn't have to know. When I woke up I wasn't bleeding at all, so I thought maybe there was a mistake, that they missed me somehow and that I was still pregnant. So I went home and for months I didn't get a period, so I believed that I was still pregnant. But I didn't get any bigger, and finally I did get a period. I cried for weeks then."

This patient also told of how she had continued to have a fantasized relationship with her deceased fetal child by doing such things as volunteering with children roughly the same age as the one who had been aborted. When the therapist asked the patient if she had any thoughts about the characteristics of the embryo (being careful to use the same terms as the patient did to describe it), the patient said she thought it was a girl, and admitted that she still had the sonogram picture. In regard to her grief and claimed inability to let go of the man she had dated, she acknowledged, "I guess it's just really hard to let go of him; he's the only other living tie to my baby. We are the only ones that knew she existed, except for the doctors."

The patient's search behaviors were evident as she continued to vascillate between the finality of the separation and her wish to recoup her loss; for example, she stated her desire to adopt a girl the same age her baby would have been. The patient was helped to interpret her behaviors as a possible sign of continued attachment to her deceased fetus/embryo, and as a means of trying to search for and reinstate the loss; she opened up even more in an environment where no judgment was made of how that loss occurred or of her need to hold on to what she had rejected. The patient admitted to attempting to recoup her loss and to survivor guilt. A more straightforward path for grieving and working through the guilt was suggested: The patient was encouraged to no longer deny either the existence of the attachment or the guilt over its disruption; thus each could be directly addressed. Both were addressed as real problems needing real resolution (i.e., the need to grieve the previously denied loss, and thereby end the persisting psychological attachment, and the need to address the guilt through a process of forgiveness appropriate to the patient's belief system), and resolution strategies were successfully implemented. The patient ended therapy with no further signs of depression or searching behaviors.

Putting the Search Fantasy to Rest

Bowlby (1979) wrote that the bereaved who is displaying the attachment behavior of searching for the lost attachment will often not respond well to statements of reality, for example, that the deceased cannot be found because death has occurred. It is more helpful to support the search process, thereby allowing what has in most cases been a primarily unconscious process to find its way into conscious thoughts where the bereaved will gradually come to terms with the two competing conclusions: one of feeling the need to search, the other of knowing that searching is futile. Generally when the search is brought out into the open and all reasonable avenues of searching are exhausted the bereaved begins to settle into a more straightforward grieving process that is no longer dominated by an unconscious, and often even conscious, denial of a final and irreplaceable loss. In terms of pregnancy loss trauma, where a strong attachment to the fetal child has occurred, this process can be facilitated immediately at the time of the pregnancy loss or later if it becomes the focus of a therapeutic encounter.

Immediately after the loss, the health care professional should be aware of the potential of a strong attachment to the fetal child, and if such exists, should aid in helping the bereaved to relinquish the psychological attachment to the fetal child (i.e., help in creating congruence between psychological and physical boundaries) as the fact of the fetal death is faced. Means of facilitating this process include honoring requests by the bereaved to hold or see the fetal remains or providing a picture, memento, lock of hair, and/or clear image that the pregnancy is indeed over, that death has occurred. After the fact, this process is aided by the health care provider's recognizing the bereaved's subtle (and often not so subtle) clues to the existence of a persistent attachment, and addressing it while simultaneously offering help in coming to terms with the traumatic realization that the attachment has been physically, at least, ended, and must be relinquished on a psychological level as well.

In either immediate or delayed intervention the reality of the loss needs to be recognized so that no persistent attachment can continue. This means that if an attachment was present that defines the pregnancy loss as a death, this must be recognized so that the psychological attachment to the fetal child is relinquished and that energy is redirected into other present relationships. In the absence of this complete recognition of death, a psychological attachment to, and a search for, the lost fetal attachment can persist literally for years after the event.

BOUNDARY AMBIGUITY AND FAMILY SYSTEMS ISSUES

Boundary Ambiguity and Projected Identity in the Family System

Grief over pregnancy loss is often conveyed across generations through the ways in which future and present relationships are defined and allowed to evolve in reaction to the loss, and the ways in which unresolved grief often interferes with current and new attachments, particularly in the symbolic meanings attached to siblings of the deceased. Ambiguous boundaries with their unclear role assignments and unsevered attachments persisting on an unconscious level often create difficulties in subsequently conceived pregnancies: The normal bonding that occurs in pregnancy and at birth is overshadowed by the need to recoup the lost attachment. This is primarily due to the continued search and survival guilt preventing the new attachment from being formed simply on the basis of who is uniquely present.

A pregnancy conceived subsequent to one that ended in traumatic death of the fetus/embryo will often be the object of projections (on the part of the bereaved) about the prior pregnancy and resentment when on some level it is recognized that the fetal child has not returned. This projecting of identity and resentment when the child does not become the former attachment figure creates a scenario for the potential of rejection in pregnancy, at birth, and for as long as the identity of the deceased continues to be projected onto the subsequently conceived child.

This ambiguous situation in which, in the minds of the bereaved family members, it is unclear who is, and who is not, included in the family forebodes trouble for all, because children born into these circumstances are not given a fair chance to form their own identities; instead they are molded to fit into an idealized image of a former nonsurviving sibling. A child who grows up with the projected identity of a nonsurviving sibling, especially one that has really only existed in terms of attachment in fantasy, is doomed to failure because no child is ever going to be able to successfully compete with the idealized image of a deceased sibling that he or she is supposed to become.

Moreover, when the pregnancy that terminated traumatically had been itself the object of yet another level of projection about a lost attachment figure(s), the ambiguity and certainty of failure on the part of the subsequently conceived child to ever be able to live up to the many projected identities placed upon him or her is virtually guaranteed.

Disorders of Attachment in Surviving Siblings in Families Where Traumatic Pregnancy Loss Has Occurred

When one takes a family systems perspective on individual pathology, traumatic pregnancy loss is often evident as a contributing issue to the development of attachment disorder in surviving siblings of families in which a traumatic pregnancy loss(es) has occurred. In taking a family history it is often possible to trace back generations of problems in attachment between parents and a sibling(s) born after a stillbirth, miscarriage, or abortion. Survivor guilt, unresolved grief, and trauma responses often create extremely ambiguous boundaries in a family system in which all are affected by the continued psychological presence of a physically absent (i.e., deceased) member, and this situation often disrupts or prevents bonding to siblings of the deceased fetal child.

In adults who grew up in such circumstances it is often evident that the traumatic grief of their parents was never overcome, forever interfering with the normal attachment process between the adult (as a child) and his or her parent. Thus an adult child of a parent bereaved by pregnancy loss may carry the marks of traumatic grief forward into his or her own future long after the parent is deceased. This is often evidenced in an inability to form the sorts of secure bonds of attachment that were lacking in the individual's own childhood.

When treatment addresses the bereaved parents' likely traumatic grief over a stillbirth, miscarriage, abortion, or series of such, it is easier for the surviving sibling to admit the hurt of the incomplete or disordered attachment because the disruption and/or failure in parental attachment is no longer perceived as personal rejection. Instead, the incomplete bonding to the surviving sibling is able to be recognized and grieved as a primary loss to the patient, that was secondary to mother or father's loss, and the resultant attachment disorder may be addressed with less shame to the individual involved.

A 24-year-old woman sought out therapy in regard to her responses to her mother's persistent traumatic grief over an abortion that occurred when the patient was 7 years old. The patient described an almost overnight change in her mother after the abortion—from nurturing to yelling and screaming and eventually being hospitalized for months. Describing her mother's attempts to undo her pregnancy loss, she recounted, "She had two more babies. I guess to try and get her baby back, but she didn't even hold them. My sister was so neglected she was diagnosed with failure to thrive."

In her therapy, the patient's primary issues revolved around grief over the sudden loss of her mother following the abortion. That time period seemed to the patient to be like the psychological death of her nurturing mother, who was replaced with a wildly angry, neglecting creature. "It was like she was there one day, and gone the next—like she was two different people. She changed overnight and I didn't know why." When the patient later learned of her mother's abortion, she was angry at her mother for not nurturing the life of her "would be" sibling and for neglecting her living children. In dealing with her mother in the present, the patient needed help recognizing and extricating herself from her mother's continued attempts to recoup the losses that had begun with the abortion trauma. Her mother made frequent requests for her to return to live at home, and the patient was tempted to do so because of her own fears about attaching to others. The patient was fearful of making new attachments because to do so cued her deep feelings of shame surrounding how the traumatic pregnancy loss and its aftermath had resulted in a sudden and traumatic disruption of her relationship with her mother, and what had felt to her like a complete and total psychological abandonment.

Working through grief and shame was accomplished as the patient sorted through her emotional reactions to her mother's abortion, coming to an understanding of the forces that motivated the decision and her mother's consequent inability to handle the emotional trauma that ensued. Likewise, she grieved the loss of her mother during the years of her mother's traumatic grief, recognizing both her mother's and her own desire to attempt to undo it by having the patient return to a prior dependent state. In coming to peace with the familial losses, she realized that her task was to build herself and her relationship to her mother on an adult-to-adult level and to understand that the loss had occurred for reasons outside of herself and that she was only prolonging the grief process by trying to recapture or undo the past traumas and losses, which could never be undone.

Differing Responses by Family Members

Because trauma is a meaning-driven response, individuals, even those in the same family, may have very different responses to the same event. This is of particular significance for couples, and for families with children, because the experience of pregnancy loss can be perceived so differently from the differing perspectives of sex and age. For instance, women often draw very different boundaries around the event of pregnancy loss, and reexperience traumatic loss physiologically in ways that their male partners cannot, which can result in misunderstandings and hurt feelings.

A couple in their late 30s presented for marriage therapy for support in dealing with a miscarriage that had occurred at 17 weeks gestation 4 months previously. The husband complained that his wife seemed unable to "get over it" and that she was irritable and angrily lashed out at him in ways she had never done previously. Feeling defensive, the wife needed support to explain to her husband that the anniversary of the "would be" due date was very real in her mind, as she had envisioned carrying out very different roles than the ones she was presently occupying, whereas her husband's career plans had not been seriously disrupted by the pregnancy or by the miscarriage. Likewise, although both were very shaken by the idea of having possibly conceived an ill-formed baby, the wife relived dissociated aspects of the miscarriage with every menses, feeling horrified and saddened as her uterine contents were again expelled.

As the couple passed the due date and began to try and conceive yet again, the wife continued to have a very different experience with the continued assault, perceived by both parties, to their hoped-for fertility. With each menstrual cycle she envisioned the changes pregnancy would thrust upon her, and with each menses she felt the lost opportunity for those changes to occur within the time frame she had envisioned. The husband had no such time frame and as a result had a very hard time relating to his wife's feeling that the loss was still present and ongoing. For him the pregnancy failure was not an ongoing event; it was already in the past. He needed help to understand how hard it was for his wife to continually open herself to adjusting her life to what seemed to be not under their control and her drastic disappointment each time it seemed, to her, that again their pregnancy had failed.

PREGNANCY AND PREGNANCY LOSS AS A TRIGGER TO THE REEXPERIENCE OF PREVIOUS TRAUMAS AND DISRUPTIONS OF ATTACHMENT

Previous Losses/Trauma as Complications to Postpartum Grief

Evidence of a persistent attachment and/or a search process following pregnancy loss gives rise to questions about what sort of attachment existed to the fetal child in the mind of the bereaved. Often, if the fetal child was internally formulated as an important attachment figure, or as a symbolic means of undoing past attachment traumas, previous family dynamics of the bereaved become evident in the projections made upon the fetal child. Thus for grief to be adequately resolved these current and past attachment issues on the part of the bereaved often need to be understood and addressed with as much significance as the traumatic pregnancy loss itself. Likewise, because a fetal/embryonic death often symbolically signifies to the bereaved more than the death event at hand, it is necessary to work through the meanings attached to the fetal child (by the bereaved) in order for grief to be resolved.

In many cases the hopes associated with the conception of new life can be significantly linked to mastering old traumas or previous childhood issues, most significantly those involving previous relationships to important attachment figures. When this is the case and pregnancy fails, the hoped-for mastery does not occur and the loss is compounded. Similarly, because attempts to master unresolved childhood issues or previous trauma are usually unconscious, grief over failures to gain mastery is often also not open to conscious resolution. Thus the present loss is intensified by feelings of grief and survival guilt over the previous loss(es) and frustration at the failure to gain mastery over both.

Childhood Attachment Issues with One's Parents

The many childhood attachment issues and previous traumas that could become entangled with the meanings connected to a successful or unsuccessful pregnancy are beyond the scope of this chapter. However, one issue that deserves particular mention is a woman's childhood relationship with her own parents and specifically any ambivalence that may have existed about how she came into the world. A rejecting or ambivalent relationship with one's parent(s) is at times reenacted, or reexperienced, in a traumatic pregnancy loss, thus passing the legacy of one generation on to the next. Likewise, the childhood experience of parental rejection, ambivalence, or abandonment may be reenacted in elective abortion or reexperienced with miscarriage or stillbirth, if the fetal child is projectively identified with the childhood self or with one's parents and the woman feels that she was abandoned or that her fetal child has been somehow rejected or abandoned.

For example, women who have traumatic elective abortion losses may refer to the experience in terms of enacting a symbolic suicide in which the fetal child was projectively identified as self and rejected by mother. Similarly, women who were adopted or conceived illegitimately sometimes use a pregnancy experience to reenact and attempt to gain mastery over unresolved childhood issues regarding rejection and being worthy of another's care and nurturing. When pregnancy fails for reasons outside the woman's control, or the pregnancy is terminated, these unconscious attempts at gaining mastery also fail.

In some cases the woman's own mother may be drawn into a reenactment scenario when ambivalence over whether or not a pregnancy should be carried to term is discussed with her. Naturally, if the woman is symbolically trying to overcome childhood rejection or feelings of unworthiness (especially if they stem from having been relinquished for adoption or conceived illegitimately and kept), advice to abort carries tremendous symbolic import, whether or not it was intended to, and may feel like advice to disown, rather than claim, the self. Likewise, carrying through with an abortion under such circumstances is experienced as solidifying a rejection of self and identifying oneself with the abuser, that is, the rejecting parent.

Previous Pregnancy Loss(es)

Another significant factor to consider in assessing how a pregnancy loss may be handled is the occurrence of any previous pregnancy loss(es). Miscarriage and abortion are such common occurrences in our culture: One in five women of childbearing age is estimated to have had an elective abortion and approximately one out of five pregnancies ends in miscarriage (Forrest, 1987). However, because the grief over each of these experiences is usually disenfranchised it is not uncommon that previous pregnancy losses are often overlooked in dealing with a current one. Similarly, shame over an abortion experience often results in a woman's not mentioning it to her physician and/or therapist or, if it is mentioned, in the physician's reluctance to note it in her medical charts or the therapist's failure to recognize that an importance piece of information has been conveyed.

Thus previous pregnancy losses are often not considered as potential complicating factors in coping with a current pregnancy and/or loss. Practioners should understand that a woman who has undergone a previous pregnancy loss has in many cases invested a great deal of emotional meaning in the successful outcome of her current pregnancy, and a further failure may be taken by her as a signal of infertility, a punishment for previous actions, or an inability to nurture life; alternatively, a further failure may simply create a new perception of a previous loss that she had heretofore held in a benign, or less significant, perspective.

A 26-year-old woman came for therapy following a stillbirth at 24 weeks. Six months previously the patient had miscarried twins at 11 weeks gestation. In giving a history the patient described a process of mental unraveling that began after the loss of the twins. The patient had been married for 6 years but remained childless by choice until she became pregnant with the twins. The marriage had followed a stormy courtship in which the couple had aborted two pregnancies, each at less than 12 weeks gestation. The patient recounted that she had not experienced much guilt or grief over the abortions until recently; now the abortions were all she could think of. However, in her narration it appeared that strong feelings of grief and guilt over the abortions had been dissociated until the present situation had caused those feelings to resurface.

Describing her psychic numbing over the abortions, the patient told how she had tried to block out her feelings over the first one and been able to do so to some degree. Describing the second abortion, she told how it was harder to block her feelings, particularly guilt, but how she had eventually been able to numb her feelings. The psychic numbing, however, resulted in an unspoken rule in her marriage: The spouses never discussed the abortions or the possibility of having children. Admitting that she had been afraid to become pregnant again after she married, the patient related how she overate for years, keeping herself at a weight that allowed her to harbor a fantasy of still being pregnant. The patient began to see how, over the years, she had been caught between two thought processes, conscious and unconscious, of wanting to be pregnant but avoiding pregnancy out of fears that she might revisit her guilt and grief over the aborted pregnancies.

Describing her reaction when she finally did conceive again and found she was pregnant with twins, the patient said she had felt as though the twins were making up for the "babies" she had aborted, that she was forgiven. Linking the conception of twins to her previous losses, she acknowledged unresolved and lingering evidence of survivor guilt and grief triggered by the miscarriage of the twins.

Returning for advice to her doctor, who did not recognize the signs of her psychological traumatization over the losses, the patient was encouraged to try to become pregnant again. Upon becoming pregnant again, the patient became very upset that she had conceived only one embryo, not two, and immediately emotionally rejected the pregnancy. Unable to explain her feelings of grief and guilt to others, the patient said, "I was so numb inside, but I wanted the pain to go away. I guess I thought if I got pregnant again maybe things would work out, but as soon as I did I didn't want the baby. I couldn't tell anyone. Everyone kept asking me, aren't you happy? But I was sick inside. When they listened for the heart-tones, there was only one. I was wishing so much that there would be two. Then I'd go home and I'd think I can't love this baby. I can't bond to it. I just can't love it. It must have suffered, I was so cold. And then at 24 weeks I had another abruption."

In this patient's case, if the twins had survived, she likely would have made peace, through their birth, with her guilt over the abortions. However, it appeared that her pregnancies subsequent to the abortions were both lost as a result of the physiological reexperience of dissociated trauma over the abortions. As the patient pieced together what had happened, she realized that each pregnancy had stirred up dissociated aspects of the previous abortion experiences, especially on the anniversary dates of the abortions, times when her guilt and traumatic reexperiencing were at their peak. Both losses began with strong uterine contractions that had occurred when the patient had been triggered on, or near, the anniversary dates of the abortions by unconscious traumatic reexperience of the painful dilation procedure and contractions involved in her abortions. The patient later reexperienced conscious recall of the abortions, each of which had involved excruciatingly painful cervical dilation and uterine contractions, which she physiologically reexperienced at the time of "remembering" the traumatic abortions, as well as when she lost her subsequent pregnancies.

The patient's physician, likewise, felt quite certain that her abruptions had been psychosomatically induced by the meanings the patient had attributed to certain anniversary dates and developmental milestones, which appeared to have caused a physiological reaction of uterine contractions to the reexperience of the abortions. The patient had recently been examined both times and was healthy. All of the fetuses had also been healthy and the pregnancies had progressed well up to the point of the patient's reexperiencing the dissociated trauma.

SURVIVOR GUILT AND CONTROL SCHEMAS

Although survivor guilt is ubiquitous following traumatic death events, it is especially problematic in two populations: (a) survivors who are truly implicated in some way for having survived when others did not, as can be true in some cases of war, pregnancy loss, accidents, neglect, etc., and (b) childhood survivors of traumatic death.

When the traumatic death of an important attachment figure occurs in childhood, cognitive schemas may continue to be operational years after the event, even into adulthood. The origin of these schemas, which often rely heavily on a perceived need for control, is the need of the child to defend against the overwhelming psychic overload of recognizing his or her complete vulnerability and utter defenselessness in the face of the death of an important attachment figure. Populations of adults who operate with these sorts of unhealthy control schemas (based upon their previous traumatic loss experiences) often wrongly suffer survivor guilt when they encounter yet another experience with the traumatic death of an attachment figure. In these cases the survivor guilt cannot usually be adequately addressed by addressing the current traumatic death experience only. Instead, the schema itself, which existed before the current event and was used to process the responses to the death, must itself be reworked in order for the survivor guilt to be inactivated.

For those who are not operating with control schemas formed in response to previous traumatization, the survival guilt that is activated by pregnancy loss usually occurs in direct proportion to the degree of volition that the traumatized individual accords to the event. Elective and therapeutic abortion are particularly difficult because they carry the most volition, and thus there is often a high degree of survival guilt, which is often expressed in some need to compensate for the loss, to attempt to undo it, to prevent others from making a similar choice, or to make sure, at any cost, that the reasons for the abortion are carried through (e.g., when an abortion is elected so that the woman can continue college or a career).

Feeling responsible for a stillbirth or miscarriage is also frequent, although in some cases not objectively warranted. Some cases are thorny, when no clear understanding of how the loss occurred is available. For example, some patients recount stories of going into early labor resulting in a stillbirth after an intensely emotional argument, intense crying episodes, or flashbacks of previous traumas. In each of these cases the women felt responsible for the resultant fetal death and experienced acute survival guilt.

Sometimes survival guilt is present in persons who could not even remotely be held responsible for the pregnancy loss. In these cases the guilt is most often a manifestation of survival guilt over previous traumas or a turning inward of anger that the survivor is too frightened to direct outward. In most cases this anger is felt toward an authority figure, such as a physician who is felt to be at least partly responsible for the loss, or toward a nonsupportive spouse.

When survivor guilt is recognized by both therapist and patient it can be worked through in a straightforward manner, taking into account whatever belief system the patient may refer to as a resource for expiating guilt. The therapist should be aware of how differing belief systems support, and also may hinder, resolution of guilt and should feel comfortable addressing such topics or providing adequate spiritual counseling resources for adjunctive treatment. It is not unusual in this phase of treatment for a patient to begin examining how his or her belief system addresses good and evil, if there is an afterlife, what (if any) sort of afterlife is available to fetal children, what must be done to attain a positive afterlife, and how forgiveness, when deemed necessary, can be attained. The professional who is uncomfortable addressing these spiritual issues may hinder the patient, who is often implicitly looking for permission to explore these difficult areas that are crucial to being able to lay the guilt and often the attachment, in terms of final responsibility to the fetal child, to rest.

When survivor guilt goes unrecognized or untreated it often creates major difficulties. In the case of survivor guilt over abortion in a young woman who has not yet borne children, the survivor guilt can often become built into the identity of the woman in terms of subsequent fertility roles. This phenomenon has been described in numerous clinical reports, in which young aborters later report emotional difficulties in subsequent childbearing: fearing infertility, fetal malformation, and stillbirth as potential punishments for having aborted a previous pregnancy(ies) (Speckhard, 1985, 1987a, 1987b; Speckhard & Rue, 1992, 1993). In these populations, when any of these above difficulties do occur, the reason is often attributed to proof of, and punishment for, their guilt. Likewise, a mother who has miscarried or had a stillbirth is likely to be plagued with fears and self-doubt in later pregnancies, and working through the survivor guilt often can release her to trust herself and others again.

Reenactment is present in all aspects of trauma work (Chu, 1991) and in terms of survival guilt following pregnancy loss is most obviously present in women who cycle through repetitive elective abortion experiences, each time using the conception, attachment, and severing of attachment experiences as attempts to gain mastery of an earlier trauma (Speckhard, 1985, 1987a, 1987b). Survivor guilt in these cases is very often the driving factor that must be addressed to end the repetition compulsion. Similarly, there is often trauma that must be worked through for each pregnancy, with the most difficult guilt often only being admitted to layer by layer as information about each additional abortion is disclosed. In these cases a clinician is often tested to see how he or she handles disclosure of yet another abortion in the history (Speckhard, 1985, 1987a).

IMPLICATIONS FOR TREATMENT

Assessment of Traumatic Pregnancy Loss

Societal denial of the perception of traumatic death in pregnancy means that few practitioners routinely include pregnancy histories in their clinical intake interviews (Donovan & McIntyre, 1990), and the reproductive histories of women seen in psychiatric outpatient and inpatient settings are often completely overlooked as relevant to assessment or treatment. As Stotland (1989) noted, "Recent pregnancy loss or delivery may be buried in a woman's history rather than highlighted as a possible factor in her illness and decision to seek psychiatric care" (p. 9). Researchers at the National Institutes of Health Statistics have found denial on the part of women who had abortions as problematic. More than one out of two women is estimated to have denied their abortion experiences in federal reproductive surveys (Koop, 1989) and this denial rate (of approximately half of all aborters) has been replicated in other surveys as well.

Thus for traumatic pregnancy loss to come to light in the therapeutic process the practitioner must overcome the influence of societal denial and social disenfranchisement over what is considered important by the both the patient and practitioner. Likewise, as in all cases of trauma, the patient's dissociative defenses come into play in assessing and processing the traumatic event(s).

When a pregnancy loss, even one by abortion, is learned of in the therapy process, simple bereavement cannot always be assumed. If trauma responses are present, as defined according to standard DSM-IV criteria for trauma, a more thorough evaluation is called for to assess whether the pregnancy loss was experienced as a traumatic death event. As with the treatment of other traumas, the assessment procedure is often plagued by dissociative defenses that prevent the patient from calling either the traumatic event or symbolically important aspects of it to the clinician's attention.

Thus a clinician encountering a patient who skims over a pregnancy loss experience; adheres closely to and becomes agitated if thrown off the course of a "canned" story; or avoids telling about a pregnancy loss should not be misled into dismissing the event as unimportant. When trauma has occurred, the defenses of denial, repression, and dissociation are often active, and in the case of pregnancy loss the bereaved has in the past probably encountered disenfranchising statements from others that have reinforced her defenses and disinclination to share her traumatic loss with others who may not see it as such.

Hence, a level of trust and openness on the part of the practitioner to explore the event and to view it as traumatic, if it was indeed experienced traumatically, must often be established before the therapeutic safety can exist for the individual to admit to having been traumatized by her pregnancy termination and to be willing to begin to address its traumatic effects. Harris (1986) wrote that in the case of pregnancy loss, an active rather than a passive role on the part of the practitioner assessing for trauma must often be adopted.

When assessing for a traumatic response to pregnancy loss, therapists should note the most clear determinants of risk:

1   the strength, valence, and consistency of attachment to the fetus/embryo that existed at the time of the loss;

2   the degree of humanity that was perceived as present in the fetus/embryo, and is now perceived (rightly or wrongly), and the interaction of the two;

3   the degree of human volition involved in the loss;

4   the degree of violence perceived; and

5   the symbolic meanings connected to both the experience of pregnancy and its loss that have been incorporated into the identity of the bereaved individual.

Model for Treatment

Treatment of traumatic death in pregnancy follows the standard protocol of any trauma-based treatment strategy. Although theoretically assessment and treatment can be separated for purposes of discussion, in practice the two are inseparably intertwined. A traumatized patient giving clear evidence of trauma may not allow access to the trauma for purposes of assessment or treatment until a safe, nurturing therapeutic environment has been created in which the dissociative barriers containing the traumatic material can be permeated. Thus the first step of any trauma-based treatment is to create a therapeutic alliance in which trust and safety can be established, maintained, and reestablished throughout the therapy process.

With traumatic pregnancy loss this requires that the practitioner create an environment that is open to exploring a pregnancy loss event as potentially involving trauma to the patient, despite the practitioner's beliefs as to whether or not trauma should have occurred. Likewise, the patient's beliefs about and attachment to the fetus/embryo even in the very early weeks (or days) of pregnancy must be respected in order to have an understanding of how disruption of this early, perhaps heavily symbolically laden or ambivalent attachment could be experienced as trauma.

Once the patient feels comfortable in admitting to attachment to the fetus and trauma upon disruption of that attachment, the therapy can progress to establishing safety around the issue of how attachment behaviors may have been enacted following the disrupted attachment. Beliefs about where the deceased depart to and continued contact with the deceased often must be explored to uncover the search process and aspects of survivor guilt and to put both to rest.

To facilitate this process the practitioner must be comfortable exploring in detail the beliefs of the patient regarding death, afterlife, and putting guilt and grief to rest. The same is true with regard to survivor guilt: Beliefs about how guilt may be remediated, etc., must often be explored to help the patient come to terms with his or her actions in regard to the traumatic death event. When the attachment trauma is uncovered, search behaviors are made evident, and survival guilt surfaces, the practitioner must work within the belief system of the patient, while also gently challenging those areas that may keep the patient trapped in dysfunctional behaviors.

As grief becomes consciously acknowledged, the mourning process usually progresses unhindered as long as it is supported, and the patient is freed to make and extend new attachments. This is often the point in therapy at which patients who have other children tell of having withheld attachment to their other children or projected the deceased's perceived "identity" upon another child. Having resolved these issues, the patients now see their living children in a completely different light, and thereby are free to bond at a much deeper and more rewarding emotional level. Likewise, when guilt is put to rest the patient is freed to define the self in a more positive manner. Treatment at this point becomes supportive and is usually very straightforward, with dysfunctional behaviors quickly becoming replaced with new, more adaptive functional behaviors.

Self-Help and Therapeutic Pregnancy Loss Groups

Women who experience traumatic pregnancy loss often do so alone and unsupported. It is not unusual for women to miscarry alone at home, into a bed or toilet, thus coming into sensory contact with the fetal/embryonic remains. The trauma inherent in experiencing this type of fetal/embryonic death and of perhaps handling the remains is often minimized by health care providers when they fail to address the experience as a human death event.

Likewise, the fact that a human death occurs in abortion is often minimized by abortion providers before, during, and after the event, the rationale being that to address abortion beforehand as involving human death is considered by some to constitute harassment or to have the potential to engender psychological trauma in those who do not recognize it as a death event. When psychological trauma is expressed by a patient during an abortion, abortion providers are rarely willing to address it because once an abortion is under way the procedure cannot be stopped without significant risks. Allowing open expression of trauma responses during an abortion is viewed as neither conducive to continuing a procedure nor supportive to others who might also be traumatized by hearing such responses (i.e., other patients, support staff, and/or the abortion provider). Traumatized abortion patients who begin to express terror over their recognition of a death event frequently report having been told to "be quiet," "don't scream," "don't disturb the others," and "it will be over soon."

Thus women who experience trauma over a miscarriage, stillbirth, or abortion may often do so alone and unsupported, greatly increasing their risk for developing PTSD coupled with complicated mourning over the fetal death event. Only recently have the resources of such groups as RESOLVE been incorporated into hospital protocols and made available to patients who miscarried, delivered stillborn children, or whose infants died near or at birth, and there are still many hospitals that do not use their materials. Groups for those traumatized by abortion death have sprung up, although they are usually highly polarized in their pro-life and religious views and far less organized in their self-help efforts, an exception being Project Rachel of the Catholic church. Women who undergo therapeutic abortion often have nowhere to turn, because groups who rail against abortion do not support those who need to come to peace with this difficult choice. Nor do such women find acceptance in groups dealing with infertility and fetal death, because many of the participants in these groups would be glad to have been able to have even a handicapped child.

Thus there is a real need for hospitals, clinics, and large group practices to run or support self-help groups for women traumatized by abortion death, induced and/or therapeutic, and to take an active interest in those that are run in their communities to ensure that they are healthy and helpful to those that attend. Self-help and therapeutic groups are an economical means to deliver support, early diagnosis, and prevention efforts to women (and those whose lives they influence) who, when isolated and unsupported, may suffer for years after a pregnancy loss. Likewise, materials from groups such as RESOLVE need to be made available to women undergoing miscarriage and stillbirth, and materials addressing abortion trauma should be provided to postabortive patients, to help those traumatized by the event to recognize their symptoms and obtain help before a significant post-traumatic decline is set in motion.

CONCLUSION

Pregnancy loss as a death event with potential traumatic implications has long been overlooked in the clinical and research literature. Also overlooked has been the manner in which the normal attachment processes occur during pregnancy, as well as the many symbolic meanings that are frequently assigned to a pregnancy experience and its manner of termination. Showing that these issues are central to understanding the subjective experience of traumatic death in pregnancy has been the focus of this work. Attachment does occur in pregnancy, and the strength, valence, and consistency of the bonds of attachment as well as the symbolic meanings that are connected to the events of conception, pregnancy, and its termination must be understood in order to be able to assess and treat effectively traumatic reactions to pregnancy loss. Moreover, the individual's unique history, psychodynamic makeup, and family and social systems dynamics affect and are affected by a pregnancy loss experience(s), often contributing to it being experienced as trauma.

Although feminine psychology is an emerging field, the experience of pregnancy loss is presently understudied. In the conclusions of her study of the psychological process in women during pregnancy, Leifer (1980) stated that these areas of feminine psychology and medicine have long been overlooked, relegated to unimportant status, negated as real problems (e.g., PMS), or distorted by largely male views imposed upon very real feminine processes. In explaining her findings, Leifer noted that "these findings are an indication of the ways in which feminine psychology has often been misunderstood or distorted to present a picture of passivity when, in fact, active psychological processes aimed at adaption are occurring." In even more stinging criticism of the neglect women's health issues have suffered in medical and psychological research, former National Institutes of Health (NIH) administrator Bernadette Healy described the lamentable dearth of scientific investigation into women's health care issues by referring to them as the "Yentl diseases." More and better research is needed in the area of pregnancy loss in general. There is no excuse for not knowing how many women are traumatized by their pregnancy loss experiences, and without this knowledge, the need for remedial and preventative programs is easily ignored.

Although more research is sorely needed to address the normal psychological processes of attachment and adaptation that take place in pregnancy, and of disruption of attachment when pregnancy fails, there is a growing body of literature on trauma and grief that describes in great detail the processes likely to be present when pregnancy loss is experienced as a traumatic death. Rando (1993) noted that even normal grief processes are often pathologized and that in cases where grief is disenfranchised, parental death of a child occurs, and/or the death event is unexpected or traumatic a complicated mourning process often ensues. Likewise, trauma researchers and clinicians have presented many models explicating how post-traumatic decline occurs. Certainly these models apply to the experience of pregnancy loss as a traumatic death experience and can be extrapolated to such, as they have been in this chapter. As the subject of traumatic death in pregnancy is addressed in both clinical and research settings, more women and their families will find relief from the effects of traumatic pregnancy loss experiences that for too many years have been given too little recognition.

REFERENCES

American Psychiatric Association. (1987). *Diagnostic and statistical manual of mental disorders* (3rd ed., rev.). Washington, DC: Author.

American Psychiatric Association. (1994). *Diagnostic and statistical manual of mental disorders* (4th ed.). Washington, DC: Author.

Barnard, C. A. (1990). *The long-term psychosocial effects of abortion* [monograph]. Portsmouth, NH: Institute for Pregnancy Loss.

Benedek, T. (1970). The psychobiology of pregnancy. In E. J. Anthony & T. Benedek (Eds.), *Parenthood—its psychology and psychopathology*. Boston, MA: Little Brown.

Bibring, G. (1961). A study of the psychological processes in pregnancy and the earliest mother-child relationship. *Psychoanalytic Study of the Child, 16*, 9–44.

Borg, S., & Lasker, J. (1989). Prenatal diagnosis and the unwanted abortion. In S. Borg & J. Lasker (Eds.), *When pregnancy fails* (pp. 43–45).

Boss, P. G. (1985). Family stress: Perception and context. In M. B. Sussman & S. Steinmetz (Eds.), *Handbook on marriage and the family* (pp. 695–723). New York: Plenum.

Bowlby, J. (1979). *The making and breaking of affectional bonds*. New York: Routledge.

Cavenar, J., & Spaulding, J. (1978). Psychiatric sequelae of therapeutic abortion. *North Carolina Medical Newsletter, 39*, 101–104.

Chu, J. (1991). The repetition compulsion revisited: Reliving dissociated trauma. *Psychotherapy, 28*(2), 327–332.

Condon, J. (1986). The spectrum of fetal abuse in pregnant women. *The Journal of Nervous and Mental Disease, 174*(9), 509–516.

Deutsch, H. (1945). *Psychology of women* (Vol. 2). New York: Grune and Stratton.

DeVeber, L., Ajzenstat, J., & Chisholm, D. (1991). Post abortion grief: Psychological sequelae of induced abortion. *Human Medicine, 7*, 203–209.

Doka, K. (1989). Disenfranchised grief. In K. Doka (Ed.), *Disenfranchised grief: Recognizing hidden sorrow* (pp. 3–11). Lexington, MA: D.C. Heath.

Donovan, D., & McIntyre, D. (1990). *Healing the hurt child: A developmental-contextual approach*. New York: Norton.

Donovan, D. M. (1991). Traumatology: A field whose time has come. *Journal of Traumatic Stress, 4*(3), 433–436.

Donovan, D. M. (1992). Traumatology: What's in a name? *Journal of Traumatic Stress, 6*(3), 409–411.

Erikson, R. (1989). *Abortion as post traumatic stress*. Paper presented at the annual meeting of the Society for Post Traumatic Stress Studies, San Francisco, CA.

Forrest, J. (1987). Unintended pregnancy among American women. *Family Planning Perspectives, 10*, 76–77.

Freud, S. (1957). On narcissism: An introduction. In J. Strachey (Ed. and Trans.), *The standard edition of the complete psychological works of Sigmund Freud* (Vol. 14, pp. xx–xx). London: Hogarth Press. (Original work published in 1914)

Furlong, R., & Black, R. (1984). Pregnancy termination for genetic indications: The impact on families. *Social Work Health Care, 10*, 17–34.

Gilbert, K., & Smart, L. (1992). *Coping with infant or fetal loss: The couple's healing process*. New York: Brunner/Mazel.

Hanley, D., Piersma, H., King, D., Larson, D., & Foy, D. (1992). *Women outpatients reporting continuing post-abortion distress: Preliminary inquiry*. Paper presented at the annual meeting of the International Society for Traumatic Stress Studies, Los Angeles, CA.

Harris, B. (1986). Induced abortion. In T. Rando (Ed.), *Parental loss of a child* (pp. 241–256). Champaign, IL: Research Press.

Hern, W., & Corrigan, B. (1978, October). *What about us? Staff reactions to the D & E procedure*. Paper presented at the 1978 meeting of the Association of Planned Parenthood Physicians, San Diego, CA.

Hill, R. (1971). *Families under stress*. Westport, CT: Greenwood Press. (Reprinted from *Families under stress*, by R. Hill, Ed., 1949, New York: Harper & Row)

Kaltreider, N., Goldsmith, S., & Margolis, A. (1979). The impact of midtrimester abortion techniques on patients and staff. *American Journal of Obstetrics and Gynecology, 135*, 235–238.

Klauss, M., & Kennel, J. (1976). *Maternal-infant bonding.* St. Louis, MO: Mobley Press.

Kohn, I., & Moffitt, T. (1992). *A silent sorrow: Pregnancy loss.* New York: Delta.

Koop, C. E. (1989, March 16). Testimony before the Human Resources and Intergovernmental Relations Subcommittee on Government Operations, U.S. House of Representatives. In *Medical and psychological impact of abortion* (pp. 193–203, 218, 223–250). Washington, DC: U.S. Government Printing Office.

Laing, R. D. (1969). *The politics of the family and other essays.* New York: Vintage Books.

Leifer, M. (1980). *Psychological effects of motherhood: A study of first pregnancy.* New York: Praeger Special Studies.

Magyari, P., Wedhouse, B., Ifft, R., & Callahan, N. (1987). A supportive intervention protocol for couples terminating a pregnancy for genetic reasons. *Birth Defects, 23*, 75–83.

Ney, P. (1982). A consideration of abortion survivors. *Child Psychiatry in Human Development, 13*, 168–179.

Ney, P., & Wickett, A. (1989). Mental health and abortion: Review and analysis. *Psychiatric Journal of the University of Ottawa Press, 14*(4), 506–516.

Peppers, L. (1987). Grief and elective abortion: Breaking the emotion? *Omega, 18*, 1–12.

Peppers, L. (1989). Grief and elective abortion: Implications for the counselor. In K. Doka (Ed.), *Disenfranchised grief: Recognizing hidden sorrow* (pp. 135–145). Lexington, MA: D.C. Heath.

Peppers, L., & Knapp, R. (1980). Maternal reaction to involuntary fetal/infant death. *Psychiatry, 43*, 155.

Rando, T. (Ed.). (1986). *Parental loss of a child.* Champaign, IL: Research Press.

Rando, T. (1991, June). *Complicated bereavement.* Paper presented at the Eastern Regional Conference on Abuse and Multiple Personality Disorder, Alexandria, VA.

Rando, T. (1993). *Treatment of complicated mourning.* Champaign, IL: Research Press.

Rue, V. (1981, November 5). *Abortion and family relations.* Testimony presented before the U.S. Senate Judiciary Committee, Subcommittee on the Constitution, Washington, DC.

Rue, V., & Speckhard, A. (1992). Post abortion trauma: Incidence and diagnostic considerations. *Medicine and Mind, 6*(1–2), 57–74.

Sears, W. (1982). *Creative parenting.* New York: Dodd Mead.

Selby, T. (1990). *The mourning after: Help for post abortion syndrome.* Grand Rapids, MI: Baker Book House.

Shostak, A., & Mclouth, G. (1984). *Men and abortion: Lessons, losses, and love.* New York: Praeger.

Speckhard, A. (1985). *The psycho-social aspects of stress following abortion.* Doctoral Dissertation, University of Minnesota.

Speckhard, A. (1987a). *Post abortion counseling.* Institute for Pregnancy Loss, Portsmouth, NH.

Speckhard, A. (1987b). *Psycho-social stress following abortion.* Kansas City, MO: Sheed & Ward.

Speckhard, A. C. (1989, March 16). Testimony before the Human Resources and Intergovernmental Relations Subcommittee on Governmental Operations, U.S. House of Representatives. In *Medical and psychological impact of abortion* (pp. 193–203, 218, 223–250). Washington, DC: U.S. Government Printing Office.

Speckhard, A., & Rue, V. (1992). Post abortion syndrome: An emerging public health concern. *Journal of Social Issues.*

Speckhard, A., & Rue, V. (1993, Fall). Complicated mourning: Dynamics of impacted post abortion grief. *Pre- and Peri-Natal Psychology Journal*, 5–32.

Stotland, N. (1989). Psychiatric issues in abortion and the implications of recent legal changes for psychiatric practice. In N. Stotland (Ed.), *Psychiatric aspects of abortion* (pp. 1–16). Washington, DC: American Psychiatric Press.

Chapter 5

Couple Coping with the Death of a Child

Kathleen R. Gilbert

The death of one's child is a death out of sequence, one that seems to defy the natural order of things. Parents often find themselves coping with their own pain, confusion, and anger over the death while also coping with its impact on their marriage. In addition to other changes that result from the loss, their roles as parents and as spouses are no longer the same (Raphael, 1983). Even if one spouse is less affected, the changes in his or her partner will result in an altered relationship. Thus, the death of their child affects them directly through the loss of the child, indirectly through the change in their partner, and together by disrupting their relationship (Gilbert, in press).

This chapter draws on available literature to explore the experience of marital couples as they cope with the death of a child. There may be similarities in the process described here to the dyadic grief and coping processes of other nonmarital couples. Limited research has been done on nontraditional couples (e.g., gay and lesbian and unmarried heterosexual couples) who lose children.

In this chapter, the marital couple is viewed as an interactive grieving system in which partners cope with individual and relational concerns that result from the death of their child. When considering the couple, we need to remember that spouses are both individuals and partners. The loss of their child affects them in both capacities and both must be taken into account. As will be shown in this chapter, these simultaneous "self" and "partner" identities are especially important, particularly when we consider the effects of the loss on the assumptions, perceptions, and beliefs of bereaved couples (Broderick, 1993).

GRIEF AS A PROCESS—AN OVERVIEW

Death is a "choiceless" event, and this choicelessness adds to the pain of loss (Attig, 1991). For parents, who "should" be able to protect their children and keep them from harm, the pain of loss is particularly acute. Losing one's child has been identified as one of the worst possible events in adult life (Owen, Fulton, & Markusen, 1982–83; Sanders, 1979–80) and has been recognized as one of the losses most likely to lead to complicated grief (Rando, 1992–93). Raphael and Middleton (1988) have described such an event as a personal disaster, encompassing "shocking, overwhelming personal experiences that test the individual beyond his adaptive capacity and bring major stresses and sometimes changes to his life" (p. 281). If the child's death is sudden and unanticipated with little or no time for parents to prepare, the impact of the loss is especially intense (Figley, 1989) and bereaved parents are left feeling out of control, helpless, and confused (DeFrain, 1991). Because the death is out of sequence, it is accompanied by a sense of untimeliness, a perception of injustice that such a thing should have happened (Janoff-Bulman, 1992). In addition, parents report a strong sense of guilt for their inability to protect and nurture their child (Sanders, 1979–80).

With their child's death, parents are faced with a senseless event. Yet, they also feel a strong need to make sense of it, must attribute meaning to their loss (Gilbert, 1996; Green, Wilson, & Lindy, 1985; Janoff-Bulman, 1992). The grief response of these parents is seen here as an active coping process centered on regaining control and predictability in one's life while also working to make sense of the loss and integrate it into one's interpretive structures (Attig, 1991; Gilbert & Smart, 1992). These interpretive structures are a generalized set of beliefs within which people operate on a day-to-day basis, allowing them to organize information encountered in the environment and to reasonably anticipate future events. These sets of beliefs have been referred to by such terms as the *assumptive world* (Janoff-Bulman, 1992; Parkes, 1972), as the *world of meaning* (Marris, 1982), and as one's *personal construct theory* (Hoagland, 1984; Neimeyer, Epting, & Krieger, 1984). For simplicity's sake, the term *assumptive world* is used in this chapter.

Grief, then, results from the loss of meaning and is a process of reconstructing the assumptive world. The bereaved may adjust their view of the loss so that it becomes consistent with existing assumptions or they may modify existing assumptions (Fowlkes, 1991; Janoff-Bulman, 1992; Marris, 1982; Parkes, 1972).

According to Janoff-Bulman (1992), the death of a loved one affects core beliefs held by almost everyone. She has identified three of these as a belief in personal invulnerability, a view of oneself in a positive light, and the perception of the world as orderly and predictable. Because of the nature of the parent–child relationship, these beliefs are extended to one's children (Gilbert & Smart, 1992). In order to make sense of the death of their child, parents must consider and reconsider these and related beliefs. This process of questioning results in psychological upheaval for parents (Janoff-Bulman, 1992) and, as is discussed later in this chapter, also can lead to disruption of dyadic processes.

NEED FOR A PERSONAL HEALING THEORY

Attributing meaning to a loss is essential to grief resolution, and some sort of explanation, a personal or "healing" theory, must be developed (Figley, 1989; Taylor, Lichtman, & Wood, 1984). By constructing such a healing theory, bereaved parents modify the assumptive world to incorporate the loss, thereby achieving a new sense of normalcy and purpose. In this way, they are able to reestablish a sense of control and predictability and gain an understanding of their loss (Borg & Lasker, 1988; Taylor, 1983).

The drive to establish a healing theory is so strong that, should the bereaved parents attempt to avoid doing so, they will experience repetitive, intrusive images of the loss that are accompanied by strong emotions (Raphael, 1983, 1992). Horowitz (1979, 1986) has proposed that this compulsion to define the event is powered by what he has called the *completion tendency*, a drive to integrate new information with one's existing assumptive world and to establish consistency between old and new views. Until this consistency is established, Horowitz posits that intrusive thoughts about the loss will recur.

While this drive to establish consistency is active, parents may find the resulting images to be too painful to consider and they may attempt to avoid or suppress them. If the parents do this, episodes of intrusive images will alternate with avoidant behavior and will continue until the loss has been integrated and closure has been achieved (Horowitz, 1986).

Parents have reported recurrences of intense grief long after the death of their child. This clearly has been seen to occur as a result of drug (Spurgeon, 1984) and AIDS (Colburn & Malena, 1989) deaths, homicides (Rinear, 1988), and suicide (Bouvard, 1988). Even when the loss is not as horrifying, similar, albeit generally less intense, recurrences have been reported. This has been the case, for example, long after a perinatal or infant loss (Gilbert & Smart, 1992; Peppers & Knapp, 1980; Rosenblatt & Burns, 1986).

DYADIC GRIEF

As they work to make sense of their loss and construct a healing theory, bereaved parents turn to others around them for help. The need to receive social confirmation for their developing healing theory is quite strong (Gilbert, 1996; Patterson & Garwick, 1994) as is evidenced by the sometimes overwhelming need to talk with others about the loss (Fowlkes, 1991; Janoff-Bulman, 1992). Spouses are in a unique position to help in this regard (Berger & Kellner, 1964/ 1992; Reiss, 1981). Both partners have experienced the loss, and their shared lives, with their common history and established pattern of interaction, may facilitate understanding.

As Lifton (1971) has stated, people feel a strong need for "connection, for meaningful ties to people, ideas and symbols, derived from the past and projecting into the future" (p. 284). If marital partners are able to develop a shared view within their marriage, they can reduce their ambiguity and uncertainty about who and what has been lost, how they are to cope with that loss, and how they are to go on with their lives (Gilbert, 1996; Gilbert & Smart, 1992; Patterson & Garwick, 1994). By validating each other's subjective views of the loss, these views may be seen to be more real (Fowlkes, 1991; Gilbert, 1996; Patterson & Garwick, 1994).

The loss of a child will have a "ripple effect" through other aspects of their lives that extend beyond the death and its immediate effects. Couples may find themselves questioning the nature of their marriage as an entity. They may need to reassess their roles and the way in which they view each other (Raphael, 1983). Thus, the loss of their child could result in their questioning their marriage and their view of themselves and their spouse in such roles as parents, partners, nurturers, caregivers, and protectors.

Dyadic System of Beliefs

In his discussion of the family's construction of reality, Reiss (1981) referred to fundamental beliefs, assumptions, and orientations shared by family members as their family paradigm; here we refer to this as the *dyadic paradigm* of the couple. Reiss conceptualized this as a system-level phenomenon in which "assumptions are shared by all family members, despite the disagreements, conflicts, and differences that exist in the family" (p. 1). Similarly, family definition of stressor events (Hill, 1949), family perceptions (McCubbin & Patterson, 1983), and the family's world view (Patterson & Garwick, 1994) have been proposed as belief systems held by whole families.

The view taken here is consistent with that of Broderick (1993), who wrote that "only an individual can have a belief or value or world view or an understanding of something" (p. 186). Partners are hampered by the fact that they cannot know, absolutely, what their spouse is thinking. Yet, even though they may not share a reality in the sense that their views are identical, the need to believe that the loss has comparable meaning for both of them appears to be strong. This is borne out by the tremendous difficulty parents have with accepting that their spouse is grieving in a way that is different from their own (Gilbert, 1996; Gilbert & Smart, 1992; Peppers & Knapp, 1980).

Couples exist in an interactive system of confirmation and disconfirmation of beliefs expressed by each partner. Each of them adopts an "as if" quality in their observations and interactions with their spouse so that they can function as if they both agree (or agree to disagree) on the meaning of the loss. Behaviors are interpreted, comments are assessed, all within the context of each partner's assumptions about how their marriage should progress. It is within the context of this dyadic paradigm that marital partners recognize the loss as a couple, reorganize the way in which they function as a system, and reinvest themselves toward the future. This dyadic paradigm is more complex than the individual's assumptive world, as it encompasses each partner's perceptions of the loss as well as expectations and perceptions of each other and themselves as spouses. The emphasis is on the closeness of the partners' expressed views of the situation and their ability to work together to reestablish a stable sense of meaning in a couple context.

Dyadic Healing Theory

As individuals form a healing theory to explain the loss, the couple also collaborates to form a dyadic healing theory after a catastrophic event (Figley, 1989; Fowlkes, 1991). Again, partners enter an "as if" state with each other and, in this process, they interact with each other to attempt to confirm the reality of the loss, to legitimize one another's reactions, and to initiate the healing process (Fowlkes, 1991). In the ideal, the dyadic healing theory would fit into the new, modified dyadic paradigm (Figley, 1989), just as the personal healing theory would fit into the new, modified assumptive world of each parent (Janoff-Bulman, 1992).

If successful in their efforts, partners mutually generate overlapping healing theories that serve as the basis for their dyadic healing theory. Such a dyadic theory would facilitate communication, provide structure and meaning to their interactions, and serve as the basis for dyadic coping behavior (Figley, 1989; Fowlkes, 1991; McCubbin & Patterson, 1983; Patterson & Garwick, 1994; Reiss, 1981).

NEGATIVE COUPLE COPING—INCONGRUENT GRIEVING AND THE MARITAL DYAD

Unfortunately, bereaved parents may find it difficult, if not impossible, to provide each other with mutual validation and support (Borg & Lasker, 1988; Frantz, 1984; Peppers & Knapp, 1980; Rando, 1983, 1984). Parents have said that, in addition to losing the child, it seemed as though they had lost their spouse for a time (Rando, 1983), or that their spouse was the least helpful person in coping with the death (Frantz, 1984). Rosenblatt, Spoentgen, Karis, Dahl, Kaiser, and Elde (1991) also noted that if two people experience a mutual loss, as when parents lose a child, they are the least likely to be able to help each other. Rather than helping them to grieve together, the "baggage" of their relationship and the relationship each had with their child who has died impedes mutual grief resolution. In addition, disparate experiences with death and other losses prior to the death of their child may contribute to dyssynchronous expectations on the part of the partners (Silver & Wortman, 1980), which may then contribute to a perception of their grieving as incongruent (Gilbert & Smart, 1992; Peppers & Knapp, 1980). Partners might question their own or the other's perceptions and formation of a shared reality would be made more difficult. When spouses are unable to affirm each other's expectations, they feel less stability and control and are less satisfied with their communication (Fowlkes, 1991).

Spouses grieve differently, in many ways having experienced different losses; yet, unless they accept these differences, they may be unavailable to each other to work through the grief of their loss (Gilbert, 1996).

The loss of a child results in what Klass (1988) has called a "paradoxical bond" between parents in which both partners simultaneously experience their own loss while also sensing that their spouse may be experiencing the loss in very different ways. The partners are joined, yet are also estranged, by their loss.

Each spouse must struggle with his or her own unique loss while attempting to cope with changes in his or her partner and in their relationship. As noted above, this is because the spouses likely will experience different losses. In a sense, they will not have lost the same child; each will have had a different relationship with their child and it will be the loss of that relationship, that connection, that they will feel most keenly. As Rando (1984) has suggested, this relationship need not have been a warm, loving one; a conflictual relationship may result in a more complicated pattern of grief. This pattern of complication may extend to the couple's relationship after the loss if one parent had a conflictual relationship with the child while the other parent's relationship with the child was a positive one.

The interaction of these differences and related conflicts may come together to place tremendous strain on the couple (Miles, 1984). Indeed, conflict between spouses comes primarily from disagreements about how they should grieve (Gilbert & Smart, 1992; Miles, 1984; Peppers & Knapp, 1980). Given that partners have only each other's behavior and imperfectly communicated information on which to base their interpretation of each other's grief states, it is not surprising that such conflicts occur. Even if one spouse attempts to be supportive of the other, the interpretation by the other spouse may be negative (Gilbert & Smart, 1992). This can act as a "second injury" (Symonds, 1980), adding to the pain of the loss.

Differing Meaning of the Loss

As noted before, each parent has a unique relationship with his or her child; thus when that child dies, the loss will have special meaning for each of them. As a result, the impact of the loss will be distinctive to each parent. Beliefs directly affected include what the child symbolizes for each parent, the importance of the parent role, the unnaturalness of a child predeceasing the parent, and the response of the support network (Rando, 1984). The specific assumptions, the tenacity with which the parents hold them, and the fact that these assumptions must be faced over and over again after their child's death can have an effect on the dyadic grief process (Gilbert & Smart, 1992; Janoff-Bulman, 1992; Peppers & Knapp, 1980; Rosenblatt & Burns, 1986). Although both parents have experienced the same objective loss of a child, each loses a different symbolic child. This then leads to different grief experiences, and possibly to dyadic conflict (Gilbert, 1996; Rando, 1984).

Spouses often expect to support each other, yet they may be unable to provide this support to each other. Because of their unique relationship with their child and their idiosyncratic coping style, each spouse will deal with the loss in his or her own way. One spouse may not wish to dwell on the death while the other wishes to discuss nothing else. It is also possible that one spouse may not have experienced the loss to be as painful as the other had.

Just as they each had a different past with their child, partners may be surprised to discover that they did not share the same imagined future for their child. This also contributes to discrepancies in what each spouse has to resolve in the grieving process (Klauss & Kennel, 1976).

Impact of Uncertainty   The situation can be made more complicated if there is ambiguity about the death. Ambiguous losses, those that lack clarity (Boss, 1991), can lead to sharply different assessments of exactly who or what has been lost (Klauss & Kennel, 1976; Rinear, 1988; Rosenblatt & Burns, 1986). Ambiguous losses receive little or no public recognition, and if members of the social network are unable to recognize the loss as real, they will not be able to validate the grief felt by the parents, possibly leading to a more complicated form of grief (Rando, 1992–93; Silver & Wortman, 1980). If a loss is seen as irreconcilable, that is, one or both partners cannot come to terms with the loss, the formation of a meaningful explanation for the loss may be impossible.

Contrasts in the Way in Which They View Themselves as a Couple

In losing their child, partners may come to view their marriage differently from the view they held prior to the loss. For example, before the loss, they might have seen themselves as sharing common interests, goals, and values. They also might have established a system of dealing with normal day-to-day life in which each fulfilled role behaviors that included supporting and comforting one another. After the loss, each partner has to consider his or her reaction to the loss and his or her spouse's reactions. This can cause one or both of them to question assumptions about their marriage, their spouse, and themselves in rela-tion to their spouse. While struggling with individual needs, parents may find themselves overburdened by their own efforts and simultaneously attempting to provide comfort, support, and a willing ear to their spouse. The result can be a perception of distance in the relationship.

Because of the obvious pain involved in discussions of the death, spouses may attempt to protect and end up overprotecting one another (Cornwell, Nurcombe, & Stevens, 1977; Gilbert, in press; Gilbert & Smart, 1992). Weitzman and Kamm (1985) found that this overprotectiveness diminishes the ability to communicate. Yet, effective communication is considered essential to successful dyadic func-tioning (Epstein & Westley, 1959; Figley, 1983, 1989). Therefore, by avoiding discussions of their loss, they may contribute to a "domino effect" in which more and more topics are not discussed. This might cause each of them to feel isolated and without support.

Differing Individual Experiences of Loss

As Lindemann (1944) has said, grief involves work and this "grief work" of bereaved parents is exhausting. Yet, even though both mothers and fathers report this exhaustion, they often attribute it to different causes. For example, a mother might experience disabling episodes of guilt for not preventing her child from driving through a dangerous part of town, while a father might find himself coping with episodes of rage at his child's carelessness.

In addition to their own loss, men often express a desire to protect their wives, and this may contribute to their loss. At the same time, social support from outside the marriage will most likely be directed toward the wife, and the husband will be expected to be "the strong one" for her sake, because she is the person who is perceived by others as the one who has experienced a loss (Cook, 1988; Peppers & Knapp, 1980).

Each parent likely will go through some experiences that will be highly specific to him or her; this often contributes to a feeling of estrangement (Silver & Wortman, 1980). These likely will result in unique triggers of recurrences of grief for each parent (Green, Wilson, & Lindy, 1985), can contribute to the feeling that their spouse does not understand, and can lead to isolation (Horowitz, 1986).

It is important to remember that the subjective interpretation of these experiences is what makes them uniquely upsetting; the same experience that distresses one parent would not necessarily bother another (Silver & Wortman, 1980). Examples include one parent identifying their child's body while the other spouse is unable or unwilling to do so, making the decision about terminating life support, or going alone to the mortuary to make funeral arrangements. Each parent deals with at least some memories that are singularly distinctive to him or her.

Disagreements About the "Right Way" to Grieve

At the time of loss and as they attempt to come to terms with the death of their child, each parent implements certain behaviors to cope with the loss; these combine to form a unique and idiosyncratic approach toward coping with grief. This frequently leads to a high degree of disparity between spouses. In addition, partners bring different ideas with them about the best way to respond to the loss. The end result often is a clash over how they should act.

Husbands and wives may see themselves as unable to agree on the way to regain a sense of stability and meaning in life. This could be complicated by changes over time of the meaning of the loss for each partner. One spouse may see emotional displays as appropriate only during the funeral; the other may view such displays as the best way to grieve months or years after the loss.

New information about the cause of death or exposure to a triggering agent might cause a recurrence of the pain of grief, sometimes intense, for one spouse, that is accompanied by an increase of grieving behavior (Gilbert, in press; Horowitz, 1986) as well as symptoms of post-traumatic stress disorder (Rinear, 1988). Such a change in behavior could be seen as frustrating and counterproductive on the part of the other parent.

Marital partners may avoid sharing feelings and thoughts because of role expectations about appropriate behavior (Cook, 1988; Gilbert & Smart, 1992) or in an effort to protect each other. They may also avoid each other, or use hurtful comments to create distance, because they feel overwhelmed by their own grief and unable to provide support (Gilbert, in press) or because the other person's grief triggers their own (Cornwell et al., 1977; Gilbert & Smart, 1992). This is especially true when one partner feels that he or she has "moved on" and either that person does not want to be "pulled back" into grief or the other resents his or her "abandonment" of grief (Gilbert & Smart, 1992). The inability of the partners to talk about the loss (and validate their growing healing theories with each other) inhibits reconstruction.

One aspect of grief that may cause conflict between partners is the need of one partner to be alone. This can contribute to a feeling on the part of the other spouse that he or she has been rejected and is alone in his or her grief. It is important to remember that the spouse who wishes to be alone does not always need to physically leave. Sometimes, he or she will remain present, but will mentally isolate him- or herself. This can cause problems if the other spouse wants the two of them to be together and to talk about the loss. Most often, it is men who need more solitary time to work through their grief, whereas women need to process their grief in a social environment (Cook, 1988).

Interpreting Each Other's Behavior in a Negative Light   As noted previously, each spouse uses the couple context to confirm his or her own experience of the loss. As they do this, they use their own previous knowledge, experiences, and observations to identify certain behaviors as productive in grief resolution (Broderick, 1993; Gilbert, 1996). Their spouse's actions may be seen as different, contradictory, and unproductive. They may also be interpreted as unhealthy and inappropriate to the situation. These assumptions, along with the related sense of unpredictability, are highly stressful to both parties. At the same time, the person whose behavior is being evaluated will likely feel judged, angry, isolated, and frustrated at the lack of sensitivity on his or her spouse's part.

The nature of the mother–child and father–child relationships as well as social constraints on gender-appropriate behavior are contributing factors to these differences. Fathers have been seen as more likely to avoid going through the grieving (i.e., emotional) process than mothers (Frantz, 1984), to be less willing to talk about the loss (DeFrain, 1991), and to experience a less intense grief that is resolved more quickly than mother's grief (Osterweis, Solomon, & Green, 1984). Mothers express more sorrow and depression, and fathers indicate that they feel more anger, fear, and loss of control (DeFrain, 1991). Mothers have also expressed more guilt (Peppers & Knapp, 1980). These patterns of gender differences are consistent cross-culturally, with women generally more expressive of their emotions and men more restrained (Haig, 1990; McGoldrick, Almeida, Hines, Rosen, Garcia-Presto, & Lee, 1991).

Men commonly find themselves caught in a "double-bind" in that they are taught to contain their emotions "like a man" while also being expected, after a loss, to express their emotions "like a woman." Regardless of how they respond to the loss, they will experience some form of censure for acting inappropriately (Cook, 1988). Indeed, the cognitive, solitary grief that predominated among the men in Cook's study of fathers grieving the death of a child to cancer has been seen as unhealthy and counterproductive to grief resolution.

Disparate Images of Appropriate Mourning   Couples may also be unable to agree about appropriate mourning, defined here as the public display of grief (Stephenson, 1985). Most commonly, one spouse feels that the other is engaging in some public display of emotion that is not seemly, such as openly weeping or involving others in continued discussion of the deceased. In other cases, one spouse may be upset because the other seems to have stopped mourning too soon and seems to have stopped caring about the deceased child.

If they maintain their sense of combativeness over these behaviors, they may be unable to agree on such activities as attending public functions or entertaining after the death of their child. Holiday gatherings are particularly difficult. One spouse might see a holiday party as a way to get out and relax, while the other sees it as a reminder that their child is no longer there to participate. As is the case with private behavior, different meanings that these gatherings hold for each spouse are the source of their conflict. The couple may choose not to attend public events. Unfortunately, such avoidance of outside social contact can reduce the available social support to the couple (Silver & Wortman, 1980) and increase the interpersonal strain felt by the couple Gilbert & Smart, 1992), adding to the impact of the trauma (Silver & Wortman, 1980).

Problematic Pattern of Grief Resolution—Being "Out-of-Synch"   In addition to conflicts over specific grief behaviors, the pattern through which the couple moves to resolve their grief may cause problems for them. As Bowlby (1980) suggested, if there is a great disparity in grief resolution, stress is placed on the marital relationship.

Disagreements may also arise when one spouse has reached a point in his or her own grief resolution process where he or she feels the time for emotion is gone and it is no longer productive to "dwell on the past." At this time, these spouses find themselves less sympathetic to their partner's need to talk and process emotions.

Disagreement on Family Goals—Which to Set and When   Conflict over setting family goals is related to conflicting patterns of grief resolution. Given the differences in the meaning of the loss and the style of grieving, one partner likely will be ready to begin to plan for the future sooner than the other. In addition, even when each partner is able to look to the future, the focus of their planning often will be different. Arguments can result when one person pushes the other to accept and focus on a specific family goal while the other person feels unready.

Disagreement About Who/What to Blame   Depending on the nature of the relationship with the child and with each other, and events surrounding the death, parents may blame each other for the death (Rando, 1984). Self-blame is also quite common with the death of a child (Worden, 1991), as it is with other forms of trauma (Janoff-Bulman, 1992).

Interestingly, if couples have been sensitized to the risk of other and self-blame (Janoff-Bulman, 1992), they may engage in an alternative approach to the attribution of blame for the loss. In this, a sort of "nonblame" argument may take place in which one of the parents sees him- or herself as at fault for the death and the other parent then responds with arguments that are intended to persuade the self-blamer that he or she is not at fault. If the self-blamer is unable or unwilling to give up the self-blame, the couple will then argue over the legitimacy of such a view (Gilbert & Smart, 1992).

When Synchronous Grieving Causes Problems—Resonating Grief

A type of emotional triggering has been seen in the mutual secondary traumatic stress reaction between spouses (Gilbert, in press). In this case, both husband and wife have experienced the same trauma (the death of their child), and through repeated exposure, their behaviors come to serve as a trigger for each other. In this, simple exposure to a spouse exhibiting strong emotion sets off the same in the observing spouse. Unfortunately, the end result of this may be that each spouse hides his or her emotions, hoping that this will make the loss easier for his or her spouse. If, on the other hand, resonating grief goes on, the spouse being triggered may avoid the other, contributing to their mutual sense of isolation.

Cornwell et al. (1977) also described a type of resonating grief in which husbands and wives influence each other's emotional state. In this, partners are emotionally sympathetic, that is, their emotions are close to the surface and they easily set each other off. This resonating grief may cause one partner, who is less comfortable with emotions, to avoid the more expressive spouse (Cook, 1988).

POSITIVE COUPLE COPING—WORKING
TOGETHER TO RESOLVE GRIEF

Although many couples go through a difficult period when they struggle to cope with their loss and its impact on themselves and their marriage, many couples survive the loss and its effects. Gilbert and Smart (1992) found a strong desire among participants to maintain their marital relationship. Marriage was important to the couples in the study and participants expressed a commitment to marriage, either as an institution or as a central relationship in their life.

In order to regain their function as a couple while they resolve their grief, marital partners need to accomplish three tasks: They must recognize the loss of their child and what that loss has meant for each of them, reorganize their marriage and their family so that the roles carried out by the child will be reassigned within the family, and reinvest themselves in their marriage and their family (Jordan, 1990; Walsh & McGoldrick, 1991). The following section addresses the ways in which couples resolve differences and work together toward these three tasks.

Marital Communication

The ability to engage in open and honest communication has often been seen as essential to recovery from loss (Figley, 1983; Gilbert & Smart, 1992; Rando, 1984; Raphael, 1983; Silver & Wortman, 1980). If the loss is to be acknowledged by the couple as real and the experience of grief shared, partners must be able to communicate clearly with each other (Jordan, 1990). Supportive communication facilitates discussion of emotions and development of healing theories, increasing the likelihood of understanding and acceptance in the marriage (Figley, 1983; Walsh & McGoldrick, 1991). Partners are able to comingle their separate realities through communication (Broderick, 1993). Finally, communication also facilitates adjustment within the couple when they experience a loss (Raphael, 1983).

In Gilbert and Smart (1992), when participants were asked about what they saw as most helpful in their relationship, the most common answers were tied to marital communication. This ability to communicate with one another was seen as particularly important because these couples frequently felt ostracized by others. Their ability to talk with one another gave them a sense of being connected and allowed them to test and confirm their growing healing theories. Even those persons who were relatively taciturn agreed with this position.

Information Exchange   The exchange of information increases a sense of mutuality, understanding, and shared concern. One parent might gather medical information explaining the child's death. The other parent might find out about support resources in the community or about the process of grief. The ability to convey accurate information to each other would be helpful to answer questions that the couple might have about the death and about each other. As they attempt to make sense of the death, the ability to discuss their evolving theories about what had happened would then be a valuable coping tool.

As noted before, each parent grieves the loss of a unique relationship with his or her child (Rosenblatt, 1988). Talking about their memories of their child and the future they had planned or visualized could contribute to understanding and acceptance of differences. For those couples with highly disparate images of their child, this could be a revealing experience.

Expressing Emotions   As suggested by Helmrath and Steinitz (1978), the ability to cry together and display deep emotions in each other's company is frequently seen as helpful. The strong emotions generated by the loss may be surprising. Several of the men in the Gilbert and Smart (1992) study were amazed at the intensity of their emotional response at the death of their child in pregnancy or infancy. Seeing someone else as apparently distressed as they are could validate their emotions.

Openly expressing their own emotions may be particularly difficult for some marital partners, especially men (Cook, 1988). For these individuals, listening to their spouses and observing their emotions may be more beneficial than attempting to express their own emotions. If they can then feel they can safely express themselves, their spouses may find this to be extremely meaningful. One way in which they can do this is through the use of support groups as long as they are treated as a "safe haven" where the partners are able to show emotions. Another way is through the use of agreed-upon rituals that allow both parents to express their feelings in a nonthreatening environment (Bowen, 1991; Imber-Black, 1991).

Listening   A common theme among bereaved parents is the need for one or both partners to have the other spouse listen nonjudgmentally. Women, in particular, seem to find their need to talk about the child and the loss to be almost compulsive (Peppers & Knapp, 1980). This need is often exacerbated by the sense of isolation and stigmatization generated by the unwillingness of others outside the marriage to allow them to talk about their child.

A drawback, however, is that listening to one's spouse expressing strong and painful emotions can contribute to the stress of the listener, especially if the result is conflicted feelings on his or her part (Cornwall et al., 1977; Gilbert, in press). Yet, even though this results in increased personal stress, listeners often persist because, in their view, they are helping their spouse to come to terms with the loss. Indeed, their willingness to do this often is viewed by the other spouse as very meaningful because it validates the legitimacy of his or her feelings and the acceptance of their differences. This acceptance can be extremely important because of their different attachments to the child and emotions at the death of the child. Additionally, listening can facilitate the resolution of conflicts in expectations held by the partners.

Nonverbal Communication   Spouses find it difficult, at times, to speak of their thoughts or emotions to one another. At these times, nonverbal means of communicating can be used instead of or in addition to verbal means. A touch or a glance, when based on a dyadic history, can carry a great deal of information. In addition, nonverbal communication may be emphasized over verbal communication for spouses who prefer to deal with their emotions in a more private way.

Code Words and Signals   Another means of communication is a system of verbal and nonverbal shorthand that allows partners to communicate with one another without letting others know. These private systems of communication allow them to exchange a great deal of information, using single words or phrases.

A Positive View

In Gilbert and Smart (1992), one of the most distinctive characteristics found among couples who reported very little conflict was the positive view they held of each other and their relationship. Indeed, the degree to which the couple had moved to a positive view seemed to be a key to determining the depth of their continued grieving and its impact on their relationship. It appears that an optimistic view predisposes the parents to seeing positive aspects of their relationship and of each other's behavior, thus allowing them to build positive on positive.

It may be necessary for one or both partners to "bottom out" before they are able to begin to look for anything positive in life. Alternatively, the shift to a more positive view may take place without drama. Initially, only certain aspects of their relationship may be framed in a positive light; later this may lead to an expansion of their positive view.

Reframing   A coping skill that is extremely useful in the move toward a positive view is reframing (Nichols, 1984). It involves changing the conceptual or emotional viewpoint of family members. The result is a change in the meaning attributed to behavior of family members without having the family member change the actual behaviors themselves (Watzlawick, Weakland, & Fisch, 1974). By positively reframing their spouse's behavior, individual partners can then alter their general perception of their spouse. This is a natural and automatic process for some couples (Gilbert & Smart, 1992). The urge to put their spouse's behavior in a positive frame can be quite strong, with individual spouses spontaneously reframing each other's behavior in a more positive light as they review each other's behavior.

In addition to creating a more positive image of their spouse, reframing can be used to "seal over" information about their spouse or the relationship that conflicts with expectations that had existed prior to the loss (Smith, 1981). By putting a positive frame on the aspects of his or her spouse's behavior that are contrary to expectations, the reframing spouse can move past disagreements and rebuild the marital relationship.

Sharing the Loss

The ability to develop a shared view is considered important to resolution of stress in the family (Reiss, 1981) and particularly important for traumatic stress (Figley, 1989). When marital partners are able to see the loss as shared—not necessarily as the same experience, but one in which they feel they have been and are available to each other—they experience a greater sense of connection.

By sharing the loss, partners can help one another to answer their questions about the death and get on with their lives. This also facilitates individual grief resolution and self-empowerment, because the ability to help another person serves as an indicator that bereaved parents have reached a point in grieving where they are able to focus on something other than their own loss.

Grieving Together   Couples who grieve together are physically available to each other, hugging and touching and, occasionally, talking. Grieving together does not mean that couples are at an identical point in their grief resolution, but that they spend a great deal of time in each other's company. This facilitates communication, because by being together, they are exposed to more information about each other's grief and have a stronger contextual base for interpreting each other's experience. This increases the likelihood that they will accurately interpret each other's behavior.

Exclusivity   Spending time with each other, without any other obligations, is very helpful, especially in the days or weeks immediately following or surrounding the death. It is important to be aware that an extended period of isolation is not helpful. Spending time alone at first, however, allows couples who need it time to establish the loss as their own.

Shared Focus   Having something to focus on outside their marital relationship allows couples to work as a team, to concentrate on something other than themselves, and to emphasize their identity as a couple. A shared focus on surviving children is very helpful for many couples in coping with their grief. Helping other family members with their grief (especially bereaved grandparents and siblings of the child who died) or working together to help other bereaved parents or to prevent other children from dying the same way their child did may be other points of mutual focus.

In addition to working as a team to solve some problem outside the dyad, couples often build a shared focus within their marriage. This shared focus might include joint rituals (Broderick, 1993; Imber-Black, 1991), such as regularly visiting the grave, which would legitimize their connection to the child and give a socially approved location to express their grief.

Common Goals/Common Values   Another way couples can pull together as a unit is by directing their efforts toward some common end. Initially, the effort to identify a common goal may serve as a source of conflict, if one party identifies a goal with which the other parent is not comfortable. However, once both parties feel that they have contributed to selecting a goal and feel ready to carry it out, strain on the relationship frequently is reduced.

In addition, common values, especially religious values, are important. This need for a common faith may be due to the fact that religious beliefs serve as the basis for much of the couple's organization of reality. Given that religious beliefs frequently are used to explain new and confusing phenomena, a couple's shared religious values serve to shape their perception of the loss. The nature of the beliefs themselves are not as critical for the marital relationship as is the commonality of these beliefs. Thus, as far as marital strain is concerned, consistency between partners' beliefs about the religious meaning of the loss is more important than the form these beliefs take.

Another important shared value that facilitates positive couple coping is seeing marriage as important, both as an institution and as a relationship. In the Gilbert and Smart (1992) study, at least one person in each couple spoke, with great emotion, about the importance of marriage.

Flexibility

Flexibility is the ability to change in response to need or to accept some type of information that contradicts previously held beliefs. This information can come from observation of or interaction with each other.

Acceptance of Differences   As indicated previously, incongruent grieving is common as couples attempt to cope with their own loss experience. In time, however, if couples become aware of the bases for these differences, they may learn to be more tolerant of one another.

For some couples, this realization may come very early in the grieving process; other couples may slowly move toward acceptance of each other; still others may need to "bottom out" before they can do so. Partners might see that, even though their grief experience is a shared one, it is necessary to grieve separately too. Even when spouses experience different emotions and have contradictory views of the loss, having the differences acknowledged and accepted by each other is viewed as helpful. This acceptance reduces the strain between them and allows each to stop feeling guilty over not grieving in the "appropriate" fashion.

Role Flexibility   Role flexibility, the easy ability to shift role performance within the couple, would allow partners to take turns and allow each other to "take a break" from responsibilities. If this was a normal part of their relationship prior to their child's death, the shift is easier and the couple can reorganize more easily (Jordan, 1990).

Sensitivity to Each Other's Needs

Another way in which partners try to reduce marital strain is by watching for cues as to what their spouse needs from them. This is successful when the spouse receiving the support confirms its helpfulness. These are often the "little things" that their spouses do that make them feel important. These can also validate the emotional connection to the child.

Sometimes, these efforts are done to reduce tension in the home. Helping one's spouse and focusing on meeting his or her needs can also benefit the person doing the helping. To some extent, this support of the spouse serves a dual purpose. Focusing on the other spouse may be helpful because it serves as a distraction. The spouse that is being helped also may learn new ways of coping by observing the helping spouse. Finally, helpers may experience a sense of movement toward recovery because they are able to help another person rather than needing help themselves.

Finally, in addition to being aware of their spouse's needs, by accepting their own limitations, recognizing their own needs, and not trying to be everything to their spouse, both partners can benefit. They can encourage their spouse to go to appropriate resources outside the marriage, such as a friend, a clergy member, a therapist or counselor, or a support group.

INTERVENTION TO FACILITATE POSITIVE COUPLE COPING

The death of a child can be devastating, both to the parents as individuals and as a couple. Couples commonly experience tremendous conflict over the nature of their grief, what it means for each partner, and how their individual approaches to the loss fit together. This also may contribute to a feeling of estrangement from their spouse, possibly a sense that their spouse "is no longer the person I married."

Figley (1989) has suggested a five-step treatment program for focusing on the development of a publicly declared and communally recognized healing theory. It involves building commitment to the therapeutic objectives, framing the problem, reframing the problem, developing a family healing theory, and reaching closure. Using such an approach builds the couple's sense of working together to resolve their grief. It also promotes the sense that they have achieved a common baseline of understanding in their relationship as a safe environment. As noted earlier, even though partners do not share an identical view of the loss, they have a strong need to see themselves sharing thoughts, attitudes, and values with each other.

Another system-based approach, based on the theoretical concepts of Viktor Frankl, includes five very similar stages: establishing the treatment system, remembering terror, recovering meaning in trauma and terror, making use of meaning potentials, and terminating and celebrating. As with the program proposed by Figley, this intervention involves both partners as they work together in resolving their loss (Lantz & Lantz, 1991).

CONCLUSION

As they work to rebuild their assumptive worlds and their dyadic paradigm, the couple can recognize several things to help them survive the loss. Awareness of these before (if possible) or at the time of loss may "inoculate" the couple against some relational strain. In the context of postloss intervention, recognition of these points may facilitate resolution of marital conflict.

1   The loss of a child is one of the losses that is most likely to result in complicated grief.

2   When their child dies, marital partners do not experience the same subjective loss. Each has specific issues to be worked through that are related to the unique character of his or her subjective loss. It may be possible for one spouse to experience the loss as devastating, while the other is far less affected.

3   It is far more the norm for parents to grieve differently from each other than to grieve similarly. Such differences can be painful to acknowledge, because so much implicit information is attributed to one's spouse's behavior. Yet, if they are able to reframe differences from "incongruent" (i.e., a weakness) to "diverse" (i.e., strengths) partners may be able to learn from and draw on each other's capabilities.

4   Underlying everything else they do is a need for the couple to build and maintain open lines of communication between each other and with others outside the marriage.

5   Marital partners benefit from holding or developing a positive view of themselves and their marriage. Reframing, as suggested by Figley (1989), is a useful tool in moving to this positive view.

6   The perception that they have shared a loss and participation in activities with each other facilitate their sense of being a couple. As they reassess their roles and relationship with each other, shared time allows them to negotiate how these new or modified roles will be carried out.

7   Partners need to strive for flexibility in their relationship and a sensitivity to each other's needs. Because each of them has experienced a different loss, and because each has a different style of grieving, each will have his or her own issues to work out. One or both of them may need to have some time to be alone. One partner may need outside resources (e.g., support groups or individual therapy) more than the other.

Marital partners may find the death of their child overwhelming and beyond belief and their marital bonds may be tested by the aftermath of their loss. The couple-focused model of parental coping with the death of a child presented in this chapter can be integrated into prevention or intervention with bereaved parents, particularly if the focus is on bolstering or improving the relationship between spouses.

REFERENCES

Attig, T. (1991). The importance of conceiving of grief as an active process. *Death Studies, 15,* 385–393.

Berger, P., & Kellner, H. (1964/1992). Marriage and the construction of reality: An exercise in the microsociology of knowledge. *Diogenes, 46,* 1–25. Reprinted in J. M. Henslin, Ed., *Marriage and family in a changing society* (4th ed.), New York: Free Press.

Borg, S., & Lasker, J. (1988). *When pregnancy fails: Families coping with miscarriage, stillbirth and infant death* (2nd ed.). New York: Bantam.

Boss, P. (1991). Ambiguous loss. In F. Walsh & M. McGoldrick (Eds.), *Living beyond loss: Death in the family* (pp. 164–175). New York: W. W. Norton.

Bouvard, M. (1988). *The path through grief: A practical guide.* Portland, OR: Breitenbush Books.

Bowen, M. (1991). Family reactions to death. In F. Walsh & M. McGoldrick (Eds.), *Living beyond loss: Death in the family* (pp. 79–92). New York: W. W. Norton.

Bowlby, J. (1980). *Attachment and loss* (Vol. III). New York: Basic.

Broderick, C. B. (1993). *Understanding family process: Basics of family systems theory.* Newbury Park, CA: Sage.

Colburn, K., & Malena, D. (1989). Bereavement issues for survivors of persons with AIDS: Coping with society's pressures. *Advances in Thanatology, 1,* 126–131.

Cook, J. A. (1988). Dads' double binds: Rethinking fathers' bereavement from a men's studies perspective. *Journal of Contemporary Ethnography, 17,* 285–308.

Cornwell, J., Nurcombe, B., & Stevens, L. (1977). Family response to the loss of a child by Sudden Infant Death Syndrome. *Medical Journal of Australia, 1,* 656–658.

DeFrain, J. (1991). Learning about grief from normal families: SIDS, stillbirth, and miscarriage. *Journal of Marital and Family Therapy, 17,* 215–232.

Epstein, N., & Westley, W. (1959). Patterns of intrafamilial communication. *Psychiatric Research Reports, 11,* 1–11.

Figley, C. R. (1983). Catastrophes: An overview of family reactions. In C. R. Figley & H. I. McCubbin (Eds.), *Stress and the family: Coping with catastrophe* (Vol. 2, pp. 3–20). New York: Brunner/Mazel.

Figley, C. R. (1989). *Helping traumatized families.* San Francisco: Jossey-Bass.

Fowlkes, M. R. (1991). The morality of loss: The social construction of mourning and melancholia. *Contemporary Psychoanalysis, 27,* 529–551.

Frantz, T. T. (1984). Helping parents whose child has died. In T. T. Frantz (Ed.), *Death and grief in the family* (pp. 11–26). Rockville, MD: Aspen Systems.

Gilbert, K. R. (in press). Understanding the secondary traumatic stress of spouses. In C. R. Figley, (Ed.), *Burnout in families: Secondary traumatic stress in everyday living.* Delray Beach, FL: Saint Lucie Press.

Gilbert, K. R. (1996). "We've had the same loss, why don't we have the same grief?" Loss and differential grief in families. *Death Studies, 20,* 269–283.

Gilbert, K., & Smart, L. (1992). *Coping with infant or fetal loss: The couple's healing process.* New York: Brunner/Mazel.

Green, B. L., Wilson, J. P., & Lindy, J. D. (1985). Conceptualizing post-traumatic stress disorder: A psychosocial framework. In C. R. Figley (Ed.), *Trauma and its wake: The study and treatment of post-traumatic stress disorder* (pp. 53–69). New York: Brunner/Mazel.

Haig, R. A. (1990). *The anatomy of grief: Biopsychosocial and therapeutic perspectives.* Springfield, IL: Charles C. Thomas.

Helmrath, T. A., & Steinitz, E. M. (1978). Death of an infant: Parental grieving and the failure of social support. *The Journal of Family Practice, 6,* 785–790.

Hill, R. (1949). *Families under stress.* New York: Harper.

Hoagland, A. C. (1984). Bereavement and personal constructs: Old theories and new concepts. In F. R. Epting & R. A. Neimeyer (Eds.), *Personal meanings of death: Application of personal construct theory to clinical practice* (pp. 89–109). Washington, DC: Hemisphere.

Horowitz, M. (1979). Psychosocial response to serious life events. In V. Hamilton & D. M. Warburton (Eds), *Human stress and cognition* (pp. 237–264). New York: Wiley.

Horowitz, M. (1986). *Stress response syndrome* (2nd ed.) New York: Jason Aronson.

Imber-Black, E. (1991). Rituals and the healing process. In F. Walsh & M. McGoldrick (Eds.), *Living beyond loss: Death in the family* (pp. 207–223). New York: W. W. Norton.

Janoff-Bulman, R. (1992). *Shattered assumptions: Towards a new psychology of trauma.* New York: Free Press.

Jordan, J. (1990, August). *Loss and family development: Clinical implications.* Paper presented at the 98th Annual Convention of the American Psychological Association, Boston, MA.

Klass, D. (1988). *Parental grief: Solace and resolution.* New York: Springer.

Klauss, M. H., & Kennel, J. H. (1976). *Maternal-infant bonding.* St. Louis: Mosby.

Lantz, J., & Lantz, J. (1991). Franklian treatment with the traumatized family. *Journal of Family Psychotherapy, 2,* 61–72.

Lifton, R. J. (1971). *History and human survival.* New York: Random House.

Lindemann, E. (1944). Symptomatology and management of acute grief. *American Journal of Psychiatry, 101,* 141–148.

Marris, P. (1982). Attachment and society. In C. M. Parkes & J. Stevenson-Hinde (Eds.), *The place of attachment in human behavior* (pp. 185–204). New York: Basic Books.

McCubbin, H. I., & Patterson, J. M. (1983). The family stress process: The double ABCX model of adjustment and adaptation. *Marriage and Family Review, 6*(½), 2–38.

McGoldrick, M., Almeida, R., Hines, P. M., Rosen, E., Garcia-Presto, N., & Lee, E. (1991). Mourning in different cultures. In F. Walsh & M. McGoldrick (Eds.), *Living beyond loss: Death in the family* (pp. 176–205). New York: W. W. Norton.

Miles, M. S. (1984). Helping adults mourn the death of a child. In H. Wass & C. A. Corr (Eds.), *Childhood and death* (pp. 219–239). Washington, DC: Hemisphere.

Neimeyer, R. A., Epting, F. R., & Krieger, S. R. (1984). Personal constructs in thanatology: An introduction and research bibliography. In F. R. Epting & R. A. Neimeyer (Eds.), *Personal meanings of death: Applications of personal construct theory to clinical practice* (pp. 1–10). Washington, DC: Hemisphere.

Nichols, M. P. (1984). *Family therapy, concepts and methods.* New York: Garden Press.

Osterweis, M., Solomon, F., & Green, M. (1984). *Bereavement: Reactions, consequences and care.* Washington, DC: National Academy Press.

Owen, G., Fulton, R., & Markusen, E. (1982–83). Death at a distance: A study of family survivors. *Omega, 13,* 191–225.

Parkes, C. M. (1972). *Bereavement: Studies of grief in adult life.* New York: International University Press.

Patterson, J. M., & Garwick, A. W. (1994). Levels of meaning in family stress theory. *Family Process, 33,* 287–304.

Peppers, L. G., & Knapp, R. J. (1980). *Motherhood and mourning: Perinatal death.* New York: Praeger.

Rando, T. A. (1983). An investigation of grief and adaptation in parents whose children have died from cancer. *Journal of Pediatric Psychology, 8,* 3–20.

Rando, T. A. (1984). *Grief, dying, and death: Clinical interventions for caregivers.* Champaign, IL: Research Press.

Rando, T. A. (1992–93). The increasing prevalence of complicated mourning: The onslaught is just beginning. *Omega, 26,* 43–59.

Raphael, B. (1983). *The anatomy of bereavement.* New York: Basic Books.

Raphael, B. (1992, April). *Counseling after a catastrophic loss.* Keynote address at the 1992 Annual Meeting of the Association for Death Educators and Counselors, Boston, MA.

Raphael, B., & Middleton, W. (1988). Personal disaster. In J. G. Howells (Ed.), *Modern perspectives in psychosocial pathology* (pp. 281–304). New York: Brunner/Mazel.

Reiss, D. (1981). *The family's construction of reality.* Cambridge, MA: Harvard University Press.

Rinear, E. (1988). Psychosocial aspects of parental response patterns to the death of a child by homicide. *Journal of Traumatic Stress, 1*, 305–322.

Rosenblatt, P. C. (1988). Grief: The social context of private feelings. *Journal of Social Issues, 44*, 67–78.

Rosenblatt, P. C., & Burns, L. H. (1986). Long-term effects of perinatal loss. *Journal of Family Issues, 7*, 237–253.

Rosenblatt, P. C., Spoentgen, P., Karis, T. A., Dahl, C., Kaiser, T., & Elde, C. (1991). Difficulties in supporting the bereaved. *Omega, 23*, 119–128.

Sanders, C. M. (1979–80). A comparison of adult bereavement in the death of a spouse, child and parent. *Omega, 10*, 303–321.

Silver, R. L., & Wortman, C. B. (1980). Coping with undesirable life events. In J. Garber & M. E. P. Seligman (Eds.), *Human helplessness: Theory and applications* (pp. 279–340). New York: Academic.

Smith, J. R. (1981). *Veterans and combat: Toward a model of the stress recovery process.* Paper presented at the Veterans Administration Operation Outreach Training Program.

Spurgeon, D. (1984). *And I don't want to live this life.* New York: Ballantine Books.

Stephenson, J. S. (1985). *Death, grief and mourning: Individual and social realities.* New York: Free Press.

Symonds, M. (1980). The "second injury" to victims. *Evaluation and Change*, 36–38.

Taylor, S. E. (1983). Adjustment to threatening events: A theory of cognitive adaptation. *American Psychologist, 38*, 1161–1173.

Taylor, S. E., Lichtman, R. R., & Wood, J. V. (1984). Attribution, beliefs about control and adjustment to breast cancer. *Journal of Personality and Social Psychology, 46*, 489–502.

Walsh, F., & McGoldrick, M. (1991). Loss and the family: A systemic perspective. In F. Walsh & M. McGoldrick (Eds.), *Living beyond loss: Death in the family* (pp. 1–29). New York: W. W. Norton.

Watzlawick, D., Weakland, J., & Fisch, R. (1974). *Change: Principles of problem formation and problem resolution.* New York: W. W. Norton.

Weitzman, S. G., & Kamm, P. (1985). *About mourning: Support and guidance for the bereaved.* New York: Human Sciences Press.

Worden, J. W. (1991). *Grief counseling and grief therapy: A handbook for the mental health practitioner* (2nd ed.). New York: Springer.

Chapter 6

Death as Trauma for Children: A Relational Treatment Approach

Arlene Steinberg

The death of a parent, by violence or otherwise, presents many issues for the children who are left behind, as well as for surviving parents, other family members, and the therapists who are treating them. The question of when death is traumatic for children is a complicated one that has been argued in the literature (Eth & Pynoos, 1985b; Raphael, 1983). Clinicians have consistently described the devastating effect on children of losing parents (Moody & Moody, 1991), siblings (Adams & Deveau, 1987; Pole, Wass, Eyberg, & Chu, 1989), friends (Klingman, 1989), or even important community figures, such as Christa McAuliff of the Challenger disaster (Blume, 1986; Stevenson, 1986). Yet the debate continues as to whether children can and do grieve like adults.

This chapter focuses mainly on parental loss, and also mentions briefly the impact of the deaths of a sibling or friend (Krupnick & Solomon, 1988). This choice was made in order to address the most extreme form of loss, because the loss of a parent or caretaker is most likely to threaten the basic security and stability of the child's world. However, the traumatic effect of a sibling or friend's death should not be minimized; here, it is mainly discussed in terms of its influence on the child's feelings about his or her own mortality.

Some of this controversy begins with the question of when children can realistically comprehend death. Robert Furman (1964) believes that 2- and 3-year-old children, because they have attained object constancy, can realistically understand death, and thus can mourn. In contrast, Nagera (1970), Wolf (1958), and Wolfenstein (1969) believe that children are incapable of mourning because they do not attain the ability to think abstractly until adolescence. This professional debate is in keeping with the lack of attention children have received in the family arena. Bowlby (1980), Rando (1984), and Raphael (1983) describe the difficulties of surviving parents in dealing with their children's pain as contributing to the denial of the child's mourning. This difficulty is shared by others who come in contact with these youngsters, such as teachers and therapists. Bowlby (1980) describes the painful struggle of bereaved children in his seminal work on loss in children. He emphasizes the bereaved child's greater helplessness as compared with a grieving adult in that children rely on their parents for help and cannot independently seek assistance.

TRAUMATIC IMPACT

Bereaved children have symptoms that strikingly resemble those of traumatization even though the extent to which death is traumatic for children continues to be discussed, questioned, and debated. They experience dysphoria, somatic symptoms, sleep disturbances (including nightmares), anxiety states, guilt feelings, enuresis, separation reactions, and phobias. In some cases, Bowlby (1980) has seen depersonalization and dissociative states, symptoms commonly associated with trauma, among bereaved children. He described the case of Geraldine, whose mother died of cancer a week before her eighth birthday. At age 10, she was found in a fugue state away from home. She did not know who she was nor where she lived. She was ultimately taken, at her own request, to a hospital and with the help of the police was returned to her family. Although Bowlby believes that dissociative symptoms are relatively rare, he nevertheless attributes them to the parental loss. Similar to trauma survivors, children who have lost a parent often experience an increase in symptoms at the anniversary of the death or when they reach the age of their parent's death (Epstein, 1982; Raphael, 1983). It is surprising that the impact of death on children continues to be questioned, particularly in light of the similar and serious symptomatology that bereaved children demonstrate. This may be partly due to the lack of confirmatory data on bereavement symptomatology (Raphael, 1983). Considering the similarity between and overlap of bereavement and post-traumatic stress symptoms, many now suggest that bereaved children also suffer from post-traumatic stress with the death being considered the traumatic event. Additionally, many writers emphasize the contribution of several factors to the traumatic impact, implying that the issue is not whether the child was traumatized, but rather the degree of trauma. The degree of the trauma is affected by the circumstances prior to and following the death, as well as by the death itself. Bowlby (1980) described the relationship patterns before the loss, the circumstances of the death, and the family relationships and/or support systems available after the loss as part of the trauma matrix. Included is the extent of existing ambivalence between child and parent (Rando, 1984); the continuity of care prior to the parent's death; the suddenness of the death; and the ability of the surviving parent or caretaker to adequately care for the child's needs, including the emotional need to grieve after the parent dies.

Elizur and Kaffman (1983), Hilgard, Newman, and Fisk (1960), and Kaffman and Elizur (1983), in their studies of parentally bereaved children, describe certain protective factors that mitigate the impact for the children. In addition to the stability of the home prior to the loss, the surviving parent's ability to foster tolerance of separation, along with the child's ability to mourn (Barnes, 1964) and to use a support system, can buffer the experience of trauma. Previous exposure to the death of more distant figures in the child's life can also contribute to the child's resilience in the face of the death of a loved one. This is because the child has already experienced losing someone and has confronted death in a situation where the stability and security of his or her own world was not threatened as it is when losing a close family member, such as a parent. The post-traumatic stress literature similarly addresses the effect of previous exposure to traumatic experiences in gradual doses on the individual's resilience in the face of serious traumata and catastrophe. Other writers (Eth & Pynoos, 1985a; E. Furman, 1983; Galante & Foa, 1986) not only underscore the importance of family support, but also emphasize the mediating impact of resuming the family routine as soon as possible after any traumatic event, including death.

DEVELOPMENTAL CONSIDERATIONS

Children of different ages display grief in varying ways. Raphael (1983) addresses the influence of age on the child's experience of loss, and states that children under age 2 are capable of experiencing the beginning of grief. At this age, children may insist on the return of the lost parent and reject any substitute. It is important that the surviving caretaker remain consistently available in order for the child to accept the loss and for the pain to ease.

The child's relationship with the deceased parent is tinged with meaning and fantasy among 2- to 5-year-olds. Raphael (1983) believes that these children can understand death with assistance. Their matter-of-fact curiosity about it requires adult honesty. Children, particularly at this age, tend to think concretely and can develop fears from metaphoric explanations that analogize death with sleeping or sickness. Besides the previously described symptomatology, they are also more likely to experience regressive symptoms, including bedwetting and soiling.

Children aged 5 through 8 are capable of feeling guilt. According to Raphael (1983), parental death may be linked in the child's mind to his or her own actions or inactions, or magical thoughts or wishes, with the latter being more intense among younger children. Guilt feelings are greater if the relationship with the deceased parent was ambivalent, because the child may have harbored murderous thoughts that he or she unconsciously believes caused the parent's death. Children of this age, similar to younger ones, tend to deny their traumatic experience.

The affective responses and defenses of children aged 8 through 12 are similar to those of adults: They understand the irreversibility of death, and they also become concerned about their own mortality as well as that of the surviving parent. Because of their fears for themselves, children of this age may particularly fear sleep, darkness, and disease, especially in situations when a sibling died (Cain, Fast, & Erickson, 1964).

Raphael's (1983) developmental considerations are consistent with Eth and Pynoos's (1985a) observations of traumatized children. They both describe the role of fantasy in the reparative enactments of preschoolers as well as the guilt-ridden concerns about their own actions or inactions among school-aged children. Both writers also describe the propensity of adolescents to enact the trauma or loss in their everyday lives in order to work it through. Separation struggles are most profound in this age group. Death, as the ultimate separation, can exacerbate the already quite difficult separation conflicts experienced by children of this age.

THERAPEUTIC CONSIDERATIONS

The debate in the intervention literature reflects the confusion regarding when death is traumatic as discussed above. Eth and Pynoos (1985b) are noted for their work on the post-traumatic stress disorder of children who witness the violent death of a significant other. Therefore, they consider death within the context of post-traumatic stress. However, they view only violent death as traumatic and believe that it is the violence that interferes with the grief work because the violent images inhibit the child's reminiscing, an essential aspect of the mourning process. Eth and Pynoos (1985b) do not address the traumatic imagery that more than likely occurs in situations of nonviolent death, as with a parent's very visible deterioration from cancer. Although acknowledging commonalities between traumatized and bereaved youngsters as they have defined them, Eth and Pynoos (1985b) distinguish the psychotherapy of bereavement from that of post-traumatic stress. Nevertheless, they state that both groups are plagued by intrusive thoughts, painful affects, and fears of being overwhelmed, and that they are helped by focal brief psychotherapy.

The approach suggested by Eth and Pynoos (1985b) is more structured than the open-ended psychodynamic intervention models commonly used with bereaved youngsters (E. Furman, 1974, 1983; Lopez & Kliman, 1970; Smith, 1991). Although both approaches emphasize reexperiencing the traumatic events or loss, in psychodynamic work it is considered necessary for the reexperiencing to occur within the therapeutic relationship. For instance, Lopez and Kliman (1979) describe their work with Diana, who would repeatedly fall in sessions, comparing these falls with her mother's suicidal leap to her death. Diana needed the secure context of the therapeutic relationship to work through her complex feelings toward, and identification with, her mother. The reenactments, described by others as well (see Barnes, 1964), can be seen as defensive mechanisms for mastering feelings of vulnerability and helplessness (Dietrich, 1989). These vulnerable and helpless feelings can come from witnessing either a violent death of a parent through suicide, murder, or disaster (Eth & Pynoos, 1985b) or a parent's deterioration or sudden death from illness.

Most younger children use play as a vehicle both for reexperiencing their loss and for expressing their rescue fantasies aimed at combatting their sense of helplessness (Smith, 1989). Both bereaved and traumatized youngsters also use post-traumatic play (Terr, 1989) as a form of remembering that enables them to cope with difficult emotions, label their feelings, and work through their problems. They can enact, often in a repetitive, monotonous, or even dangerous way, the death, the burial, or any other aspect of the loss, including their own rescue fantasies, which they hope will undo the damage. Children's play allows them to express conscious and unconscious themes without having to verbally acknowledge, or even have a conscious awareness of, the painful aspects that older children and adolescents are more likely to deal with in words.

Because one of the main things that has been lost to the children discussed in this chapter is their relationship with a parent, the psychotherapeutic relationship becomes particularly important and can provide a secure place for children to reexperience and integrate their traumatic loss.

ASSESSMENT

As in any treatment, the initial phase of the work is assessment. It is important to recognize the symptomatology of the traumatized individuals in order to properly treat them. To consider loss within the context of post-traumatic stress can lead to a greater focus on symptoms than traditionally discussed in the bereavement literature. Therefore, assessing symptoms and their disruptive effect on an individual's life becomes more crucial. Evaluation can include direct clinical interviews (Pynoos & Eth, 1986), projective measures, meetings with parents (Altschul, 1988; E. Furman, 1974), psychological assessments (Pruett, 1979), or standardized self-report measures (Malmquist, 1976; McNally, 1991; Yule & Williams, 1990).

In the Pynoos and Eth (1986) structured interview, children are initially engaged in drawing a picture or telling a story, while the rest of the interview focuses on the creation of the picture or story. The children's affective and perceptual experience of the traumatic event, as well as present and future life plans, are elicited via the picture or story. Pynoos and Eth (1986) recommend one interview. Yet, particularly because of the increased emphasis on the therapeutic relationship as proposed in this chapter, more interviews would be optimum.

Although the assessment phase proposed in this chapter, consistent with psychodynamically oriented bereavement writings, is generally less structured than Pynoos and Eth (1986) suggest, there are some general guidelines for inclusion. First, an assessment of preloss history of both children and parents should include the quality of the relationship with the deceased, because, as mentioned earlier, prior feelings of ambivalence can impede mourning. Second, the atmosphere of the home following the death, including the availability of a support network, is another factor that can influence adjustment. Death holds a particular meaning for each child. This meaning is embedded in the world in which the child lives at the time of the loss and subsequently. Third, an evaluation of the child's future life plans can provide an assessment of the extent to which he or she is involved with his or her surroundings, and also provide a measure of pathological bereavement.

If a more formalized assessment is desired, standardized self-report scales, such as the Impact of Events Scale, can measure the intrusive and avoidant symptoms of post-traumatic stress (Horowitz, Wilner, & Alvarez, 1979) and grief (McNally, 1991). These standardized scales have a tendency to be skewed toward conscious material, which can lead to neglect of more unconscious experience. Nevertheless, reactions children do not report directly for fear of upsetting their parents can be elicited. Also, the use of these scales allows comparison of the significance of their distress with that of their peers. In spite of these benefits, less structured methods of assessment are generally recommended in psychodynamic treatment because of the need to examine the underlying, unconscious fears, wishes, and thoughts in order to facilitate working them through.

AN INTERVENTION APPROACH

Particularly because family members too often deny childhood mourning, it is not surprising that most writers in the field stress the need to work with surviving parents as an essential and sometimes initial step in working with bereaved children. Barnes (1964) describes therapeutic work with a girl and her grandmother. In this case, treatment with the caretaker was sufficient to help the child cope with the loss of her mother. Raphael (1983) describes caretakers' needs for support to facilitate their own grief so that they have better resources to respond to their children. Although parent guidance is frequently sufficient to assist caretakers, family therapy is sometimes recommended. A family therapy format can provide opportunities for family members to share with one another feelings and memories surrounding both the death itself and the person lost to them. Raphael (1983) also reports that freeing feelings within the family system decreases the isolation of members, enables them to confront one another, and demonstrates that the powerful feelings of grief will not destroy the family system.

Guidance sessions can provide surviving parents and caretakers with some understanding of the confusing symptom picture presented by the bereaved children in their care. Caretakers often have difficulty accepting a child's seemingly short sadness span. For instance, a request for ice cream after being told of the death may be considered insensitive. Yet this request is more likely a seeking of reassurance on the child's part that his or her needs will continue to be met. It is important to help caretakers understand the meaning of the symptoms. A preschooler's sadness can be either a reaction to the loss itself or an identification with a close relative's grief when the child simply does not quite understand what has occurred. Caretaker intervention in the former situation may involve acceptance of the child's feelings; in the latter case, providing concrete information may be crucial.

It is very important for parents and others to answer children's questions in a simple and concrete way rather than in an abstract, religious, or philosophical manner. Children can feel confused rather than comforted by statements like "Daddy's in heaven" or "God took him away." E. Furman (1974) describes a case of one little boy who refused to walk down the street, fearing that God would take him away too. Using the term *rest in peace* can lead to confusion between resting and death. Because children tend to concretize abstract explanations, heaven may be viewed as a faraway, physical residence. Providing children with accurate information often clarifies their misconceptions. Rando (1984) encourages the inclusion of children in formal rites in order to include them in the family's mourning experience and to concretize the loss they are also experiencing.

Family members frequently find educational information about the symptoms of childhood loss as well as guidelines about what to say to children enormously helpful (Pruett, 1979). For instance, while putting children to sleep, they are encouraged to say, "Mother used to do this; now I am," in order to reassure the children that, although their mother is gone, their needs will continue to be met. Resuming routines quickly and maintaining them after the loss can also be comforting in the same way. In addition to educating caretakers as to how to interact with the children, helping caretakers tolerate children's anger may be necessary, particularly if caretakers hold their own ambivalent and guilty feelings toward the deceased.

Overall, children need a caretaker not only to recognize their grief, but also to reassure them that they will continue to be loved and taken care of, and that they are not in danger of dying themselves. When parental counseling is not sufficient to help the caretaker with this task because of the severity of his or her own grief, a referral for individual psychotherapy for the caretaker may be necessary. The therapeutic relationship can provide caretakers as well as children with a safe arena for grieving. This can even be true in the parent counseling format.

Children usually need their own private place to work through their grief. They are often reticent in family sessions (Terr, 1989) because they are fearful of upsetting the surviving parent with their own distress (Yule & Williams, 1990). Therefore, traumatized parents should be careful when acknowledging their own vulnerability and difficulties (Terr, 1989). It is very important for children to receive the specific individual support they need (Raphael, 1983).

Because children react differently to their loss, their needs for therapeutic intervention vary. The therapist can serve as a backdrop, an active participant, or both at varying points in the treatment. Sarnoff (1987) states that often little active intervention is needed in psychotherapy. However, Pynoos and Eth (1986) describe the therapist as actively structuring the treatment. Perhaps the children Pynoos and Eth (1986) discuss, who have experienced violent death, need greater input from their therapist to support them in their confrontation with the violent intrusive imagery.

Whether children utilize their therapist as a sounding board for their feelings, to test the reality of their perceptions, or for specific guidance, the therapeutic relationship can be a safe place for children to relive and ultimately integrate their loss. The therapist must always keep in mind that children can designate the therapist as a replacement for the lost object or they can withdraw from contact, fearing a reexperience of the loss. Beneath a child's initial presentation can lie a myriad of feelings including sadness and anger. Bereaved children, like trauma victims, can view the therapist as the inflictor of trauma, either the one who took the parent away or the parent who left.

COUNTERTRANSFERENCE

Complex countertransference feelings can arise. The emotionally demanding nature of clinical work with trauma survivors has been described and empirically demonstrated in the post-traumatic stress literature (Danieli, 1980). However, issues of countertransference are not directly addressed in bereavement writings. As with clinicians who treat trauma survivors, being viewed as the inflictor of trauma can raise a variety of conflicting feelings for the clinician who treats the bereaved. Countertransference feelings can include guilt over replacing the parent in the therapeutic role and in the child's fantasy, sadness over the child's loss, anger at the parent for leaving, and the desire to rescue the child. It is imperative that clinicians be aware of these feelings; otherwise the feelings are likely to interfere with the work. The emotionally taxing nature of this work may lead clinicians to seek outside assistance from either supervisors or colleagues to help them deal with these complex emotions. The therapist's ability to accept and understand both the child's feelings and their own countertransference facilitates the creation of the stable holding environment (Winnicott, 1986) that is necessary for healing.

Children's methods of coping with grief, as has been discussed, vary with age, as do their therapeutic needs. Preschoolers repetitively ask questions about the details of the death, seeking not only facts but also reassurance that the story has remained the same. Although they use play in therapy to work through their loss, concrete explanations may provide them with the reassurances they are seeking. Children in this age group may blame themselves for the death and need to be told it was not their fault. They also can use play to work through the loss without conscious awareness of their struggle.

Given the concrete understanding of school-aged children, they too demand concrete explanations. Euphemisms should be particularly avoided with this age group (e.g., "we lost grandma") because they taunt the child's literal understanding and can result in a search for grandma. Because these children often blame themselves, they too may need to be told that it was not their fault.

Although adolescents have the clearest understanding of the universality and inevitability of death, their struggles with separation–individuation may make them feel particularly abandoned by the deceased or guilt ridden about their striving for independence. The identity struggles of adolescents can result in greater identification with the deceased and increased concerns about their own mortality. This can particularly occur when the individual who died was a peer or sibling. In addition, caretakers tend to underestimate the emotional needs of adolescents and expect them to handle the loss as an adult might. Teenagers look to the therapeutic setting as a place where they can express their feelings. They may also need the therapist to provide reassurance and understanding about their own health as well as help in sorting out the confusing messages they receive from caretakers.

Children often benefit from group therapy in addition to or, as in the case of resistant youngsters, instead of individual therapy. Structured, time-limited creative therapy groups are suggested by many (Moody & Moody, 1991; Zambelli, Clark, Barile, & deJong, 1988). The expressive art format allows children to express feelings they cannot put into words, and the presence of other bereaved children is comforting. These groups generally do not offer opportunities to work through concerns and conflicts that predate, but were aroused by, the loss, but can be extraordinarily helpful as a beginning step.

Another course of intervention is with school personnel, who often need assistance understanding the bereaved child's behavior. Classmates identifying with the grieving youngster often develop similar symptomatology. School personnel are faced not only with helping the bereaved child reintegrate into the classroom (Pynoos, Nader, & Frederick, 1987), but also with assisting peers with the prospect of a parent's death (McDonald, 1964). Death not only occurs in the lives of bereaved children, but affects those with whom they come in contact as well.

Certain types of loss, such as suicide and catastrophe, affect many students in a school setting. Organized programs of mental health consultation in schools are described by such authors as Klingman (1989) (high school–based intervention programs dealing with adolescent suicide) and Stevenson (1986) (community-wide losses such as the Challenger disaster).

Observations of successful interventions with bereaved children have been described in the literature (Lopez & Kliman, 1979). Yet, outcome studies of their effectiveness are lacking (Raphael, 1983). One empirical study (Van Erdewegh, Bieri, Parilla, & Clayton, 1982) notes instead the relative underutilization of services, with bereaved parents being less likely to take their children to a physician than those in a control group. This is attributed to their preoccupation with their own grief and their failure to perceive and recognize the significance of the child's symptoms (Raphael, 1983). Despite the numerous case studies cited in the literature, it appears that more empirical work in this area is needed.

CASE ILLUSTRATIONS

Despite the need for more systematic research to demonstrate quantitatively the effectiveness of accepted models of intervention, case illustrations can provide excellent qualitative support. Two cases, differing in terms of the age of the children, the suddenness of the loss, and the proximity of the children to the moment of death, are presented. The two cases—those of a preschooler whose mother committed suicide and an adolescent whose mother and brother died after slowly deteriorating from AIDS—illustrate the treatment approach presented here.

Erica, the second oldest of four children, lost her mother at age 5, when her mother took her own life by overdosing on antidepressant medication as the children stood nearby. Erica's grandmother, who always wanted to have several children but had only the one daughter, became the children's legal guardian. Erica had an early history of erratic maternal care; her mother would leave the children in her own mother's charge for days at a time. Both parents were teenagers when they had the four children, and Erica's father was never considered to be capable of reliably caring for them.

At that time, Erica presented with a host of post-traumatic symptoms displayed at home and at her day care center, including fears, enuresis (she had previously mastered toilet training), nightmares (including her mother's apparition in her room), sleep difficulties, and reenactment of her mother's death.

Erica's treatment involved weekly individual sessions, meetings with her grandmother, and school contact. The sessions with the grandmother were more frequent when her own feelings of guilt and deep sorrow over the loss of her daughter interfered with her ability to handle the children's fluctuating needs. She needed guidance in dealing with the children's grief as well as help with her own difficulties in grieving. The goal of phone contact and visits to the day care center was to facilitate the child's reintegration into that setting. When Erica's physical fighting and traumatic enactments (including running out of the center into onrushing cars on the street) disrupted the center's routines, visits provided reassurance to Erica and guidance to her teachers, and eventually led to symptom abatement.

Individual sessions provided Erica an arena in which she could express her thoughts, fears, and wishes and reenact many of her anxious concerns as well as her experience of her mother's traumatic death. She playacted death and endangered herself by climbing high and jumping to the floor. Erica's risky behavior may have demonstrated an identification with a self-destructive mother. Bereaved children frequently identify with parental behaviors as a way of both remembering their parent and gaining control over their helplessness in the face of their parent's death. However, identification with her mother was particularly problematic. She physically resembled her mother, and Erica's grandmother, who also identified her in this way, frequently questioned whether Erica was suicidal as well.

Erica's therapeutic play revealed her struggles to comprehend her mother's whereabouts. She announced in one session that her mother had died, made stars with white Play-Doh, described the twinkling of the stars in the sky as mother saying good-bye, and wondered if she would say good-bye to her again. These concerns were mirrored in her worries about parting upon leaving sessions. Erica insisted on both getting her own appointment slip and taking various objects from the office home. These objects served as transitional objects to hold onto until the next session, providing her with a sense of security. Erica would also declare before leaving a session that she was no longer coming, then ask in the next sentence when the next appointment was. Erica frequently questioned the whereabouts of her mother, and seemed confused and troubled when the family visited the cemetery. Frank discussion of the details of her mother's death and burial reassured her.

Erica fluctuated rapidly between positive feelings and angry feelings toward her mother. She frequently questioned whether her mother could have cared for her and yet have left. These fluctuating feelings were reflected in her transference reactions. She quickly attached to the therapist, expressing anger at her mother and at others. The positive nature of the initial therapeutic relationship could be seen as a necessary stage around which she could crystallize her wishes for reunion with the lost object (Lopez & Kliman, 1979) and that would hold her (Winnicott, 1986) through the angry storms. The tentative nature of this bond was demonstrated when Erica did not like something that the therapist said, at which time her angry feelings would emerge. She would empty out the contents of games and act in a mocking, taunting way. During the therapist's vacation, Erica was furious at the therapist for abandoning her, angry feelings she could not express to her mother. The therapist's consistent presence and empathic involvement helped her express and integrate these negative feelings. With time, she also needed less reassurance of this consistency, eventually not needing her own appointment slips between sessions and seeming to more fully trust the therapist's presence. The therapist's verbal acceptance and understanding of Erica's ambivalent feelings and post-traumatic play were important elements in Erica's healing.

Work with Erica's grandmother was essential in diminishing her identification of Erica with her dead mother as well as helping her accept Erica's symptoms as a normal reaction to an abnormal event. The grandmother got angry with Erica's insensitivity, and needed guidance to accept the age-appropriate short-sadness span. The grandmother's own incomplete grieving process interfered with her ability to help the children. She felt enormously guilty that her only daughter had died and left the four children in her care, particularly because she enjoyed caring for them. The grandmother would frequently relive her relationship with Erica's mother through Erica. The therapeutic relationship, by providing a safe arena for Erica's grandmother to express and sort out her own intense feelings, diffused the intensity of this identification, buffered her projections, and helped her differentiate Erica from the child's mother. The grandmother seemed to view the therapist as a calm provider of nurturance, which she needed. She also utilized the guidance sessions to work through her profound guilt feelings that her attempts to rescue her daughter had failed.

Contact with the day care center helped them understand and contain Erica's frequent enactments and deal with the secondary traumatization of her peers. She would frequently reenact her mother's funeral, requiring other children to play her dead mother, resulting in traumatic symptoms among her peers.

As therapy progressed, Erica became better able to integrate the profound loss of her mother into the fabric of her everyday life. Each new developmental phase threatened this integration, but the sense of reliability and consistency provided in therapy helped her to weather the new anxieties that arose. She grew better able to verbalize her reactions rather than acting them out. Although she feels sad and misses her mother, she no longer enacts the loss. She knows that she physically resembles her mother, and yet no longer feels compelled to act out self-destructively as her mother had. In addition, the post-traumatic symptoms of fears, sleep disturbance, enuresis, and behavioral reenactments have diminished. She is viewed as a gifted child at school who is able not only to concentrate on but also to enjoy the academic curricula, and she is well aware of her own skills and mastery.

Sixteen-year-old Lila began individual psychotherapy at the urging of her maternal aunt and caretaker, who was concerned about Lila's withdrawn behavior and poor academic performance. Lila's mother and 3-year-old brother were dying of AIDS. Her mother seemed to have contracted the virus from the father of Lila's brother and passed it on to the child. Lila had an early history of neglect, which led to her aunt's gaining custody. She had mainly grown up in her aunt's stable home, and was doing well socially and academically until the illness. Her mother died several months after Lila began treatment, heightening the issues of loss and abandonment that she had already begun to work on.

Consistent with her age, Lila expressed her feelings in sessions through words rather than action or play. Lila used the stability of the therapeutic relationship to cope with and integrate the loss. The therapist served as a bridge between Lila's age-appropriate need for individuation and her desire to stay connected to her family and their shared grief. She used her sessions to express her feelings of sadness as well as her need to get away from the sadness of the home and pursue social involvement outside the home. Lila, as an adolescent, seemed to understand the facts about the death but was confused by her guilty feelings. The therapist's acceptance and clarification of her contradictory feelings enabled her to use the therapeutic arena for working through her loss at her own pace. Her periodic missing of sessions, not unusual for her age, probably reflected a need to distance herself from her own painful feelings and also served as a transferential enactment of her frequent absences from her home, because she had difficulty tolerating her aunt's grief. She also feared that the therapist would push her to experience her painful feelings, as her aunt did, rather than accept her equally important, self-protective need to distance herself. By expressing and working through these feelings with the therapist, Lila developed a deeper understanding of the struggle, and became less withdrawn at home and school. Her school work also improved.

In these two case examples, Erica's grandmother and Lila's aunt struggled with understanding the children's distancing and denial, which they perceived as callousness. Erica's grandmother developed a greater sensitivity to her granddaughter's age-appropriate needs to play, and became better able to perceive Erica's indirect expressions of grief in this activity. Lila's aunt began to accept her niece's need to stay out of their house and be with friends. Both women struggled with their fears of danger befalling the children and their own overprotectiveness related to the traumatic deaths of their loved ones. Erica's grandmother frequently overdressed the children and did not allow them to play outside; Lila's aunt worried that Lila's absences from home and her staying with friends resembled her mother's antisocial behavior patterns. Instead, Lila needed to maintain her social life and some distance from the sadness of the home. Therapeutic contact with these caretakers provided them with guidance and practical information about the age-appropriate reactions of children to loss. The stability of the therapeutic relationship enabled them to discover and work through their own complex feelings and projections related to the lost family member that were displaced onto these children. Both women ultimately pursued their own treatment to continue the important work begun in these sessions.

Parents' or caretakers' grief may not only disrupt children's lives but, if unresolved, additionally burden the children by spilling over into their parenting of the children. Therefore, parental counseling and, if needed, referral of caretakers for more intensive treatment are essential parts of treating the bereaved child.

CONCLUSION

Bereaved children can be helped via the therapeutic relationship to integrate traumatic losses into the fabric of their lives so that their psychological development is not impeded. Therapeutic contact with caretakers can provide them with guidance and ensure that their own concerns do not interfere with the child's healing. The resultant diminishing symptomatology of the child may be a measure of the child's healing.

The tendency of family members and other adults of significance to deny the pain experienced by bereaved children has been described. The theoretical debate over whether children mourn has also contributed to camouflaging their pain and suffering by focusing on labeling their experience rather than exploring what they actually feel. Whether this grieving process is identical to adult mourning or some variation thereof does not diminish the profound grief youngsters feel, at times requiring therapeutic assistance. Case studies like those presented in this chapter reflect the emotional struggles of bereaved children. Given the dearth of empirical work in this area, more research is recommended in order to substantiate the clinical claims made. In the meantime, children let us know about their emotional struggles and pain through their behavior, their play, or their words depending upon their age, and it is imperative that we know how to listen. Only then can we begin to understand and try to help them.

REFERENCES

Adams, D., & Deveau, E. (1987). When a brother or sister is dying of cancer: The vulnerability of the adolescent sibling. *Death Studies, 11*, 279–295.

Altschul, S. (1988). *Childhood bereavement and its aftermath.* Madison, CT: International Universities Press.

Barnes, M. (1964). Reactions to the death of a mother. *Psychoanalytic Study of the Child, 19*, 334–357.

Blume, D. (1986). Challenger 10 and school children: Reflections on the catastrophe. *Death Studies, 10*, 95–118.

Bowlby, J. (1980). *Loss: Sadness and depression.* New York: Basic Books.

Cain, A., Fast, I., & Erickson, M. (1964). Children's disturbed reactions to the death of a sibling. *American Journal of Orthopsychiatry, 34*, 741–752.

Danieli, Y. (1980). Countertransference in the treatment and study of Holocaust survivors and their children. *Victimology: An International Journal, 44*, 611–619.

Dietrich, D. (1989). Early childhood parent death, psychic trauma and organization, and object relations. In D. Dietrich and X. Shabad (Eds.), *The problem of loss and mourning* (pp. 277–335). Madison, CT: International Universities Press.

Elizur, E., & Kaffman, M. (1983). Factors influencing the severity of childhood bereavement reactions. *American Journal of Orthopsychiatry, 53,* 668–676.

Epstein, A. (1982). Mental phenomena across generations: The Holocaust. *Journal of the American Academy of Psychoanalysis, 10,* 565–570.

Eth, S., & Pynoos, R. (1985a). Developmental perspective on psychic trauma in childhood. In C. R. Figley (Ed.), *Trauma and its wake* (Vol. 1, pp. 36–52). New York: Brunner/Mazel.

Eth, S., & Pynoos, R. (1985b). Interaction of trauma and grief in childhood. In S. Eth & R. Pynoos (Eds.), *Post-traumatic stress disorder in children* (pp. 171–186). Washington, DC: American Psychiatric Press.

Furman, E. (1974). *A child's parent dies: Studies in childhood bereavement.* New Haven, CT: Yale University Press.

Furman, E. (1979). Filial therapy. In J. Noshpitz (Ed.), *Basic handbook of child psychiatry* (Vol. 3, pp. 149–158). New York: Basic Books.

Furman, E. (1983). Studies in childhood bereavement. *Canadian Journal of Psychiatry, 28,* 241–247.

Furman, R. (1964). Death and the young child. *Psychoanalytic Study of the Child, 19,* 321–333.

Galante, R., & Foa, E. (1986). An epidemiological study of psychic trauma and treatment effectiveness for children of a natural disaster. *Journal of the American Academy of Child Psychiatry, 25,* 357–363.

Geller, J. D. (1988). The process of psychotherapy: Separation and the complex interplay among empathy, insight and internalization. In J. Bloom Feshbach & S. Bloom Feshbach (Eds.), *The psychology of separation and loss* (pp. 459–514). San Francisco: Jossey-Bass.

Hilgard, J. R., Newman, M., & Fisk, F. (1960). Strength of adult ego following childhood bereavement. *American Journal of Orthopsychiatry, 30,* 788–798.

Horowitz, M., Krupnick, J., & Kaltreides, N. (1981). Initial psychological response to parental death. *Archives of General Psychiatry, 137,* 316–323.

Horowitz, M., Wilner, N., & Alvarez, W. (1979). Impact of Events Scale: A measure of subjective stress. *Psychosomatic Medicine, 41,* 209–218.

Kaffman, M., & Elizur, E. (1983). Bereavement responses of kibbutz and nonkibbutz children following the death of the father. *Journal of Child Psychotherapy and Psychiatry, 24,* 435–442.

Klingman, A. (1989). School-based intervention following an adolescent's suicide. *Death Studies, 13,* 263–274.

Krupnick, J., & Solomon, F. (1988). Death of a parent or sibling during childhood. In J. Bloom Feshbach & S. Bloom Feshbach (Eds.), *The psychology of separation and loss* (pp. 345–371). San Francisco: Jossey-Bass.

Lopez, T., & Kliman, G. (1979). Memory, reconstruction and mourning in the analysis of a 4 year old child. *Psychoanalytic Study of the Child, 34,* 235–271.

Malmquist, C. P. (1986). Children who witness parental murder: Post-traumatic aspects. *Journal of the American Academy of Child Psychiatry, 25,* 320–325.

McDonald, N. (1964). A study of the reactions of nursery school children to the death of a child's mother. *Psychoanalytic Study of the Child, 19,* 358–376.

McNally, R. (1991). Assessment of post-traumatic stress disorder in children. *Psychological Assessment, 3,* 531–537.

Moody, R., & Moody, C. (1991). A family perspective: Helping children acknowledge and express grief following the death of a parent. *Death Studies, 15,* 587–602.

Nagera, H. (1970). Developmental reactions to the death of important objects: A developmental approach. *Psychoanalytic Study of the Child, 25,* 360–400.

Pole, J., Wass, H., Eyberg, S., & Chu, L. (1989). Communicating with dying children and their siblings: A retrospective analysis. *Death Studies, 13,* 465–483.

Pynoos, R., & Eth, S. (1986). Witness to violence: The child interview. *Journal of the American Academy of Child Psychiatry, 25,* 306–319.

Pynoos, R., Nader, K., & Frederick, C. (1987). Grief reactions in school age children following a sniper attack at their school. *Israel Journal of Psychiatry and Related Sciences, 24,* 53–63.

Pruett, K. (1979). Home treatment for two infants who witnessed their mother's murder. *Journal of the American Academy of Child Psychiatry, 18,* 647–657.

Raphael, B. (1983). *The anatomy of bereavement.* Northvale, NJ: Jason Aronson.

Rando, T. (1984). *Grief, dying and death: Clinical interventions for caregivers.* Champaign, IL: Research Press.

Sarnoff, C. (1987). *Psychotherapeutic strategies in the latency years.* Northvale, NJ: Jason Aronson.

Smith, I. (1991). Preschool children "play" out their grief. *Death Studies, 15,* 167–176.

Stevenson, R. (1986). The shuttle tragedy, "community grief" and the schools. *Death Studies, 10,* 507–518.

Terr, L. (1989). Treating psychic trauma in children. *Journal of Traumatic Stress, 2*(1).

Van Erdewegh, M., Bieri, M., Parilla, R., & Clayton, P. (1982). The bereaved child. *British Journal of Psychiatry, 140,* 23–29.

Winnicott, D. W. (1986). *Home is where we start from.* New York: Norton.

Wolf, A. (1958). *Helping your child understand death.* New York: Child Study Association of America.

Wolfenstein, M. (1969). Loss, rage and repetition. *Psychoanalytic Study of the Child, 24,* 432–460.

Yule, W., & Williams, R. M. (1990). Post-traumatic stress reactions in children. *Journal of Traumatic Stress, 3,* 279–295.

Zambelli, G., Clark, E., Barile, L., & deJong, A. (1988). An interdisciplinary approach to clinical intervention for childhood bereavement. *Death Studies, 12,* 41–50.

Chapter 7

Minimizing the Impact of Parental Grief on Children: Parent and Family Interventions

John E. Baker

Children are deeply affected by the death of a parent or sibling. However, studies of bereaved children show that they are actually reacting to a series of stressful events (E. Furman, 1974). In addition to their reactions to the loss of a family member, they also show powerful reactions to other events that occur in the family as a result of the loss. The most important of these "secondary" losses are changes in the parent's behavior, family routine, and lifestyle.

This chapter focuses on changes in parental behavior after a death in the immediate family, the child's reactions to those changes, and how to address those reactions therapeutically. These are reactions not to the loss of a family member per se, but to the loss of emotional involvement with the parent because of the parent's own grief reaction. Any disruption of parental involvement will lead the child to feel more insecure in his or her attachment relationship to the parent. The child's reactions to the parent's behavior can be considered as a "secondary" type of traumatic stress response (Figley, 1983).

Primary grief reactions are the child's reactions to losing a person whom he or she loved. Secondary grief reactions are reactions to the parent's grief, to the increased fear of losing another attachment figure, and to other losses that result from the death. In practice, it may be difficult to differentiate between primary and secondary reactions to loss in children. However, this distinction does have implications for therapeutic intervention with bereaved children and their parents. If a child is reacting to changes in other family members after a loss, the most effective therapeutic intervention includes some type of parent or family treatment. This chapter describes techniques of parent guidance and family therapy that can be helpful in the treatment of bereaved children and their families.

CHILDREN'S GRIEF AND THE IMPACT OF PARENTAL GRIEF

Children commonly experience four primary emotional reactions to death: fear, anger, sadness, and guilt. Especially powerful are feelings of fear and anxiety: The world has suddenly become to them a very unsafe place in which beloved people can disappear forever. Baker, Sedney, and Gross (1992) have conceptualized the earliest tasks of grieving as understanding and self-protection. To accomplish these tasks the child must both make sense of the death and find a way to feel protected from any danger that may be associated with the death. Children's understanding of death is limited by their level of cognitive development, and may be distorted by unrealistic and magical notions concerning death and its causes.

Middle-phase tasks of grieving for children consist of, first, fully acknowledging the reality of the person's death and all of its myriad implications; second, rethinking and reworking their own relationship to the person who died; and third, bearing the pain and sadness that come when they realize the full implications of the person's death (Baker, Sedney, & Gross, 1992).

Parents experience many of these same emotions and reactions after a death. Bereaved parents often feel depressed and emotionally drained, with little energy to face the difficult practical tasks of family life after a death. They often feel helpless, fearing that they and their children will not be able to survive without the family member who died. They may also be feeling a great deal of guilt because of angry conflicts with the deceased that existed prior to the death.

How does a grief reaction affect the parenting abilities of these bereaved parents? First, they are likely to be emotionally preoccupied for periods of time, which would lead them to be less responsive and nurturant toward their children (Hummer & Samuels, 1988; Osterweis, Solomon, & Green, 1984). Children almost invariably notice these changes in their parent's behavior, which threaten their sense of having a secure attachment to the parent. As a result, children often feel more sad and lonely because of the parent's emotional preoccupation and unavailability. This may be expressed through a variety of behaviors such as a depressive withdrawal from the parent, an anxious demanding attitude toward the parent, or an increase in angry, disruptive behavior that is meant to reengage the parent emotionally.

Second, bereaved parents are likely to be emotionally labile and inconsistent both in their behavior and in their discipline. Children often are made anxious because of the parent's inconsistency. It increases their sense of the world being an unpredictable place where frightening and painful things can happen without warning.

Third, the parents may appear emotionally vulnerable and weak at times, causing their children to worry about the parent's well-being. After a death in the family, children become especially concerned about the health and welfare of other attachment figures, fearing that they too could die. This anxiety about further loss is thus exacerbated by the parent's obvious vulnerability. In addition, children may feel guilty about placing demands on a parent who seems so tired and overextended, or about irritating or angering the parent. This reaction may exacerbate the strong but irrational feelings of guilt that children often experience after a death in the family.

Fourth, parents may avoid talking about the person who died (Bowlby, 1980). This can accentuate the child's feelings of sadness and longing for the deceased. To children, it is natural to reminisce out loud about a person they miss, but that kind of reminiscing can be intolerably sad for the parent.

A fifth aspect of parenting after a death concerns the parent's ability to support his or her child's grieving process. Bowlby (1980) emphasized the strong effect of a child's emotional environment on his or her ability to grieve. He states that children are better able to successfully mourn a loss if four conditions are present: (a) a secure relationship with parents existed prior to the loss; (b) prompt and accurate information about the death is provided; (c) there is an opportunity to participate in family grieving rituals; and (d) the comforting presence of a parent or parent-substitute is available following the death. These are ways in which bereaved children need extra support from a parenting figure in order to tolerate their reactions to loss. When parents are themselves disabled by grief, they may be unable to provide that extra support.

COMPARISON WITH OTHER TYPES OF POST-TRAUMATIC STRESS IN FAMILIES

There has been relatively little research to date on the effect of other types of post-traumatic stress disorders (PTSDs) on parenting behavior. Silver and Iacono (1986) reported a study of Vietnam veterans that included their perceptions of their immediate family environment. Veterans who reported more severe symptoms of PTSD also reported more family conflict, less emotional expressiveness and cohesiveness in their current families, and less closeness to their children. These changes in family environment appear to parallel in part the preoccupation and emotional lability found in many bereaved parents. The actual effect on the children of these veterans was not measured, however. Solomon et al. (1992) documented the negative impact of a spouse's PTSD on the wives of Israeli war veterans, thus supporting the concept of secondary traumatization.

McFarlane (1987) studied the effects of a natural disaster on family functioning and found higher levels of conflict, withdrawal, and maternal overprotectiveness in these families, according to questionnaires filled out by parents. The severity of post-traumatic symptoms in both the mothers and the fathers, especially recurrent thoughts that interfered with their functioning, was most highly correlated with the observed changes in the family environment. Once again, the actual effect of these changes on the children was not measured. These studies do provide some preliminary support for the notion that PTSD reactions in parents lead to distinct changes in family environment that can have a secondary impact on children.

THERAPEUTIC INTERVENTION FOR SECONDARY TRAUMATIC GRIEF REACTIONS: REVIEW OF THE LITERATURE

There are several therapeutic techniques that address the reactions of children to their parents' grieving. Child psychotherapy, family therapy, parent guidance, and individual parent psychotherapy are all ways that can improve children's coping with their parent's grief. When it is clear that the child is reacting to a change in parental behavior, the most effective techniques are those that involve the parent directly—either to assist the parent with his or her own grieving, or to help the parent understand and address the needs of his or her children more effectively. This chapter focuses specifically on the use of parent guidance and family therapy as ways of helping children with their secondary grief reactions.

Parent Guidance

Parent guidance is a form of intervention that was developed in conjunction with individual psychotherapy with bereaved children. On the basis of individual treatment of bereaved children, clinicians developed a better understanding of the needs, reactions, and common misunderstandings of these children. Aspects of parent guidance for the bereaved were initially described by Robert Furman (1964a), and further illustrated in his paper on the reactions of a 6-year-old boy to the death of his mother (1964b). Overall, however, there have been relatively few papers devoted to actual methods of parent guidance.

Erna Furman (1974) published an in-depth study of childhood bereavement that includes a discussion of how surviving parents can best help their children to mourn a parent's death. Furman's suggestions for helping bereaved children incorporate the following ideas. First, she notes the importance of helping the child to understand the actual circumstances of the death and to distinguish reality from the child's fantasies about possible causes of the death. Second, she emphasizes the importance of reassuring the child that his or her needs will continue to be met, that life will maintain continuity and stability, and that other important relationships in his or her life will not be lost. Third, she describes how the child needs the physical presence of as well as an emotional connection with the surviving parent (or parent-substitute) in order to cope with feelings of grief whenever they may arise in the course of everyday life.

Knight-Birnbaum (1988) states that the goals of parent guidance are helping the parent to stabilize family life, to facilitate the child's adjustment to the loss, and to understand the child's developing capacity for mourning. Parent guidance involves advice giving, reassurance, and managerial suggestions. Another component is to educate the parent about children's reactions to loss, and then to integrate that understanding into his or her care of the child. In addition, Knight-Birnbaum notes that the therapist can play a supportive emotional role for the surviving parent.

Family Therapy

The literature on family therapy includes very little about the treatment of loss in families. According to Walsh and McGoldrick (1991), this omission stems from the focus of family therapists on the "here-and-now" functioning of family members, with a corresponding deemphasis on historical influences on the family such as loss. Walsh and McGoldrick specify four tasks that are relevant for bereaved families: a shared acknowledgment of the reality of the death; a shared experience of loss, and of putting it into a meaningful context for each family member; reorganization of the family system; and reinvestment in other relationships and life pursuits. A similar model of developmental recovery tasks has been presented by Jordan (1990).

A review of the family literature indicates that most family approaches emphasize one or more of the following goals. The first goal is identifying a previous loss as a major influence on the family's current functioning, and helping the family understand this influence. McGoldrick (1991) presents a number of cases of adults who presented with psychological problems related to losses in childhood.

A second goal of family therapy is encouraging the communication of feelings among different family members, especially feelings about the loss. In most families, the death of a family member severely disrupts the family communication process (Silverman & Silverman, 1979). A depressed or preoccupied parent is less communicative, but may also react with irritation, anger, or a sudden outburst of tears. This makes it less safe for children to express their feelings, and normal parent–child protective and nurturing functions are interrupted.

A third goal is helping the family reorganize its structure following the loss, to reassign important role functions and to restore appropriate generational boundaries. For example, Hare-Mustin (1979) described a family that had lost a child to cancer for which her treatment goals were to move the oldest child out of the role of the "parental child," and to support the mother in her own role functioning, thus reestablishing appropriate generational boundaries in the family. A more comprehensive analysis of family roles after bereavement is presented by Poussaint, Shapiro, and Gross (1982) and Shapiro (1994).

A final goal of family therapy after a death is addressing developmental tasks that were not accomplished because of the disruptive influence of the loss, especially the task of helping children to separate and individuate in adolescence and early adulthood. Issues related to family development and the family life cycle are addressed by a number of authors, including Gelcer (1983) and Solomon and Hersch (1979). Jordan (1990) presents a model of family development as a cyclical process, with periods of greater and lesser interdependence. McGoldrick and Walsh (1991) present a comprehensive outline of the family life cycle, and of the effect of bereavement on family members at different points in the life cycle.

Many family therapists maintain that grief work with the bereaved parent is often an essential part of a family approach. Hare-Mustin (1979) and Gelcer (1983) used individual sessions to help a bereaved parent with issues of unresolved mourning. Rosen (1988–89) recommends that, in families where one parent seems to be grieving "interminably" for a lost child, a period of individual therapy with the grieving parent should precede family sessions.

Black and Urbanowicz (1987) present a method of time-limited family therapy for bereaved families. The aim of the therapy, which lasted only six sessions, was to promote mourning in both the children and the surviving parent, primarily by improving communication among family members about the death. The therapist asked each family to review the events that led up to the parent's death, and to bring in photographs and other mementos to aid in reminiscing about the deceased parent.

Figley (1989) has developed a model of family therapy that applies to families that have experienced a variety of traumatic stresses, including traumatic loss. He stresses the importance of building relationship skills in all family members, including communication, problem solving, and conflict resolution skills, as well as educating all family members about stress reactions. Another important aspect of Figley's approach is his focus on reframing the meaning of the loss in a more optimistic and growth-enhancing light.

ASSESSMENT PROCESS

Parent Interviews

Assessment usually begins with a parent interview. The assessment should include, first, a detailed description of the events surrounding the death. The status of all family members, their relationship to the deceased, and their location at the time of the death are all important. If the death was violent, the presence of any family members at the scene of the death has an especially strong impact on post-traumatic reactions (Eth & Pynoos, 1985). If there was a preexisting illness, the changes brought about in the ill person and the role of each family member in helping that individual are important to establish. The rituals that followed the death are important to understand, including the participation of each family member in these rituals. A child's experience of loss is strongly colored by the context of the loss and by the reactions of other family members.

Family history is a second focus of the parental assessment. Preexisting family problems may heighten the family's response to loss and indicate the absence of sufficient resources for effective coping with loss. Previous losses in the family, or in the childhood of either parent, can also indicate a vulnerability to an exaggerated reaction to loss.

Third, the psychological functioning of the surviving parent or parents should be carefully assessed. Symptoms of shock, depression, crying spells, preoccupation, and irritability all have a strong impact on children. Inability to talk about the deceased individual or the converse, frequent rumination about the individual, has very different effects on the children. Any pathological grief reactions—such as an inability to believe in the reality of the death—are also important to assess. The presence of intense traumatic anxiety or separation anxiety in the parent is significant, because anxiety is rapidly transmitted among family members and can lead to overprotection and overinvolvement. Parents are often aware of their symptoms, and seek treatment to help them provide the best care and support they possibly can to their children.

Family Interviews

One or more family interviews should also be done as part of the assessment process. The family interview adds to an understanding of how each family member is processing the events around the death. Family interviews also provide a way of assessing how easily the family can communicate about the death and about their own reactions to it. Some family members may become extremely constricted in the interview, suggesting a need either to control their own intense feelings or to protect others. An initial family interview can also have a positive therapeutic impact on a family, providing a sense of unity and cohesiveness that had been absent (Sedney, Baker, & Gross, 1994).

Figley (1989) uses family interviews to assess how functional a family's coping skills are. His interview protocol addresses a variety of coping skills, including the ability to accurately perceive current family stresses, the tendency to blame one or more individuals for the stress, the ability to tolerate differences, the ability to communicate openly, the flexibility of family roles, and the tendency to use substances to cope.

Child Interviews

An interview with each child in the family is also recommended as part of the assessment process, even if family or parent therapy becomes the preferred method of treatment. Although children may participate actively in family meetings, they may withhold significant perceptions or interpretations of events that they believe are not shared by other family members. Because a child's reaction to loss is so strongly colored by his or her understanding of the causes and consequences of the death (Baker, Sedney, & Gross, 1992), an individual interview can provide very important information about children's functioning that would not be otherwise available. Information can be drawn either from the children's actual statements, from their nonverbal behavior, or from their play.

Psychometric Measures

A variety of self-report measures have been recommended by Figley (1989) and by Carroll, Foy, Cannon, and Zwier (1991). Figley uses his own Traumagram questionnaire; the Purdue PTSD Scale; the Purdue Social Support Scale; and the Brief Symptom Inventory (Derogatis & Spencer, 1982), which measures current symptoms of stress. Another measure of PTSD symptoms is the Impact of Events Scale (Horowitz, Wilner, Kaltreider, & Alvarez, 1980). Family measures include the Family Environment Scale (Moos & Moos, 1981) and the Family Adaptability and Cohesion Evaluation Scale (Olson, Russell, & Sprenkle, 1983).

PARENT GUIDANCE METHODS

There are several important aspects of parent guidance. First, parent guidance is a supportive type of therapy for the parent. Second, it is a psychoeducational process with an emphasis on helping the parent to understand children's emotional reactions to loss and to make parental decisions on that basis. A third aspect is the importance of behavior management, which should be based on the parents' increased understanding of their child. A fourth aspect, which runs throughout all other aspects of the work, is therapeutically helping a parent cope with his or her reactions to the mourning process.

Supportive Aspects

Parent guidance aims to support parents both as individuals with emotional needs of their own, and as parents with numerous responsibilities with which they need help. Some sessions explore the parent's personal reactions to the loss, but the parenting responsibilities are always present in the background. The parent's trust in the therapist is based both on the therapist's ability to be compassionate and sensitive, and on the therapist's importance as an expert to whom he or she can turn for advice on parenting matters.

When a parent has died, the surviving parent comes to treatment in a state of great emotional distress. The surviving parent often feels extremely helpless and greatly overburdened by the responsibilities of managing a family without assistance from his or her spouse. Because of the extreme distress of these parents, a strong therapeutic relationship can be formed very quickly (Kliman et al., 1969; Knight-Birnbaum, 1988). The therapist provides a "holding environment" in which parents can feel safe and protected, and where they feel able to express the feelings of anxiety, guilt, and inadequacy that they rarely feel they can confide to other adults.

When a child has died, the parents often become highly anxious about the well-being of their other children (Cain, Fast, & Erickson, 1964). Because the loss of a child is often experienced by them as a parenting failure on some level, parents may lose their sense of parental competence. For these parents, the therapist can challenge the self-concept of the parents as failures, and help them find ways to reestablish a sense of their own competence. The therapist can also inform them that each parent will cope differently and that each should be allowed to do so. This challenges the usually unconscious notion of parents that their partner should feel exactly the same in such a time of crisis and emotional need (Rando, 1980).

Psychoeducational Aspects

Bereaved parents feel an enormous pressure to help and protect their children after the death of a family member. Yet they often feel unsure of the best course of action. These parents are often very eager to better understand what their child is going through and how they can best help as a parent. Thus the psychoeducational aspect of parent guidance after bereavement is extremely important.

Parents often need education about how their child understands death and all of its implications. A description of how children's cognitive development affects their understanding of death is an essential part of the therapist's educative interventions. Even more useful is a description of the different misunderstandings that children can have about death. Usually the parent has heard some of the child's remarks and questions, and these can be used as a basis for discussing which aspects of the death are most puzzling or disturbing to the child.

Important notions in this context are the young child's belief that the deceased person will come back again; the child's fear that another family member, especially one of the parents, could also die; the child's fear of any place or thing that he or she associates with the death and that could put him or her in danger; and the child's frequent feelings of guilt and responsibility about the death or his or her failure to prevent it. A good overview of these issues can be found in E. Furman (1974), Lonetto (1980), Fox (1985), Sekaer (1987), and Baker, Sedney, & Gross (1992).

Along with a description of how children understand death, it is useful to give parents a description of how children ask questions and process the information they have received. Parents are often surprised when, after a lengthy conversation, a child comes back some weeks later with an identical question or concern. It is helpful for parents to know that understanding is a process in children, that it takes time for them to integrate what they have heard, and that sometimes they can only take in so much information at a time (Osterweis, Solomon, & Green, 1984).

It is extremely important for the therapist to stress the child's need for accurate information about the person's death and its causes. Parents feel a strong need to protect their children and to avoid hurting them through disclosing information that would be painful or destructive. Yet if a child is not given accurate information, he or she is more likely to construct a distorted and inaccurate picture of the death. The role of the therapist is to reassure parents that they will not be harming their children by telling them the truth. Instead, they will be strengthening the child's ability to use his or her intellectual skills in a constructive way to achieve some degree of cognitive mastery of a situation over which he or she otherwise has no control.

A related issue has to do with how the parent communicates with the child about the death. Parents are often reluctant to talk openly about the dead family member or to share their own feelings and memories about that person (Silverman & Silverman, 1979). This reluctance may be an attempt to avoid facing the reality that the loved one is dead, or to avoid facing the feelings of loss and grief that might be unleashed if they spoke openly with their children. The parents' silence tends to intensify the children's feelings of loneliness and longing for the person who died, and can also serve as an unspoken prohibition against the children's voicing their own feelings about the loss. Parent guidance sessions can enable parents to talk more easily to their children about the person who has died. This encourages the child's own mourning process, even though the feelings involved may be quite different.

Another crucial aspect of the psychoeducational work focuses on the child's need for stability, continuity, and reassurance after a death in the family. Although it may be more convenient for a parent to make certain changes in routine after a death, the parent should be made aware of the child's need for a stable routine, and the possibility of inducing psychological distress by making any major changes in routine. This is especially true for preschool children, who have a weaker sense of internal security and rely on the predictable occurrence of everyday events to shore up their sense of self-identity. Younger children feel much less anxious if they are assured that their family will stay together, that no other major changes will be made for a while, and that their own needs will be attended to despite the traumatic loss of a family member (E. Furman, 1974).

In a larger sense, parents often need to understand that one of the most powerful things they can offer their children after a death is their own affection, caring, attention, and nurturance. These are what help children feel secure in their ongoing attachment relationship to the parent (or parents), and an intact sense of internal security is what protects children from their exaggerated fears of loss after a death.

One final element of parent education is to explain that children and adults have different timetables for grieving (Knight-Birnbaum, 1988). Whereas adults go through a process of acute grieving during the first 1 or 2 years, mourning in children often takes place over a much longer period of time. Thus even though parents may have passed through the most intense period of their own grief, their children may ask questions and react to problems that the parents have long since resolved. This does not mean that the child has not been grieving;

rather it means that the grieving process is considerably slower for children, and that it is accomplished piece by piece over a longer period of time. With this knowledge, parents can be more patient with the questions their children ask. They can also reduce their expectations for the child, and accept the slower and more uneven process of grieving in the child without trying to accelerate it unnecessarily.

Behavioral Management Aspects

Bereaved parents commonly have certain difficulties in managing their children's behavior. If they feel bereft and disoriented themselves, they have difficulty maintaining a consistent pattern of response to their children's behavior. If they feel less confident as parents, they distrust their own instincts. If they feel weak and vulnerable, they find it harder to be firm. Perhaps most important, bereaved parents feel deprived and see their children as equally deprived. This makes it very hard for them to deprive their children of anything for disciplinary reasons.

A therapist can be of special assistance to parents in making decisions about their children during the crisis period that comes immediately after a death. During this period family routines are usually disrupted, and many decisions must be made about what to tell the children and whether to let them participate in the funeral and other mourning rituals. A therapist can help the parent decide what to tell the children, how to preserve some sense of routine, and how to include them as much as possible in the family events that take place. An excellent discussion of these issues can be found in E. Furman (1974).

A key area of behavioral problems comes from the intensified separation anxiety that is experienced by bereaved children (Knight-Birnbaum, 1988). Anxiety about loss is usually very intense after a death in the family. Young children have particular difficulty separating from their parents in order to go to school or day care, and this leads to scenes of great distress for parent and child alike. Bedtime is another time of separation from the parent. When parents are feeling guilty, they are more likely to give in to a child's demands to be comforted after bedtime, and to allow the child to share their own bed—even when this conflicts with the child's own developmental needs. The frequency with which parents share their bed with a child after a death was noted by Kliman et al. (1969). Ultimately it is not appropriate or desirable for the parent to be with the child at all times, despite the child's resistance to separation after the stressful experience of loss.

Often the most effective response to these fears is for the parent to acknowledge and verbalize children's fears of loss and feelings of sadness, and to reassure them that they are safe where they are and that they will see the parent again soon. Extra time for calming and reassuring the child is often necessary, but otherwise the usual rules and routines about separations and bedtimes should be maintained. It is also useful to help parents distinguish their own feelings of distress at these times from those of their children. Separation from the child may intensify the parents' own feelings of longing for the person that died, and cause the parents to have separation difficulties of their own.

Sometimes bereaved parents become overly protective and solicitous of their children, and worry constantly about their whereabouts and safety. This overprotectiveness is an aspect of the parent's own grief, as it protects against further loss, and atones for any guilt they may feel about the death. Over-protectiveness is especially common in families that have lost a child (Krell & Rabkin, 1979). Overly protective parenting can give children the opposite message, however, implying that indeed they are not safe and are constantly in danger. This message reinforces the child's own irrational fears related to death.

Parent guidance can help the parents test the reality of their fears, understand the repercussions of their protectiveness for their children, and relax their hypervigilant attitude while remaining attentive and emotionally available to the children. Through therapy the parents may also come to understand the functions this behavior has served in their own attempts to cope with feelings of grief.

A final issue that frequently arises is the parents' difficulty setting limits on their children's negative and defiant behavior. Many parents tend to be overly lenient and believe, as noted above, that their children have suffered enough and that discipline would place an additional burden on them. If a child's behavior is out of control, however, the child begins to feel guilty as well as frightened by the parent's failure to respond appropriately.

Parents often need support in order to place firm but reasonable limits on their children's behavior. Children need to know that their parents are strong and can function in their parental role despite the enormity of the loss, but can also be understanding of their feelings as well. Children draw a sense of security from the consistency and structure provided by their parent's rules and methods of discipline. Consistent limits and structure also reassure children that even if they are unable to control their own feelings and behavior, the parent will be able to help them reestablish control in this way.

Therapeutic Aspects

Therapeutic elements are significant throughout the guidance process. Part of the therapist's support is to acknowledge that parents are going through their own grieving process, and that the parents' own personal feelings affect their ability to respond to different aspects of the child's behavior. Parent sessions can provide an opportunity for parents to discuss their unresolved feelings about the loss.

Helping parents distinguish their own feelings of distress from those of their children, and to understand how their children's feelings are different from their own, is one of the most important therapeutic elements in parent guidance work. Indeed, the parents' awareness of their children's grieving can stimulate them to be more aware of their own feelings of grief, and to sort out which feelings are their own and which belong to their children.

It should be acknowledged that some parents need to undergo individual psychotherapy in addition to parent guidance, depending on their level of functioning and the presence of emotional issues that need to be addressed in depth.

The following case example shows how parent guidance helped a woman find appropriate means of coping with her children's grief after the death of her husband.

A 40-year-old woman was referred for parent guidance 10 months after the death of her husband by suicide. Mrs. Miller had two daughters, aged 6 and 8, who were already being seen in individual play therapy at the time of the parent referral. There had been a lengthy period of marital and family conflict prior to the suicide, which was precipitated by Mrs. Miller's decision to separate from her husband and initiate divorce proceedings. At the time of referral, the older daughter was still exhibiting a variety of fears and anxieties, along with a refusal to talk about her father in any but the most general terms. The younger daughter exhibited no unusual fears, but her behavior was at times defiant and manipulative at home.

Mrs. Miller was aware of several changes in her parenting since her husband's death. In general she felt she was more angry and impatient with her children, and she became especially angry if one of the children did something of which she disapproved. At the same time she was reluctant to discipline the children; she saw them as being deprived by the loss of their father, and she felt unable to further deprive them by taking away any of their privileges. Instead of discipline, she engaged the children in lengthy conversations about the reasons behind their behavior. However, she did not talk with the children about their father, because she did not know what to say. She also had difficulty tolerating the older daughter's expressions of sadness about her father's death.

Mrs. Miller became constantly concerned about her children's safety and welfare, and overly close in her attentiveness and emotional reponsiveness to their statements. She had particular difficulty handling her older daughter's expressions of fear and anxiety at bedtime. She tended to overidentify with her daughter's fears, and had difficulty remaining calm and reassuring to her daughter at those times. She even slept in the hallway outside the children's room so she could be available should they become frightened.

Parent guidance had to be done carefully, in the context of Mrs. Miller's extreme sensitivity to criticism about her parenting skills. She and the therapist did identify a focus on the older daughter's anxieties at night. Mrs. Miller's usual response was to ask questions of the child and ask her to explain why she was feeling so frightened. The therapist suggested that she limit the length of these conversations and advised her to focus on reassuring the child of her safety rather than understanding the reasons for her fears. It was especially important that Mrs. Miller encourage her daughter to be more independent in developing ways to soothe herself when frightened rather than calling immediately for her mother. As the mother encouraged greater separateness, she also began to sleep in her own bed rather than outside the children's room. The child's response was to become less fearful at bedtime, and even to sleep through the night on some occasions.

Mrs. Miller was also advised to talk with her older daughter about any possible connections between her fears on the one hand, and her feelings about her father's death on the other. Although the daughter had previously refused to talk about her father, she responded positively to her mother's inquiries and began to come to her mother with very appropriate questions about her father and his death. The girl also began to show more overt signs of sadness and grieving, in contrast to her earlier phobic presentation.

Mrs. Miller also worked on other ways to allow her children greater independence and autonomy. Since her husband's suicide, she had become overly protective and overly involved with her children. She needed help in determining when she had done enough to help her children in a given situation, and when she needed to allow them to manage their own behavior and resolve their own conflicts. By adopting this viewpoint she was better able to handle her own feelings of disappointment when they did not behave the way she wanted them to.

Addressing the children's need for consistent discipline was more difficult, mainly because of the mother's fragile self-esteem in this area of parenting. Although she hesitated to discipline the children directly, she clearly showed her displeasure with their behavior and would subject the children to lengthy questioning about why they did what they did. Extensive discussion of different types of parent–child situations, both actual and hypothetical, allowed her to ask for ideas and approaches from the therapist without feeling overly criticized or controlled by his suggestions. Gradually she became more able to set consistent limits on the children's behavior, and to feel more confident about this aspect of her parenting.

FAMILY THERAPY METHODS

The primary goal of family therapy with the bereaved is to facilitate communication among different family members. Communication often has been disrupted by the self-protective reactions of each family member to the pain and anxiety of loss. With the structure and leadership of a therapist, families often are able to talk together openly about the death for the first time, and to share their feelings and memories about the loss. Success in communicating can strengthen supportive emotional bonds between family members, which is particularly important for children, who need that support to face the painful aspects of grieving. It also helps all family members to hold and tolerate their feelings of sadness and loss, rather than avoid and deny them in a way that can lead to dysfunctional behavior.

It is useful to devote one of the first sessions to inviting the family to tell the story of the death that has occurred. Although a parent may often take the lead in this account, all family members present should be encouraged to report their recollections as well as their emotional reactions at the time. The importance of this process is described in greater detail by Sedney, Baker, and Gross (1994). Telling the "story" of the death can help parents regain their sense of purpose and competence, and can help all family members see that talking about the loss is bearable. It provides some emotional catharsis and relief for all family members, and also promotes a feeling of togetherness and cohesiveness in families that have been splintered by the loss. Johnson (1987) gives examples of how families tell the story of a death.

In family sessions, family members are encouraged to think about the different ways in which each copes with his or her feelings about the loss. The goal of this process is to help the family to allow for differences in coping styles among different family members. Different ways of coping often seem insensitive or unsupportive to other family members. The open acknowledgment of differences among family members reduces the level of tension in the family and makes it less necessary to "put up a front" in order to keep important feelings hidden.

Family sessions also provide a forum for discussing the role that was played in the family by the person who has died, and how the family can respond to their absence (Walsh & McGoldrick, 1991). When the family is encouraged to identify the ways in which family life has changed since the death, the roles played by the deceased person are clarified. This awareness stimulates family members to discuss different ways of compensating for the lost role functions, and of doing this in a way that all family members are comfortable with.

The family therapist should also help the family to make connections between their recent experience of loss, and their reactions to other losses in the past. Family members can be more sympathetic and supportive of one another if they can better understand how their reactions to loss are related to their previous experiences. Often the major difficulty they are having with the recent loss is the same as the difficulty that was left unresolved in past losses. For example, a parent may come to identify a previous loss in his or her life that came unexpectedly and led him or her to feel guilty about neglecting that person prior to the death. The parent then may be able to see how the excessive sense of guilt left over from that past loss is being acted out in his or her guilt-ridden, overprotective style of parenting after the more recent loss.

The developmental tasks of the family also need to be addressed in therapy. Family members benefit from being able to see the family as having a future. If the therapist can help them identify the life cycle tasks they have been unable to complete, the family sessions can be used to discuss different ways that the family can proceed in the future. This is especially true in helping individual family members to become more independent and self-sufficient. The bereaved family often chooses togetherness over independence in a way that can stultify the developmental growth of individual family members (Solomon & Hersch, 1979). In understanding togetherness and independence as opposing and yet equally important goals, the family often is able to work toward a better balance between them.

Family sessions often stimulate the grieving process in individual family members. Talking about the death with other family members makes the death more real to each of them, and interferes with the tendency to deny the loss. Parents, who may have focused all of their attention on their children, find that family meetings stimulate their own grief work in a constructive way. Conversely, as children learn more about the death and receive permission to grieve, they too can move ahead in the mourning process.

Family sessions should also include psychoeducational material when appropriate. Psychoeducational issues were delineated in the section on parent guidance, but are equally important in family treatment.

A case example demonstrates family therapy after the death of a child.

A family requested treatment for their 6-year-old boy nearly 2 years after another son had died from complications due to a serious heart defect. Chris, the surviving son, experienced anxieties and phobias, had problems in school, and made statements at times about wanting to die. After an initial evaluation of parents and child separately, family treatment was initiated. Communication in the family was very indirect, and seemed designed to hide information from the children and to avoid upsetting Chris. The parents were relieved that the therapist saw the boy's symptoms as being related to his brother's death. Nevertheless, they were reluctant to talk about the child who died unless Chris confronted them with specific questions.

Family sessions addressed several topics. First, they focused on obstacles to communication among family members. This included the therapist's making a rule that any family member could say whatever he or she wanted in the sessions. Chris objected strongly to this rule at first, and became overtly aggressive and even provocative in the next several family meetings. This behavior was not in character for Chris, who tended to be fearful and controlled at home.

Second, family sessions included periodic discussions of the deceased brother, the nature of his illness and heart defect, and memories of the time of his illness. The parents acknowledged the close relationship between Chris and his brother and the similarities in their behavior and their fears. In many ways, Chris had taken on the role of his sick brother in the family. During one family discussion it became clear that Chris did not understand what was wrong with his brother's heart and whether or not he himself had the same defect. With encouragement from the therapist, the parents gave a detailed description of the brother's illness to Chris and his younger sister, and this seemed to relieve Chris greatly.

Third, Chris's rejection of his parents' support was examined and reframed as an insistence on doing all the parenting of himself. This was connected to his parents' loss of confidence in their own parenting. They were encouraged to be more persistent and assertive, pushing Chris to communicate when he resisted doing so and working toward a resolution of conflict rather than an avoidance of it. This led to Chris's open expression of anger both in family sessions and at home. Anger became a major focus of the family sessions. The parents then revealed how angry their sick child had been in the months before his death, and were able to connect this to their avoidance of dealing with issues of anger after his death. The boy had correctly perceived their inability to tolerate his anger, and tested it out in therapy first before directing it toward his parents at home.

A final issue had to do with differences between the mother and father in their preferred coping styles. This became especially clear on the 2-year anniversary of their child's death. The father was rather subdued and sad throughout the day, whereas the mother spent much of the day focused on Chris and his difficulties in school. When she later looked for her husband and found him unavailable, she reponded with anger and disappointment. This led to a discussion of the parents' differing reactions to their son's death. While the father felt somewhat sad and guilty and wondered if maybe there was something else they could have done to keep the child alive, the mother was uncompromising in her anger and bitterness toward the doctors who she felt had mishandled the boy's surgery leading to lethal complications.

Over 6 months of family treatment, changes were noted in the way that parents and children communicated. The parents became more direct and less secretive, while Chris was able to show anger much more openly in the family sessions. In subsequent weeks Chris began to seek his parents more often for comforting, even accepting physical affection at times, which he had refused previously. As the boy became more emotionally expressive, he at times became weepy at home and in school. In general his behavior at home and with peers improved, and he appeared less phobic, avoidant, and rigid.

EFFECTIVENESS OF TREATMENT METHODS

No outcome studies measuring the effects of parent guidance therapy for parents have been done. Only one study has examined the effectiveness of time-limited family therapy. Black and Urbanowicz (1987) delivered six sessions of family therapy to a sample of 21 families (38 children) in which one of the parents had died. They found slightly greater improvement in the treated families after 1 year than in the control families, in that the parents appeared less depressed and the children showed fewer signs of restlessness in their behavior. By 2 years some of these effects were still present but not at a statistically significant level. Clearly further research is needed on the effectiveness of parent and family treatment.

CONCLUSION

This chapter has examined different methods for helping to minimize the effects of loss on children. Children often show strong emotional reactions to a loss, and they also respond to the way in which their parents cope with the loss. This chapter has concentrated on methods of treatment that, in the context of the parents' own grief, help them to provide the special kind of care needed by their distressed children, and encourage types of family communication that are emotionally supportive. Parent guidance and family therapy are the two treatment methods that were presented in some detail in this chapter. The practicing therapist should be familiar with these methods, but should also feel free to use other techniques in their treatment of bereaved families. Parent sessions, child sessions, and family sessions may be beneficial at different times and for different purposes.

REFERENCES

Baker, J. E., Sedney, M. A., & Gross, E. (1992). Psychological tasks for bereaved children. *American Journal of Orthopsychiatry, 62,* 105–116.

Black, D., & Urbanowicz, M. A. (1987). Family intervention with bereaved children. *Journal of Child Psychology and Psychiatry, 28*, 467–476.

Bowlby, J. (1980). *Attachment and loss: Loss, sadness and depression* (Vol. 3). New York: Basic Books.

Cain, A., Fast, I., & Erickson, M. (1964). Children's disturbed reactions to the death of a sibling. *American Journal of Orthopsychiatry, 34*, 741–752.

Carroll, E. M., Foy, D. W., Cannon, B. J., & Zwier, G. (1991). Assessment issues involving the families of trauma victims. *Journal of Traumatic Stress, 4*, 25–40.

Derogatis, L. R., & Spencer, P. M. (1982). *The brief symptom inventory (BSI): Administration, scoring and procedures, manual I.* Baltimore: Johns Hopkins University.

Eth, S., & Pynoos, R. S. (1985). Interaction of trauma and grief in childhood. In S. Eth & R. S. Pynoos (Eds.), *Post-traumatic stress disorder in children* (pp. 169–186). Washington, DC: American Psychiatric Press.

Figley, C. R. (1983). Catastrophes: An overview of family reactions. In C. R. Figley & H. I. McCubbin (Eds.), *Stress and the family: Coping with catastrophe* (Vol. 2, pp. 3–20). New York: Brunner/Mazel.

Figley, C. R. (1989). *Helping traumatized families.* San Francisco: Jossey-Bass.

Fox, S. S. (1985). *Good grief: Helping groups of children when a friend dies.* Boston: New England Association for the Education of Young Children.

Furman, E. (1974). *A child's parent dies: Studies in childhood bereavement.* New Haven: Yale University Press.

Furman, R. A. (1964a). Death and the young child: Some preliminary considerations. *Psychoanalytic Study of the Child, 19*, 321–333.

Furman, R. A. (1964b). Death of a six-year-old's mother during his analysis. *Psychoanalytic Study of the Child, 19*, 377–397.

Gelcer, E. (1983). Mourning is a family affair. *Family Process, 22*, 501–516.

Hare-Mustin, R. T. (1979). Family therapy following the death of a child. *Journal of Marital and Family Therapy, 5*, 51–59.

Horowitz, M., Wilner, N., Kaltreider, N., & Alvarez, W. (1980). Signs and symptoms of post-traumatic stress disorder. *Archives of General Psychiatry, 37*, 85–92.

Hummer, K. M., & Samuels, A. (1988). The influence of the recent death of a spouse on the parenting function of the surviving parent. In S. Alschul (Ed.), *Childhood bereavement and its aftermath* (pp. 37–63). Madison, CT: International Universities Press.

Johnson, S. E. (1987). *After a child dies: Counseling bereaved families.* New York: Springer.

Jordan, J. (1990). *Loss and family development: Clinical implications.* Paper presented at the annual convention of the American Psychological Association, Boston, MA.

Kliman, G., Feinberg, D., Buchsbaum, B., Kliman, A., Lubin, H., Ronald, D., & Stein, M. (1969). *Facilitation of mourning during childhood.* Paper presented at the annual conference of the American Orthopsychiatric Association, New York.

Knight-Birnbaum, N. (1988). Therapeutic work with bereaved parents. In S. Altschul (Ed.), *Childhood bereavement and its aftermath* (pp. 107–143). Madison, CT: International Universities Press.

Krell, R., & Rabkin, L. (1979). The effects of sibling death on the surviving child: A family perspective. *Family Process, 18*, 471–477.

Lonetto, R. (1980). *Children's conceptions of death.* New York: Springer.

McFarlane, A. C. (1987). Family functioning and overprotection following a natural disaster: The longitudinal effects of post-trauma morbidity. *Australian and New Zealand Journal of Psychiatry, 21*, 210–218.

McGoldrick, M. (1991). Echoes from the past: Helping families mourn their losses. In F. Walsh & M. McGoldrick (Eds.), *Living beyond loss: Death in the family* (pp. 50–78). New York: Norton.

McGoldrick, M., & Walsh, F. (1991). A time to mourn: Death and the family life cycle. In

F. Walsh & M. McGoldrick (Eds.), *Living beyond loss: Death in the family* (pp. 30–48). New York: Norton.

Moos, R., & Moos, B. S. (1981). *Family Environment Scale manual.* Palo Alto, CA: Consulting Psychologist Press.

Olson, D. J., Russell, C. S., & Sprenkle, D. H. (1983). Circumplex model VI: Theoretical update. *Family Process, 22,* 69–83.

Osterweis, M., Solomon, F., & Green, M. (Eds.). (1984). *Bereavement: Reactions, consequences, and care.* Washington, DC: National Academy Press.

Poussaint, A. F., Shapiro, E., & Gross, E. (1982). *Grief as a family process.* Paper presented at the annual meeting of the American Orthopsychiatric Association, San Francisco.

Rando, T. A. (1980). The unique issues and impact of the death of a child. In T. A. Rando (Ed.), *Parental loss of a child.* Champaign, IL: Research Press.

Rosen, E. J. (1988–89). Family therapy in cases of interminable grief for the loss of a child. *Omega, 19,* 187–202.

Sedney, M. A., Baker, J. E., & Gross, E. (1994). "The story" of a death: Therapeutic considerations with bereaved families. *Journal of Marital and Family Therapy, 20,* 287–296.

Sekaer, C. (1987). Toward a definition of "childhood mourning." *American Journal of Psychotherapy, 41,* 201–219.

Shapiro, E. (1994). *Grief as a family process.* New York: Guilford.

Silver, S. M., & Iacono, C. (1986). Symptom groups and family patterns of Vietnam veterans with post-traumatic stress disorders. In C. Figley (Ed.), *Trauma and its wake: Traumatic stress theory, research, and intervention* (Vol. 2, pp. 78–96). New York: Brunner/Mazel.

Silverman, S. M., & Silverman, P. R. (1979). Parent-child communication in widowed families. *American Journal of Psychotherapy, 33,* 428–441.

Solomon, M. A., & Hersch, L. B. (1979). Death in the family: Implications for family development. *Journal of Marital and Family Therapy, 5,* 43–49.

Solomon, Z., Waysman, M., Levy, G., Fried, B., Mikulincer, M., Benbenishty, R., Florian, V., & Bleich, A. (1992). From front line to home front: A study of secondary traumatization. *Family Process, 31,* 289–302.

Walsh, F., & McGoldrick, M. (1991). Loss and the family: A systemic perspective. In F. Walsh & M. McGoldrick (Eds.), *Living beyond loss: Death in the family* (pp. 1–29). New York: Norton.

Chapter 8

Treating Traumatic Grief in Systems

Kathleen O. Nader

Studies of children's traumatic responses have provided evidence of both independence and interaction between trauma and grief reactions (Eth & Pynoos, 1985a; Nader, Pynoos, Fairbanks, & Frederick, 1990; Pynoos et al., 1987). When there is a traumatic death, a child who is affected must contend with the symptoms of trauma, of grief, and of the interaction between the two. The response to traumatic death is further complicated by the fact that catastrophic events can affect entire communities. An entire family, classroom or group, school or agency, or community may grieve over the traumatic loss of one or more individuals.

Thus the traumatic nature of such deaths complicates the treatment and recovery process. Treatment for bereavement alone following a traumatic death can be ineffective and can have harmful effects (Nader & Pynoos, 1993). Chapter 2 describes the interaction of trauma and grief; this chapter describes incidents of traumatic death at three elementary schools and the specific intervention programs and methods used to assist the children and their caretakers following the events.

TRAUMATIC DEATHS AT THREE ELEMENTARY SCHOOLS

The following are descriptions of three catastrophic events in which elementary school children were killed under three very different sets of circumstances. Because seeing horrible sights and witnessing injury or threat, as well as experiencing them directly, can result in traumatic responses, the following descrip-

The author would like to thank the school administrators, staff, and treatment and screening teams for our work together at a number of sites, including Newburgh, New York, and Los Angeles and Orange County, California. Appreciation is extended also to Dr. Robert Pynoos for our years of collaboration and for the opportunity to work with a variety of traumatized and grieving children both across this country and in other countries.

tions include some of the graphic images as well as the experiences to which the children were exposed.

In the first catastrophic event, one classmate and a stranger were killed by sniper fire in a low-income, high-crime area of south central Los Angeles.

A man in his 20s had, as a teenager, lost eight members of his family in the Jonestown massacre in Guyana and suffered from traumatic grief. Later complaining of depression, he applied for treatment at a local mental health agency and was placed on a waiting list. He became attached to a woman, who had him put her name on his checking account and then took his money and left him. Neighbors called the police after he began shooting into the air at passing airplanes. Because of existing laws, he was not arrested or placed in a psychiatric facility; his gun was not taken from him. He lived across the street from an elementary school.

At the end of a school day in February, from the second story window of his home, this young man opened fire on the crowded elementary school playground. Using high-powered ammunition that penetrated metal doors and monkey bars and shattered windows in the school, he killed one fifth-grade child and one passerby, and injured more than 14 others, including one school staff member. Children witnessed the sight as bullets went through one side of a fifth-grade girl, exiting the other side along with lung and heart tissue. The passerby was cut open across his abdomen by the same automatic gunfire, and intestines emerged from his abdomen. Some of the other children's injuries were severe. The sniper appeared to be shooting at any moving target, and many children were pinned down on the playground or behind nearby barriers that protected them only from the sniper's sight. Children looking out through windows on the sniper's side of the school sometimes saw severe, bloody injury through the windows or were frightened by bullets breaking through them. Children in classrooms on the other side of the school saw their teachers tape paper over windows or were ordered to hide in closets or under desks. They feared gang members were attacking the school and would enter to kill them.

One month after the sniper attack, 77% of children present on the playground under direct attack and 67% of children in the school had moderate to severe post-traumatic stress disorder (PTSD). In contrast, 74% of children no longer at school at the time of the attack and 83% of children on 3-week vacation from this year-round school had mild or no PTSD. Within each exposure level, children who knew the deceased child had significantly more symptoms of PTSD (Pynoos et al., 1987). Fourteen months later, children with greater exposure to the shooting continued to have significantly more symptoms and significantly greater severity of traumatic reactions. Children with lesser exposure had higher trauma scores if they knew the child who was killed or if they reported guilt. Grief scores were associated with greater acquaintance with the deceased classmate independent of exposure to the sniper attack (Nader et al., 1990).

In the second catastrophic event, the death of the child's family in a plane crash affected school faculty and staff as well as children and parents from the deceased child's third-grade classroom.

During a holiday trip, while traveling between islands in Hawaii, a family went down in a small aircraft over the ocean. There was one distress call from the plane.

The plane and bodies were never recovered. (The Coast Guard explained that often when a plane goes down over the ocean it "quickly ditches" and does not break up but sits on the water for a while and then sinks. There is no oil slick and no way to locate the crash site.) Family members tried to get a court order to continue the search but were unsuccessful. One young elementary school child, Robby, was among the deceased.

As is common following sudden or traumatic loss, misinformation and rumors were spread. One administrator at Robby's school received a call in the middle of the night telling her that another administrator with the same name as the dead mother had been killed. After learning about the crash, teachers and administrators became concerned about the children in their school. Some felt overwhelmed by their own reactions to the crash and subsequently were more sensitive about their performance or others' evaluations of their projects. Some described a real sense of aloneness; for example, one teacher lamented that her husband was not as touched by the deaths as she was. Some adults and children believed that surely the family was safe on an island somewhere and would be rescued.

The school was small, and families knew each other. Parents became distressed, and they also worried about the safety of their own children. Some parents and children began to collect every newspaper article about the tragedy. Parents and children were concerned about the last moments for the family before the plane crashed. They openly speculated about what it must have been like to know you were going to crash and not be able to do anything to protect your child or yourself. Parents described a variety of reactions: for example, disbelief and fear of flying. Some reacted by wanting to do something but felt helpless because they had no way, and no one, to help: "When the whole family goes like that . . . there isn't anybody to comfort." Parents and children reviewed the last contact they had had with the family. Some had envied them their vacation to Hawaii. A few parents thought that there could not be a funeral because the bodies had not been found; others felt relieved that a funeral was, in fact, planned.

Additionally, parents were concerned about how to handle their children's responses and questions following the crash: "It's not easy to know how to be a parent in those situations." One child started to play plane crash with a bar of soap in the bathtub. Children asked questions they had not asked before—for example, about death and its permanence, about whether the family members had all died at once or if anyone had been "broken up" first and in pain, about what would happen to the toy that had been left at Robby's house, about how someone so young could die, about whether airplanes were safe, about what would happen to Robby's turtle and dog and house. A few parents were concerned that their children showed no reaction. For example, one boy focused only on happy memories of Robby and his family—for example, playing Nintendo, going to Mardi Gras. This boy's mother described feeling upset that her child had not cried. Another mother said that it made her sad to hear anyone discuss the good times with the dead family.

While some parents struggled with how to tell their children, some of the children found out over the phone from friends. The children had been studying airplanes and airports in class before the holiday; this event gave new meaning to those studies. A few children began to talk about other tragedies instead of or in addition to the crash—for example, a bombing in Nevada. Robby's close friend Johnny was now scared to be upstairs alone. He said, "We have to have Simon over soon, before he dies too"; the three boys had played together. For many weeks after the crash, another classmate, Bill, spent 5 minutes before going to sleep each night talking about death or the accident. He was concerned about what had happened to the bodies and asked, if the bodies were finally found, if the Coast Guard could give them oxygen and revive them. In response to a television story about a 3-year-old girl who had survived when her parents had died, Bill decided that the girl should die too. He felt some sense of comfort that Robby had not died alone. Bill decided he would not become a pilot because of this accident.

At school, the classmates of the child who had died were preoccupied with what must have happened after the plane went down. During art session, there were drawings of bones at the bottom of the ocean. They began to play radar tower in the schoolyard—traumatic play aimed at rescuing a wayward plane. They also engaged in grief play as a group: They began to find dead animals in the wooded area near the school and to bury them ceremoniously. His class decided as a group to keep the dead child's desk in place. Who would have his toys and other items became an issue to them. As advised, teachers set aside specific times to discuss Robby in the classroom. In one of the younger classrooms, children for the first time were able to discuss losses in their own families. These discussions became therapeutic for the children; one child who had been struggling with a previous loss began to improve.

The third catastrophic event occurred at a school in rural New York, where 10 schoolchildren died as a result of a tornado.

A tornado struck the double-block wall of an elementary school cafeteria, blowing out windows and knocking down two layers of brick and block on to tables of children. Nine children were killed; one's face was flattened beyond recognition. One teacher and at least 13 other children were injured, a few severely. Some children were trapped under fallen debris. Children had limbs caught under large blocks or between cafeteria benches. One child was hit in the face by a flying table. Children who could not get out of the cafeteria immediately saw limbs sticking out from under parts of the wall or limp bodies lying atop some of the debris. Some children outside of the cafeteria, or recently escaped from the cafeteria, watched as bleeding children were carried through the hallway or as school staff attempted futilely to resuscitate a child. The roof had lifted during the tornado, and there was some concern about the integrity of the building.

Teachers and community members joined the rescue efforts to dig children out from under blocks and debris, to carry the injured to the nurse's office or to ambulances, or to move children to safe areas. Desperate attempts were made to revive one child who was dead. One child died in a car accident in the congested traffic outside of the school.

The effects of the event reached well beyond the school. Community members, administrators, staff, and teachers as well as children were all contending with their own traumatic reactions. An architectural flaw was found in the school building, which had contributed to the wall collapse. Community members were distressed about the number of dead children and that the school might not be safe for their children.

After the tornado, children were afraid not only of the cafeteria but also of the gym, which now served as cafeteria, and of windows that were cracked or that rattled. They became upset whenever there were clouds or wind. Even in the unexposed classrooms, teachers reported an inability to teach for the first 2 months following the event. The number of deaths seemed to affect the course of response; the intensity of the experience and the number of dead children seemed to prolong the initial numbing period. Children were still numb during the first Christmas after the event; the second Christmas was more difficult for most of them.

THEORETICAL PERSPECTIVE

The specific specialized methods of trauma treatment described in this chapter began, under the tutelage and supervision of Dr. Ted Shapiro at Cornell University, in the form of a semistructured research interview. The interview included a draw-a-picture, tell-a-story method and a set of research questions developed by Dr. Shapiro, Dr. Karen Gilmore, and Dr. Robert Pynoos (K. Gilmore, personal communication, August 1994; R. Pynoos, personal communication, 1985; T. Shapiro, personal communication, August, 1994). This research interview was first used by a group of colleagues at Payne Whitney Medical Center at Cornell University with children whose parents had attempted suicide; later it was used in Los Angeles as a diagnostic interview with children exposed to violence (Eth & Pynoos, 1985b). The initial specialized interview for traumatized children with innovations by Drs. Pynoos and Eth and additions by this author was first published in detail in 1986 (Pynoos & Eth, 1986). It has continued to evolve in its clinical diagnostic and therapeutic use in response to the needs of the traumatized child in sessions (Nader, 1994a; Nader & Pynoos, 1991; Pynoos & Nader, 1993; Pynoos, Nader, & March, 1991). There are similarities between this method and the methods used in abreactive therapy (Levy, 1938) and those discovered as effective for use with Israeli children following traumatic exposures (Ayalon, 1979).

Therapeutic approaches to PTSD nearly all incorporate cognitive and emotional reprocessing of traumatic memories (Pynoos et al., 1991). Children can be assisted in exploring their subjective experiences thoroughly and in understanding the meaning of their responses. They can be helped to develop a new relationship with their cognitive, affective, and physiological traumatic memories as well as with the aspects of self disrupted by the traumatic experience.

Premises of Treatment and Intervention

Following are some of the basic principles underlying this method of directive and interactive childhood trauma intervention (Nader, 1994a; Nader & Pynoos, 1991; Pynoos & Eth, 1986; Pynoos & Nader, 1989, 1993). The premises of treatment and intervention include those that have been used primarily in the former University of California at Los Angeles Trauma, Violence, and Sudden Bereavement Program and additional premises. Because Nader, Pynoos, and Eth have worked separately, differences in their styles and uses of the method have emerged. Additional premises and elaborations of the basic premises that have become apparent in the process of the present author's work are included below, as well.

The following description assumes a working knowledge of basic psychotherapeutic principles and techniques. It assumes the use of good skill, timing, and intuition in the implementation of these methods.

1   Response and recovery processes following traumatic events suggest the need for specific phases of prevention and intervention (Nader, 1994b, see "Phases of Intervention," this chapter). These phases may include measures of primary and secondary prevention, immediate and secondary first aid, and initial and ongoing interventions (see Nader & Pynoos, 1993). Assessment of the traumatic situation and initial response permits planning for the appropriate methods of aid or intervention following traumatic events. In a situation of ongoing trauma, such as inner city violence or war, the phase of the trauma itself may have an effect on the intervention process (see "Multiple or Ongoing Trauma"). Varying levels of intervention are indicated depending on the circumstances. For example, moderate to severe PTSD reactions suggest the need for individual interventions. There is evidence that failure to resolve moderate to severe traumatic reactions may result acutely and over time in a variety of significant psychological disturbances (see Nader, 1996).

2   Cultural differences may result in differences in approach, style, or method at each phase of intervention (Nader, 1994b; Nader, Dubrow, & Stamm, in preparation). Community or school interventions necessitate an understanding of cultural differences to be effective. Among the issues that require an understanding are the following: (a) views about death, (b) views about mental health response and intervention, (c) styles of approaching a goal, (d) issues of power and authority, (e) views of outsiders, (f) moral issues, and (g) views about victimization. For example, initially, fears about the dead and beliefs about their possible return may need to be addressed (see Chapter 2). After shootings on a school ground in Stockton, California, it was essential to perform a ceremony for the removal of angry dead souls before a large population of Vietnamese Buddhist children would return to school. Cultural differences may affect ongoing aspects of intervention such as the expression of fantasies of intervention (e.g., revenge) or the engagement of support from others. The grandfather of an adolescent girl who had been raped in wartime reported that, a year after the rape, she finally had the courage to tell her family. Her brother murdered her 2 days later. Hers was a culture where a woman who is raped is considered contaminated.

3   The clinician acts as an advocate or involves others as advocates for the traumatized child to minimize secondary adversities (Nader, 1994a; Nader & Pynoos, 1993). In the immediate aftermath of a traumatic event, children need protection from unnecessary reexposure. A child may need additional assistance within the community, at school, at court, with peers, and within the

family. For example, a boy who was severely traumatized and badly injured in the tornado was returned to the classroom on a gradual basis. He was given a customized curriculum and was thus eased back into the classroom and into his studies. He became upset when curious peers wanted to gather around him and ask questions; his peers were helped to understand his sensitivity to noise and to motion. The therapy team and parents advocated within the community so that specific memorials were placed for optional viewing to prevent involuntary constant confrontation with these reminders of the event.

4 The ability of adults to restore a school or community to pretrauma levels of functioning is influenced by their own levels of distress and recovery (Nader & Pynoos, 1993). Effective interventions for children, therefore, necessitate attention to the needs of all members of the traumatized community.

5 The support of others has been found to be therapeutic following loss (Marris, 1991) and following exposure to tragic events (Nader et al., 1990). Several post-traumatic circumstances can interfere with the giving of support. The patient's loss of energy for normal interactions and/or preoccupation with the deceased may be factors. Over time, the stressful atmosphere following a traumatic event may create new or exacerbate already existing rifts between groups. This divisiveness can interfere with the therapeutic support that community members can provide for one another following traumatic events. It can, in fact, be an additional source of tension (Nader & Pynoos, 1993).

Different rates of recovery may affect available support (Pynoos & Nader, 1990). Knight-Birnbaum (1988) has observed that adults and children have different timetables for grieving. Differing exposures and courses of response within groups or families may add to ill-timed or missing supportive behaviors. Teachers who have not been as traumatized by an event or who have had none of the dead or injured children in their classrooms have sometimes become intolerant of prolonged traumatic and grief reactions in other teachers and in children. Among siblings of children hospitalized with catastrophic illness (Stuber, Nader, Yasuda, Pynoos, & Cohen, 1991) or with traumatic injury, over time worry about the sibling may be replaced by anger at the loss of parental attention and loss of other resources now applied to the ill child. One and a half years after the tornado described above, less affected members of the community began to complain about the continued attention and resources allocated to the affected school.

6 Separate intervention efforts, unless cooperative and well coordinated by well-trained clinicians, can add to any loss of support or divisiveness in a school or larger community. After one school disaster, a separation developed between the parents of the deceased children and supporting friends and the parents of the survivors. Parents of the deceased were concerned that their lost children be memorialized in such a way that they would never be forgotten. Parents of the survivors were concerned about their children's daily exposure to vivid reminders of their horrible experience. The battle over the number and placement of memorials interfered with the support that the two groups of com-

munity members could have given each other. It was ultimately determined that there should be "optional viewing" of the memorial for the traumatized children: It was placed in front of the school outside the principal's office and was surrounded by shrubs and trees so that anyone who wanted to see it needed to enter to do so. Repairing the division between community groups was difficult and was most effective after clinicians who understood the interaction of trauma and grief became involved with the grieving families.

7   There is evidence of both independence and interplay between traumatic and grief reactions, regardless of exposure (Eth & Pynoos, 1985a; Nader et al., 1990; Pynoos et al., 1987). Traumatic aspects of death may hinder or complicate recovery from the loss. For example, attempts to reminisce and grief dream work may be thwarted by traumatic response; the process of identification with the deceased may be complicated by the nature of the death; estrangement, avoidance, and post-trauma complications may interfere with healing interactions; and overlapping symptoms may be intensified (e.g., the sense of isolation that often follows traumatic experience and also often accompanies loss may be more pronounced following a traumatic death). Moreover, there may be multiple losses during a traumatic event; a child may be grieving for the loss of individuals, property, aspects of self, and aspects of a continuing relationship, all at once (see Chapter 2). To be effective, treatment must address traumatic reactions, grief reactions, and the interaction between the two. Some trauma resolution may be necessary before initial grief work can be successful. The child or adolescent patient will establish a rhythm by which trauma and grief issues must be addressed.

8   The goals of treatment include both the repair of the injured aspects of the child and the recovery of, recognition of, and reconnection with the healthy aspects of the child—which may have taken a backseat to symptoms and an altered self-concept. For example, Bobby was an 8-year-old boy who had watched helplessly while several of his classmates were shot, one fatally, in their classroom. He had carefully watched the woman with the gun and determined that she looked intently at a child before shooting him or her. He had known his friend across the room would be shot after the friend had moved, drawing her attention. When she had turned her focus to Bobby, he had promptly run for cover and slid like a baseball player behind the file cabinet, effectively saving himself. He experienced a greatly diminished self-image until he recognized the competence with which he had saved his own life. High levels of fragility and high levels of personal strength can coexist in individuals who are moderately to severely traumatized. It is essential to recognize both in the process of ongoing treatment and recovery.

9   The goal of effective individual intervention is to hear everything, including the worst. Especially during the initial interview, any reluctance to discuss a child's experience directly may lead to disturbances in memory and cognition related to the event. Trauma review is not a simple retelling. It is essential to elicit, sensitively and skillfully, the whole of the child's experience,

including his or her affective responses, rather than encouraging a journalistic retelling (Nader, 1994a; Pynoos & Nader, 1993). Both initially and as numbing reduces and the child's confidence and ego strength improve, it is essential to push through difficult moments, to find the physiological, affective, and perceptual aspects of the experience as well as any lost portion (Nader, 1994a).

10   Children's initial retelling of an event may include distortions, omissions, spatial misrepresentations, and desired actions (Johnson & Foley, 1984; Pynoos & Nader, 1989; Terr, 1979, 1991). Inasmuch as memory is improved by reinstating the original cognitive or physical context in which an event occurred, children's recall of the event's details can be assisted by permitting re-creation of the original scene. Children are also assisted when provided a strategy of recall (Pynoos & Nader, 1989; see also Johnson & Foley, 1984). This goal must be accomplished with care taken not to jeopardize any potential court case.

11   During one traumatic event, there are multiple visual and perceptual experiences. In the case of traumatic events, children's recall is not organized as a single episode, but rather as multiple traumatic episodes within a single event (Pynoos & Nader, 1989). Step-by-step reexamination of the event permits understanding of individual episodes of the event in context of, for example, life experience, attitudes, desires to act. After the tornado and wall collapse, Lisa remembered as separate episodes of her experience: (a) seeing the window blow out and then the wall begin to fall; (b) getting up to run for safety and being pulled down by her best friend; (c) having her foot smashed under a table; (d) seeing her friend smashed under the table and apparently not breathing; (e) calling for help and waiting for rescue while bits of debris from the ceiling continued to drift down; (f) being rescued; (g) going to the hospital; and (h) hospitalization.

12   Emotional meaning becomes embedded in the details of an event. Spatial and temporal registration, affective and cognitive responses, sets of perceptions, intervention fantasies, and psychodynamic attributions differ for each moment and memory anchor point (Nader & Pynoos, 1991; Pynoos & Eth, 1986; Pynoos & Nader, 1989, 1993). Specific traumatic moments should be addressed in treatment as they appear in the child's play or drawings, writings, recount of dreams, or other verbalizations (Nader & Pynoos, 1991; Pynoos & Nader, 1993). A child invariably gives some clue about the episode of his or her experience, the traumatic symptom, or the related issue that is currently of importance for review and processing. Specific traumatic episodes or moments may be of particular importance to the grieving process—for example, realizing that the deceased was wearing something of the child's when he or she died or hearing what the deceased said before being killed. In the sniper attack, when Marta said, "I'm hit," Rashadah laughed, thinking she was joking. Realizing there were real bullets, Rashadah ran for safety. She later became preoccupied with having run for safety instead of helping her now dead friend to the nurse's office.

13   This method of treatment recognizes the intensity of traumatic moments. Conditioning that elicits a specific response to a specific stimulus nor-

mally takes many repetitions; but behaviors that occur only once during a traumatic experience may result in such conditioning (possibly related to an increase in the secretion of specific neuropeptides). Consequently, sounds, sights, bodily postures, pains, and specific emotions occurring during a traumatic event may become linked to traumatic symptoms or to each other (see Chapter 2). Additionally, behaviors, wishes, or fantasies may become embedded with intensity into levels of a child's consciousness; the result may be a compulsion to repeat or to complete these specific actions, wishes, or fantasies. Moreover, intense wishes to assist others or to protect oneself may go unrecognized when fear or a sense of failure prevail. When realized, these wishes may provide relief to the child's condemning superego (see Nader & Pynoos, 1991).

14 A child's mind remains extremely active during and after a traumatic event (Nader & Pynoos, 1993; Pynoos & Nader, 1989, 1993). The child looks for the next appropriate action, methods of undoing the threat, ways of intervening, or means of repairing the damage. Ongoing intervention fantasies include the child's fantasies during and after the event of preventing or stopping harm, of challenging the assailant, and of repairing damage (Nader, 1994a; Pynoos & Eth, 1986). When children's desires to act during an event go unresolved, the result can be a major change in behavior and personality (Nader & Pynoos, 1991; Pynoos & Nader, 1993). For example, a 12-year-old boy who had spent much of a 72-hour massacre thinking about punching out the sniper later began to provoke fights and attack others in response to traumatic reminders. Similarly, before the sniper attack, the brother of a 7-year-old boy (who did not witness the attack) had been bullied by some boys at the same school into swallowing a nickel. The brother subsequently died after the nickel ate through his stomach lining. After the sniper attack, the boy recalled wishing that he had beat up the boys and kept them from harming his older brother. When asked what he wanted to do when he grew up, he said, "Beat up people." His mother reported his increased aggressive behavior and defiance (Nader & Pynoos, 1991).

15 Desires or fantasies as well as successful actions may be recognized and facilitated in the safety of therapeutic sessions (Nader, 1994a; Pynoos & Eth, 1986). The consequence is usually the expression of prohibited affect or the enactment of a desire or fantasy with its associated affect. Done effectively, this process leads to the reduction of the sense of helplessness and the recognition of the child's good intentions or effective behaviors. For example, Ralph (see the case example in Chapter 2) experienced a sense of relief following sessions in which he depicted aggression toward someone who represented the sniper. He subsequently demonstrated a reduction in external aggression. Bobby, the boy who slid to safety (see above, number 8), enacted how he had anticipated the woman with the gun and promptly run sliding for cover. He became so thrilled with the recognition of his success that he later had to be given permission to choose a career other than professional baseball.

It is of assistance to some adolescents to facilitate behaviors that recognize their desires for adult status. For example, assisted court testimony, controlled reenactments and/or, at least initially, expression of wishes for intervention or revenge from the third person perspective may be helpful. Using the third person perspective is also effective when the perpetrator of the crime is someone the child feels a need to protect (e.g., a parent or an injured person whom the child attempted to assist; see Nader, 1994a). Controlled reenactments include demonstrating, in the intervention session, aspects of the event (e.g., the clinician may provide toys or objects replicating the trauma or make him- or herself available for demonstration of what happened). Other controlled reenactments include taking the child, when psychologically ready, back to the site of the crime or disaster and creating a metaphorically similar situation. The enactment of wishes and fantasies must be well timed and appropriately facilitated so as to remain harmless and effective.

16 It is essential to reinforce a child's impulse control while permitting the expression of rage or revenge. Unresolved revenge fantasies may be expressed in activities, play, or reenactments that express rage or revenge. The expression of fantasies of revenge or assistance is often more difficult for adolescents who, even in the privacy of the therapeutic session, are embarrassed or afraid of appearing silly. Skillfully assisting expression or enactment of these fantasies in session often reduces a sense of helplessness and the need for repetitive reenactment. For example, the boy who had been in the restaurant massacre began to attack the ants outside the treatment office during a break. He attacked imaginary men in army fatigues (like the sniper) in the area behind the hospital on one occasion. After expressing his revenge in sessions over time, he stopped dangerous reenactment behaviors such as provoking fights or taking life-threatening risks. It may be necessary to assure a child or adolescent that the clinician knows he or she would not actually hurt anyone and that it does not actually hurt the other person to enact revenge in a clinical session.

17 The therapist takes an active role in addressing the impact of the traumatic experience (Nader, 1994a; Pynoos & Nader, 1988). Although children may need assistance in understanding the influence of prior life experiences on current traumatic response, it is essential to maintain a primary focus on the child's full subjective experience and its impact. For example, a 12-year-old girl who had witnessed the public suicide of a woman who had held her and her peers hostage at school also had previous issues related to early abandonment by her father. The primary focus of treatment remained on the girl's traumatic recollections, including her fears, her friends crying, the teacher's actions, the accidental shot that almost hit a child, the woman's dictated suicide note, the woman shooting herself, the blood spurting from the woman's head and mouth, and other episodes of her experience and its aftermath. Life themes may become a part of the process of traumatic resolution. A year later, after much trauma resolution, the abandonment issues became a central focus. She was unable to address her traumatic rage without first addressing abandonment by her father (Nader, 1994a).

18 Attention must be given to achieving the proper closure at the end of each interview to prevent leaving the child with renewed anxiety and an unnecessary avoidance of the therapeutic situation itself (Nader, 1994a; Pynoos & Eth, 1986). Moreover, it is advisable to make certain that children are reoriented to the present at the end of the session. During a session, children, adolescents, and adults may become entranced with aspects of the trauma. For example, during treatment, a young woman described how, at age 5, wheelbarrows full of rocks crashed onto her head and body from atop a building. The cracking sound in her head from the rocks was like the sound of gunfire near her head in a recent near-miss shooting. Although the session focused on the shooting, she had entered the session entranced with the experience at age 5, feeling like "a little child" and thinking of the earlier event. At the end of the session, there was closure regarding the shooting. However, when she stood up to leave, her right leg went out from under her; psychologically, her leg was still buried under the rocks. It was a simple matter to bring her fully back to the present.

19   Trauma recovery is often characterized by progress and periodic exacerbation of symptoms. The child lends meaning to specific traumatic moments and puts them in the context of his or her life. During the course of recovery, there may be a reduction in numbing and a complementary exacerbation of intrusive symptoms. This increase in symptoms must be recognized as a sign of therapeutic progress rather than a failure of treatment and as an indication that further exploration of specific moments is necessary (Nader, 1994a). For example, Joanie had been molested by the robbers who tied her up and went in and out of her room, bringing items from the house, while her father read unknowingly in his room. The robbers had sharpened a knife in front of Joanie, then gone to stab her father. Only after she symbolically assisted her father in her treatment session was she able to face issues of the molestation. At that time, her symptoms increased.

20   Each child establishes his or her own rhythm(s) of trauma review and focus on the issues of bereavement (Nader, 1994a). Some children need periodically to stop and focus on secondary post-trauma changes or traumatic moment complexes with thorough attention to new issues, definitions, or responses, and/or the deeper meanings of their experiences. The clinician must be willing to move in rhythm with the child's need to process trauma or grief issues and to re-review aspects of the event in search of the child's reprocessing. An example of the need to review occurred in the case of Sandy who, 18 months after a disaster, appeared to be functioning well. The clinician wanted to be certain that nothing was left unaddressed and began re-review of the disaster with moments just prior to the destruction and Sandy's injury. At one point, the clinician observed that Sandy kept her visual focus on the corner of the room. The clinician's attention to what Sandy saw in a corner, where the trauma had occurred, revealed a continued deep sadness about her helplessness to move herself and her friends to safety once the debris began to fly.

21   Sympathy or attachment toward the deceased or the perpetrator may

hinder resolution of anger or a revenge fantasy. For example, a woman entered a fifth-grade classroom and held the class and teacher at gunpoint. She accidently fired the gun, barely missing one child. The teacher attempted to talk her out of killing herself. The woman said that she had to do it because she had had bad doctors and killing herself in front of the children would gain the publicity to expose the doctors. The teacher asked the children if they wanted the woman to live, and they all yelled "Yes." When this strategy was ineffective, the teacher asked the children to put their heads down and pray that the woman would not shoot herself. The woman shot herself in the temple; blood poured from the side of her head and then from every opening in her face. Compassion toward the woman made it difficult for both teacher and children to express anger or revenge toward her. Children were helped to divide themselves into two parts, the one who felt sorry about the woman and the one who was forced to watch this horror in fear of their own lives or the lives of others.

22   Children may take one of several roles in their play and actions following traumatic events, for example, victim, perpetrator, rescuer, or witness. They may also place the clinician in one of these roles while they work through aspects of their experiences. Children may primarily focus on one role at a time, but shift over time or as issues are processed. These roles may be intertwined with issues of grief. For example, in the early phases of his treatment, the boy who was in the massacre at the restaurant often took the role of victim or of assailant (see Chapter 2). Taking these roles assisted him in relinquishing the post-traumatic behaviors of self-mutilation, provoking fights, and attacking others. Prior to the clinical sessions he spent mutilating a doll he had dressed to look like himself, he was banging his head and poking the sites of his wounds on the hospital ward. In clinical sessions, after discussing the death of his friend, he played at killing ants; he played with soldiers fighting to the death; he became a sniper and sneaked up on soldiers to kill them. (The murderer had worn army fatigues.) Although his rage was not resolved, the aggressive behaviors had almost disappeared before he prematurely discontinued his treatment in response to peer pressure. Two years later, he was primarily exhibiting the rescuer role and was described as a protector to his friends. He had really wished that he could have saved his best friend from death during the massacre. On one occasion when he was in a fight, he was so intent on saving his friends that he did not realize he had been stabbed until the fight was over and he discovered the blade sticking out from between his ribs. Resolution of these roles and identifications was eventually assisted by appropriate interpretations, facilitation of desires and fantasies, linkage of traumatic reminders and symbols to specific current behaviors, recognition of the child's strengths and positive desires, and provision of a safe and therapeutic environment for the expression of positive and negative affects as well as for regressions and developmental progressions.

23   Specific symptoms may serve as methods of avoiding or denying an intense sense of helplessness or the reality of a traumatic event. Children, like adults, may experience real guilt (for an actual action or omission that resulted

in harm) or imagined guilt (for something that they could not have prevented or accomplished) about: (a) things they wish they had done, (b) things they wish they had not done, or (c) survival or faring better when others died or were badly injured (Pynoos & Nader, 1988). Similarly, self-aggression may occur when children (a) turn anger inward, (b) feel self-deprecation as a result of a sense of damage or of not being more successful in preventing harm to themselves or others, or (c) feel the need to attack the symbols or marks of the injury or harm. For example, when the boy in the restaurant massacre poked at the sites of his wounds with sharp objects and banged his head, he was contending both with a sense of anger at his own helplessness and with the symbols of the same. On the other hand, symptoms such as aggression toward the self or unrelenting imagined guilt may serve to maintain the illusion that the traumatic event was preventable. These symptoms suggest that the horror could have been stopped and that the individual him- or herself could have stopped it. Attempts to bring reality to the guilt or to link self-aggression to aspects of the traumatic event may be unsuccessful if the patient's unconscious goal is to remain oriented to before the event or to maintain the illusion that the event was preventable. As long as the child's focus remains on "I could have prevented the event," it is possible for him or her to avoid facing the actuality of the event and his or her intense helplessness.

24   Both boys and girls entertain strong wishes or fantasies of revenge during and following traumatic events. Although aggression has been observed most prominently in boys following the death of a significant other (Krupnick, 1984; Raphael, 1983), this treatment method acknowledges, permits, and facilitates expression of anger/rage and fantasies of revenge or intervention by both genders in the safety of the treatment session.

MULTIPLE OR ONGOING TRAUMA

This method of intervention was initially developed as an assessment tool and evolved as an intervention for traumatized children exposed to a single traumatic incident. In the past few years, there has been much discussion about the differences between children exposed to a single traumatic incident and those exposed to ongoing traumas (Nader & Stuber, 1992; Terr, 1991). Discussions of long-standing traumas have most often addressed the reactions of abused and molested children.

There are many factors that determine a child's reactions to an event or events. Consequently, clearly determining accurate profiles for children exposed to ongoing versus single-incident experiences is complicated. The nature of an ongoing trauma affects outcome. Some traumas are endured essentially alone, others in a group. For example, in both the ongoing trauma of war and large-scale single-incident traumas, the horrors are endured as a group; there are many known and unknown individuals who have shared the experience with the child survivor and who may understand his or her plight. Similarly, shame is more prominent for some traumas than for others (e.g., molestation). Issues of betrayal vary. The child who has undergone continual abuse or molestation is likely to react differently than a child who has gone through the repeated and ongoing horrors of war. In the former, the betrayal is often by someone known to the child (e.g., a family member or family friend). In the latter, the enemy is usually another nation or group; if betrayal is involved, it is less personal and has different implications for the lovableness and basic personal worth of the child.

Observations have been made of children in various phases of ongoing trauma; the phase of the trauma is an additional factor influencing reaction to it. For example, children in Kuwait in 1991 after the Gulf War was over seemed to be in a different phase of their reactions than refugee children in Croatia in 1992 while the war there continued (Nader, 1993). Kuwaiti children became focused on the extent of the physical and psychological damage that had occurred, on rebuilding, and on issues of accountability. In contrast, Croatian children were still focused on surviving the war and its horrors; they found watching the news and staying informed to be useful coping mechanisms. Numbing appeared to be prevalent; often, symptoms appeared to be warded off or ignored because there was quite possibly more to endure.

Children suffering abuse with no end in sight and inner-city children enduring violence with no end in sight, like the Croatian children exposed to ongoing war, may of emotional necessity ward off symptoms until "the war is over." The question then becomes the nature and intensity with which avoidance occurs and whether avoidance has become a lifestyle. When children exposed to single incidents of violence were compared with children exposed to ongoing painful treatments for catastrophic illness (including bone marrow transplantation), the most prominent differences were the predominance of avoidance and the reduced number of arousal symptoms in the catastrophic illness patients (Nader & Stuber, 1992).

There is some evidence that the impact of traumatic experiences is most pervasive during the first decade of life and diminishes with age (van der Kolk, Roth, Pelcovitz, & Mandel, 1993). Moreover, the phase of development may influence the importance of a symptom or the degree to which a child experiences it. For example, disruptions to impulse control and issues of aggression may be more significant for children who have recently gained a measure of control over their impulses and for adolescents who are entering a stage of feeling invulnerable. Although trust (e.g., trust in one's safety in the world; trust of the integrity, protection, and goodwill of others) may be an issue for all of those experiencing traumatic events, trauma may be more damaging to the trust of very young children who are either just learning to trust or who still believe in the absolute ability and desire of adults to protect and care for them. In addition, more than one single-incident trauma or trauma combined with death of a significant other, like repetitive or ongoing traumatization, may intensify the damage to trust.

Terr (1991) has provided a preliminary profile of children exposed to single-incident versus long-standing traumas. She has divided these experiences into

Type I and Type II childhood traumas, respectively. The former are marked by extreme fear and intense surprise, the latter by prolonged and sickening anticipation. Both types of trauma include: (a) repeated, intrusive thoughts or images of the event; (b) repeated traumatic play or reenactment; (c) trauma-specific fears; and (d) changed attitudes toward people, aspects of life, and the future. Type I traumas generally meet the American Psychiatric Association's (1994) *Diagnostic and Statistical Manual of Mental Disorders* (DSM-IV) criteria for PTSD and are characterized by (a) full, detailed, "etched-in" memories; (b) retrospective reworkings, attribution of reasons, cognitive reappraisals, and turning points; and (c) misperceptions and mistimings. Type II traumas generate attempts to protect the psyche such as massive denial, dissociation, repression, self-anesthesia, self-hypnosis, identification with the aggressor, or aggression toward the self. The emotional consequences of Type II traumas may include (a) an absence of feeling, (b) a sense of rage, and (c) unremitting sadness (Terr, 1991). Terr has suggested that when a single psychological shock is combined with the death of a parent; consequent homelessness, handicap, or disfigurement; or prolonged hospitalization and pain, the child may develop Type II characteristics as well as the features of Type I trauma.

The specific differences in symptomatic results for Type I and Type II experiences are still in the formulation phase. Rage, unremitting sadness, momentary dissociations, identification with the aggressor and, occasionally, self-anesthesia and the absence of feeling have been clinically observed in severely traumatized children after a single catastrophic incident. Some of these reactions (e.g., unremitting sadness) may be more likely if a friend or relative has died or if a death has been witnessed whether or not the deceased was previously known. Others may be most common when there is danger or injury to personal physical integrity (e.g., momentary or longer dissociations, self-anesthesia). For example, a child who witnessed an unknown woman shoot herself experienced ongoing sadness. A child who was hit in the face by a table, an adolescent who was raped, and a child who was in an explosion with her classmates had periods of dissociation and subsequent amnesia for specific moments of their experiences. Aggression toward the self, including self-mutilation, has been observed following a single traumatic experience when the child has had a prior unrelated single-incident trauma or a prior loss. More information is needed to discover if self-aggression may occur for specific children following a single severe trauma. Delunas (1992) has suggested that the tendency toward some of these specific symptoms or disorders is related more to personality style than to experience. The intensity and nature of the experience, however, seem to be factors in the outcome.

DESNOS or Complicated PTSD

The DSM-IV field trials examined three groups of traumatized adults: victims of interpersonal violence (sexual and/or physical assault) that began before age

14, victims of interpersonal violence that began after age 14, and victims of natural disasters (van der Kolk et al., 1992). Several main symptom clusters, or disorders of extreme stress not otherwise specified (DESNOS) were examined: (a) alterations in regulating affective arousal, including chronic affect dysregulation, difficulty modulating anger, self-destructive and suicidal behavior, difficulty modulating sexual involvement, and impulsive and risk-taking behaviors; (b) alterations in attention and consciousness, including amnesia and dissociation; (c) somatization; and (d) chronic characterological changes such as alterations in self-perception (e.g., chronic guilt, shame, self-blame, ineffectiveness, being permanently damaged), alterations in perception of the perpetrator (e.g., distorted beliefs, idealization), alterations in relations with others (e.g., inability to trust or maintain relationships, tendency toward revictimization, victimization of others), and alterations in systems of meaning (e.g., despair, hopelessness, loss of previously sustaining beliefs). A group of symptoms in addition to PTSD were found to occur most particularly when trauma began at an early age, was prolonged, and was interpersonal in nature. The symptoms included chronic affect dysregulation, aggression against self and others, dissociative symptoms, somatization, and character changes. The younger the age at onset, the more likely the occurrence of current PTSD and of DESNOS. There was also a linear trend between the diagnosis of lifetime PTSD + DESNOS and duration of the trauma. The symptoms tended to occur in association with one another rather than in isolation. PTSD + DESNOS has come to be known as "complicated PTSD" (Roth, 1992; Herman, 1992).

There is clinical evidence that, in addition to repetitive interpersonal traumas such as sexual or physical abuse, dual or multiple unrelated traumas or a single trauma combined with previous loss may result in the more complicated forms of traumatic response. More complicated and prolonged reactions have also been observed in a small number of female victims of a single incident of violence. As a subgroup of victims of crime, these women were described as having been extremely competent and self-sufficient before the traumatic experience; they had been accustomed to dealing with life stresses successfully (J. Kent, personal communication, March 1992). Similarly, a child who was well liked, a good student, and used to dealing competently with normal life stresses was on the playground under gunfire during the sniper attack. She subsequently exhibited symptoms of complicated PTSD.

Treatment of Ongoing or Multiple Traumas

Children who have been previously traumatized often respond differently to the initial specialized treatment session described in this chapter. Resistance and avoidance are more prominent; trust is more difficult. This treatment recognizes the need for levels of numbing and periods of avoidance as a child's ego strength and trust are restored. Treatment may become more directive as the child's tolerance increases. Inasmuch as the child's rhythms and timing are respected in the course of this treatment, the clinician recognizes, for example, a child's need or readiness to regress, express revenge or intervention fantasies, or engage in repetitive play of the trauma with appropriate interpretations.

Long-term treatment may be more appropriate for a child who has had more than one traumatic experience. In addition to trust, specific aspects of the developing ego may have been injured. It may be necessary periodically to strengthen weakened aspects of character and personality before continuing with trauma work. During long-term treatment, the basic premises of this chapter's treatment method should be observed and combined with the use of transference and basic psychotherapeutic techniques (Nader & Pynoos, 1991).

When there have been dual or multiple individual traumas or a trauma and a loss, treatment should include attention to relevant aspects of each event. Depending on the emotional impact of each event, some children may need first to address a previous trauma before attending to the current event; others may be reminded of the previous trauma and undergo symptoms related to each. One 7-year-old boy who had been in a safe area just outside the school door during the sniper attack had, as a younger child, badly burned his hand. He found it difficult to discuss the sniper attack until he had first described in detail the incident in which he had been burned. In contrast, a young woman with multiple traumas came to treatment after a man pointed a gun at her and told her to get out of her car, then fired at her twice as she tried to drive away. When specific traumatic moments of this attempted assault and robbery were addressed in treatment, aspects of the other traumatic events appeared in relationship to them: When she described the large hands of the man with the gun, she recalled the large hands of the uncle who had touched her inappropriately when she was a child. When she described the assailant's eyes before he shot at her, she recalled the frightening eyes of the dog that had viciously attacked her and bit her thumb almost off. When she recalled the bullet sounds cracking through her head, she recalled the rocks that had fallen on her head and body as a child (see above, number 8). Both the current and the earlier traumatic moments were addressed as they came up in the course of treatment.

Additionally, issues that were of relevance in the earlier trauma or traumatic sequence (e.g., abandonment, betrayal, victimization) are likely to appear as issues in the current trauma or traumatic episode. If treatment begins soon after the event or repeated episode, these matters may appear within main trauma themes, or as side or associated issues. Over time, these issues may require direct focus before the treatment can continue with main trauma themes (see above, number 6).

As ego strength returns, with direct focus, forgotten issues (lost traumatic moments or periods) representing moments too horrible to recall initially are often recovered and thoroughly addressed. These moments may be addressed early in the treatment, as they become relevant to recovery, or as they are identified by the child. Directing the focus of treatment to the full force of traumatic rage and/or helplessness may have to wait until some recovery has been accomplished (Nader, 1994a). Over time, aspects of the trauma take on new meaning for the child as he or she enters a new developmental phase or as life unfolds. These issues are then worked through in the context of this new meaning or reappraisal (Nader & Pynoos, 1991; Pynoos & Nader, 1993).

Periodic meetings with parents are important to a child's progress. Often both teachers and parents are included in the ongoing treatment process. Parents may need assistance to adjust to regressions and other changes in the child and to establish a rhythm with the child that enhances recovery. For example, following traumatic experiences, trust is an important issue for children. Severely traumatized or retraumatized children may need to reestablish a sense of trust, especially toward adults. A child who trusts is easier to like than a child who distrusts. Distrustful behaviors may result in the discomfort, rejection, or annoyance of others. These reactions may contribute to or perpetuate the distrust. Parents may need assistance in recognizing that some traumatized children's behaviors are both measures of self-protection and cautious attempts to regain love and trust. The distrustful and annoying conduct is the noise that covers an intense desire to be loved and protected, combined with an intense fear of continued betrayal and harm.

SCHOOL COMMUNITY INTERVENTIONS

Phases of Intervention

Primary intervention: Disaster proofing, disaster preparedness, preventing exposure.

Secondary prevention: Preventing reexposure or additional exposure, restoring safety (rescue efforts, moving children to safety, locating and tracking children), restoring the location of the event.

Immediate first aid: Providing accurate and age-appropriate information, restoring a sense of safety, providing comfort, reuniting family members.

Secondary first aid: Returning to appropriate location, providing accurate and age-appropriate information, dispelling rumors, permitting discussion, providing realism and normalization of responses, providing comfort, beginning return to normality.

Initial intervention: Restoring community (e.g., large group meetings), interventions for adults (e.g., parents, teachers, administrators), interventions for children (e.g., class-room exercises, family sessions), Phase 1 of training for screening and treatment teams (if needed), assessment of post-trauma reactions and risk factors.

Ongoing intervention: Ongoing group planning and education meetings (e.g., planning committee, administrators, parents, teachers, community), preparation for individual and group course of response and for special circumstances, individual treatment (children and adults), group treatment (e.g., grief, injured, family, peer), ongoing assessment.

The scope and nature of intervention programs are determined by the needs of the affected population as well as by the availability of appropriate personnel and funding, and administrative and political considerations. Following the sniper attack described earlier, a sampling of children from the entire school was completed at 1 and 14 months. A specialized clinical interview was conducted with specific identified children at each of those phases, and referrals were made to nearby agencies. Trauma clinicians provided interventions to the children and parents for approximately 2 years.

The plane crash off Hawaii also resulted in sudden tragic deaths and a sense of traumatic loss. There was, however, no direct witnessing of the horror and no direct life threat to the children. One extended parents meeting and one teachers meeting was conducted to discuss suggestions to assist the children and parents in the recovery process. Consultation was given to the teacher of Robby's class and to administrators so that they might assist the recovery process at school.

Following the tornado, cooperative efforts between state, county, and local agencies (to provide personnel and specialized funding) and the efforts of the school district made possible a comprehensive intervention program. Consultation visits were made once a week approximately every 2 months to train interviewers and clinicians, to hold group and planning meetings, to provide specialized interventions, and to monitor the progress of children and adults.

Schools and communities are often prepared to provide assistance up to and including "secondary first aid." After severe catastrophic events affecting large groups, ongoing prevention efforts are well served by creating a comprehensive school intervention program that addresses all post-traumatic reactions including grief (see Pynoos & Nader, 1988). Although childhood traumatic response occurs primarily in relationship to exposure to traumatic phenomena regardless of adults' experiences, recovery of the adult community affects the recovery of children. A comprehensive mental health program includes periodic groups for administrators, for school personnel, and for parents; individual treatment for identified adults and children; and small groups for grieving children and, if possible, for injured children. Coordination of helping groups and individuals is necessary for an effective overall effort and to prevent the formation of community subgroups working at cross purposes (see Nader & Pynoos, 1993). Following are descriptions of some of the initial and ongoing interventions for schools.

"SECONDARY FIRST AID": INITIAL CLASSROOM INTERVENTIONS

During and after violent events, disasters, or severe accidents, children need to be moved to safety, to be reunited with other family members as quickly as possible, and to have their whereabouts tracked (Nader & Pynoos, 1993). After initial cleanup, restoration of the school's physical safety must precede school return. Children may be relocated until this goal can be accomplished.

Prior to the entry of invited consultants into the school, school psychologists or other mental health professionals have often provided an early presence in the classroom, furnishing factual information and emotional support to the children and teachers.

At home and after their return to school, children need to be given accurate information that is not beyond their need or ability to understand. Rumors are common in the aftermath of traumatic events (Pynoos & Nader, 1988). For example, there may be rumors about the number and nature of deaths or injuries as well as about continued danger. Trauma-specific issues affecting recovery must be anticipated.

In this initial phase, less exposed children can be encouraged to support their peers; they can be deterred from further upsetting their peers, for example, by the use of humor to relieve their own tension. In one elementary school, after two children and their mother were shot to death by their father, children who had not been at the site of the shootings and who were not close to the dead girls played at shooting other students in the head with their fingers. This behavior by less exposed children was very distressing to their traumatized and grieving peers.

SCHOOL-BASED TREATMENT PROGRAM

A comprehensive school intervention program is characterized by a cooperative effort between consultants, administrators, teachers, school nurses, staff members, and mental health professionals.

Administrators

Administrators can provide support by increased visibility on site, by acting as a buffer between the traumatized school population and the media, by backing the treatment team, and by anticipating special needs (Nader & Pynoos, 1993). With the assistance of a trauma consultant, administrators can help to orchestrate effective therapeutic efforts by school personnel and trauma team members. For example, after the sniper attack, the principal provided rotating space for specialists to conduct prereferral diagnostic and therapeutic interviews with children and voiced his continued support at faculty meetings. He assigned the school psychologist to provide consultants with needed information and assistance in contacting parents to arrange interviews. Similarly, after the tornado, the school superintendent read about childhood trauma so that he could anticipate possible needs. He became involved in fund-raising efforts and cooperated with the trauma consultant and mental health agencies to plan and implement a comprehensive intervention program. With his support, regular visits were made by the consultant to the site every 2 months to provide ongoing training for the trauma team, to conduct regular teacher and parent meetings, to problem-solve, and to anticipate and plan for future needs.

Teachers

Teachers have the task of restoring normal functioning—a sense of safety and order—to the classroom after a disaster. They need assistance with their own traumatic and grief reactions so as to be able to assist the treatment effort effectively. Teachers often feel that protecting children is an important part of their role (Nader & Pynoos, 1993). Teachers and school administrators have often expressed guilt over not having saved children in situations when they in fact did all they could do. Guilt has been associated with intensified traumatic and grief reactions (Nader et al., 1990; Pynoos et al., 1987; Raphael, 1983) and may complicate recovery (see Chapter 2).

During the school day, the protective shield normally provided by parents is transferred to the school, principal, and teachers. Following a traumatic event, restoring this sense of protection is important. It can, however, be carried to an extreme: After one violent event at a school, the teacher in a deceased child's class took extreme measures to reinstate this protective shield. She did her best to isolate the children in her class from outsiders. She attempted to deal with their psychological reactions herself and sometimes interrupted clinical interviews with trauma specialists in attempts to bring the children back to the classroom.

Teachers may, like children, have trouble contending with traumatic reminders and emotions as well as their own grief reactions (Nader & Pynoos, 1993). Teachers should be prepared to use the mental health team effectively during the intrusion of traumatic reminders (e.g., during the next bad weather, when there are gunlike sounds, on the week of the anniversary) and to anticipate and respond to specific personal and child reactions. A few months after the sniper attack, the unexpected arrival of a celebrity to the community was accompanied by sirens and a police escort. The children and school personnel responded with renewed traumatic symptoms indicating their uncertainty if another sniper attack was in progress (Nader & Pynoos, 1993). After the tornado, teachers needed assistance in responding to siblings of the deceased and in handling their own reactions when reminded of the dead and of the tornado experience. For example, a few months after the tornado, construction began to rebuild the cafeteria and the fallen wall. Some of the teachers and students were startled by the loud noises and were upset by thoughts of the cafeteria. The treatment team made arrangements to warn the teachers when loud noises would occur and requested that the construction team complete as much construction as possible outside of school hours.

Intervention Team

One of the most important details of post-catastrophic event intervention is the thoroughness and sufficiency of training for those who are to provide the intervention. They need to understand traumatic response, grief reactions, and the interaction of the two, as well as a variety of associated reactions. When there is an offsite consultant, one team member should coordinate efforts and oversee the implementation of planned interventions and events in the absence of the consultant.

Using the school as a site of intervention can enhance the chances of an effective program by providing easy access to clinicians and consultants. Placing the treatment team at the school site for the first 2 years after a severe trauma and gradually moving services offsite can prevent the sense of premature loss of support. After the tornado, for example, trauma team clinicians were next door to the nurse's office for the 2 years following the collapse of the wall. Clinicians provided individual and group treatment, saw children and teachers at difficult times (e.g., the anniversary of the event, the Christmas after the anniversary, the beginning of reconstruction of the cafeteria, reentry into the cafeteria), and consulted with teachers regarding the special needs of children. In the third year following the trauma, clinicians were moved into an adjoining building, and in the following summer they began to move back to their respective agencies (county or state mental health agencies) leaving one full- and one part-time school psychologist from the treatment team in the adjoining building.

INITIAL INTERVENTIONS: SECONDARY CLASSROOM INTERVENTIONS

The first month following a catastrophic event at a school is usually allocated to restoring the school community, planning services, and preparing administrators and teachers for current and future needs. After the sniper attack, the tornado, and the plane crash, meetings were held first with administrators and then with teachers to allow them to discuss their experiences and their traumatic and grief reactions. A program was then implemented for the children, which included the training of screeners and clinicians and plans for classroom exercises and interviews. Classroom exercises permit normalization of responses, preparation for common post-traumatic and grief reactions, addressing fears and rumors, and screening for PTSD and grief (Pynoos & Nader, 1988). Within the first 2 weeks following an incident, some initial symptoms (e.g., bad dreams, fears) may disappear for those who are not traumatized. Moreover, the initial numbing and denial may reduce so that assessment may be more accurate at 3 to 5 weeks following the event.

Classroom Exercise

The classroom exercise begins with a draw-a-picture, tell-a-story technique, in which the children draw anything they want and then tell a story about it. The drawing and story become vehicles for establishing rapport with the children and may include traumatic imagery or traumatically based omissions. Children often spontaneously draw peaceful scenes, designs, and pictures with some link to the traumatic event. Traumatic links and avoidances may be addressed in prelude to formal screening for traumatic symptoms. The use of play and drawing in the group setting, however, must be psychologically sound. It is inadvisable, for example, to engage children in their revenge fantasies in the group setting (Nader & Pynoos, 1991). Pictures of a single item, such as a face, a flower, balloons, or a cross may serve as remembrances or tributes to the dead and often suggest a need to inquire about a sense of loss. Some of these items may also appear in children's grief play. After the tornado, one child asked for helium balloons. She first played games that she had played with her dead friend and then released the balloons one at a time into the sky. She later said that she hoped that her friend would catch one and know that it was a message from her.

When children visualize and draw damage to persons or property, the opportunity to depict repair can prove therapeutic. Children have been visibly relieved, for example, after restoring in their drawings the physical integrity of an injured person, such as drawing a mother without the bloody knife wound that killed her. Galente and Foa (1986) have described the benefit to children of drawing their reconstructions of the damage after an earthquake. Reconstruction is essential to counteract the traumatic helplessness evoked by depicting the destruction (Nader & Pynoos, 1991).

The classroom can be an excellent site for addressing issues of dying and loss (Nader & Pynoos, 1991). Although it is commonly expected that by the third grade children understand the finality of death, after a traumatic loss allowance must be made for regression and confusion. After the plane crash, third-graders inquired about the possibility of resuscitation long after the event. Furman (1973) has suggested that without recognition of the physical reality of death there can be no grieving. The classroom exercise provides a chance to discuss specific issues of loss. Concrete and symbolic representations of the finality of death can assist children. Playing out the funeral may be especially effective when a body is not recovered after a traumatic loss. In one elementary school after a child suddenly dropped dead, a classroom exercise (without screening for PTSD) was conducted with her classmates. This occasion permitted open discussion of previous losses, reminders of the dead child, and emotional reactions to the loss. Children were prepared for the differences in course of recovery that could occur.

In such discussions, children reveal aspects of their grieving and related traumatic issues such as their disbelief, reunion fantasies, anger, emotional pain, sadness, depression, restlessness, separation anxiety, fears, and loss of a sense of safety. After a father murdered his two daughters and his wife in their church parking lot, many surviving children became concerned about their relationships with their fathers. There were rumors that the man had shot his 8-year-old daughter in the back of the head because he could not bear to look at his favorite daughter when he killed her. He had, however, looked his teenage daughter in the face and shot her. Children worried when their fathers became angry or if there were weapons in their homes. They discussed the difficulty of contending both with these fears and with their sense of loss and horror for their dead friends.

Assessment

Initial triage and screening for trauma reactions has included the use of the Childhood Post-Traumatic Stress Reaction Index (CPTS-RI; Frederick, Pynoos & Nader, 1992), a brief Grief Inventory (by Pynoos), and an exposure and coping questionnaire (by Nader). These semistructured interviews are conducted with individual children during the classroom exercise and are generally followed by group discussion. The 20-item CPTS-RI with a brief exposure questionnaire has taken 20 to 40 minutes with American children and 45 to 80 minutes with children exposed to war conditions using the more extensive exposure questionnaire. (Time varies with level of traumatic symptoms.) Other screening instruments for children permit diagnosis of PTSD or complicated PTSD (see Nader, 1996; Stamm, 1996).

These instruments permit screening of individuals, groups, or samples of children for their PTSD and grief reactions. Representative sampling permits the generalization of traumatic and preexisting factors contributing to a group's traumatic response. When the number of children affected prohibits the interviewing of all children, representative sampling permits use of the exposure questionnaire alone with a larger number of children to identify those with risk factors. Additional risk factors and protective factors can be assessed through questions on the exposure questionnaire, interviews with parents, or school records. These factors include, for example, child intrinsic factors, previous psychopathology, previous traumatic or loss experiences, family factors, and relationship to deceased victims. The initial clinical interview is both diagnostic and therapeutic in nature. It permits assessment of specific traumatic moments and their effects on the child, his or her traumatic reaction, and his or her grief response. It also permits the development of a strategy of recall that helps to enable any future treatment, including delayed treatment. It provides the child with an initial sense of relief, and often with some regaining of a sense of control.

Changes in Classroom Needs

Classes from which students have been killed or injured are often the most affected classrooms in the school. The teachers may also be among the most traumatized. Particular attention is required to meet all of the recovery needs of these classes. For example, at the school that experienced the tornado, classmates sat together for lunch; consequently, when the cafeteria wall collapsed, one class that sat next to the wall had numerous dead and injured children and an injured teacher. This classroom was given an assistant teacher. It had many children in individual treatment and a few children in grief groups.

After a traumatic loss, a class may need to establish periodic times to discuss the deceased. Confining these formal discussions to established times and returning the class to normal functioning at other times (Nader & Pynoos, 1993; Pynoos & Nader, 1988) can assist children to learn to postpone focus on their reactions without having to suppress them. Because the school promptly sought intervention after the loss of the family in the plane crash, parents were afforded the opportunity to share their reactions with experts in the field of traumatic stress. They were first assisted with their own responses and then helped to see the parallels in their children's reactions. At set times, classmates of the boy discussed the death and their dead friend as a class. They made decisions together about his desk and toys and discussed the need to find times to remember him.

ONGOING INTERVENTIONS: INDIVIDUAL TREATMENT

It is essential to provide individual treatment for parents, teachers, staff, and administrators in an injured school community as well as for the children. The specialized trauma interview and treatment methods (Nader, 1994a; Nader & Pynoos, 1991; Pynoos & Eth, 1986; Pynoos & Nader, 1993) can assist by counteracting traumatic hindrances to normal functioning and development and by restoring normal ego functioning. The interview assumes a trusting relationship between the child or adult and the therapist that permits the child or adult to engage in reconstructions of the event in the therapy room. Timing is important in the use of interpretation as well as in the introduction of play or drawings as therapeutic tools. The interview (a) permits step-by-step reexamination of the experience; (b) imparts a strategy of recall; (c) uses play and drawings to restore the provoking situation, reexamine and give new meaning to aspects of the event, permit reexperiencing and reworking of the memory and emotion, and reassess the emotion-laden moments and any new meanings attributed to them over time; (d) reenters the fantasy—examines and magnifies desires to act—a process that can provide relief and may allow a sense of completion; and (e) observes the patient's own rhythm in processing the moments and components of his or her traumatic and grief reactions.

Reworking of the memories of the event may include both abreaction and reentering a fantasy toward completion of a desired act. The availability of objects similar to those used in an event (e.g., a toy knife, cafeteria tables, windows, an ambulance, a fire truck, schoolchildren and adults, guns, airplane, soldiers, tanks) permits the restoration of the anxiety-provoking situation in play and a reentering of the child's fantasy associated with the event (see Levy, 1939; Nader & Pynoos, 1991). The act can be repeated until the fears or anxieties are released, for example, in aggression. Replicating the initial event and reentering the fantasy associated with it permit both release and a sense of completion (see the case example at the end of this chapter).

The emotions as well as the means of coping are embedded in the details of children's play and drawings. Mental representations as depicted in children's drawings may include spatial misrepresentations (e.g., proximity to the danger), omissions (e.g., an empty television screen), exaggerated focus (e.g., the eyes, blood), elements of censoring (e.g., large locked cabinets), and opposite situations (e.g., rainbow, happy scene). After the sniper attack, a boy's mother described how tired her son now became after his play and how much more he needed her attention. He repeatedly played games of running and chase. Later, he enacted for the clinician his horror as he had desperately tried to run for safety after the sniper fire began. Just before the interview with his mother (he was interviewed the next day), the same child enacted a funeral pretending that his sister's daughter had died. He and his sister used the ironing board and a doll and acted as pallbearers. They ceremoniously took the body into the living room and stood over and then covered it. They then talked to each other of the "child's" death. Months later, with the same clinician, this boy was able, in his play, to prevent violent disasters at all of the schools in the surrounding area by using the helicopter and ground police and firemen to intervene. Afterwards, he was pleased and animated: He had experienced at least a temporary sense of relief from the helplessness engendered by the sniper attack.

Brief treatment may last for several months and go beyond the first anniversary of a traumatic event. Repetitions of the same play may change slightly over time to incorporate aspects of the event. A 6-year-old girl saw her father kicked and stabbed in the leg with a knife. She was very upset about all of the blood and thought it meant that her father was dying. The father drove himself to a hospital, where the little girl had to wait in the lobby. Weekly she played at disasters—people getting hurt in, for example, car accidents or falls from high places. Over time, the girl added more elaborate injury and rescue scenes. Eventually, she incorporated human-inflicted injury. She became the perpetrator, then the rescuer. She introduced relevant life issues; for example, one session included the issues of cleanliness and filth. Then she added a character named for the actual attacker. Kicking, then stabbing were added to the play. The attacker was finally stopped and punished by being stabbed himself.

Long-term treatment addresses the deeper ramifications of the traumatic event to a child's emotional life, such as specific aspects of the event, court proceedings, intrafamilial issues, and prior traumas. Severely traumatized children, especially those also suffering from traumatic grief, may need such long-term treatment. A 9-year-old boy had accidentally shot his brother while playing good guy–bad guy games with a loaded gun he had found in the closet and "emptied." He had hit an artery and been unable to stop the blood, and his brother had died. Weekly he played out "fight to the death" contests between superheroes and supermenaces. Over time he added into the play (a) resurrection of the dead; (b) the profuse bleeding; (c) a witch who was killed and who in later weeks became a good witch who was killed and then resurrected; and (d) supernatural forces to stop the bad guy from hurting "He-man." (One of the protectors was the good witch.) His play incorporated both his aggression and his idealization of his brother; transference issues, including the bad mother who had not stopped the dangerous play and the bad therapist who forced the boy to discuss the accident, then the good mother and the good therapist who helped ease the pain and helped protect the boy from his own dangerous impulses; his fantasy of undoing the harm; and themes of self-inflicted punishment (Nader & Pynoos, 1991).

SMALL-GROUP INTERVENTIONS

In this treatment method, groups are used primarily as supplements to individual intervention and as a part of ongoing community intervention. Group therapy may address specific trauma issues (e.g., grief, injury, ongoing traumatic reactions) or the needs of specific groups (e.g., parent, teacher, child).

Parents' and Teachers' Groups

Initially after a traumatic event, a large group meeting for parents and school personnel is held with the consultant(s). These meetings generally include the following: (a) discussion of the event and the clearing up of rumors; (b) discussion of the adults' reactions to the event; (c) a question-and-answer period about the children's reactions and a discussion about the possible course of traumatic and grief reactions; (d) information about the psychological first aid that parents can provide; and (e) descriptions of planned services (see Nader, 1994c). Parents also need a chance to discuss their own reactions. Moreover, understanding their own reactions assists them in understanding their children's reactions (Pynoos & Nader, 1988).

After the tornado, parent groups of up to 40 parents each were held every 2 months with the consultant. These meetings permitted parents to ask questions about their children's symptoms and behaviors; to update the consultant on the children's, school's, and community's progress and difficulties related to the wall collapse; and to problem-solve and plan for future difficulties. Similar groups were held for teachers (up to 15 per group) in the absence of administrators. These groups permitted discussion of personal reactions; personal, interpersonal, and school changes; fears regarding administrative actions or lack of continued support; classroom difficulties; behaviors and symptoms of specific children; and preparation for the future.

Weekly groups for specific parent groups (e.g., grief groups, groups for parents of traumatized survivors) can assist both parents and children throughout the children's recovery process. Grief groups for parents of the deceased may also include friends who are grieving the loss of the children or friends who can become support for the grieving parents. After the tornado, separate weekly groups were held for parents of injured children and for parents of other traumatized children.

Children's Groups

Yule and Udwin (1991) found that groups were helpful for adolescents after the sinking of a ferryboat with multiple deaths by drowning. Groups can also provide supplemental support for children undergoing individual treatment following traumatic events. Grief groups can help children establish a support system as well as permit open discussion of reactions and difficulties related to their losses. After the sniper attack, friends of the deceased fifth-grade girl met with the present author on two different occasions. Only then did they learn that other children had seen their dead classmate in dreams, had continued to cry about her, had thought they had seen her on the street, had had fears related to her, or had stopped or emphasized playing games that reminded them of her. In the group the children were able to ask questions about what happens to people after they die and whether or not a spirit can do harm to the living. Worries about harm from the dead were dispelled, and their individual beliefs about what had happened to their friend were expressed. It was a relief to them to know that others had continued to grieve and to worry. They began to be able to provide each other some support through their grieving and traumatic recovery.

After the tornado, siblings and close friends of the deceased were given the opportunity to join specific groups. The groups met weekly and consisted of four children—two grieving children and two others (sometimes one who had already recovered from a previous loss). The two children who were not close to the deceased children had to be doing well academically, so the groups did not disturb their school progress. They were picked with particular attention to their ability to be sensitive to others, and they became an excellent support system to the grieving children, who were also in individual treatment. In the group setting the children were able to discuss with their peers the times of day, the reminders, and the internal images that increased their sense of grief and aloneness. The children learned to read each other and to provide subtle or open support through the difficult times.

When staffing and time permit, groups for injured children can be similarly beneficial. Injured children may become preoccupied with both post-trauma and physical recovery and may have delayed or intermittent grief reactions. It is essential to adapt to a child's pace in processing direct injury, emotional injury, and grief. Parents may need preparation so that they are not shocked and confused at an intensified grief reaction after the child has made excellent progress in recovering from physical and emotional injuries. A long, slow process of physical recovery, emotional work, reintegration into school, and continued emotional and physical therapy may precede grief work.

Children with severe injuries may have particular difficulty reintegrating back into the classroom. They may be contending with feeling damaged as well as with concern about how their peers will view them. A boy who was shot in the eye and head in a drive-by shooting was afraid to return to school because of his eye patch. A classroom exercise to reintegrate him back into the classroom allowed discussion of what had happened to him, how he was doing, how the shooting might still bother him (e.g., reminders, poor vision with the eye patch, not feeling safe) and how the other students could help him feel comfortable returning to school. His classmates were scared by the eye patch until they understood his need to wear it and talked with him long enough to see that he was still Ramone under that eye patch.

Young children sometimes have a fear of contagion; classroom reintegration permits them to move from the role of endangered to the role of protectors and assistors. After the tornado, severely injured children were also reintegrated into school by a classroom exercise and discussion technique. For one boy who had suffered a broken pelvis and multiple breaks in his legs, classmates were helped to recognize that, initially, it was difficult for him to have other children hover around him and that he was frightened by some noises. The boy's mother was permitted to sit with him in class and was gradually moved farther away from him in the room and to fewer and fewer days per week. After she exited the classroom, she remained in the library for a few days in case he needed her and then was available by phone until he was completely adjusted to being in school again. The boy had a reduced stress tolerance and was angry about the damage to his legs. His classmates learned to allow him space and recovery time when he became overwhelmed and irritable. He seemed without grief for the first year of his recovery. The beginning of grief work introduced an emotional and symptomatic regression.

Family Interventions

When more than one family member is in treatment, weekly communication between their clinicians is essential. Whole-family sessions are generally held to assist families to understand the differences in their courses of recovery, to aid their abilities to help rather than hinder each other's recovery and to address specific post-trauma family issues. For example, a mother and her two young daughters entered treatment after the shooting death of the husband and father. Individual treatment addressed the personal traumatic reactions of each family member to the loss; occasional family sessions permitted the discussion of, for example, why Sally became so upset when her mother wanted to go to the grave regularly. Sally was in a different phase of her recovery, still contending with traumatic, intrusive images of her father's bloody body and not yet ready to grieve. Her mother and sister had not seen the body.

Conjoint work has proved helpful to children and other family members when there has been intense worry about another family member (or friend) during the traumatic event. One little girl accompanied her crying mother to the school after the sniper attack to search for her brother. Afterward she began to get up in the night to check on her brother and became anxious when he was away from home. Another little girl was very angry with her brother, who had run for safety, leaving her behind. Joint sessions with the pairs of children allowed expressions of both anger and worry. Such sessions address changes in relationships related to the worry or upset. They have assisted with, for example, estrangement and separation anxiety.

CASE EXAMPLE

On the day of the tornado, Susan, aged 7, was sitting next to her sister, Janie, aged 8, in the school cafeteria at one of the tables near "the wall." When the windows blew out and the wall started to fall, Susan yelled, "Run!" and ran out of the cafeteria, thinking Janie would run too. Janie was smashed under bricks. After they dug her out, several school staff tried at length to resuscitate her. She vomited the lasagna she had just eaten while CPR was administered long beyond the normal period of usefulness. Paramedics brought additional equipment. Janie never regained consciousness and was pronounced "dead on arrival" at the hospital.

Prior to the tornado, Janie had been a bit defiant and had required much of her mother's attention. Susan, the "good child" who needed little attention, had been jealous of Janie and had believed that her mother loved Janie more. She was despondent after her sister's death and also contended with extreme anxiety in response to wind, rattling windows, and dark skies. She reported high numbers of traumatic symptoms including intrusive imagery and dreams, attempts to avoid feelings, regression, problems with impulse control, and somatic complaints. In her initial treatment session with a beginning trainee, Susan's affect remained constricted. The trainee was unable to get Susan to draw her mental image of what Janie looked like after the wall fell or to discuss issues of her loss.

In a consultation session Susan again told the story, using the dolls and doll-sized cafeteria tables, of running out of the cafeteria to safety only to discover her sister did not make it out. The clinician recognized a subtle emphasis on the statement that she had yelled "Run!" and said, "You must have been really angry at your sister for not running when you told her to." Susan animatedly said "Yes!" then returned to her original flat affect.

Susan was directed to send the Susan doll back into the cafeteria to tell the Janie doll how angry she was that Janie did not run. She did this despondently, even the second time when she was urged to say it more forcefully. She was then told that she was saying it like a wimp and that the Janie doll was probably ignoring her because of it. She was told (in a forceful tone) to say it like she meant it. The Susan doll grabbed the Janie doll by the arms, shook her, yelled "I told you to run!" shook her some more, then slapped her and dragged her out of the cafeteria as she ran out.

Susan became animated and remained so for the rest of the session. She was then able to engage in grief play. She put Janie in a coffin, but declined when asked if she wanted to say something about Janie the way that sometimes people do at funerals. She was given the chance to let someone else speak about Janie. Susan spontaneously made two lines of mourners; each line took a turn at going up to say something about Janie. The first line talked about what a mean, bad, and yukky girl Janie was. The second line said loving and nice things and talked about how much Janie would be missed.

Before the lines finished, Susan elaborately built and fussed over a tomb using blocks in the same shape as the cafeteria table but too strong to fall down. Janie would be protected from getting smashed while in this structure. She placed Janie inside to protect her, then let the lines of mourners finish their eulogies. In the end, she hugged the Janie doll to herself and placed her back into the tomb.

CONCLUSION

There is statistical evidence of the effectiveness of a direct screening interview and primarily clinical evidence of the effectiveness of the clinical methods described in this chapter. All of the children at the school in south Los Angeles where the sniper attack occurred were seen in a classroom exercise. A sample of the children was interviewed using the CPTS-RI (16-item original version) at 1 and 14 months following their experience. An additional group of children was sampled at 14 months. In a recent analysis of these two groups of children, those who were interviewed initially showed significantly fewer symptoms than those with comparable exposures who were interviewed only at 14 months after the event.

Currently, there are no systematic studies of the use of these specialized treatment techniques. The reports of children and adults who have undergone this treatment suggest its success. Parents have relayed messages from close friends asking what was done to the children because they were happier than before the traumatic incident. Adults and adolescents have suggested the same results for themselves. In fact, the achievement of a sense of success before completion of treatment sometimes poses a difficulty: Children and adults often save the intensity of their senses of rage or intense helplessness until other issues have been resolved in treatment. When they feel improved in some ways beyond previous levels of functioning, they may wish to leave treatment prematurely both to avoid the intensity of the unresolved issues and because it no longer seems urgent to resolve anything.

There are difficulties for systematic assessment. Where possible, all moderately to severely traumatized children have been seen in treatment interviews. The only ethically reasonable way to assign children randomly to treatment versus nontreatment groups is when there are insufficient numbers of trained clinicians to treat the numbers of affected children. Such studies may be possible in Kuwait and the former Yugoslavian Republics and in other war-torn nations.

REFERENCES

American Psychiatric Association. (1994). *Diagnostic and statistical manual of mental disorders* (4th ed.). Washington, DC: Author.

Ayalon, O. (1979). Community oriented preparation for emergency: COPE. *Death Education, 3,* 227–244.

Delunas, E. (1992). *Survival games personalities play.* Carmel, CA: Sunflower Ink.

Eth, S., & Pynoos, R. (1985a). Interaction of trauma and grief in childhood. In S. Eth &

R. Pynoos (Eds.), *Post-Traumatic Stress Disorder in children.* Washington, DC: American Psychiatric Press.

Eth, S., & Pynoos, R. (1985b). Psychiatric interventions with children traumatized by violence. In D. H. Schetky & E. P. Benedik (Eds.), *Emerging issues in child psychiatry and the law.* New York: Brunner/Mazel.

Frederick, C., Pynoos, R., & Nader, K. (1992). The Childhood Post-Traumatic Stress Reaction Index (CPTS-RI), a copyrighted inventory.

Friedrich, W., Grambsch, P., Broughton, D., Kuiper, J., & Beilke, R. L. (1991). Normative sexual behavior in children. *Pediatrics, 88,* 456–462.

Furman, R. (1973). A child's capacity for mourning. In E. J. Anthony & C. Koupernik (Eds.), *The child in his family: The impact of disease and death.* New York: Wiley.

Galente, R., & Foa, D. (1986). An epidemiological study of psychic trauma and treatment effectiveness for children after a natural disaster. *Journal of the American Academy of Child Psychiatry, 25,* 357–363.

Herman, J. L. (1992). Complex PTSD: A syndrome in survivors of prolonged and repeated trauma. *Journal of Traumatic Stress, 5,* 377–391.

Johnson, M. K., & Foley, M. A. (1984). Differentiating fact from fantasy: The reliability of children's memory. *Journal of Social Issues, 40,* 33–50.

Knight-Birnbaum, N. (1988). Therapeutic work with bereaved parents. In S. Altschul (Ed.), *Childhood bereavement and its aftermath.* Emotions and Behavior monographs, No. 8 (pp. 107–143). Madison, CT: International Universities Press.

Krupnick, J. L. (1984). Bereavement during childhood and adolescence. In M. Osterweis, F. Solomon, & M. Green (Eds.), *Bereavement, reactions, consequences and care* (pp. 99–141). Washington, DC: National Academy Press.

Levy, D. M. (1938). Release therapy in young children. *Psychiatry, 1,* 387–390.

Marris, P. (1991). The social construction of uncertainty. In C. M. Parkes, J. Stevenson-Hinde, & P. Marris, (Eds.), *Attachment across the life cycle* (pp. 82–84). New York: Routledge.

Nader, K. (1996). Assessing traumatic experiences in children. In J. Wilson and T. Keane (Eds.), *Assessing psychological trauma and PTSD* (pp. 291–348). New York: Guilford Press.

Nader, K. (1993, October). *Children's traumatic grief reactions.* Paper presented at the annual meeting of the International Society for Traumatic Stress Studies, San Antonio, TX.

Nader, K. (1994a). Countertransference in treating trauma and victimization in childhood. In J. Wilson & J. Lindy (Eds.), *Countertransference in the treatment of Post-Traumatic Stress Disorder* (pp. 179–205). New York: Guilford Press.

Nader, K. (1994b, August). *Children's traumatic grief reactions.* Training workshop presented at Federal Way School District, Federal Way, WA.

Nader, K. (1994c). Psychological first aid for trauma, grief and traumatic grief, a copyrighted document.

Nader, K., Dubrow, N., & Stamm, B. H. (in preparation). *Cultural differences in the treatment of trauma and loss: Honoring differences.* Washington, DC: Taylor & Francis.

Nader, K., & Pynoos, R. (1991). Play and drawing as tools for interviewing traumatized children. In C. Schaeffer, K. Gitlan, & A. Sandgrund (Eds.), *Play, diagnosis and assessment* (pp. 375–389). New York: John Wiley.

Nader, K., & Pynoos, R. (1993). School disaster: Planning and initial interventions. *Journal of Social Behavior and Personality, 8,* 299–320.

Nader, K., Pynoos, R., Fairbanks, L., & Frederick, C. (1990). Children's PTSD reactions one year after a sniper attack at their school. *American Journal of Psychiatry, 147,* 1526–1530.

Nader, K., & Stuber, M. (1992, October). *Catastrophic events vs. catastrophic illness: A comparison of traumatized children.* Workshop presented at the annual meeting of the International Society for Traumatic Stress Studies.

Pynoos, R., & Eth, S. (1986). Witness to violence: The child interview. *Journal of the American Academy of Child Psychiatry, 25,* 306–319.

Pynoos, R., Frederick, C., Nader, K., Arroyo, W., Eth, S., Nunez, W., Steinberg, A., & Fairbanks, L. (1987). Life threat and posttraumatic stress in school age children. *Archives of General Psychiatry, 44*, 1057–1063.

Pynoos, R., & Nader, K. (1988). Psychological first aid and treatment approach for children exposed to community violence: Research implications. *Journal of Traumatic Stress, 1*, 445–473.

Pynoos, R. S., & Nader, K. (1989). Children's memory and proximity to violence. *Journal of the American Academy of Child and Adolescent Psychiatry, 28*, 236–241.

Pynoos, R. S., & Nader, K. (1990). Children's exposure to violence and traumatic death. *Annals of Psychiatry, 20*, 334–344.

Pynoos, R. S., & Nader, K. (1993). Issues in the treatment of posttraumatic stress in children and adolescents. In J. P. Wilson and B. Raphael (Eds.), *International handbook of traumatic stress syndromes* (pp. 535–549). New York: Plenum.

Pynoos, R., Nader, K., & March, J. (1991). Post traumatic stress disorder in children and adolescents. In J. Weiner (Ed.), *Comprehensive textbook of child and adolescent psychiatry* (pp. 339–348).

Raphael, B. (1983). *The anatomy of bereavement.* New York: Basic Books.

Roth, S. (1992, October). *DESNOS: Complicated PTSD.* Paper presented at the annual meeting of the International Society for Traumatic Stress Studies, Los Angeles, CA.

Stamm, B. H. (Ed.). (1996). *Measurement of stress, trauma and adaptation.* Lutherville, MD: Sidran Press.

Stuber, M., & Nader, K. (1995). Psychiatric sequelae in adolescent bone marrow transplant survivors: Implications for psychotherapy. *The Journal of Psychotherapy Practice and Research, 4*, 30–42.

Stuber, M., Nader, K., Yasuda, P., Pynoos, R., & Cohen, S. (1991). Stress responses after pediatric bone marrow transplantation: Preliminary results of a prospective, longitudinal study. *Journal of the American Academy of Child and Adolescent Psychiatry, 50*, 407–414.

Terr, L. (1979). Children of Chowchilla: Study of psychic trauma. *Psychoanalytic Study of the Child, 34*, 547–623.

Terr, L. C. (1991). Childhood traumas: An outline and overview. *American Journal of Psychiatry, 148*, 10–20.

van der Kolk, B. A., Roth, S., Pelcovitz, D., & Mandel, F. S. (1992). *Disorders of extreme stress: Results from the DSM-IV field trials for PTSD.* Unpublished manuscript.

Yule, W., & Udwin, O. F. (1991). Screening child survivors for post-traumatic stress disorders: Experiences from the 'Jupiter' sinking. *British Journal of Clinical Psychology, 30*, 279–295.

Chapter 9

Death of a Co-Worker: Facilitating the Healing

Mary Beth Williams and Lasse A. Nurmi

Healing after the death of a co-worker is an individual process that can be influenced by a variety of strategies and factors. This chapter examines organizational and individual therapeutic interventions and provides conclusions concerning the efficacy of debriefing and treatment.

On a Monday morning in September at approximately 8:00 a.m., a soldier doing his obligatory service, on leave from the military hospital where he was being treated for mental problems, approached the 23-year-old male receptionist of a large resort. He intended to rob the facility and had a handgun. A second receptionist (female, aged 30) was also present. When the soldier attempted to enter the back room, the male receptionist tried to prevent his entry, against company policy, which stated that employees should offer no resistance in case of robbery. The offender shot the young man several times, killing him immediately. The second receptionist, wounded in her side and arm, escaped into a bathroom. A courier heard the shots, arrived on the scene, and called the resort doctor. The doctor pronounced the young man dead.

At 5:00 p.m. the same day, the director of the resort called all personnel together (about 200 people) to inform them of the incident. The chief of the local police was also present to give the facts. Four days later, two large debriefings were held, led by the resort psychologist.

The receptionist co-worker, when interviewed, criticized this debriefing procedure. First, she thought it occurred too long after the incident. Second, the group sizes were too large to allow individual participation; a larger number of smaller sessions should have been held, she thought. Third, the courier who had heard the shots was particularly upset and cried during both the general meeting and the debriefing session she attended. The debriefer, however, did not attend to her needs. Fourth, during the debriefing, when the receptionist offered some sympathy for the offender, her fellow workers were allowed to vent their anger and aggression upon her. (Fortunately, she understood their feelings, because she had volunteered in emergencies with both the fire brigade and the Red Cross.) In conclusion, the worker recommended that the management develop better procedures for debriefing and future critical incidents at this large resort (e.g., suicides of customers, drownings, etc.).

Co-workers from the reception department of the resort spontaneously helped each other by peer debriefing and support—in this instance, a much more effective approach. During the funeral, these personnel sat together and held hands. The murdered young man had been very much loved, and the interviewee was one of several workers aged 30 or older who asked themselves, "Why not me instead of him? He was so young!" The offender was apprehended, tried, and sentenced to 9 years in a hospital for the criminally insane; he would probably be released in 3 to 4 years. All personnel thought his sentence to be too light.

The incident bonded the receptionist unit together. For example, during the interview, four different team members came to check on the employee being interviewed. The conclusion in this case was that spontaneously organized peer support and talking while working together provided more healing than badly planned and run debriefings.

SOCIAL SUPPORT

The death of a co-worker drastically alters the social environment of those who remain behind. If many employees were intimate with the deceased co-worker, their social networks can be devastated and suffer from network stress (Jacobs, 1993). However, the environment itself can be a source of support, moderating and mediating the resultant stress. An absence of adequate support may increase the risk of depression and post-traumatic stress disorder (PTSD), as well as reduce self-esteem (Cobb, 1976). Little research examining the role of objective characteristics of the social support system is available (Jacobs, 1993); however, the perception of the supportiveness of the system to those individuals who are grieving the loss, as it fits with the individuals' needs, is important in helping them heal (Vachon & Stylianos, 1988)

The quality of organizational social support for surviving employees may account for differential outcomes in those employees and affect the threshold of sensitivity to the death (Breslau & Davis, 1987). This support may include both emotional and material support, given through provision of information (informational support), financial remuneration for leave taken related to the death (instrumental support), encouragement and reassurance that those who grieve will not be punished (motivational support), and provision of opportunities to talk about the impact of the death (Wills, 1987). Feuer (1994) has observed that social support systems that provide stabilizing strategies for employees can serve as buffers against later reactions. An organization may also make periodic checks on employees most affected by or directly involved with the deaths, helping them to prepare to return to work or even intervening in the system to modify their duties and responsibilities upon return (Hoyt, 1993).

An organization and its management-level representatives must demonstrate a positive, caring response to promote healing. If attitudes of senior staff toward the deceased and toward grieving co-workers are thoughtless, anger and resentment often develop (Manolias & Hyatt-Williams, 1993). When co-workers have been directly involved in a death, or if a death receives high publicity or is controversial or questionable (e.g., murder, suicide), then it is the role of the organization to protect the survivors from unwanted publicity and attention. Organizations with positive attitudes do not judge traumatized employees and permit those closest to the deceased to take psychological breaks or return to duty at their own pace. Such organizations screen out vicarious thrill seekers, give all their employees basic facts, respond to a death compassionately even if it is controversial or if the reputation of the deceased is involved, and expedite administrative and/or criminal investigations.

If at all possible, an organization should have a crisis intervention plan that includes a design to help surviving employees heal. Some organizations have a sincere interest in and genuine concern for their employees. These organizations are aware of the impact of anniversaries of the death, litigation dates, potential for occurrence of similar deaths, and the significance of other life crises upon their employees and make allowances for employee performance and absence accordingly.

Just as family type may moderate the degree of development of a secondary traumatic stress reaction among wives of trauma survivor Vietnam veterans, so may type of work environment moderate the development of a secondary post-traumatic stress reaction (PTSR) or disorder among employees. Wives from conflict-oriented families whose husbands had PTSD from war experiences reported higher levels of psychiatric symptoms and social dysfunction than wives from non-conflict-oriented families (Waysman, Mikulincer, Solomon, & Weisenberg, 1993). The family, and perhaps also organizational, characteristics that have been most frequently found to lead to negative outcomes are rigidity (Williams & Williams, 1985), scapegoating of the secondary victim, and discouraging expression of traumatic symptoms (Figley & Sprenkle, 1978; Shehan, 1987). It is possible that employees who work in conflict-ridden organizations are more likely to have secondary PTSD than employees who work in organizations that encourage and support expressions of grief. If a death is ignored, if a deceased employee is quickly replaced (as if forgotten), or if persons grieving a death are isolated or discounted, secondary reactions are more likely to develop. Working in a caring, people-oriented environment contributes to resistance to traumatic stress. Thus the habitual patterns of interaction of an organization may influence the healing of its employees greatly.

USE OF DEBRIEFING

Debriefing surviving employees following a co-worker's death is a specific type of organizational consultation designed to help those employees cope with tragedy and increase their effectiveness by teaching them skills to use in the future, should a similar situation occur (Mendoza, 1993). Critical Incident Stress Debriefing (CISD) may be primarily didactic and teaching (Dunning, 1988) or may focus on the psychological impact of the death on other employees, utilizing either a cognitive restructuring model (Bergman & Queen, 1986) or a catharsis and ventilation model (Mitchell, 1988). According to Hoyt (1993), it generally involves phases of:

1   establishing ground rules and confidentiality;
2   discussing facts of the incident;
3   discussing perceptions, reactions, and feelings about the incident;
4   educating about PTSR, crisis reactions, and coping tactics; and
5   summarizing and referral.

Persons directly involved in or affected by an incident should be required to attend a debriefing. At times, individual debriefings are also necessary. It is essential to debrief co-workers following a line-of-duty death, as well as a violent or unexpected death caused by accident, medical emergency, murder, or suicide. One of the primary responsibilities of a debriefing team is *buffering*, that is, stabilizing individuals who are in acute crisis and need immediate intervention.

In some instances debriefing may be conceptualized as the means to give comfort and solace once provided by organized religion. As one psychiatrist said, debriefers are "today's priests who kick-start the grief process" (L. Nurmi, personal communication, 1992). In other instances, debriefers and clergy work together to provide psychological relief.

If the job setting involves frequent opportunities for critical incident stress, formalized post-trauma procedures should be developed and instituted. Procedures that are part of an institutional culture are more likely to be accepted by personnel because they indicate that management has a concern for the welfare of its employees.

Numerous debriefing models exist. The model used almost exclusively by many European countries is the Mitchell Model (Dyregrov, 1992; Mitchell & Everly, 1993). This model was designed as a "direct, action oriented crisis intervention process . . . a group psychological debriefing intervention . . . based upon core principles of crisis intervention . . . designed to . . . assist personnel in recovering as quickly as possible from the stress associated" with a crisis event (Mitchell & Everly, 1993, pp. 3, 7). CISD is "a useful tool for stress mitigation when applied properly" and can "accelerate recovery processes in (normal, emotionally healthy) people who are experiencing stress reactions to abnormal traumatic events" (Mitchell & Everly, 1993, pp. 59, 61).

The debriefing process is not psychotherapy; it is a team approach conducted by trained team members who have rehearsed together in advance and led by a trained mental health professional. Ideally, it should occur within 24 to

72 hours after a critical event for groups of 10 to 15 persons. It is not a cure-all for traumatic events but is one of many potentially helpful techniques. The principles of debriefing are immediacy (as quickly as possible), proximity (as close to the scene as safety allows), and expectancy (for recovery and that one's reactions after the event are normal, instilled in the victim by the debriefer).

Teams should arrive at the scene of an incident in enough time to familiarize themselves with the critical event and review any written, audio, or video information, however inaccurate or incomplete. When participants arrive for the debriefing, team members should circulate and meet them, entering into conversations containing a mixture of casual and event-related topics. This process helps participants (and team members) relax and begins to initiate trust in the team. Once this mingling has been accomplished, the team should excuse itself and plan its strategy in a short meeting, making sure that the debriefing begins at the scheduled time.

MODELS

The Mitchell Model has seven stages. During the Introduction (Phase 1), members introduce themselves and describe the parameters of debriefing. Participants are given the opportunity to point out anyone who does not belong or who is not suitable to attend. Principles of confidentiality are explained and enforced (e.g., no written notes or recordings may be made by participants). The debriefing generally lasts between 2 and 3 hours, without a formal break. If a participant must take a rest room break, he or she is asked to return immediately. It is not necessary that each and every participant talk about his or her feelings, reactions, or experiences.

Phase 2 is the Fact Phase. During this phase, participants are encouraged to discuss the facts of the incident and the relationships they had to the event (role, location, experiences). During this phase, participants "begin to tell their stories" (Mitchell & Everly, 1993, p. 93). If participants begin to reveal their emotions during this phase, it indicates the level of impact of the event upon them. It is important that team members validate the emotions but not focus on them.

Phase 3, the Thought Phase, begins immediately after the Fact Phase. In this phase the leaders ask participants to relate their first thoughts upon arrival at the site of the event, when they heard about the event, or when they became involved in the event. Sensory impressions and impressions of time are important to talk about, as well. This phase is the transition phase between cognitive facts and personal emotions.

Phase 4 is the Reaction Phase. During this phase, the majority of talking is done by participants, although leaders may ask, "What was the worst thing you experienced/felt [during the event]?" (Dyregrov, 1992). The order of participation during this phase is unstructured. Emotions may be shown subtly or openly, depending on the group or individual. Depressed, quiet persons are encouraged, but not forced, to talk. Participants are also encouraged to reveal the event's impact on their families and whether their families understand what they have gone through.

Phase 5 is the Symptom Phase, another transition phase. During this phase, team leaders move the group away from emotional reactions to more cognitive concerns. Participants are now asked to describe any stress-related symptoms they may have had during or after the event, up until the debriefing itself. This phase is generally fairly short in duration.

Phase 6 is the Teaching Phase. In this phase, team members actively point out that symptoms are part of typical PTSRs. Team members teach the participants about common courses of reactions and potential symptoms that may still occur. The team also teaches the group simple survival techniques, including ways to relax, ways to change one's diet or routine, and other strategies. Participants are also encouraged to share ways in which they can help one another as well as share their experiences with fellow workers who were not involved directly in the event.

The final phase of the model, Phase 7, is the Re-Entry Phase. The team leader summarizes and reviews what has occurred, answers questions, and closes the discussion. The team provides appropriate handouts about PTSR and PTSD and, if indicated, sets up the date for a follow-up meeting in about 3 to 4 weeks. Each member of the team makes a summary comment. After the close of the debriefing, team members may target individuals who have been exceptionally silent or exceptionally emotional. In this sense, the debriefing has served as a screening tool to determine who needs a supportive phone call or visit or, in rare cases, individual counseling. The team also may recommend counseling at the follow-up meeting for those participants who continue to have symptoms or who have had remarkable personality changes. Refreshments are served at the conclusion of the debriefing, as well. After participants leave, the team has a post-debriefing meeting to explore the process, assign specific follow-up tasks, and debrief themselves (Mitchell & Everly, 1993).

Another organizationally oriented debriefing model begins with the debriefer's assessment of the potential for action (Weisbord, 1987). In a crisis, employees are frequently in an anxious state of confusion. The debriefer must decide how to make a contribution while getting the whole organizational system into the room (or whatever location is feasible) for the debriefing process. The focus is on immediate survival as well as future coping, and the debriefer helps employees structure the tasks that revolve around the critical event: who talks to the media, who removes the deceased person's belongings, who attends the funeral. During the debriefing, the debriefer ascertains which employees have had the closest relationship to the deceased and may need additional help; who makes organizational decisions; who has skill and experience in dealing with death; and what are the ongoing environmental demands of the business, in spite of the death. The debriefer repeatedly gives as much information about the event (facts) as he or she knows or has knowledgeable persons present those facts as needed. Fisher (1991) found that police officers in general required more data and facts about death than non-law-enforcement workers. In some instances, co-workers require very little information because they are emotionally incapable of handling more. Colleagues of the deceased employee should set the "pace, timing, and level of detail" they receive during debriefings (p. 83).

Debriefing is more effective if the debriefing team has at least two members. As one leads, the other can observe and determine who needs additional help. It is also important to do follow-up with the organization at a later date, often several weeks later, to assess levels of recovery and do an evaluation of the debriefing's effectiveness.

In Nordic countries, debriefing has become part of the public health care system. At the present time, about 100 teams exist, and within 2 years there will be enough trained teams to service the entire country. Services are gratis, and teams work in any environment as needed, ranging from police settings to the social sector to Lutheran Church (the state church) settings. In the United States as well, many local mental health systems have procedures in place to assist with critical incident stress in the workplace. Smith (1986), describing the role of the San Diego County Mental Health Department's response to a variety of disasters ranging from an air crash to a massacre at a fast food restaurant, recommended the following interventions:

1 Services need to be readily and quickly available, publicized from a single access point.

2 Both crisis intervention (debriefing) and counseling referral sources need to be available.

3 Services need to be provided in the language of those involved.

4 Outreach at the job site, particularly if the incident occurred there, needs to he implemented.

5 Services need to be given beyond working hours, if needed.

6 Services involving more than one debriefer or agency need to be co-ordinated and divided appropriately, and personnel most directly suited to the incident or most appropriately trained need to be utilized.

7 Debriefers also need to be debriefed.

8 Materials need to be available on site; people appreciate handouts.

9 Each incident has its own characteristics that include cultural needs, personnel affected, and numbers of persons affected.

Systematic, controlled evaluations of the effectiveness of these debriefing models and specific debriefing interventions are beginning to be undertaken. For example, investigation will take place into the methods used to debrief the crew and passengers in a recent maritime disaster. However, such research is difficult. Weisaeth (1983) found that detailed recountings of a fire disaster within 2 days after event did not seem to prevent the development of PTSD in substantial numbers of individuals. Perhaps, however, without the interviewing and debriefing, levels of PTSD would have been even higher. Creamer (1990) found that significant levels of PTSD occurred in persons exposed to a mass shooting and homicide, even when those persons were given extensive debriefings and mental health support. Although many professionals (e.g., Pynoos & Nader, 1990) have argued for the necessity and advisability of early intervention, debriefing several weeks after an event is better than no debriefing at all.

DEVELOPMENT OF PEER SUPPORT AND PEER INTERVENTIONS

As the receptionist at the spa expressed, support among her own peer group (reference group) led to less severe survivor reactions. The employees of the spa had an unwritten role obligation to help and to depend upon one another. They saw themselves as interdependent not only as a necessity of job function but out of genuine caring and concern for one another. They developed their own rituals (e.g., at the funeral and afterwards at the spa) to demonstrate this concern. They believed the peer support was more effective in moderating the effects of the stressor event than the support offered by supervisors and friends.

Critical incident stress plans for organizations need to recognize and foster the development of peer protocols. This strategy fits with Mitchell's (1988) hypothesis that debriefing is even more effective when based on the peer support network and Solomon's (1989) observation that the stronger the victim's non-kin support systems, the greater the ability of the individual to recover. In other words, non-kin support networks safeguard fellow workers from harm (Lindy & Grace, 1985).

Development of a peer counseling program is a team-building activity. Peer counselors have the "trust, empathy and rapport" of peers and, if they know each other well, can have a great positive impact on one another (Feuer, 1994, p. 19). Peer counselors can assist with debriefings and make referrals for counseling, matching clients and clinicians. They can be assigned to liaison duties with next of kin or other survivors. Finally, they can be gatekeepers, recognizing signs of post-traumatic stress in peers after debriefings have occurred (Mitchell, 1983).

ACTS OF CONDOLENCE

Acts of condolence are healing actions honoring the life of the deceased given without expectations of gratitude (Zunin & Zunin, 1991). These legacy-producing acts may include writing a sympathy letter, eulogizing through a newspaper article (Lasso, 1991), noting special qualities of the deceased, recounting a special memory or past experience, or offering assistance to the deceased person's family (e.g., help with driving, house-sitting during a wake, making phone calls, baby-sitting).

Acts of condolence from an organization should be aesthetically pleasing and personal rather than rigid and formal. They need to highlight the positive contributions of the employee to the organization as well as positive aspects of the employee's character and personality. If possible, they should include specific offers of assistance (e.g., help with insurance, death benefits, personal effects) and include the name of a contact person. Condolences should be offered to the families of all deceased employees, even if the death is the result of suicide.

Offering condolence during the funeral is also important. Manning (1985) has noted that a funeral is a time for people to comfort one another (as did the resort employees) while celebrating the significance of the life of the deceased and dealing with the issue of death. Rituals in honor of the deceased are symbolic acts of remembrance. Certain types of rituals may be developed by an organization for use during or after the funeral services (e.g., planting a tree in honor of the deceased, placing the name of a slain officer on the front wall of the police academy). Rando (1993) and Catherall (1992) have noted that rituals make an active statement and challenge passive grieving. They provide a means of ventilation to release emotions, sanction and validate those emotions, and channel them into an activity that has a beginning, end, and clear focus. Rituals are tools to express loss in a symbolic fashion and reinforcing that the loss has actually occurred, thereby helping survivors to work through the mourning process.

TRAINING AND PSYCHOEDUCATION

Raphael (1991) has noted a substantial amount of evidence describing the protective effects of training and practice in lessening traumatic effects of critical events. Offering lectures, classes, and providing literature (bibliotherapy) to persons in high-stress occupations about the signs and symptoms of PTSR and PTSD is a proactive way to give support to employees (Williams, 1993). Holt (1985) has noted that education "often improves . . . attendance . . . leads to increased efficiency and safety . . . [and] results in awareness and prevention" (p. 26). Training can begin with lectures, demonstrations, and discussions and move on to role plays and skills practice. Courses for spouses and partners of persons in high-stress jobs can be helpful as well. All educators, for example, need training about stress and the impact of trauma. It is inevitable that they will encounter the death of a student, colleague, or parent of a student. If they are appropriately trained when such a crisis occurs, they will be more likely to respond in a positive fashion.

Training for employees concerning safety measures (e.g., security, how to deal with a robbery, surveillance techniques), organizational policies, and environmental stress factors is very helpful. Such training is particularly important after a critical incident; in many instances, employees must return to the site of a traumatic event to perform their duties. It is a normal response, of course, to want to avoid that setting (Creamer et al., 1993). If training about safety measures and PTSR and PTSD is not given, the return may be problematic and may result in early retirement or poor job performance.

SUPPORTIVE COUNSELING, POST-TRAUMATIC COUNSELING, AND INDIVIDUAL THERAPY

When PTSD has become chronic, more intense treatment may be necessary. Treatment may be individual or group-based, or it may combine modalities; it may be conducted in an outpatient or inpatient setting. Whatever the modality or setting, treatment needs to be trauma-based and to involve both cognitive and behavioral techniques and strategies of intervention. Treatment may be eclectic, with elements of hypnotherapy, short-term psychodynamic psychotherapy, or (if indicated) long-term therapy. A major component of therapy is to extract "as detailed an account as possible of the traumatic experience—bringing emotions out into the open and making avoidance impossible. Use is also made of leave-taking rituals sometimes in combination with anti-depressives" to help relieve overpowering emotions. (Gersons & Carlier, 1994, p. 15).

According to Gersons and Carlier (1994, p. 16), the aim of PTSD treatment is to "reactivate the coping process by emphasizing 'turning passive into active,' through regaining control of one's own life, one's own emotions, and restoring trust in others." If the individual is in a state of post-traumatic decline, treatment initially aims to help him or her regain some sense of control over reactions and behaviors before processing the trauma or traumas that have devastated her or him.

Literature describing the efficacy of psychotherapy for treatment of complications of bereavement is limited (Jacobs, 1993). There have been some studies indicating that professional therapeutic interventions are helpful to individuals at risk for developing further disorders, including PTSD. Marmar and colleagues (1988), for example, found that brief psychodynamic individual therapy can be beneficial to such individuals. Jacobs (1993, p. 281) has written that all psychotherapeutic treatment models in the literature incorporate "concepts of adaptation as background theory or emphasize the identification of current problems and their solution as a task of therapy." He has also noted that the basic goal of psychotherapy for acute bereavement is the reduction of "the mystery, fear, and sense of helplessness that accompanies the experience of bereavement" (p. 239). The process is "basically a process of listening and teaching" (p. 239) as persons at risk for PTSR and PTSD talk about their grief and traumatic reactions and as therapists educate them about the normal post-traumatic responses to death. Psychoeducation, including education about trauma and traumatic distress, is an important component of such therapy.

At times, bereaved individuals may also join facilitator- or peer-led support groups. In these groups, members share experiences about their co-worker's death, learn about grief and post-traumatic stress, and help one another cope with the changes that death brings. Support groups provide "education, advocacy, and friendship" (Jacobs, 1993, p. 240). Part of their function is to teach members how to maintain a relationship with the deceased co-worker by both remembering and saying good-bye.

The exact course, length, and focus of treatment, however, depend on the needs of the individual. A generic model for the treatment of PTSD that encompasses four stages—encounter and education; exploration of the trauma and its impact; skill building; and client empowerment, evaluation, and termination—has been proposed (Williams & Sommer, 1994). Each stage is characterized by a series of steps to serve as guidelines for treatment; however, rigid adherence to them is neither necessary nor desirable.

This model begins with the establishment of safety within the intervention relationship and of beginning levels of control over behaviors and emotions. Trauma work must not be done unless the clients feel secure and stable enough to endure the pain of recounting the events and experiencing the emotions associated with them. Post-traumatic therapy recognizes that the most effective method for resolving traumatic experiences is talking about the trauma with a concerned other. Once the work of trauma remembering and expressing has been done, then clients can begin to work on belief change, reentry into the social environment, and building of intimate relationships. A major goal of trauma-focused therapy is to help clients go beyond the traumatic death, putting that death into the past, recognizing that it will always have a place in their lives. This treatment protocol has been described in more detail in Williams and Sommer (1994).

Few controlled studies or reviews of treatment programs for chronic PTSD have been published (Hyer, McCranie, & Peralme, 1993). This is particularly the case for studies involving the use of cognitive processing of trauma via education, exposure, and reattribution. Blake (1993) has observed that behavioral studies are overrepresented and little has been written about psychodynamic and other therapies.

Resick, Jordan, Girelli, Hutter, and Harhoefer-Dvorak (1988) compared assertion training, stress inoculation, and supportive psychotherapy plus education in the treatment of rape victims and found that all three treatments led to "significant improvements in anxiety and depression, but no treatment was superior to any other" (p. 14). Implosive therapy has also been found to reduce symptoms of depression, impulsivity, guilt, fear, distress, intrusive memories, and avoidant behavior (Keane, Fairbank, Caddell, & Zimering, 1989; Saigh, 1987). Some clinicians advocate the use of both desensitization and abreaction (exposure) of trauma and integration (reattribution) and reappraisal (Brende, 1985).

Documented knowledge of what works and how it works, however, is lacking. It appears that treatment reduces arousal, startle, anger and intrusive symptoms of PTSD but, as Blake (1993) has written, "it is not clear whether these treatments also reduced negative symptoms of PTSD, i.e. numbing, alienation, and restricted affect" (p. 16). Studies of treatment techniques and their efficacy are therefore necessary in a wide variety of settings over a period of time. Although a variety of models describing phases of treatment exist (e.g., Herman, 1992; Loo, 1993; Williams & Sommer, 1994), the "validation and ordering of the curative components of PTSD treatment has not been adequately examined. [Models] represent clinical science at best. . . . The need for the mapping and ordering of the elements of an effective treatment process for PTSD is now ready for study" (Hyer, McCranie, & Peralme, 1993, p. 3).

CONCLUSION

There is a wide range of service and therapeutic interventions that can facilitate healing following the death of a co-worker. This chapter has addressed the use of rituals, social support, crisis intervention, peer support, psychoeducational strategies, and counseling methods, with a primary focus on debriefing. Debriefings in organizations should occur in all cases of sudden death. In law-enforcement organizations, debriefings should also occur when the death is that of a perpetrator killed by a police officer and, if possible, in cases of wounding of perpetrators or officers. The type and structure of debriefing depends on the size and culture of the organization.

Immediate or fairly prompt debriefing is just a start in the treatment process. It is a good way to begin the reconstruction of life and the world after the shock of death occurs. For some people, debriefing is the kick-start to recovery, allowing for the process of grief and bereavement. It helps people identify how the meaning of life has been shaken and guides the path to recovery from a loss. For others, debriefing merely opens the black box of memory or brings previous experiences that have been unresolved into focus. In such instances, treatment for the ensuing PTSR or PTSD is essential.

In an atmosphere of brief therapy and managed care, however, many persons are not being given the opportunity to heal from traumatic events and deaths. Four to six therapy sessions often cannot heal the pain of the senseless murder of one's partner or co-worker. Trauma must be processed if persons are to heal, and processing cannot occur unless a client feels safe. It takes time to build safety for many traumatized individuals—time that increasingly is not allocated in the limited number of treatment sessions authorized by insurance and managed care. It appears that traumatologists must give voice to the needs of their clients if healing is to occur.

To reiterate the message of Thomas Mann (quoted in Stillman, 1986, p. 145), "A man's dying is more the survivor's affair than his own." Human beings tend to live in a vacuum until the death of someone they know reminds them of their own mortality. In today's world of violence, terrorism, and fast-paced living, every company, institution, and organization needs to be ready to meet the death of an employee with a predetermined plan. When this is the case, the deceased can be accorded the best possible recognition, ceremony, and legacy, and survivors will be given the best possible support.

REFERENCES

Bergman, L. H., & Queen, T. R. (1986, May). Responding to critical incident stress. *Fire Chief*, 52–56.

Blake, D. D. (1993). Treatment outcome research on post traumatic stress disorder. *Clinical Newsletter, 3*(2), 14–17.

Brende, J. P. (1985). The use of hypnosis in posttraumatic conditions. In W. E. Kelly (Ed.), *Post-traumatic stress disorder and the war veteran patient* (pp. 193–210). New York: Brunner/ Mazel.

Breslau, N., & Davis, G. C. (1987). Post-traumatic stress disorder: The stressor criterion. *The Journal of Nervous and Mental Disease, 175*(5), 255–264.

Catherall, D. R. (1992). *Back from the brink: A family guide to overcoming traumatic stress*. New York: Bantam Books.

Cobb, S. (1976). Social support as a moderator of life stress. *Psychosomatic Medicine, 38*, 300–314.

Creamer, M. (1990). Post-traumatic stress disorder: Some diagnostic and clinical issues. *Australian and New Zealand Journal of Psychiatry, 24*, 517–522.

Creamer, M., Burgess, P. Y., Buckingham, W., & Pattison, P. (1993). Posttrauma reactions following a multiple shooting: A retrospective study and methodological inquiry. In J. P. Wilson & B. Raphael (Eds.), *International handbook of traumatic stress syndromes* (pp. 201–212). New York: Plenum.

Dunning, C. (1988). Intervention strategies for emergency workers. In M. Lystad (Ed.), *Mental health response to mass emergencies: Theory and practice*. New York: Brunner/Mazel.

Dyregrov, A. (1992). *Katastrof-psykologi*. Lund, Sweden: Studentlitteratur.

Feuer, B. (1994). The association of flight attendants employee assistance program responds to workplace trauma: A dynamic model. In M. B. Williams & J. F. Sommer, Jr. (Eds.), *Handbook of post-traumatic therapy* (pp. 310–324). Westport, CT: Greenwood Press.

Figley, C. R., & Sprenkle, D. H. (1978). Delayed stress response syndrome: Family therapy indications. *Journal of Marriage and Family Counseling, 4*, 53–60.

Fisher, C. R. (1991). Critical incident trauma treatment of an officer/son of a slain officer. In J. T. Reese, J. M. Horn, & C. Dunning (Eds.), *Critical incidents in policing* (rev., pp. 83–84). Washington, DC: U.S. Government Printing Office.

Gersons, B. P. R., & Carlier, I. V. E. (1994). Treatment of work-related trauma in police officers: Post-traumatic stress disorder and post-traumatic decline. In M. B. Williams & J. F. Sommer, Jr. (Eds.), *Handbook of post-traumatic therapy* (pp. 325–333). Westport, CT: Greenwood Press.

Herman, J. L. (1992). Trauma and recovery. New York: Basic Books.

Holt, F. (1985, November). Post-traumatic stress disorder and the firefighter. *Fire Engineering*, 24–26.

Hoyt, D. P. (1993, February). *The effects of traumatic stress on public safety personnel*. Paper presented at the IATC Conference, San Diego, CA.

Hyer, L., McCranie, E. W., & Peralme, L. (1993, Spring). Psychotherapeutic treatment of chronic PTSD. *PTSD Research Quarterly, 4*(2), 1–3.

Jacobs, S. (1993). *Pathologic grief: Maladaptation to loss*. Washington, DC: American Psychiatric Press.

Keane, T. M., Fairbank, J. A., Caddell, J. M., & Zimering, R. T. (1989). Implosive (flooding) therapy reduces symptoms of PTSD in Vietnam combat veterans. *Behavior Therapy, 20*, 245–260.

Lasso (1991, June). *Tribute to Mary Lee Tatum*. Falls Church, VA: George Mason High School.

Lindy, J., & Grace, M. (1985). The recovery environment: Continuing stressor versus a healing psychological space. In B. J. Sowder (Ed.), *Disasters and mental health: Selected contemporary perspectives*. Rockville, MD: National Institutes of Mental Health.

Loo, C. M. (1993). An integrative-sequential treatment model for posttraumatic stress disorder: A case study of the Japanese American internment and redress. *Clinical Psychology Review, 13*, 89–117.

Manning, D. (1985). *Comforting those who grieve: A guide for helping others.* San Francisco, CA: Harper.

Manolias, M. B., & Hyatt-Williams, A. (1993). Effects of postshooting experiences on police-authorized firearms officers in the United Kingdom. In J. P. Wilson & B. Raphael (Eds.), *International handbook of traumatic stress syndromes* (pp. 385–394). New York: Plenum.

Marmar, C. R., Horowitz, M. J., & Weiss, D. S., et al. (1988). A controlled trial of brief psycho-therapy and mutual help group treatment of conjugal bereavement. *American Journal of Psychiatry, 145*, 203–209.

Mendoza, D. W. (1993, July/August). A review of Gerald Caplan's theory and practice of mental health consultation. *Journal of Counseling and Development, 71*(6), 629–635.

Mitchell, J. T. (1983). When disaster strikes: The critical incident stress debriefing process. *Journal of Emergency Medical Services, 8*, 36–39.

Mitchell, J. T. (1988). The history, status and future of critical incident stress debriefings. *Journal of Emergency Medical Services, 13*, 49–52.

Mitchell, J. T., & Everly, G. S., Jr. (1993). *Critical incident stress debriefing (CISD): An operations manual for the prevention of traumatic stress among emergency services and disaster workers.* Ellicott City, MD: Chevron.

Pynoos, R., & Nader, R. S. (1990). Children's exposure to violence and traumatic death. *Psychiatric Annals, 20*, 334–344.

Rando, T. A. (1993). *Treatment of complicated mourning.* Champaign, IL: Research Press.

Raphael, B. (1991, June). *Critical appraisal of post trauma mental health services and critical incident stress debriefing.* Paper presented at the Harvard University Conference on Trauma, Boston, MA.

Resick, P. A., Jordan, C. G., Girelli, S. A., Hunter, C. K., & Harhoefer-Dvorak. (1988). A comparative outcome study of behavioral group therapy for sexual assault victims. *Behavior Therapy, 19*, 385–401.

Saigh, P. A. (1987). In vitro flooding of childhood posttraumatic stress disorders: A systematic replication. *Professional School Psychology, 2*, 685–688.

Shehan, C. (1987). Spouse support and Vietnam veterans' adjustment to post-traumatic stress disorder. *Family Relations, 36*, 65–70.

Smith, P. (1986). *Mental health involvement in the aftermath of a disaster or tragedy.* San Diego, CA: Mental Health Association.

Solomon, S. D. (1989). Research issues in assessing disaster's effects. In R. Gist & B. Lubin (Eds.), *Psychosocial aspects of disaster* (pp. 308–340). New York: Wiley.

Stillman, F. (1986). The invisible victims: Myths and realities. In J. T. Reese & H. A. Goldstein (Eds.), *Psychological services for law enforcement* (pp. 143–146). Washington, DC: U.S. Government Printing Office.

Vachon, M. L. S., & Stylianos, S. K. (1988). The role of social support in bereavement. *Journal of Social Issues, 44*, 175–190.

Waysman, M., Mikulincer, M., Solomon, Z., & Weisenberg, M. (1993). Secondary traumatization among wives of posttraumatic combat veterans: A family typology. *Journal of Family Psychology, 7*(1), 104–118.

Weisaeth, L. (1983). *The study of a factory fire.* Doctoral dissertation, University of Oslo, Norway.

Weisbord, M. R. (1987). *Productice workplaces: Organizing and managing for dignity, meaning and community.* San Francisco, CA: Jossey-Bass.

Williams, C. M., & Williams, T. W. (1985). Family therapy for Vietnam veterans. In S. M. Sonnenberg, A. S. Blank, & J. A. Talbott (Eds.), *The stress of war: Recovery in Vietnam veterans* (pp. 195–209). Washington, DC: American Psychiatric Press.

Williams, M. B., & Sommer, J. F., Jr. (1994). Toward the development of a generic model of PTSD treatment. In M. B. Williams & J. F. Sommer, Jr. (Eds.), *Handbook of post-traumatic therapy* (pp. 551–564). Westport, CT: Greenwood Press.

Williams, T. (1993). Trauma and the workplace. In J. P. Wilson & B. Raphael (Eds.), *International handbook of traumatic stress syndromes* (pp. 925–933). New York: Plenum.

Wills, T. A. (1987). Helping seeking as a coping mechanism. In C. R. Snyder & C. E. Ford (Eds.), *Coping with negative life events* (pp. 19–50). New York: Plenum.

Zunin, L. M., & Zunin, H. S. (1991). *The art of condolence: What to write, what to say, what to do at a time of loss.* New York: HarperCollins.

Part Three

Generic Treatment Approaches

Chapter 10

Treating Families with Traumatic Loss: Transitional Family Therapy

Susan H. Horwitz

This chapter uses the experiences of two families to demonstrate the far-reaching effects of the loss of a family member, particularly when families are ill equipped to handle the diverse and powerful forms of expressed and unexpressed grief. Trauma need not be sudden or dramatic to be life-altering and deeply wounding. The death of a family member, especially at a key moment in the family's life cycle, may set into motion a series of events that shift the family from its anticipated course into a new and undesirable territory, potentially leading to generations of dysfunction. Left undetected and therefore untreated, this often unpredictable and unrecognizable burden can traumatize the family system.

The diagnosis and treatment of families suffering from unresolved grief is discussed through the presentation of Transitional Family Therapy, which is based on an ecological perspective, family systems theory, network theory, and the embracing of the wisdom of a family's elders.

> John Wallen, a 14-year-old asthmatic, was first diagnosed with that condition at age 7, shortly after the death of his beloved grandfather. John's physicians deemed his asthma to be mild at that time, and it remained stable for several years.
>
> When John was 11 years old, his father lost his job and was unemployed for a long period of time. John's medical condition began to deteriorate. He would go to school in the morning and by 10:00 a.m. would be in the nurse's office struggling for breath. The nurse would call his father, who was dutifully stationed at home, and Mr. Wallen would come to pick John up.
>
> This daily ritual became a predictable pattern, necessitating a parent conference at the school. All parties consented to put John in a home-tutoring program.

He continued to do poorly, unable to respond even with one-to-one tutoring. Much of his day was spent in bed or at the computer, where he had hooked up a rather elaborate communication system through which he had established relationships with people all over the world.

The family continued to be concerned about his disinterest in his schoolwork and his failing grades. In desperation, they sought help at the University of Rochester Family and Marriage Clinic in Rochester, New York.[1]

POWER OF LOSS IN FAMILIES

Many researchers and clinicians agree that the death of a significant family member is the most powerful emotional experience families face as they journey through time (Bowen, 1976; Carey, 1977; DeFrain, 1991; Derdyn & Waters, 1981; Friedman, 1988; Gelcer, 1983; Hare-Mustin, 1979; Hepworth, Ryder, & Dreyer, 1984; Jensen & Wallace, 1967; Krell & Rabkin, 1979; Kubler-Ross, 1975; McGoldrick & Walsh, 1991; Paul, 1966; Powers, 1977; Seaburn, 1990; Soloman & Hersch, 1979; Stanton, 1977; Stanton & Coleman, 1980; Walsh, 1978; White, 1988; Williamson, 1978). Some families are able to pull together and share the experience of their pain from loss. They are able to bridge life and death by planning for the future with the help of their dying loved one, say good-bye to the deceased, and punctuate this life cycle event in a meaningful way (e.g., a funeral, memorial service, cremation). They may reassign old roles to new people and pay tribute to the deceased on anniversary dates and at other important moments in the family's life experience.

Other families, for many reasons, are unable to accept the changes necessary to make way for the family's forward movement. These families have difficulty letting go in healthy ways; they are unable to give the deceased member a special place outside the daily mainstream of life's demands and joys. These dilemmas prevent or delay reorganization of the family structure into a functional system.

In the case cited above, the therapist and her supervisors hypothesized that the Wallen family might be stuck in the grieving process. The team believed that mourning may not have been completed and that the boy's condition, although certainly medical, might also reflect the family's pain.

In fact, his particular condition was viewed as metaphoric, because the therapist thought of the family as unable to "catch its breath," therefore unable to give new life and meaning to its entire system. Another component of the hypothesis was that perhaps Mr. Wallen was experiencing some level of depression over the loss of his father, which may have been a major contributor to

---

[1]The therapy was conducted at the Family and Marriage Clinic, Division of Family Programs, Department of Psychiatry, University of Rochester Medical Center, Rochester, New York. The author was the therapist, supervised by M. Duncan Stanton, Ph.D., and Judith Landau-Stanton, M.B., Ch.B., D.P.M. This is an actual case in which names and details have been changed to protect the confidentiality of the family.

his dismissal at work. In any case, whether the loss of Mr. Wallen's job was coincidental or connected to the death of his father, it was hypothesized that John's illness was triggered by the loss of his grandfather and exacerbated by the loss of his father's job. This hypothesis was confirmed as the treatment and resolution of John's problems unfolded.

ROLE OF SYMPTOMATOLOGY AS A REACTION TO GRIEF

Few families come to the Clinic reporting that their problem is unresolved grief. In most cases, family members have no idea that there is a possible connection between their current problems and the unfinished business one or more of them may have with a significant deceased family member. They usually present a variety of other problems: anxiety attacks, sleeplessness, marital conflict, adolescent problems, shoplifting, drug and/or alcohol abuse, suicidal behaviors, compulsive disorders, school phobia, psychosomatic illness, and so on. Of course, not every symptom presented to a therapist should be presumed to be related to unresolved grief. However, in a large percentage of cases, incomplete mourning appears to be a significant complicating factor in the resolution of many family problems.

Additionally, grief work can alleviate symptomatology. At the very least, therapy resulting in productive grief work may "clear the air," so that the remaining powerful issues can be dealt with more effectively. At times, it seems as though the therapist is unraveling a knotted ball of fiber. By assisting the family to complete the mourning and grieving processes, the therapist frees the family to think differently about their losses and reevaluate previously held ideas about the meaning and cyclical nature of life and death. Their altered perspective often results in enriched interaction among all family members.

John Wallen was an adopted child, and his biological family's medical history was not readily available, but he almost certainly had a biological predisposition to asthma. It was also apparent that the stress of the loss of his special grandfather, "the family saint," as he was affectionately known in the family, with whom John had had a close and special relationship, "selected" John to become the receptacle of the family's pain.

The therapeutic plan was designed effectively to move the family beyond its "stuck" point in the grieving process. The goal was to intervene with precision between the family's inability to deal with loss (and its concomitant stressors) and the boy's symptoms.

EFFECTS OF LOSS ON FAMILIES

The effects of loss are often traumatic to individuals and families, leaving pain, emptiness, and profound sadness in their wake. The finality of death often leaves surviving individuals disoriented for a time. In some cases they become dysphoric, and in others even immobilized.

The passage of time becomes an important ingredient in how the effects of loss demonstrate themselves in family life. Some people are able to gain perspective and find ways to keep their beloved family members close to them without compromising the quality of their lives. Others are never able to separate their pain from their daily experience, no matter how much time passes. Anniversary dates can be seen as opportunities to reconnect with the deceased in a special way or, alternately, as yet another grievous moment to be borne with pain.

An obvious effect of death is the need of the family members to renegotiate their relationships with one another and with the deceased. If the deceased member was an active contributor to the family, tasks, roles, and responsibilities need to be reassigned. Agreement needs to be reached by all adults in the family as to who should assume which responsibilities. Whereas in many instances it is obvious who will inherit special tasks, there are many situations in which this process of reallocation can be painful, and even traumatic. For example, if family members have preconceived ideas about their new place in the family, only to find themselves outvoted by other, more powerful family members, long-term dissatisfaction and schisms can develop.

Renegotiation of relationships to the deceased is an essential and often a difficult task. Few people effectively complete their unfinished business with the dying family member prior to death.

John had a high IQ and, until sixth grade, had received straight A's on his report cards. His grandfather, a successful businessman, had prided himself on his grandson's achievements, particularly his prowess with the computer. (It was clear to this forward-thinking businessman that computers were the wave of the future.) John's father also had an interest in computers, which he passed on to his son. However, John's father was not successful in his chosen line of work, argued frequently with his wife, and didn't have many friends. In fact, it seemed that the only right thing he had ever done was to adopt this wonderful boy—the son his father could finally be proud of.

As a result of the cross-generational bonding, several relational issues were left unattended when John's grandfather died. First, John and his father had a distant, strained relationship. John had received much of his paternal support from his grandfather, leaving little time or space for John's father to form a close relationship with him. Second, in many ways John's presence in the family, and his achievements, were more highly valued than his father's, creating an inversion in the natural hierarchy, which more typically respects age and experience over youth. Third, it appeared that John was under enormous pressure to achieve as a means of holding on to his respected position in the family and making up for his father's failures. John felt guilty for being more respected than his father, yet compelled to fulfill grandfather's expectations.

Such unnegotiated relationship issues, spanning at least three generations in this case, are a prescription for confusion, rage, and "stuckness." If one subscribes to the theory that "the sins of the father are visited upon the son," it is no wonder that under the intensity of this pressure and stress among the three generations of males, John became symptomatic where he was most biologically vulnerable.

Children's problems are often the focus of a family's entry to treatment, mostly because children have the least amount of life experience in dealing with stress and the fewest coping skills. Young people are sensitive, loyal persons who often sacrifice themselves if they perceive the significant adults in their lives to be fragile or vulnerable (Stanton, 1977).

TRANSITIONAL FAMILY THERAPY: A SYSTEMS APPROACH TO UNRESOLVED GRIEF[2]

Transitional Family Therapy (TFT) is an integrative, interactive, brief (average of 10 sessions) problem-solving therapy approach that includes transgenerational exploration of family patterns (Boszormenyi-Nagy & Spark, 1973; Bowen, 1976, 1978; Kerr & Bowen, 1988; Stanton, 1992) punctuated by transitional therapy (Landau-Stanton, 1985; Landau-Stanton & Clements, 1993). These aspects of TFT assess multigenerational, repeating patterns of difficulty and success in making transitions from one life cycle stage to another (Carter & McGoldrick, 1988; Landau, 1982; Stanton, 1992).

A critical element in the treatment of trauma and loss is the family mapping process, identified in TFT as "transitional mapping" (Landau-Stanton, 1985; Landau-Stanton and Clements, 1993). The transitional map is co-constructed by the family and the therapist. It seeks to explore the family's history and patterns, from as far back as the oldest members can remember to the current generation. The transitional mapping process helps to locate epicenters of trauma and loss, and tracks family members' responses, suggesting to the therapist which interventions may be most helpful. The map becomes a diagnostic, even predictive tool (because patterns usually continue into future generations) as well as a powerful intervention.

Having identified a probable etiology of trauma, the therapist assists the family in grieving effectively, thus relieving its members' pain. As the pain and fear begin to drain away, their symptoms abate, leaving space for the therapist and family members to codesign appropriate methods or tools for managing traumatic events in the future.

Other aspects of TFT call for structural, strategic, and experiential interventions (Aponte & Van Deusen, 1981; Haley, 1976, 1980; Landau-Stanton et al., 1993; Minuchin, 1974; Minuchin & Fishman, 1981; Minuchin, Rosman, & Baker,

---

[2]Transitional Family Therapy (TFT) is an approach to family systems treatment designed by Judith Landau-Stanton and M. Duncan Stanton and expanded upon by their colleagues and faculty of the Family Therapy Training Program. Notable contributions have been made by Susan McDaniel, Ph.D., Pieter leRoux, Phil et Litt, David B. Seaburn, M.S., and Susan H. Horwitz, M.S. For a summary most closely associated with this chapter, see Landau-Stanton et al. (1993) and Seaburn et al. (1995).

1978; Seaburn, Landau-Stanton, & Horwitz, 1995; Stanton, 1981b; Stanton & Landau-Stanton, 1990; Whitaker & Keith, 1981). A strong emphasis is placed on joining (establishing rapport and trust with each family member, subgroups, and the whole system), both initially and throughout treatment; identifying strengths and resources; defining goals, both for treatment and for the family's future; and using the therapy within the room as an active forum for enacting and discovering new ways in which grief can be managed by the family. Sculpting (Duhl, Kantor, & Duhl, 1973), transitional sculpting (Landau, 1982), role play, simulation, and in-session tasks bring the family's pain into proper perspective creatively and productively. What the family learns in the sessions is then translated into homework tasks, specifically designed for each member, with the expectation that these tasks will be completed between sessions. Homework thus becomes the springboard for the next session. In this way, treatment is conducted in a developmental and purposeful manner.

Managing the grief experience can be an overwhelming and isolating journey. A systems therapist using TFT usually chooses to defuse the pain of loss by inviting family members to grieve and work through their pain together, as a group. He or she may choose to work with just the nuclear family or to open the process up to include significant members of the extended family, friends, clergy, medical people involved in the family's care, and others who may have a special connection to the family. The idea is to mobilize those people who are likely to be most affected by the loss and who, at the same time, have the greatest investment in the healing process (Landau-Stanton & Clements, 1993; Landau-Stanton & Stanton, 1985; Reuveni, 1979; Speck & Attneave, 1973). Everyone may be invited for the first session or for subsequent sessions. The therapist may see the group as a whole or in subgroups. These decisions are tailored to the needs of the case.

In the University of Rochester postgraduate Family Therapy Training Program, where the approach is taught, clinician trainees are trained to assess: (a) alliances and conflicts among the various dyads and triads of the nuclear and extended family; (b) the level of autonomy of the individuals and subsystems; (c) the openness and clarity of boundaries between family members; (d) the resources and structures of extended family members and the extended family system; (e) gender roles; (f) ethnic considerations; and (g) the religious orientation and spirituality of the family. Special attention is paid to symptomology. Questions such as, "Where in the system are symptoms repeated?" and "When and who are the symptom bearers?" are routinely asked.

As the family and significant others work together, the therapist assists them in identifying the special and unique qualities of their system. He or she helps them to appreciate how competent they are—as individuals, as subgroups (couples, siblings, women in the family, men in the family), and as an entire system. The awareness of their competence encourages meaningful connections among members, creates a safe place to share painful feelings, and injects hope into what may have seemed to a painful and endless process. The family is empowered and affirmed in their ability to heal themselves with direction and facilitation from the therapist (Landau-Stanton, 1985; Landau-Stanton & Clements, 1993; Seaburn et al., 1995).

Trainees are taught to assume a metaperspective as they explore a family's "terrain" over time, including the events and circumstances that brought the family to therapy. One way of thinking about a family's interactions is to view them as a series of feedback loops in which each interaction informs the others. These interactions move along a continuum while simultaneously circling back and forth. A family experiencing unresolved grief finds its movement is blocked because there is no new information; the pathway has been detoured back to a former point in the cycle. The therapist assesses the couple or family for these repetitive behavior patterns. As the clients tell their stories of how and why they have come to therapy, the therapist also explores the family's past history and current situation by asking questions and listening for the various insults to the family system that have occurred over time. These wounds are assessed to determine which, if any, have been traumatic, leaving undue pain, long-lasting negative impact, and closed doors, thereby prohibiting the family from moving forward.

Having hypothesized about the etiology of any reported traumas, the therapist looks for ways in which the family has navigated around and through the traumas. Most often, as stated earlier, if the family has been unable to find healthy solutions, it is more than likely to enter therapy with a symptomatic member.

Figure 10.1 shows the cyclical nature of the effects of trauma because of loss, demonstrating how it is possible for a family to remain stuck for many years, perhaps even generations.

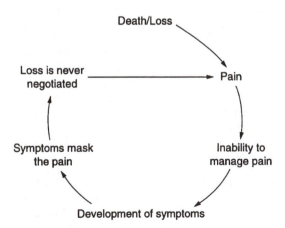

Figure 10.1 The cyclical nature of how families become *stuck* in the symptomatology of one or more of their members. These symptoms are seen as effects of trauma due to loss.

The grieving process has many implications across the family system. These effects emerge in many forms that mask trauma because of loss (Gutheil & Avery, 1977; Guttman, 1991; Krell & Rabkin, 1979; Landau-Stanton & Stanton, 1985; Paul, 1966; Paul & Paul, 1982; Stanton, 1977; Stanton & Coleman, 1980; Stanton & Todd, 1982; Walsh, 1978). Many theorists and clinicians agree that symptomatology is most likely to become exacerbated at the point of transition to a new family developmental stage (Carter & McGoldrick, 1988; Landau, 1982; McGoldrick & Walsh, 1991; Walsh, 1983). The Wallen case was no exception, in that the severity of John's symptoms did not show themselves until he reached the threshold of adolescence, a typical moment in any family's history where unresolved issues from the past are likely to surface (Haley, 1980; Stanton & Todd, 1982).

With the use of TFT, the work progresses, assisting the family to acquire tools and learn new ways of coping. Family relationships have an opportunity to realign themselves. These accomplishments become woven into the family's way of thinking about trauma, death, and the future, providing family members with the ability to reroute future encounters with pain and toxicity. The family thus becomes self-sufficient, no longer needing the therapist to guide, direct, or teach.

> Larry and Cheryl Turner entered therapy distressed and discouraged over the conflict in their marriage. They reported that their relationship would be idyllic for months at a time and then, seemingly for no reason, Larry would take up with a woman and begin an affair lasting from a single night to several weeks. When Cheryl would discover Larry's infidelity (which Larry often shared with her), she would become violent and punch his chest. Cheryl also reported that Larry was a habitual marijuana user and would occasionally strike Cheryl across the face with his open hand.
>
> After each affair ended and after each violent episode, Larry became remorseful and depressed, begging Cheryl not to leave him. Initially, Cheryl would distance herself after these occurrences, but within a week or two she would find herself feeling sorry for Larry and forgive him. Finally, after Larry's most recent girlfriend had called Cheryl to say she was going to take Larry away from her, Cheryl insisted that they seek therapy or get divorced. Larry was relieved at the suggestion to enter therapy. They came to treatment confused about what caused this untenable situation and eager to get their problems resolved.[3]
>
> Larry's initial symptoms had surfaced in adolescence at the time of his father's death. He had been a rebellious teenager who drank excessively and was often truant from school. He had married his pregnant girlfriend in his late teens, continued to drink and carouse with his friends, and divorced within a few years. Larry had settled down just before his marriage to Cheryl, but had begun this new set of behaviors (having affairs, smoking marijuana, becoming violent) shortly after the transition into marriage. As his son from his first marriage reached adolescence, Larry's marijuana use escalated, as did his extramarital flings.

---

[3]Linda Tornabene, M.S., was the therapist in this case. The author was her supervisor.

The Turners were stuck in a recursive pattern of excessive closeness and volatile explosions that served to give them distance from the intensity of their relationship. The pattern continued to repeat itself because they had no new information or skills with which to correct the cycle. Larry and Cheryl could not understand that Larry's father's sudden death (when Larry was 15 years old) and the current delinquent behavior of Larry's 16-year-old son, many years later, influenced Larry and Cheryl's marital relationship. Unresolved grief over their father's untimely had death led Larry and his brothers to an adolescence fraught with delinquency, police records, and poor school performance. The vectors of adolescence, their father's death, the subsequent loss of their father's successful neighborhood business, and the stress of caring for their invalid mother had converged all at once, creating a black hole of pain and loss with no apparent exit.

Larry's later infidelities, habitual marijuana use, and violent episodes were seen as adult symptoms resulting from years of patterned response to his unresolved grief over his father's death and the series of subsequent family losses.

Cheryl, too, had experienced trauma—from repeated incidents of sexual abuse by a trusted family member. She was clearly still wounded and had not been able to resolve the secret of sexual abuse she carried. Larry's affairs and violent behavior fueled feelings of abandonment and intrusion similar to those during her earlier abuse, setting in motion a course of mutual violent retaliation. Together the couple reacted in this unforgiving pattern with no relief.

Given the relationship between Larry's past and the repeating pattern seen in his son, one might further predict that each succeeding generation would be at risk for the same problems and the same harsh consequences. This scenario might very well perpetuate itself if some attempts were not made to discover the etiology of the problem and treat it effectively.

GOALS OF THERAPY

The therapist's efforts are channeled toward several desired outcomes: The unfinished business between deceased and living family members must be resolved in a way that allows for reorganization of the family to take place (Paul, 1966; Stanton, 1984; Williamson, 1981). Forgiveness, understanding of the deceased member's role before and after death, and redistribution of responsibilities are the work of the middle phase of treatment. When this renegotiation is accomplished, a family may continue to move forward, break its version of the cycle described above, reduce or drain away its symptoms, and learn to meet challenges with significantly less fear and anxiety.

The competence of the family needs to be mobilized by empowering its elders to assist in the healing process. The accumulated wisdom that older family members have acquired is tapped and explored during therapy sessions. Their acumen about their own particular family members is recognized and supported as valuable data. The therapist facilitates the process of the elders teaching the younger generations in the family about life and death, grieving, the development of broad perspectives, and forgiveness. The central goal is to establish credibility in the strength and wisdom of the hierarchy so that the family may learn to rely on its own members for healing. Additionally, this work gives future generations a significant gift—guidance in dealing with the potent stressors that result from loss, and a way to protect and maintain good mental health (Paul, 1966). With a functional hierarchy in place and equipped with appropriate tools, the family moves toward a successful conclusion and a reduction in the effects of the trauma of loss (Haley, 1976, 1980; Minuchin, 1974; Minuchin & Fishman, 1981; Minuchin, Rosman, & Baker, 1978; Stanton & Todd, 1982).

INTERVENTIONS USING TFT

Cases like the two described in this chapter are treated at the Family and Marriage Clinic, Division of Family Programs, Department of Psychiatry, University of Rochester Medical Center, using TFT. Although it is not possible to describe this approach fully within the framework and intent of this chapter, its essential features are listed here in an effort to summarize the theory presented above and the treatment described below. The reader should keep in mind that the approach and methodology described here represent only a portion of the interventions used by practitioners. TFT's key elements, in order, include:

1 joining with the family and other support people present (include the elders of the family whenever possible);
2 establishing goals for treatment;
3 identifying and mobilizing the strengths of the family;
4 constructing the transitional map and locating the most likely epicenters of the trauma;
5 utilizing theory and technique from various schools of systems thinking to create meaningful in-session dialogue and action-oriented interventions;
6 assigning relevant tasks to be carried out by the family members between sessions; and
7 termination.

These elements are repeated during each session, tailored to the work in progress, and expressed in ways that are meaningful to the participants and helpful to the process.

The therapist invited John Wallen, his parents, his maternal grandparents, and his paternal grandmother to the first therapy session, together with the school counselor and John's physician. After appropriately joining with everyone in the room (Key Element 1), she established the goals for treatment (Key Element 2) listed below:

1 John will return to school in September. (The initial session was in July.)
2 John will complete all school assignments and work to his potential.

3 John and the family will find more effective ways to manage John's asthma with the physician's guidance. (The physician reported John's asthmatic reactions to be more severe than his medical condition warranted.)

4 School personnel will look for creative and appropriate ways for John to reenter school smoothly, both socially and academically.

The therapist recorded a list of the family's, physician's, and school counselor's perceptions of John's strengths as well as the family's unique and special qualities (Key Element 3). A transitional map was begun (Key Element 4). Quickly, the absence of Mr. Wallen's father became the focus of conversation. The therapist hypothesized that the grandfather's absence and death were significant and needed to be attended to urgently and respectfully.

In the three subsequent sessions held with only the family present, it became clear that Mr. Wallen's father, John Sr., had been responsible for almost every decision made about John and his upbringing. He had sacrificed his social evenings with his friends, wife, and family by sending them out to dinner or a party while he remained home with John. In that way, he had ensured that no strange baby-sitter would be brought into the house. His death had been the result of a short but painful bout with cancer. He had not wanted his family to discuss his medical condition with him, and he had given them specific instructions not to grieve for him if he should die.

The therapist invited Mr. Wallen's mother to create a list of all of the special qualities and lessons about life that she thought her husband had offered the family, and specifically John. As the list grew, other family members added to it. John became more and more anxious, eventually bolting from the therapy room. Mr. Wallen was sent to retrieve him and was successful in having John rejoin the session. This incident was diagnostic in that the therapist and her supervisors could easily see the intense pressure John was under. John assumed he was expected to carry his grandfather's saintly qualities into the future as a man. It was also helpful to see John's willingness to respond to his father's authority, indicating his desire to be taken care of and remain a boy for now (Key Element 5).

The therapist continued gently, but firmly, to push the family members toward their unfinished grief, by suggesting they get together with more extended family members to celebrate John Sr.'s gifts and to create a memorial in his name. She suggested donating money and time to his favorite charity or possibly putting up a plaque. They agreed to visit the place where his ashes had been scattered to read the list of his special qualities aloud. In this way they could thank him for being such a valued member of the family. The therapist asked Mr. Wallen to officiate by contacting everyone in the extended family about the decision to honor his father, inviting them to come to the gathering. He was charged with the reading of the list the family had generated (Landau-Stanton & Stanton, 1985). The event turned out to be powerful for the family in that tears and joyful memories were shared. The family reported the event with a celebratory energy (Key Element 6).

The last (fifth) session was a reconvening of the original participants. The school counselor reported all the ways in which the school was prepared to help John as he reentered school. The physician offered several new and previously untried ways of responding to John's asthmatic attacks in school. The family reported changes they had noticed (Key Element 7). John seemed eager to get back to school. Mr. Wallen had called (prior to this last session) to say that he and his wife were communicating differently now than in the past and that they thought they might need some marital therapy. The three grandparents reported much improvement in John's condition. Even though they could not understand exactly what had changed, they were relieved to see him so much happier.

After 3 months, the therapist contacted the family to check on their status. Mr. Wallen had accepted a position in a field he had always wanted to pursue—a field requiring special expertise using computers. John had reentered school without much disruption. He had experienced two asthmatic attacks while at school, which had been handled successfully in the nurse's office, and returned promptly to class. All in all, his medical condition had vastly improved. Mr. and Mrs. Wallen were still arguing some of the time, but their relationship also had improved. There were no further requests for marital therapy.

The therapist and supervisors attributed some of these outcomes to several principles:

1 Mr. Wallen's father had become part of the daily life of the family members through their dependence upon him, even in his absence. He had given no permission for his family to grieve its loss of him and for him thereby to be put to rest. Creating the list of his special qualities brought him into the therapy room and their daily thoughts in a more legitimate way. Because he had been such an important part of their lives, this list seemed like a continuation of their own experience of him, but it pushed the process to its limit (a compression intervention), demonstrating there was an outermost boundary to the potency of this loss (Landau-Stanton & Stanton, 1983; Stanton, 1984).

2 By organizing the donations of time and money, the family was given the freedom to "pay back" its saint, relieving the family members of their feelings of guilt and obligation. By the establishment of a relationship in which there was give and take, the balance between and among family members evened out, becoming more of a peer relationship. The pressure of obligation lifted, giving way to genuine appreciation and love for the deceased (Boszormenyi-Nagy & Spark, 1972; Williamson, 1978).

3 Mr. Wallen's role in (a) retrieving his son after the boy had fled the therapy session, and (b) orchestrating the family memorial ceremony gave him the important and respected position he deserved. His leadership reorganized the family hierarchy into a functional structure.

The discussion above utilizes the theoretical perspectives and therapeutic techniques of TFT in a case in which an adolescent was identified as the patient. These principles are applied below to the Turner case, where marital discord was the presenting problem.

With the initial phase of joining under way (Key Element 1), Larry and Cheryl Turner set their goals for treatment and for their future together. They wanted to be more understanding of each other in the relationship, and they wanted to make important parenting decisions about Larry's son that would improve their family's lifestyle. Cheryl was firm in insisting that Larry have no more affairs. She also wanted Larry to stop smoking marijuana. Larry wanted the violence between them stopped (Key Element 2).

Rich in strengths as a couple, they had little difficulty recognizing that they wished to stay together to work through these difficulties (Key Element 3). They agreed, however, that if they became convinced they could not meet their goals, they would separate and divorce.

Cheryl shared the story of her abuse and her fear of talking with her mother, aunts, and sister about her experience. Cheryl had recently begun individual therapy and was working hard on her memories and the resolution of her pain, both past and present. It was important to Cheryl to work on her marriage and to maintain her own therapy at the same time. The therapist and her supervisor agreed to the arrangement as long as Cheryl gave permission to the individual therapist and the marital therapist to talk together on a regular basis. This collaboration proved fruitful and useful to both therapies as the case progressed.

As the transitional mapping process unfolded, Larry began to recognize the impact of his father's death on his family's subsequent experiences (Key Element 4). He recounted many stories about his brothers and younger sister. When offered the opportunity to bring his siblings into treatment to reminisce about life before and after his father died, he readily agreed. The session with his siblings and Cheryl was dramatic and moving as the pain and difficulties the siblings had also experienced were shared. They cried and supported each other.

The consensus at the end of the meeting was an agreement to convene again and to include their father's mother, aged 91, in the session. (The therapist recommended including their mother as well; however, Larry and his siblings declined. They thought that their issues with their mother were separate from this exploration and agreed to consider addressing those issues at a later date.) Again, the session was powerful in that their grandmother, whom they revered, was asked to tell her painful story about the loss of her son. She heard her grandchildren's account of their family life based on their memories and was able to confirm their various perceptions. She shared their sadness over a lost adolescence and, for some, a lost childhood (Key Element 5).

The family collectively agreed with the therapist's suggestions, which were twofold: (a) to make up for lost time by spending time together as siblings, with and without their marital partners, and (b) to hold a memorial service for their father. Now that they were old enough they could fashion the service in a way befitting their love and respect for him and for his legacy. Larry and his sister designed most of this service, with input from their brothers and grandmother (Key Element 6).

The out-of-session tasks—spending time together and designing the memorial service—had the obvious effect of bringing the distant, wounded siblings together in a common purpose, to rekindle old loyalties. Their efforts were well rewarded in that closeness and genuine warmth set the stage for plans to celebrate holidays together and to have a family reunion to which they would invite their father's extended family, including cousins they had never met.

Cheryl, having for the most part observed this process, reported that the marital relationship was much improved in that they were talking more about intimate issues, sharing their feelings, and supporting each other. Larry stopped smoking marijuana, astonishing Cheryl, who was skeptical about Larry's ability to "stay straight." She even took a somewhat ambivalent position, stating that he had been "more mellow" when he smoked and that she was afraid he would become tense and violent without it. He stood firm on his ability to stop permanently. He agreed that he had felt tense for the first few days but insisted he was feeling more and more calm as the days and weeks went by. He reassured her that he would not become violent.

Cheryl began to express interest in exploring her own family issues more. Through Larry's experience with his family she had recognized certain themes that might well apply to her family—issues of abandonment, isolation, and fear.

Larry and Cheryl terminated treatment with the decision to continue working on strengthening their relationship with the tools they had acquired through the therapeutic process. They looked forward to spending time with Larry's family and consciously set aside certain days to be together, alone as well as with their nuclear family. Armed with a list, generated in session, of what the danger signals for future difficulty might be, Larry and Cheryl left therapy confident and content with the present state of their relationship. They agreed to call if they felt themselves getting off track (Key Element 7).

A therapist may choose to "compress" family members toward their grief experience (Stanton, 1984), as was done in both cases above. By use of this technique, grieving, and the energy it consumes, become the most powerful focus of the treatment. The therapeutic forum becomes a safe venue for grief reactions to unfold and be monitored.

Interventions such as bringing together all concerned parties, especially nuclear and extended family members; creating the transitional map; assigning in-session and out-of-session tasks for family members; and encouraging grave-side visits (Paul & Grosser, 1965; Williamson, 1978), formal tributes to the deceased, and the establishment of memorials continue to help families make notable progress.

BASIC ASSUMPTIONS OF THIS APPROACH

1   Reaction to trauma is dependent on the state of preparedness for life events and life cycle changes of any individual or system. The effects of trauma—anxiety, fear, flashbacks, sleep disturbances, change in eating behavior, stressed interpersonal relationships, and so on—are typical and normal responses to traumatic events. However, the persistence of these effects over a long period of time, coupled with the development of symptomatology, indicates an inability on the part of an individual or family to navigate through the mire of trauma. The result is the development of a recursive cycle such as that described above.

2   A systemic approach, specifically the theoretical perspective and methods of TFT, neutralizes the effects of trauma by disrupting the cycle of pain and symptomatology. As a result, the pain decreases or drains away, and the symp-

toms become more manageable or disappear. The trauma is dismantled. The memories become an important part of a family's history, rather than its nemesis.

3 A successful outcome to the resolution of pain from trauma requires a family to "lose the loss" and award the deceased family member an appropriate and useful presence in the family's current life experience.

4 Pushing a family closer to its grief than its members would know to push themselves can assist family members in "letting go" of the pain of loss (Stanton, 1977, 1984). This pushing process and its concomitant techniques require savvy on the part of the clinician, particularly in the areas of pacing, timing, and assessing the appropriateness of an intervention. New clinicians may require supervision before proceeding with interventions that compress a family toward its pain because of the powerful effects such interventions can produce. Prior to initiating compression techniques, mental status assessments of family members (and the family as a whole) may be useful to ensure that the family and its members are stable enough to tolerate the process and benefit from its potential positive effects.

5 Dealing with the realities of the death experience demystifies the notions a family may have about death and loss. Often families do not discuss their feelings about the death of a loved one before or after the event. Misperceptions, lack of understanding, and fear block helpful grieving and keep family members isolated from each other.

Children, particularly, are often confused about the dying process and what happens to the body after death. In efforts to protect children, open discussions are often forbidden, leaving the children to conjure up their own ideas, including the worry about themselves, "Am I next?" or the feeling that somehow they are responsible for the loved one's death. These particular fears are typical of children experiencing the death of a sibling or a pet. Children's active imaginations and magical thinking can create visions that are likely to be more ghastly and terrifying than the actual circumstances (Fraiberg, 1968). Harboring the horror can lead to severe behavior changes and ultimately to painful symptomatology. When children are allowed to discuss the incident and its aftermath, the door is opened for questions, for opportunities to say good-bye, and for healthful grieving (Gelcer, 1983; Glicken, 1978; Krell & Rabkin, 1979; Kubler-Ross, 1975).

6 An equalization or rebalancing of familial relationships among a family's living members and between the living members and the deceased family member allows for effective reorganization of the hierarchy (Landau-Stanton & Stanton, 1983; Stanton, 1984; Williamson, 1978, 1981, 1982).

7 As a result of the "systems of import" (Stanton, 1981a) working through the grief experience together, the pain of loss and fear from trauma can be diffused among all family members. The resolutions reached by the group give permission to all members to move on, free from the bonds of guilt and unhealthy obligations (Boszormenyi-Nagy & Spark, 1973; Landau-Stanton &

Clements, 1993; Landau-Stanton & Stanton, 1985; Stanton & Landau-Stanton, in preparation).

ISSUES OF ASSESSMENT AND EVALUATION

Assessment is a key consideration in any form of mental health treatment. Assessment can take many forms under the rubric of TFT. As mentioned above, the transitional mapping process is an excellent assessment and diagnostic tool. Also helpful is a family's recounting of the chronology of important events, which the therapist records in the form of a timeline (Stanton, 1992). This graphic intervention assists the family in assessing why entering treatment at this moment in the family's journey is critical and potentially valuable. The timeline and transitional map together help identify those areas of greatest resistance to change by clarifying when critical events occurred in relation to the onset of symptomatology.

The therapist routinely calls the referral source to confer, with permission from the family. Additionally, all other service providers—physicians, other appropriate medical and school personnel, clergy, legal advisors, other therapists in the community, and agency personnel as well as close friends and neighbors where appropriate—are recorded as part of the intake procedure and are contacted for input, again with the family's permission. As mentioned above, many, if not all, of these people may be invited to one or more sessions to help the therapist assess the nature of the difficulty and to offer suggestions for treatment. Ongoing contact is maintained throughout therapy. Assessment is viewed as an ongoing process, rather than simply a pre- or posttreatment obligation.

A family seen at the Family and Marriage Clinic may be asked to review its goals midway through treatment to assess its progress to date and to reconstruct its goals for the rest of the therapy. Termination sessions are spent assessing progress in several ways. The original or revised goals are evaluated, and lists of accomplishments are developed by the family and therapist creatively working together. Other service providers are included to offer their input concerning the family's progress. Finally, a statistical follow-up is conducted each year on a random sample of cases and preparation for the clinic's annual review process. Some therapists follow up with their client families at 3 or 6 months and again at 1 year posttreatment.

In the case of the Wallen family, medical and school personnel were extremely helpful both in identifying difficulties and in helping to design interventions that targeted the family's goals for the son's reentry into school. The family reassessed its original goals at the fifth session, assuming a wait-and-see position until school began. The therapist checked with the family at 3 months posttreatment, thereby learning of John's medical improvement and that he had made a successful transition into school.

In the Turner case, Larry and Cheryl left treatment in the process of achieving their goals, seeing the goals as lifetime efforts, not isolated, compartmental-ized tasks to be completed and forgotten. Larry's extended family was helpful in providing the therapist with an assessment of the breadth and depth of the unresolved grieving problem in the family. The family was left to become its own gatekeeper with the on-going tasks of (a) keeping in mind that family members desired to promote closeness, and (b) mobilizing each member's own resources to ensure success.

Sometimes families lose sight of their newly acquired tools, begin experi-encing new difficulties months and years after the initial treatment, and look to the therapist to help them assess their position. With proper coaching and a successful treatment past, such families are quickly able to take on the respon-sibility for assessing the etiology of the new dilemmas and move logically, rapidly, and easily to resolution.

CONCLUSION

TFT is a paradigm that has been evolving over many years. Only recently, within the past 5 to 10 years, has the approach become more formalized. Each year clinic personnel assemble statistics related to presenting problem, length of stay, socioeconomic data, and other utilization review information for the clinic's annual report. Within the next 3 to 5 years, research should address issues of effectiveness in a systematic way, for both senior clinicians and the program's trainees. Issues of clinical experience, years of training in TFT, client satisfaction, recidivism rates, and so forth can provide valuable feedback to the practitioners of the approach.

In working with families experiencing trauma through death, a large per-centage of families treated with TFT have been helped significantly. They have become "unstuck," resolving significant difficulties and going on to live more productive lives. Client reports have validated the results at 1 year follow-up contacts.

TFT is an exciting opportunity to apply the principles discussed within this chapter to many situations involving trauma and loss. Further evidence of its effectiveness will provide an important set of data to consider as the senior clinicians and their trainees continue to meet the challenge of conducting this type of therapy.

REFERENCES

Aponte, H. J., & Van Deusen, J. M. (1981). Structural family therapy. In A. S. Gurman & D. P. Kniskern (Eds.), *Handbook of family therapy* (pp. 310–360). New York: Brunner/Mazel.

Boszormenyi-Nagy, I., & Spark, G. M. (1973). Loyalty. In I. Boszormenyi-Nagy & G. M. Spark (Eds.), *Invisible loyalties* (pp. 37–52). New York: Brunner/Mazel.

Boszormenyi-Nagy, I., & Spark, G. M. (1984). *Invisible loyalties.* New York: Brunner/Mazel.

Bowen, M. (1976). Family reaction to death. In P. Guerin (Ed.), *Family therapy.* New York: Gardner Press.

Bowen, M. (1978). *Family therapy in clinical practice.* New York: Jason Aronson.

Carey, A. (1977). Helping the child and the family cope with death. *International Journal of Family Counseling, 5*(1), 58–63.

Carter, B., & McGoldrick, M. (1988). The family life cycle and family therapy: An overview. In B. Carter & M. McGoldrick (Eds.), *The family life cycle: A framework for family therapy* (pp. 3–20). New York: Gardner Press.

DeFrain, J. (1991). Learning about grief from normal families: SIDS, stillbirth, and miscarriage. *Journal of Marital and Family Therapy, 17,* 215–232.

Derdyn, A. P., & Waters, D. B. (1981). Unshared loss and marital conflict. *Journal of Marital and Family Therapy, 7,* 481–487.

Duhl, F. J., Kantor, D., & Duhl, B. S. (1973). Learning, space and action in family therapy: A primer of sculpture. In D. A. Block (Ed.), *Techniques of family psychotherapy: A primer* (pp. 43–63). New York: Grune and Straton.

Fraiberg, S. H. (1968). *The magic years: Understanding the problems of early childhood.* London: Methuen.

Friedman, E. H. (1988) Systems and ceremonies: A family view of rites of passages. In B. Carter & M. McGoldrick (Eds.), *The family life cycle: A framework for family therapy* (pp. 459–460). New York: Gardner Press.

Gelcer, E. (1983). Mourning is a family affair. *Family Process, 22,* 501–516.

Glicken, M. D. (1978). The child's view of death. *Journal of Marriage and Family Counseling, 4*(2), 75–81.

Gutheil, T., & Avery, N. (1977). Multiple overt incest as family defense against loss. *Family Process, 16,* 105–116.

Guttman, H. A. (1991). Parental death as a precipitant of marital conflict in middle age. *Journal of Marital and Family Therapy, 17,* 81–87.

Haley, J. (1976). *Problem solving therapy: New strategies for effective family therapy.* San Francisco: Jossey-Bass.

Haley, J. (1980). *Leaving home: The therapy of disturbed young people.* New York: McGraw-Hill.

Hare-Mustin, R. T. (1979). Family therapy following the death of a child. *Journal of Marital and Family Therapy, 5*(2), 51–59.

Hepworth, J., Ryder, R. G., & Dreyer, A. S. (1984). The effects of parental loss on the formation of intimate relationships. *Journal of Marital and Family Therapy, 10,* 73–82.

Jensen, G. D., & Wallace, J. G. (1967). Family mourning process. *Family Process, 6,* 56–66.

Kerr, M., & Bowen, M. (1988). *Family evaluation.* New York: W. W. Norton.

Krell, R., & Rabkin, L. (1979). The effects of sibling death on the surviving child: A family perspective. *Family Process, 18,* 471–477.

Kubler-Ross, E. (1975). *Death: The final stage of growth.* New York: Prentice-Hall.

Landau, J. (1982). Therapy with families in cultural transition. In M. McGoldrick, & J. Pearce (Eds.), *Ethnicity and family therapy.* New York: Guilford Press.

Landau-Stanton, J. (1985). Competence, impermanence, and transitional mapping: A model for systems consultation. In L. Wynne, T. Weber, & S. McDaniel (Eds.), *Systems consultation: A new perspective for family therapy* (pp. 253–269). New York: Guilford Press.

Landau-Stanton, J., Clements, C. D., and Associates. (1993). *AIDS, health, and mental health: A primary sourcebook* (pp. 214–225). New York: Brunner/Mazel.

Landau-Stanton, J., & Stanton, M. D. (1983). Aspects of supervision with the "Pick-A-Dali Circus" Model. *Journal of Strategic and System Therapies, 2*(2), 31–39.

Landau-Stanton, J., & Stanton, M. D. (1985). Treating suicidal adolescents and their families. In M. P. Mirkin & S. L. Koman (Eds.), *Handbook of adolescents and family therapy.* New York: Gardner Press.

McGoldrick, M., & Walsh, F. (1991). A time to mourn: Death and the family life cycle. In F. Walsh & M. McGoldrick (Eds.), *Living beyond loss* (pp. 30–48). New York: W. W. Norton.

Minuchin, S. (1974). *Families and family therapy.* Cambridge, MA: Harvard University Press.

Minuchin, S., & Fishman, H. C. (1981). *Family therapy techniques.* Cambridge, MA: Harvard University Press.

Minuchin, S., Rosman, B., & Baker, L. (1978). *Psychosomatic families: Anorexia in context.* Cambridge, MA: Harvard University Press.

Paul, N. L. (1966). The role of mourning and empathy in conjoint marital therapy. In *Pathogenic social systems and family therapy* (pp. 186–205). Palo Alto, CA: Science and Behavior Books.

Paul, N., & Grosser, G. (1965). Operational mourning and its role in conjoint family therapy. *Community Mental Health Journal, 1,* 339–345.

Paul, N., & Paul, B. (1982). Death and changes in sexual behavior. In F. Walsh (Ed.), *Normal family processes.* New York: Guilford Press.

Powers, M. A. (1977). The benefits of anticipatory grief for the parents of dying children. *International Journal of Family Counseling, 5*(2), 48–53.

Reuveni, U. (1979). *Networking families in crisis.* New York: Human Sciences Press.

Seaburn, D. B. (1990). The ties that bind: Loyalty and widowhood. In E. M. Stern (Ed.), *Psychotherapy and the widowed patient* (pp. 139–146). New York: Haworth Press.

Seaburn, D., Landau-Stanton, J., & Horwitz, S. (1995). Core intervention techniques in family therapy process. In R. H. Mikeshell, D. D. Lusterman, & S. H. McDaniel (Eds.), *Family psychology and systems therapy: A handbook.*

Soloman, M. A., & Hersch, L. B. (1979). Death in the family: Implications for family development. *Journal of Marital and Family Therapy, 5*(2), 43–49.

Speck, R., & Attneave, C. (1973). *Family networks.* New York: Pantheon.

Stanton, M. D. (1977). The addict as savior: Heroin, death, and the family. *Family Process, 16,* 191–197.

Stanton, M. D. (1981a). An integrated structural strategic approach to family therapy. *Journal of Marital and Family Therapy, 7,* 427–439.

Stanton, M. D. (1981b). Strategic approaches to family therapy. In A. S. Gurman & D. P. Kniskern (Eds.), *Handbook of family therapy* (pp. 361–402). New York: Brunner/Mazel.

Stanton, M. D. (1984). Fusion, compression, diversion, and the workings of the paradox: A theory of therapeutic/systematic change. *Family Process, 23,* 135–166.

Stanton, M. D. (1992). The time line and the "Why now?" question: A technique and rationale for therapy, training, organizational consultation and research. *Journal of Marital and Family Therapy, 18,* 331–343.

Stanton, M. D., & Coleman, S. B. (1980). The participatory aspects of indirect self-destructive behavior: The addict family as a model. In N. L. Farberow (Ed.), *The many faces of suicide: Indirect self destructive behavior* (pp. 187–203). New York: McGraw-Hill.

Stanton, M. D., & Landau-Stanton, J. (1990). Therapy with families of adolescent substance abusers. In H. B. Milkman & L. I. Sederer (Eds.), *Treatment choices for alcoholism and substance abuse* (pp. 329–339). Lexington, MA: Lexington Books.

Stanton, M. D., & Landau-Stanton, J. (in preparation). *The role of ancestors in normality, nonshared environments and dysfunction, I: Family themes and balance.*

Stanton, M. D., & Landau-Stanton, J. (in preparation). *The role of ancestors in normality, nonshared environments and dysfunction, II: Family scripts.*

Stanton, M. D., & Todd, T. C. (1982). The therapy model. In M. D. Stanton, T. C. Todd, & Associates (Eds.), *The family therapy of drug abuse and addiction* (pp. 109–151). New York: Guilford Press.

Walsh, F. W. (1978). Concurrent grandparent death and birth of schizophrenic offspring: An intriguing finding. *Family Process, 17,* 457–463.

Walsh, F. W., & McGoldrick, M. (Eds.) (1991). *Living beyond loss.* New York: Norton.

Whitaker, C., & Keith, D. (1981). Symbolic-experiential family therapy. In A. S. Gurman & D. P. Kniskern (Eds.), *Handbook of family therapy* (pp. 187–225). New York: Brunner/Mazel.

White, M. (1988, MONTH). *Saying hello again: The incorporation of the last relationship in the resolution of grief.* Invited lecture.

Williamson, D. S. (1978). New life at the graveyard: A method of therapy for the individuation from a dead former parent. *Journal of Marriage and Family Counseling, 4*(1), 93–101.

Williamson, D. S. (1981). Personal authority via termination of the intergenerational hierarchical boundary: Part II—The consultation process and the therapeutic method. *Journal of Marital and Family Therapy, 8*(2), 23–37.

Chapter 11

Eye Movement Desensitization and Reprocessing: A Therapeutic Tool for Trauma and Grief

Roger M. Solomon and Francine Shapiro

Eye movement desensitization and reprocessing (EMDR) is an integrative client-centered approach that is presently widely used in the treatment of trauma. Use of this method within a comprehensive treatment plan can significantly accelerate recovery from a recent traumatic event, hasten the working through of unresolved past events, and facilitate the client's incorporation of adaptive beliefs, emotions, and behaviors. Furthermore, treatment effects appear to be stable over time. The following example illustrates the utilization of EMDR to treat unresolved grief.

A 20-year-old woman driving over a mountain pass on a snowy day with her 18-year-old sister hit a pocket of ice and skidded out of control into a light pole. After determining that she was uninjured, she looked for her sister. She was confronted with the horrible sight of her dead sister, who had been thrown against the pole.

The woman dissociated the accident, feeling as if she were out of her body looking at her sister and herself. Getting help from passing motorists, the ride in the ambulance, and the ordeal at the hospital all added to her trauma.

She blamed herself for her sister's death, reasoning that she had been driving and should have been better able to control the car. She coped with the incident by avoiding thoughts and reminders of it. Nevertheless, over the years, she suffered mild to moderate depression and anxiety, as well as intrusive images of the accident and nightmares. She went to a few sessions of psychotherapy a year after the accident and was able to talk about it. However, her self-blame, feelings of guilt, nightmares, and other intrusive images continued.

Five years later, she became engaged to a police officer but was reluctant to marry him because of his potential for being hurt or killed on the job. She believed she could not handle dealing with the death of another loved one. Several months after they became engaged, her fiance killed a gunman who had been about to shoot him. She reacted strongly, starting seriously to question her engagement. One of her worst fears had been realized: Her fiance had almost been killed. She was again flooded with overwhelming emotions related to her sister's death and again experienced strong feelings of guilt, intrusive imagery, and nightmares about the accident.

The first author visited with the fiance immediately after the shooting and again 2 days later. Although the situation was tragic to the officer, it was not traumatic. He realized he had had no choice but to shoot the gunman, and he had previously worked through the possibility of having to use lethal force. His main concern was the emotional well-being of his fiancee.

An appointment was quickly scheduled for the woman. After taking a history and assessing the client, the therapist chose EMDR to help her resolve her emotional distress. After 2 intense hours, the vivid images of her sister faded and her level of emotional tension greatly lessened. She realized that her sister's death was not her fault and that she had done all she could to control the car. She now had a sense of distance from the incident; it was over and in the past.

Follow-up evaluation showed that she could recall her sister with fondness, no longer experiencing the guilt or traumatic imagery. One of the hallmarks of EMDR is the generalization of treatment effects to other related problems. In this instance, the 2-hour session was sufficient not only to resolve the woman's prolonged grieving for her sister, but also to put her fears regarding her fiance in perspective. Although it was possible for him to get killed, she realized he had survived the gun fight and would continue to do all he could to avoid getting hurt. She remained asymptomatic 6 months later, even after her marriage to the officer.

EYE MOVEMENT DESENSITIZATION AND REPROCESSING

EMDR was initially introduced with a controlled study of Vietnam veterans and rape or sexual molestation victims (Shapiro, 1989a), which indicated that the procedure could rapidly desensitize traumatic memories, provide a cognitive restructuring of irrational thoughts and negative self-attributions, and significantly reduce symptomatology (e.g., anxiety, intrusive thoughts, flashbacks, nightmares). These research results have been replicated (Grainger, Levin, Allen-Byrd, & Fulcher, 1994; Levin, Grainger, Allen-Byrd, & Fulcher, 1994; Renfrey & Spates, 1994; Silver, Brooks, & Obenchain, 1995; Solomon & Kaufman, 1994; Vaughan et al., 1994; Wilson, Becker, & Tinker, 1995; Wilson, Covi, Foster, & Silver, 1995). In addition, other successful studies of cases that used EMDR have been published (Carlson, Chemtob, Rusnak, & Hedlund, 1996; Cocco & Sharpe, 1993; Cohn, 1993; Forbes, Creamer, & Rycroft, 1994; Goldstein & Feske, 1994; Greenwald, 1994; Kleinknecht, 1992, 1993; Lipke & Botkin, 1992; Marquis, 1991; McCann, 1992; Pellicer, 1993; Puk, 1991; Shapiro & Solomon, 1995; Shapiro, Vogelmann-Sine, & Sine, 1994; Spector & Huthwaite, 1993; Thomas & Gafner, 1993; Wernick, 1993; Wolpe & Abrams, 1991; Young,

1994). Clinical observations and study have concluded that EMDR has no racial or cultural biases (Lipke, 1992).

It is important to keep in mind that the following description of the EMDR method is not instruction on how to use it; training is necessary for its competent and ethical use. The EMDR treatment of post-traumatic stress disorder (PTSD) includes procedural stages involving a desensitization to the emotional effects of trauma and a subsequent cognitive restructuring of clients' views of themselves and their participation in the event. In addition, during the treatment phases clients usually generate insights and recognitions of life patterns that assist them in the future. Consistent with the recent trend toward integration of psychological practices (Goldfried, 1980; Norcross, 1986), the implementation of EMDR includes elements of psychodynamic, interactional, and body-oriented therapies along with cognitive-behavioral elements. Consequently, the 4-day supervised training is considered important not only to teach the protocols and procedures distinct to EMDR practice, but to upgrade the clinicians' skills in these diverse disciplines. Because clinical skills are necessary in effectively utilizing EMDR, only licensed mental health professionals may be trained.

EMDR is an eight-phase treatment method that should always be used within a comprehensive treatment plan. The first phase is History Taking. It must first be determined whether a client is suitable for EMDR treatment, because the reprocessing of traumatic material may precipitate intense emotions. The client's ability to deal with high levels of disturbance, personal stability, and life constraints are evaluated. If it is determined that the client is appropriate for EMDR treatment, the clinician obtains the information needed to design a treatment plan. The clinician evaluates the entire clinical picture, including the dysfunctional behaviors, symptoms, and characteristics that need to be addressed. The clinician then determines the specific targets that need to be reprocessed, including events that initially set the pathology in motion, present triggers that stimulate the dysfunctional behaviors, and the kinds of positive behaviors and attitudes that are important for adaptive future functioning.

Phase 2 is Client Preparation. This phase involves establishing a therapeutic alliance, explaining the EMDR process and its effects, dealing with the client's concerns, and teaching the client relaxation techniques for coping with high levels of emotions. Informed consent about the possibility of intense emotions being evoked is obtained. The preparation phase also includes briefing the client on the theory of EMDR and the procedures involved, and explaining what the client can realistically expect.

The third phase is Assessment. In this phase the clinician identifies the components of the target to be treated and takes baseline measures before reprocessing begins. The client is asked to select the image that best represents the traumatic memory. (In the case described above, the woman recalled vivid images of her sister lying dead with a bloody head wound.) Then the therapist assists the client in identifying the negative cognition that expresses the dysfunctional, negative self-attribution related to participation in the event. (In the same example, the woman's negative cognition was, "I am to blame.") Then, the therapist identifies a positive cognition or a more rational, realistic, and empowering self-assessment. The positive cognition is later used to replace the negative cognition in the Installation phase (Phase 5), but its initial purpose is to provide a therapeutic direction. (In this example, the positive cognition was, "I did the best I could.") To provide a baseline measurement, the client is asked to report how valid the positive cognition feels on a 7-point Validity of Cognition (VOC) Scale, with 1 = *it feels totally false* and 7 = *it feels totally true.*

The client and therapist also explore the emotions and physical sensations associated with the traumatic experience. (In the above example, the woman felt deeply guilty. She experienced physical sensations in her chest and upper stomach.) The client is asked to rate the intensity of the emotion on a 10-point Subjective Units of Disturbance (SUD) Scale, with 0 = *neutral* and 10 = *the worst it could be,* to provide a baseline from which to assess changes during the procedure.

The next three phases have to do with the accelerated processing of information. During these phases there is simultaneous remediation of negative affect, cognitive restructuring, and the generation of insights to guide the client in the future. The individual phases are designated according to the elements used to determine treatment effects. For instance, the Desensitization phase uses the SUD Scale, the Installation phase uses the VOC Scale, and the Body Scan phase uses the evaluation of body sensations. However, all treatment effects are viewed as by-products of accelerated information processing, which is described in the next section. Sets of eye movement, alternate taps on the client's palms, and the therapist snapping his or her fingers alternately on each side of the client's head are utilized to stimulate information processing according to appropriate protocols.

The fourth phase is Desensitization. This phase focuses on the client's negative affect, with clinical effects measured by the SUD Scale. While the client holds in mind the visual image, the negative cognition, and the emotions associated with the image, processing is activated during a focused clinician–client interaction involving sets of eye movement (or other stimulation) until the SUD level is reduced to 0 or 1, or higher if appropriate to client circumstance.

Phase 5 is Installation. After the distress level has dropped to 0 or 1 on the SUD Scale, the focus becomes enhancing and strengthening the positive cognition identified earlier (or a more appropriate cognition that may have arisen spontaneously) as the replacement for the original negative cognition. Clinical effects are evaluated on the basis of the 7-point VOC Scale. This phase is complete when the positive cognition feels valid in relation to the incident, that is, when the cognition reaches a VOC rating of 6 or 7.

Phase 6 is the Body Scan. The client is asked to hold in mind both the target event and the positive cognition and scan his or her body for residual tension in the form of body sensation. As in the work of van der Kolk (1994), body sensations may indicate that additional information is dysfunctionally stored. Upon adequate processing, usually the tension simply resolves itself, but it is not uncommon for additional targets to be revealed.

Phase 7 is Closure. The client must be returned to a state of emotional equilibrium at the end of the session, whether or not the reprocessing is complete. Relaxation and other coping skills learned during the preparation phase can be utilized when the client is experiencing discomfort. The client is briefed as to the possibility of other memories, feelings, or images emerging as the material continues to be processed between sessions. The client is asked to keep a journal so that what comes up may be discussed in the next session.

Phase 8 is Reevaluation. EMDR is not a one-shot therapy. It is important to review treatment results to evaluate if the effects of reprocessing are maintained. At the next session, the log is reviewed and the client is asked to reaccess the previously targeted material. This reevaluation determines whether there are new aspects of the problem that should be addressed, if other issues have arisen, and future therapeutic direction.

EMDR is not a rigid protocol but a highly interactive procedure individualized for each client. It involves an eight-phase treatment approach of which the eye movement itself is only a small part. Competent clinical skills and knowledge on the part of the clinician are needed for the successful utilization of EMDR. Identifying appropriate negative and positive cognitions is an exercise in case formulation. Knowledge of personality dynamics and psychopathology are necessary for the therapist to identify the beliefs and self-attributions underlying symptoms. Establishing rapport, eliciting a complete history, assisting the client in accessing traumatic memories, and steering the EMDR process require a strong clinical background.

Again, it must be emphasized that supervised training is essential for the proper use of EMDR. There is potential risk to the client if a clinician attempts the procedure without it. In the example described above, for example, the client initially remembered the tragedy from a dissociated perspective, seeing herself and her sister in the situation. Dissociation may be viewed as an attempt to ward off overwhelming emotions (van der Kolk & Kadish, 1987). During EMDR, as the memory processed, the dissociative perspective changed and the client experienced the emotions, sensations, and feelings associated with the event intensely. Training and experience with EMDR enabled the woman's clinician to understand what was happening and to deal appropriately with the abreaction. Although abreactions are not unique to EMDR, their suddenness of onset and the manner in which they manifest during EMDR require special knowledge to work them through rapidly. If the clinician had not had proper training, the woman's abreactive experience could have been prolonged and intensified.

THEORETICAL FRAMEWORK

Whereas EMDR protocols and procedures are empirically derived, the treatment effects may be theoretically explained by the Accelerated Information Processing Model formulated by Shapiro (1991, 1992, 1993, 1994, 1995).

The Accelerated Information Processing Model is compatible with a number of other information theories that have great merit (Chemtob, Roitblat, Hamada, Carlson, & Twentyman, 1989; Foa & Kozak, 1986; Horowitz, 1976; Litz & Keane, 1989). However, it is distinct in that it is based on and guides the application of EMDR treatment sessions. Specifically, the observation of thousands of EMDR sessions led to identification of patterns of information processing and memory association that led to the Accelerated Information Processing Model. The principles of this model, in turn, led to the continued development and refinement of EMDR procedures and protocols.

The Accelerated Information Processing Model posits an innate information-processing system that is physiologically configured to facilitate mental health in much the same way the rest of the body is designed to heal itself when injured. When the system operates effectively, it takes the perceptual information from a distressing event and brings it to an adaptive resolution (i.e., useful information is stored with appropriate affect and is available for future use). Thus, ideally, if something disturbing occurs, the individual thinks, talks, reads, and/or dreams about it until he or she has learned what can be learned from it, after which it resides simply as a memory without undue attendant distress.

According to the Accelerated Information Processing Model, an individual's information-processing mechanism may be blocked by a traumatic event. The result is that the information taken in at the time of the trauma becomes stored in the state-specific form of disturbing pictures, thoughts, sensations, beliefs, and the like, and cannot progress through the normal steps of adaptive integration. The continual activation of this information by external or internal stimuli, or perhaps because of an attempt by the mechanism to complete its own reprocessing, results in the nightmares, flashbacks, and intrusive thoughts associated with PTSD. This information is viewed as dysfunctionally stored because it is incapable of connecting with more adaptive, salient information.

EMDR appears to catalyze the information-processing system, making possible the appropriate metabolization and integration of the dysfunctional information. For instance, with molestation victims and Vietnam combat veterans, the incidents that occurred 20 years previously may be dysfunctionally stored along with inappropriate feelings of excessive grief, guilt, and powerlessness. Once a client accesses the pivotal memories, EMDR helps the processing mechanism to become active and dynamic, and the client progresses spontaneously through the appropriate stages of affect and insight, coming to realizations about such fundamental issues as (a) appropriate levels of responsibility, (b) present safety, and (c) availability of future choices (see Shapiro, 1995).

The desensitization and cognitive restructuring apparent in EMDR treatments may be viewed as a result of effective processing, which also includes a shift of somatic response, a remission of pronounced symptomatology, and often a spontaneous emission of insights, a recognition of life patterns, and an assumption of new, more appropriate behaviors. Until traumatic information is appropriately processed, a client remains in a pathological state in which a variety of stimuli are capable of triggering the traumatic information—flooding the body and consciousness with feelings of inadequacy, danger, and helplessness that have been held physiologically in their original and highly disturbing state-specific form.

Death can be a traumatic event for the survivors. The victim of excessive grief, although not necessarily involved in a traumatic situation meeting the criteria for PTSD (i.e., outside the range of normal human experience), is often bombarded with negative images of the death scene or unresolved earlier events involving the loved one, which are especially disturbing because of concomitant issues of guilt or powerlessness. Essentially, if trauma is defined as an event having a substantial emotionally discordant effect, the client with excessive grief may be said to be suffering from a "post-traumatic stress configuration."

For instance, one client requested treatment from the second author because of prolonged grief over the death of her father in a nursing home 2 years before. Although she had many positive and neutral memories associated with her father, any deliberate attempt by the client to remember him (or any externally stimulated thought of her father) induced vivid images of his suffering and death. The use of EMDR to focus on these negative images allowed the client to reprocess the memories of the events in the nursing home along with her associated feelings of guilt and helplessness. The client was then asked to think of her father, and what emerged were pictures of the two of them laughing together at a party. Clinical effects remained stable 4 years after treatment.

According to the Accelerated Information Processing Model, the highly charged, disturbing memories of the father in the nursing home were stored at a dysfunctional level in the client's neuro network (see Shapiro, 1995) associated with her parent. These easily elicited images, therefore, become the only memories available. Accessing and reprocessing the memories of the father's death in the nursing home resulted in the client's incorporation of more adaptive information and made the metabolized events accessible by choice, not by dysfunctionally charged activation.

This same pattern has been observed in a number of clients whose family members have committed suicide. Once the negative imagery is reprocessed, other, more pleasant memories associated with the loved one can emerge. The attendant rebalancing of the information-processing system allows the recovery process to proceed unimpeded.

RESOLUTION OF TRAUMA AND GRIEF

Recovery from a traumatic experience or a loss involves a period of adjustment and adaptation. However, many obstacles can interfere with this recovery and prolong emotional pain and disabling symptoms. As previously mentioned, three major themes that commonly need to be addressed by the victims of traumatic experiences are: (a) responsibility for the event, (b) personal vulnerability, and (c) feelings of control and self-efficacy.

Issues of responsibility and self-blame are often central following a tragedy (Janoff-Bulman, 1992; Herman, 1992). Traumatized people often take undue responsibility for the events and blame themselves for outcomes beyond their control. Many hold a core belief that they are in control of whatever happens to them (Janoff-Bulman, 1992). Hence, when a tragedy occurs that is beyond control, a person may believe he or she did something wrong. A victim often thinks, "Because of what I did [or did not] do, this happened. . . . If I had done something different, it would not have happened." Underlying such thinking is the assumption, "I'm supposed to be in control." Guilt, depression, low self-esteem, feelings of inadequacy, and low self-efficacy may result from such thinking.

Issues of personal safety may also be paramount after a critical incident. In the aftermath of a traumatic event, its victims come face to face with their own mortality. Intense feelings of vulnerability may be experienced not only after one's safety is threatened, but also after one has witnessed a tragedy or experienced a significant loss.

Issues of control may also be central following a tragedy. Dealing with the realization that one has no control over disasters and tragedies often stimulates feelings of helplessness and powerlessness. A crucial part of recovery is recapturing a sense of empowerment and efficacy. People may not be able to control what goes on around them, but they can control their responses to a situation; in other words, they have choices.

The aftermath of a tragedy may revolve around one or more of these three issues of responsibility, vulnerability, and control. EMDR may help resolve such issues and, when integrated in an overall treatment plan, it can facilitate clients' emotional recovery, as the following three case examples illustrate.

Late at night, a husband and wife were sleeping when they heard a noise in their living room. The husband got up to investigate. The wife heard five gun shots and her husband scream. She called the police and reported what happened. She wanted to go to her husband, but the police dispatcher told her to stay on the phone because the gunman could still be in the house. Her husband called out her name. Again, she wanted to go to him, but again she was told to stay on the phone for her own safety.

The police arrived 6 minutes after she called. When they told her it was safe to come out, she saw her dead husband on the living room floor. The killer was never caught.

The woman felt intensely guilty for not going to her husband after he was shot. She wondered if she could have done something to save him or at least comfort him. She also blamed herself for not taking better precautions to prevent a break-in. She became very frightened and concerned over her personal safety. Her severe post-traumatic stress reactions included flashbacks and nightmares of seeing her husband mortally wounded on their living room floor. She also was flooded with feelings of guilt and loss. Although her work supervisors were very supportive, she realized after 6 months that she needed to quit her job because she had difficulty functioning.

The woman received counseling twice a week for 4 months and then had sessions once a week. She also attended two different support groups. Although the counseling and support groups were very helpful, she still experienced significant feelings of guilt and fear and found it difficult to make life decisions. She missed her husband tremendously, but found it difficult to have any positive memories. Thinking of him only brought up the traumatic imagery of him lying on the living room floor and the guilt that she had let him down.

Six months after the murder, the woman was referred for EMDR treatment in addition to sessions with her regular therapist and support group meetings. The initial focus for EMDR was the image of her husband lying dead on the floor and her feeling of guilt for not going to his side. She realized, after 60 minutes, that it was all right for her to have stayed in the bedroom. She wished she had gone to his side but realized her reasons for not going were legitimate. She believed her husband would not have wanted her to place herself in jeopardy. Furthermore, the memory of her husband lying on the carpet had diminished in detail and had a more distant perspective, and the emotional intensity associated with the image had significantly diminished.

The next session occurred a week later. The gains of the first session had been maintained. She reported thinking of her husband more often and said that she was remembering more positive experiences. She greatly missed him and the relationship they had had. She now found herself, however, preoccupied with what he must have felt when he was shot and how much fear and pain he must have experienced before he died. The EMDR process started with her focusing on her image of her husband in pain and her accompanying emotions. By the end of the session, she was able to accept that his death had probably been painful and he indeed might have experienced much fear; however, the event was now in the past. Furthermore, when she thought of the fatal evening, she now had the image of him lying on the living room floor unconscious, feeling no pain, and at rest.

The same session also dealt with her feelings of guilt for not taking better precautions to prevent the break-in. Although she knew that she had taken the same precautions as others in the neighborhood, she believed that the tragedy would not have happened if she had done even more. After EMDR, she realized that she had not done anything wrong or inappropriate. She thought that she, and most people, were naive in thinking that such a tragedy could not happen to them. Her attribution of naïveté was understandable to the client, and much less distressing than the guilt she had been experiencing.

At the next session 2 weeks later, she reported having intense feelings of vulnerability and fear for her own safety. She feared she would never be able to protect herself fully from tragedy. Even while she was practicing appropriate safety measures at home and when she traveled during the day, she focused on the possibility that she was still vulnerable to attack. The EMDR process began with her focusing on her fear. At the end of the session, she realized that although she was vulnerable, she was not helpless. She determined that she was taking adequate precautions and making intelligent decisions regarding her safety and could continue to do so. A tragedy could indeed happen again, but she felt more in control knowing she could minimize the probability of an attack.

The next session was 2 weeks later. She reported that her ability to function and engage in life had greatly increased. She had now put up a large reward for her husband's murderer. Although he might never be caught, she could now say with conviction that she had done everything she could. She started looking for part-time work, made decisions to uncomplicate her life, and increased her social activity.

At the final session, 3 weeks later, she reported maintaining her improved functioning. She felt back in the flow of life. She reported that she still greatly missed her husband but now had positive memories and feelings when she thought of him. EMDR was utilized further to help her to gain access to more positive memories and feelings.

In summary, EMDR helped her process the trauma of her husband's death. Her intrusive imagery was eliminated, as were her feelings of guilt. She was no longer vicariously experiencing the pain and fear of her dying husband. She felt back in control of her life and able to make appropriate safety choices. She could now recall her husband with positive memories and feelings. She was still grieving, but her processing of the death was no longer impeded by traumatic circumstances.

The previous example illustrates how guilt stemming from grief and traumatic loss can be treated by EMDR. EMDR can also be useful in the treatment of guilt and inappropriate self-blame that often results from a critical incident. The following example illustrates the application of EMDR to a situation where the client was assuming blame for a situation beyond his control.

A railroad engineer saw a car speed up as it approached the track. He knew the driver was trying to beat the train across the intersection. He applied the emergency brakes and blew the whistle. The car kept coming, but it lost the race. The engineer made eye contact with the driver, a 17-year-old male, just before impact. The minute it took the train to stop seemed an eternity to the engineer. When the train stopped he went back to the mangled car. The driver of the car was dead.

The engineer's sick time increased after the accident. When on the job he was overly cautious, slowing down if he saw any car approaching a crossing, and was also more irritable and touchy. He had difficulty at the intersection where the accident had occurred, because the sight of it triggered negative images and feelings of guilt.

For 3 years, the engineer had intrusive imagery of the eye contact made before impact. He described this image as continually "in my face." He also had intrusive imagery of what the youth looked like after he was killed. He felt responsible for the death because, after all, he had been running the train. He thought he should have been able to do something more; if he had been going faster or slower during the trip, the timing would have been different, and he would never have encountered the youth's car.

The engineer received treatment with EMDR 3 years after the accident. The worst intrusive image, the eye contact with the driver right before impact, was the initial focal point. His negative cognition reflected his belief about being responsible for the accident: "It was my fault." The positive cognition was "I did the best I could." The major feeling associated with the incident was guilt.

During EMDR, the imagery changed as the client jumped to different parts of the experience. After the gory images of the youth's body spontaneously came up and were reprocessed, feelings of anger arose. The engineer was angry at the youth for racing the train and causing the accident. After the anger was reprocessed, the thought "There was nothing I could do" spontaneously occurred, with associated feelings of powerlessness. Targeting this thought and the associated feelings led the engineer to focus on his actions and thoughts prior to, during, and after impact. The engineer realized he had done all he could do, that he had had no control over the driver's decision.

Several changes occurred within 25 minutes of the start of EMDR. The images of the youth's face prior to impact and of the youth after the accident were smaller, more distant, and less detailed. The event no longer felt alive and in the present. The engineer no longer felt responsible for the accident. The thought "There was nothing I could do" changed to "There was nothing MORE I could do"—a statement that felt very empowering. He felt good that he had done all that he possibly could have done by blowing the whistle, putting the train into an emergency stop, and then checking to see if he could help. He knew another accident could happen in the future because he could not control another person's decision. But he felt in control of his actions and believed he would once again do what he could do to prevent an accident in the future.

Follow-up evaluations at 2 and 10 months showed that the treatment effects had been maintained. The engineer no longer experienced intrusive imagery or guilt. When he passed the crossing where the accident occurred, he remembered it as a past event that was over.

DELAYED REACTIONS

A current traumatic incident may trigger feelings associated with past unresolved traumatic events. The combined emotional impact of old and new situations may seem so overwhelming that a person's ability to deal effectively with any incident suffers. Even a person who has become symptom-free after a traumatic incident can be vulnerable to reactivation of traumatic symptoms when exposed to stimuli that are directly reminiscent of the original trauma (Hiley-Young, 1992). In terms of the Accelerated Information Processing Model, the current trauma not only can be dysfunctionally stored in the brain, but can trigger similar dysfunctional information from previous incidents associatively stored within the same neuro network. The following example illustrates that EMDR can treat the past unresolved trauma as well as the present critical incident.

A police officer responded to an accident in which had been people were killed. Two of the deceased people, who were burned, reminded the officer of two buddies killed during a covert military mission 19 years earlier. The officer, who had never dealt with the incident (and had been ordered not to talk about it), was flooded with intense memories of his combat experience as well as the accident. He sought treatment after a month of vivid nightmares; active thrashing during sleep, which woke up both the client and his wife; intrusive images and flashbacks of the combat experience; uncontrollable crying; and feelings of intense grief.

EMDR was used to deal with the memories and images of the combat experience. The initial target was the intrusive image of his buddies being killed in combat. The negative cognition associated with this image was, "I am powerless." The positive cognition was, "We tried our best." The feelings accompanying the image were fear, inadequacy, and loss. During the session he relived the combat experience moment by moment, experiencing feelings of rage, terror, guilt, and grief. At the conclusion of the session, which lasted 90 minutes, he reported feeling some relief.

After two more sessions in the next 10 days, his symptoms subsided. When he thought of the combat experience he still could see his dead comrades, but the images were distant and faded. His thoughts were now "We did our best" and "It happened and it's over." He slept normally, with only an occasional dream about the incident; crying spells ceased; and he could recall and talk about the combat experience in a controlled manner. In addition, intrusive images significantly dropped in both frequency and intensity.

The treatment effects from the reprocessing of the combat experience generalized to the recent accident. When he was asked to think of the accident, he reported that the images had significantly faded and lost their emotional intensity. (Such generalization of treatment effects to other situations associatively connected to the treated incident was first reported by Shapiro [1989a].)

Psychotherapy continued weekly for another month to deal with the officer's grief and help him work through his combat experience further. It then tapered to bimonthly sessions for another 2 months. A follow-up session a year later showed treatment gains to be stable.

VICARIOUS TRAUMATIZATION THROUGH OVERIDENTIFICATION

At times, a person can identify very deeply with a traumatic incident that happens to someone else. The identification may be particularly deep if there is a significant relationship with the victim. If the victim dies, the bereaved, in identifying with the loved one and trying to understand what was experienced, can imagine horrible images so vivid that they interfere with, and prolong, the grieving process. EMDR can be helpful in dealing with these situations, as the following example illustrates.

A police officer was brutally beaten, stabbed, and left dead in the middle of the street. The widow requested, and was told, the complete circumstances of his death. Although she saw no pictures, she thereafter developed a vivid, gory image of what he must have looked like. The image was in color, with much blood. The expression on his face in the imagined image showed great suffering. This negative image continually intruded and caused her distress whenever she thought of her husband or was reminded of him, even 3 years after his death.

The focal point for EMDR was the imagined negative image of her husband. The image became distant, blurred, and smaller after about 40 minutes; when asked to think of the image, the widow saw a body in the street, but with little detail and no blood. The picture, now in black and white, was no longer of her husband and held no emotional charge. When she was asked to think of her husband, positive images immediately came to her mind. The treatment results were stable after 2 years.

The extent to which people identify with a tragedy is an important contributor to the degree of emotional trauma they experience. Many emergency personnel experience powerful emotional reactions when dealing with death, especially when children are involved (Dyregrov & Mitchell, 1992). Reactions can be particularly acute if the helper has small children and vividly imagines, "This could be my child." Such intense identification can lead to vicarious traumatization (McCann & Pearlman, 1990). EMDR can help emergency workers deal with such traumatic experiences, as the following case example illustrates.

> An emergency room nurse was part of the medical team working on a 6-month-old baby who had been badly injured in an auto accident. Despite intense, prolonged efforts on the part of the medical staff, the child died. The nurse had a 2-year-old child at home. Although she realized she had done all she could for the infant, she was plagued by images of the incident and became fearful that her own child might be killed. Consequently, she became anxious and overly protective of her child.
>
> She was referred for EMDR 2 years after the incident, because she was still very bothered by it. The worst image of the situation, the moment of the child's death, was the initial target for EMDR. After several sets of eye movements, she reported that the superimposed image of her child's face had lifted from the face of the dead child she had worked on. She had not been conscious of the superimposed image previously. The incident then seemed like a past incident, and her negative affect was greatly reduced.
>
> At a follow-up meeting 6 months later, the nurse reported that she was no longer haunted by images of the deceased patient. She noted that the death of the baby had indeed been a tragedy, but not her personal tragedy; her own family had not been involved. She now experienced a sense of emotional distance that she had not had before. Furthermore, she described that she was no longer overly protective of her child.

WHAT IS THE MEANING OF TIME IN THE RECOVERY PROCESS?

The use of EMDR invites the clinician to reexamine fundamental issues regarding the purpose of time in therapy. Conventional wisdom tells us that "time heals all wounds," yet clinical experience indicates that excessive grief often persists for decades.

According to the Accelerated Information Processing Model, recovery occurs because information is processed on a physiological level by the dynamic connection of appropriate neural networks. Clearly, because neural networks are in close proximity, the function of time for recovery becomes comparatively irrelevant in this process. However, if clinicians can come to accept that remission of PTSD effects is possible within a few sessions, they then must decide when to attempt EMDR with a client who is trying to recover from grief.

Because it has been suggested that even simple desensitization and exposure techniques may eliminate appropriate fears (Kilpatrick & Best, 1984; Kilpatrick, Veronen, & Resick, 1982), it is important to address the possibility that the EMDR client may be prevented from progressing through appropriate stages of recovery. However, clinical experience with EMDR appears to indicate that the method takes away nothing that is appropriate or healthful for the client. Thus, the client can safely be treated with EMDR upon request.

When recovery from the death of a loved one is unimpeded, an individual gradually comes to terms with the painful experience of loss and, over time, is able to think back on various aspects of shared experiences with a wide range of feelings, including an appreciation of positive times spent together. In the case of pathological grief, the application of EMDR appears to accelerate the processing of information held dysfunctionally and to allow appropriate insights and emotions to emerge. The method does not force clients through stages by neutralizing appropriate emotions or truncating individual growth. Coming to terms with the loss of a loved one or responsibility for a death in the line of duty still proceeds "organically," but without inappropriate impediments to recovery. Indeed, continued processing of information and progression through the various phases of recovery by the client may be apparent following a treatment session. Therefore, clinicians need not judge how long a client should suffer before attempting EMDR, but can feel free to apply it without restricting the manner in which relief may be subjectively achieved. Allowing the interaction of client and method to dictate the necessary time parameters can remove an inappropriate burden of responsibility from the clinician. This point is especially important, because no clinical model can definitively predict the appropriate recovery time for any individual client—nor can a clinician fully appreciate the depth of pain experienced by a client who is requesting relief.

Three weeks after his wife died from cancer, a husband and his 11-year-old son requested intervention. The couple had enjoyed a good relationship, except for a very stormy few months prior to the birth of their child when the husband had decided to leave the relationship. He felt very guilty for this decision and for his treatment of his wife during that period. After an EMDR session, the stormy period of time felt much farther in the past. With the strong realization that things had worked out, he felt in touch with the pleasant times of their marriage. Over the next year he continued to grieve for his wife, but without self-recrimination or guilt.

The 11-year-old son had felt sad and guilty that he had not told his mother he loved her before she died. He had visited her at the hospital daily and said at the end of each visit, "I'll be back tomorrow." When the day had come that he could not visit her tomorrow, he felt sad that he had not told her he loved her. With EMDR, he spontaneously realized, "Every time I said I'd be back tomorrow, I was telling her I loved her, and she knew it."

In this scenario, both the father and son had experienced significant loss, and both felt encumbered by their separate issues. EMDR enabled each to arrive at his own unique and appropriate resolution. EMDR removed the pathological elements while the father and son retained what was useful and meaningful, allowing relief to be attained after only 3 weeks. They continued to grieve over time, but they were now on an unimpeded path to recovery.

CONCLUSION

EMDR is a useful therapeutic method that facilitates the working through of dysfunctionally held information. Traumatic memories, with associated images, thoughts, feelings, and physical sensations, can be processed relatively quickly through EMDR compared with traditional methods of psychotherapy. In addition, there is a high level of generated insight and incorporation of adaptive behaviors. In essence, accelerated information processing can be defined as accelerated learning.

It must be emphasized that EMDR does not work in a vacuum. It is a highly interactive method, demanding a high level of clinical skill and sensitivity, and it must be tailored to each individual client. Integrated in one's therapeutic framework, EMDR enhances therapeutic skills. The clinical method, however, demands a redefinition of the role of the therapist. Instead of attempting to dictate the form or substance of a positive treatment effect, the therapist uses EMDR to set in motion clients' own processing resources and allows them to determine the direction and the speed of approach to their own mental health.

REFERENCES

Carlson, J. G., Chemtob, C. M., Rusnak, K., & Hedlund, N. L. (1996). Treatment of combat PTSD. *Psychotherapy, 33,* 104–113.

Chemtob, C., Roitblat, H., Hamada, R., Carlson, J., & Twentyman, C. (1989). A cognitive action theory of post-traumatic stress disorder. *Journal of Anxiety Disorders, 2,* 253–275.

Cocco, N., & Sharpe, L. (1993). An auditory variant of eye movement desensitization in a case of childhood posttraumatic stress disorder. *Journal of Behavior Therapy and Experimental Psychiatry, 24,* 373–377.

Cohn, L. (1993). Art psychotherapy and the new eye treatment desensitization and reprocessing (EMD/R), an integrated approach. In E. Dishup (Ed.), *California art therapy trends.* Chicago: Magnolia Street.

Dyregrov, A., & Mitchell, J. T. (1992). Work with traumatized children—psychological effects and coping strategies. *Journal of Traumatic Stress, 5,* 5–17.

Foa, E. B., & Kozak, M. J. (1986). Emotional processing of fear: Exposure to corrective information. *Psychological Bulletin, 99,* 20–35.

Forbes, D., Creamer, M., & Rycroft, P. (1994). Eye movement desensitization and reprocessing in posttraumatic stress disorder: A pilot study using assessment measures. *Journal of Behavior Therapy and Experimental Psychiatry, 25,* 113–120.

Goldfried, M. R. (1980). Toward the delineation of therapeutic change principles. *American Psychologist, 35,* 991–999.

Goldstein, A., & Feske, U. (1994). Eye movement desensitization and reprocessing for panic disorder: A case series. *Journal of Anxiety Disorders, 8,* 351–362.

Grainger, R. K., Levin, C., Allen-Byrd, L., & Fulcher, G. (1994, August). *Treatment project to evaluate the efficacy of eye movement desensitization and reprocessing (EMDR) for survivors of a recent disaster.* Paper presented at the 102nd annual meeting of the American Psychological Association, Los Angeles, CA.

Greenwald, R. (1994). Applying eye movement desensitization and reprocessing (EMDR) to the treatment of traumatized children: Five case studies. *Anxiety Disorders Practice Journal, 1,* 83–97.

Herman, J. L. (1992). *Trauma and recovery.* New York: Basic Books.

Hiley-Young, B. (1992). Trauma reactivation assessment and treatment: Integrated case example. *Journal of Traumatic Stress, 5,* 545–555.

Horowitz, M. J. (1976). *Stress response syndromes.* New York: Jason Aronson.

Janoff-Bulman, R. (1992). *Shattered assumptions.* New York: Free Press.

Kilpatrick, D. G., & Best, C. L. (1984) Some cautionary remarks on treating sexual assault victims with implosion. *Behavior Therapy, 15,* 421–523.

Kilpatrick, D. G., Veronen, L. J., & Resick, P. A. (1982). Psychological sequelae to rape: Assessment and treatment strategies. In D. M. Doleys & R. L. Meredith (Eds.), *Behavioral medicine: Assessment and treatment strategies.* New York: Plenum.

Kleinknecht, R. (1992). Treatment of post-traumatic stress disorder with eye movement desensitization and reprocessing. *Journal of Behavior Therapy and Experimental Psychiatry, 23,* 43–50.

Kleinknecht, R. (1993). Rapid treatment of blood and injection phobias with eye movement desensitization. *Journal of Behavioral Therapy and Experimental Psychiatry, 23,* 43–50.

Levin, C., Grainger, R. K., Allen-Byrd, K., & Fulcher, G. (1994, August). *Efficacy of eye movement desensitization and reprocessing (EMDR) for survivors of Hurricane Andrew: A comparative study.* Paper presented at the 102nd annual meeting of the American Psychological Association, Los Angeles, CA.

Lipke, H. (1992). *Preliminary survey results of 1200 EMDR-trained clinicians.* Paper presented at the annual meeting of the International Society for Traumatic Stress Studies, Los Angeles, CA.

Lipke, H. J., & Botkin, A. L. (1992). Brief case studies of eye movement desensitization and reprocessing (EMD/R) with chronic post-traumatic stress disorder. *Psychotherapy, 29,* 591–595.

Litz, B. T., & Keane, T. (1989). Information processing in anxiety disorders: Applications to the understanding of post-traumatic stress disorder. *Clinical Psychology Review, 9,* 243–257.

Marquis, J. N. (1991). A report on seventy-eight cases treated by eye movement desensitization. *Journal of Behavior Therapy and Experimental Psychiatry, 22,* 187–192.

McCann, D. L. (1992). Post-traumatic stress disorder due to devastating burns overcome by a single session of eye movement desensitization. *Journal of Behavior Therapy and Experimental Psychiatry, 23,* 319–323.

McCann, D. L., & Pearlman, L. A. (1990). Vicarious traumatization: A framework for understanding the psychological effects of working with victims. *Journal of Traumatic Stress, 3,* 131–150.

Norcross, J. C. (Ed.). (1986). *Handbook of eclectic psychotherapy.* New York: Brunner/Mazel.

Pellicer, X. (1993). Eye movement desensitization treatment of a child's nightmares: A case report. *Journal of Behavior Therapy and Experimental Psychiatry, 24,* 73–75.

Puk, G. (1991). Treating traumatic memories: A case report on the eye movement desensitization procedure. *Journal of Behavior Therapy and Experimental Psychiatry, 22,* 149–151.

Renfrey, G., & Spates, C. R. (1994). Eye movement desensitization and reprocessing: A partial dismantling procedure. *Journal of Behavior Therapy and Experimental Psychiatry, 25,* 231–239.

Shapiro, F. (1989). Efficacy of the eye movement desensitization procedure in the treatment of traumatic memories. *Journal of Traumatic Stress, 2,* 199–223.

Shapiro, F. (1991). Eye movement desensitization and reprocessing procedure: From EMD to EMD/R—a new treatment model for anxiety and related traumata. *The Behavior Therapist, 12,* 133–135.

Shapiro, F. (1992). Stray thoughts. *EMDR Network Newsletter, 2,* 1–2.

Shapiro, F. (1993). Commentary: The status of EMDR in 1992. *Journal of Traumatic Stress, 6,* 417–421.

Shapiro, F. (1994). EMDR: In the eye of a paradigm shift. *The Behavior Therapist, 17,* 153–157.

Shapiro, F. (1995). Eye movement desensitization and reprocessing: Basic principles, protocols and procedures. New York: Guilford Press.

Shapiro, F., & Solomon, R. M. (1995). Eye movement desensitization and reprocessing: Neuro-cognitive information processing. In G. Everly & J. Mitchell (Eds.), *Critical incident stress management* (pp. 216–237). Ellicott City, MD: Chevron Publishing.

Shapiro, F., Vogelmann-Sine, S., & Sine, L. (1994). Eye movement desensitization and repro-cessing: Treating trauma and substance abuse. *Journal of Psychoactive Drugs, 26,* 379–391.

Silver, S. M., Brooks, A., & Obenchain, J. (1995, January). Eye movement desensitization and reprocessing treatment of Vietnam war veterans with PTSD: Comparative effects with bio-feedback and relaxation training. *Journal of Traumatic Stress, 8,* 337–342.

Solomon, R. M., & Kaufman, T. E. (1994, March). *Eye movement desensitization and reprocess-ing: An effective addition to critical incident treatment protocols.* Paper presented at the 14th annual meeting of the Anxiety Disorders Association of America, Santa Monica, CA.

Spector, C., & Huthwaite, M. (1993). Eye-movement desensitization to overcome post-traumatic stress disorder. *British Journal of Psychiatry, 163,* 106–108.

Thomas R., & Gafner, G. (1993). PTSD in an elderly male: Treatment with eye movement desensitization and reprocessing (EMDR). *Clinical Gerontologist, 14,* 57–79.

van der Kolk, B. A. (1994). The body keeps the score: Memory and the evolving psychobiology of posttraumatic stress. *Harvard Review of Psychiatry, 1,* 253–265.

van der Kolk, B. A., & Kadish, W. (1987). Amnesia, dissociation, and the return of the repressed. In B. A. van der Kolk (Ed.), *Psychological trauma* (pp. 173–193). Washington, DC: Ameri-can Psychiatric Press.

Vaughan, K., Armstrong, M. F., Gold, R., O'Connor, N., Jenneke, W., & Tarrier, N. (1994). A trial of eye movement desensitization and reprocessing compared to image habituation training and applied muscle relaxation post-traumatic stress disorder. *Journal of Behavior Therapy and Experimental Psychiatry, 25,* 283–291.

Wernick, U. (1993). The role of the traumatic component in the etiology of sexual dysfunctions and its treatment with eye movement desensitization procedure. *Journal of Sex Education and Therapy, 19,* 212–222.

Wilson, S. A., Becker, L. A., & Tinker, R. H. (1995). Eye movement desensitization and repro-cessing (EMDR) treatment for psychologically traumatized individuals. *Journal of Counsel-ing and Clinical Psychology, 63,* 928–937.

Wilson, D., Covi, W., Foster, S., & Silver, S. M. (1995, May). *Eye movement desensitization and reprocessing and ANS correlates in the treatment of PTSD.* Paper presented at the 148th annual meeting of the American Psychiatric Association, Miami, FL.

Wolpe, J., & Abrams, J. (1991). Post-traumatic stress disorder overcome by eye movement desen-sitization: A case report. *Journal of Behavior Therapy and Experimental Psychiatry, 22,* 39–43.

Chapter 12

Thought Field Therapy: Aiding the Bereavement Process

Roger J. Callahan and Joanne Callahan

This chapter describes a relatively new therapeutic method called Thought Field Therapy (TFT). Using this method with or without a comprehensive treatment plan can significantly accelerate the bereavement process by dramatically decreasing a client's emotional suffering.

Recovery from the death of a close friend or loved one involves more than emotional pain; it involves regrets about lost opportunities—past, present, and future. TFT enables the bereaved client to recover faster by focusing on and eliminating the emotional suffering associated with the loss, including the additional issues of guilt and anger. Although the memories remain, the pain is greatly reduced or eliminated altogether.

All therapy is based, either implicitly or explicitly, on some sort of philosophy; and it is important for therapists to state their positions explicitly. It is recognized that professionals may differ in their points of view. The present authors believe that it is beneficial to reduce human suffering.

The ability to reduce suffering and pain allows the therapist a choice, thereby admitting value judgment into the treatment domain. If there were no methods available to reduce the acute pain of personal loss there would be no choice in the matter, but the newer therapies investigated in Figley and Carbonell's (1994, 1995) research appear to introduce the choice of whether to remove the psychological pain in bereavement (or other traumas). Differing points of view, of course, deserve a hearing.

The painful emotions entailed in the loss of a loved one are considered quite normal and appropriate. The present authors consider bereavement to be a specific type of post-traumatic stress disorder (PTSD). All forms of PTSD result in disturbed emotions, which differ significantly from the emotions in what are seen as psychological problems, where the keynote is that the negative emotion is considered inappropriate, even by the client. The emotions involved in PTSD, including bereavement, are considered normal and quite appropriate to the traumatic situation or loss.

TFT AND OTHER THERAPIES

If a therapist of any school of psychotherapy would like to help a client reduce the suffering of bereavement, the choice of TFT, although unusual, is not likely to interfere with the goals of any other therapy in use. The treatment is targeted for specific problems and gives immediate therapeutic power to the therapist, who may have many other goals. On the other hand, if the therapist would like to increase therapeutic power for a larger number of problems, the therapy provides algorithms for many of these problems.

TFT: AN ORIENTATION

New discoveries require new concepts to describe the newly uncovered facts. Some of the major concepts of TFT are thought field, perturbation, psychological reversal, and apex problem.

Thought Field

What is a thought? It is so commonplace that it is difficult to define. In TFT, a *thought* refers to a delimited domain of consideration and focus. For example, a client may be thinking about a football domain when it pops into his awareness that his father loved football. This change of thought can transform the client from a calm and quiet state to one of pain over the absence of his father.

The concept of a field, common to psychology today, was first introduced in the last century by Michael Faraday, a self-educated and brilliant creative scientist. The field concept has become commonplace and quite useful and has been extended to many of the sciences. Embryologists such as Conrad H. Waddington imagined a field surrounding an embryo and posited the existence of a chreode (necessary path) in that field to account for time and the pathways of specific morphology. British biologist Rupert Sheldrake defined *field* (1989, p. 367) as "a region of physical influence. Fields interrelate and interconnect matter and energy within their realm of influence. Fields are not a form of matter; rather matter is energy bound within fields. In current physics, several kinds of fundamental fields are recognized: the gravitational and electromagnetic fields and the matter fields of quantum physics." Sheldrake added that fields carry information and have memory. He referred to "psychological fields"; the term *thought field* is more compatible and precisely related to the procedures developed for TFT.

The concept of field has been used in various psychological approaches.

Practitioners of gestalt psychology (not to be confused with Gestalt Therapy) such as Kohler introduced the field notion as a perceptual field; this field was presumed to be subject to certain predisposing "gestalt" forces that influenced perception. Kurt Lewin used the field concept to portray and represent social forces, and Carl Rogers, Donald Snygg, and Arthur W. Combs used the concept of "phenomenal field" to indicate the aspect of consciousness that interested them. Snygg and Combs were fond of stating that "all behavior, without exception, is due to the phenomenal field of the behaving individual." Snygg and Combs were advocates of the Rogerian or "client-centered" type of psychotherapy and believed that the phenomenal field was fundamental to understanding human behavior.

Clinical psychologists are interested in thought fields—specifically, thought fields that generate negative or disturbing emotions. Webster's *New Collegiate Dictionary* includes a definition of field that seems applicable to this use: "a complex of forces that serve as causative agents in human behavior." Thought fields may be intrusive and automatically present, especially in cases of recent bereavement, or they may not be consciously present but become present when a client "tunes" or thinks about the situation that has generated his or her disturbance.

Perturbation

Because the same thought field that is tuned before therapy with great upset can be tuned without upset after successful therapy, it is logical to assume that there is something different about the thought field after therapy. The tuning is generated by the simple request that the client "think about the loss."

The element that is different after therapy can be called a perturbation. A *perturbation* is an isolable aspect of a disturbing thought field that contains the information and capacity for triggering negative emotions such as fear. (The dictionary definition of perturbation is simply "a cause of mental disquietude.") It is proposed that perturbations in thought fields are the fundamental cause of all negative emotions, whether warranted by a situation or not. Perturbations are the basic and fundamental source of input into the system. The relevant subsystems include the nervous system, the brain, and the hormonal system, which generates or triggers the sequence of events that leads to negative emotions. It is further proposed that negative emotions are triggered by specific perturbations in thought fields. When the perturbations are quieted by effective treatment, then the basic cause of the disturbed emotions is gone, and the rest of the system (i.e., the nervous system, hormones, brain chemicals, and cognitive system) no longer reacts in the pretherapy (disturbed and upsetting) manner.

Psychological Reversal

Psychological reversal is a most fascinating phenomenon and too complex to be described fully here; it is sufficient to note that it is a state that, when present, blocks what would otherwise be a successful treatment. The blocking effect of psychological reversal may be witnessed when treatment is given and a subject reports no improvement at all: Then the treatment for psychological reversal is given, and the same treatment that did nothing a moment before is suddenly able to work, as indicated by the subject's report. Some practitioners like to treat routinely for psychological reversal prior to beginning treatment; this procedure is not recommended, because it obscures this most important phenomenon from the serious professional. The psychological reversal state is associated with self-sabotaging attitudes and behavior, and in some cases the mere correction of psychological reversal can not only allow an effective treatment to work but can alter this self-defeating program.

A mini-psychological reversal is a reversal or block to effective treatment that has its onset during treatment and prevents treatment from being completed. The correction for mini-psychological reversal is given in the algorithm (below). If a client progresses from a 10 but gets stuck at a 4, for example, and the mini-psychological reversal correction is given, the client can usually proceed to a 1 when the algorithm is repeated after the correction.

Apex Problem

A most interesting and highly predictable reaction to the rapid changes that occur during TFT is the occurrence of the phenomenon called the *apex problem*. When treatment is dramatically successful, a client often reports the improvements accurately but then appears to have a compulsion to explain them away by claiming that he or she was distracted or stating that the treatment is some sort of placebo, suggestion, or hypnosis. Early clinical research has ruled out these factors, and those other modalities have very low success rates.

The apex phenomenon seems similar to what Gazzaniga (1985) reported with his split-brained subjects after surgery; he called it the "left brain interpreter." Similar reactions are observed in hypnosis with posthypnotic suggestions that induce amnesia for the suggestions. The subject, who seems compelled to carry out some induced act and whose behavior evidently makes no sense to him, compulsively invents (and evidently believes) "explanations" for his strange behavior. The split-brain subject never offers the possibility that perhaps his behavior is because of his or her recent surgery; the hypnotized subject does not offer his hypnosis experience as a possible cause; and the successfully treated client does not offer the therapy as the reason for his or her radically improved state of being.

This phenomenon is called the apex problem because the mind does not appear to be operating at its apex at that moment; something familiar from the past is used for explanation even though it does not fit the situation. This occurrence most definitely is the result not of a problem in intelligence but of a problem in dealing with new, unexpected, and unfamiliar material in the psychotherapy domain. As the power of TFT becomes generally known and familiar it can be expected that the apex problem will disappear; but until then the practitioner should be on the lookout for this common reaction to the treatment.

TREATMENT PROCEDURES

The TFT approach has the client focus on the emotional pain that is most disturbing to him or her in the grieving process, such as sadness or loss when recalling the deceased. The TFT therapist asks the client to attune to the targeted emotion and, while experiencing this feeling, go through a specific set of procedures that usually takes a matter of only a few minutes. Prior to and following the procedure, the therapist determines the client's Subjective Units of Distress (SUD) by telling the client, "Tune in to, or focus on, the most disturbing part of your grief. When you think of the loss, indicate the degree of distress, discomfort, or pain that you feel. Use 10 to indicate the most distress possible for you and 1 to indicate that there is no trace of upset at this time." (The present is always emphasized in treatment, because the future must remain unknown until it becomes the present. Although therapy is an implicit prediction that the treatment will hold over time; only the passage of time will tell how successful the prediction is for an individual.)

When it is close in time to a tragic event, the attuning is ever present in the client, and painful thoughts typically have an intrusive element. Thinking about the loss usually generates pain that provides a baseline from which to assess the effect of treatment. In the TFT system, the brief experience of pain is a means to an end—the rapid removal of that pain.

The procedure involves having the client tap specific points on his or her body (see Figure 12.1) while tuning in to the upsetting emotions. Some of the tapping is done while simultaneously performing certain activities, such as directional eye movements, humming (possibly right brain activity), and counting (possibly left brain activity). The sequence of the procedures can be critical and should be followed in the prescribed fashion. The common algorithm for traumatic stress is presented below. It is possible that a particular client may feel guilt and/or anger as part of the sum of grief reactions; algorithms for each of these complications are included as well.

There are specific diagnostic procedures that have facilitated discovery of a common sequence for relief of the pain and trauma associated with bereavement, and there are three levels of treatment developed from the more complex diagnostic procedures: the algorithm or recipe level; the in-person diagnostic level, where the treatments are determined through a rather involved procedure; and the voice technology level, which is more precise and also beyond the scope of this chapter.

Algorithm for Emotional Loss

It was discovered some years ago that a simple treatment algorithm or recipe could yield a rather high level of success with a general population of bereaved

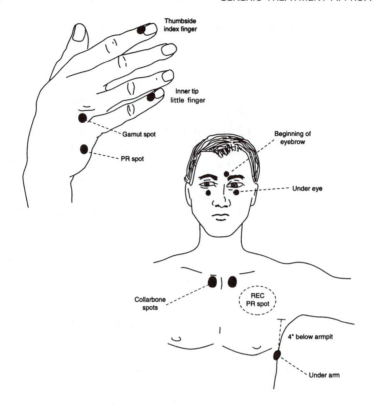

Figure 12.1 TFT treatment points.

subjects. The success rate of the algorithm runs between 80% and 90%. It is an interesting fact that most people respond well to a very simple series of treatments—which, however, were developed and finely honed over time, based on the authors' experience with bereaved subjects.

No special training is required for practitioners other than studying and carrying out the correct procedures as presented. Practitioners experiencing high failure rates may wish to study the procedures again, because high success rates are expected and commonplace. Because the treatment is a series of physical steps (while the client is attuning the appropriate thought field), video or in-person instruction is helpful. A decade and a half of practice, by many individuals using the procedure, has brought to light no harmful effects. It is important to note, however, that the tapping procedure should not be done hard enough to cause bruising or pain. Following are case studies that illustrate the use of these procedures.

A 26-year-old woman, Linda, came into the office for help with severe post-traumatic stress reactions of daily flashbacks, uncontrollable anger, and nightmares.

The intrusive imagery and anger had been triggered by the death of her father a year before. When she was a young girl, Linda's parents had divorced, and her mother and stepfather had not allowed her to communicate with her father, with whom she was very close. The stepfather sexually had molested her off and on over a 5-year period until she reached her mid-teens and was able to move out of the house.

She had gone through eclectic psychotherapy for several years in her early 20s to deal with the issues of molestation by the stepfather and anger at her mother for not doing anything about it and not allowing her to communicate with her father for all those years. This therapy had been of considerable help; she had developed an understanding of her feelings, the nightmares had decreased, and she had been able to resume her relationship with her father.

Two years later, her father got very ill and passed away. She was overcome with emotions of grief, loss, and uncontrollable anger and resentment toward her mother. The nightmares resumed, got much worse in content, and increased in frequency; and she had flashbacks of being molested two or three times a day.

Linda was referred by her therapist to TFT for specific help with the severe reactions while she continued to see the regular therapist. After taking a brief history of her problems and the past therapy, the therapist was ready to administer the TFT procedures.

Before the beginning of treatment, a careful and sensitive explanation was offered to Linda, to the effect that the loss of a loved one to death is irreplaceable and can never be compensated. The emphasis of therapy is on the effort to help the bereaved become as strong as possible in the face of the tragedy and to facilitate the wholesome survival of the family. It is vital to explain in this context that "breaking down" is normal and acceptable.

The following is from the transcript of Linda's first treatment session (verbatim):

Therapist: *Linda, first let's work on the trauma of losing your father. Think about your father's death and tell me how upset you feel on a scale of 1 to 10, 10 being the most upset possible and 1 being not upset at all.*
Client [tears streaming down her cheeks]: *10.*
Therapist: *Okay, think of your father's death and tap the beginning of your eyebrow, five solid taps. Now tap under your eye five taps, that's right. Now tap under your arm, directly below the arm pit, about 4 inches. Good, now tap the collarbone spot five times, either spot—it doesn't matter which side. Now, think about your father's death, and on that 1 to 10 scale how much upset do feel right now?*
Client: *It's less, maybe a 6.*
Therapist: *Good. Now we are going to do the nine gamut treatments. I will lead you through them today, but I want you to learn them so you can do them from memory. I want you to tap the gamut spot on the back of your hand—it doesn't matter which hand—use whichever is most comfortable. While you keep tapping, I will lead you through the nine gamut treatments. Okay, start tapping and keep your eyes open. Keep tapping and close your eyes, thinking about your father's death. Open your eyes and point them down and to the left, now down and to the right. Keep tapping; now whirl your eyes around in a circle. Okay, now whirl them in the*

opposite direction. Keep tapping and hum any tune—we believe this activates the right brain. Now count to five—this activates the left brain—and hum again. Now when you think of your father's death, how would you rate your upset?

Client: It's gone down a little more, probably a 4.

Therapist: *Good. Now we will repeat the sequence that we did in the beginning. Focus on your father's death and tap the beginning of your eyebrow, then under your eye, under your arm, and the collarbone spot. Where is your upset now?*

Client: Well, I don't feel the pain right now, but I feel really angry about all those years I missed with him.

Therapist: *On a scale of 1 to 10, how high is that anger?*

Client: An 8½.

Therapist: *Focus on that anger and tap the inner tip of your little finger. While you tap I want you to say, "I accept and forgive them for what they did."*

Client: But I don't.

Therapist: *That's okay, I understand how you feel, but you don't have to believe it; just say it three times while you tap the inner tip of the little finger.*

Client: All right. [Begins tapping and saying the affirmation.]

Therapist*: Now tap the collarbone spot. Okay, now focus on that anger, and how high is it now?*

Client [hesitating]*: About a 5.*

Therapist: *Now let's do the nine gamut treatments again. I'll help you. Start tapping the gamut spot on your hand. Eyes open, eyes closed, down left, down right, hum, count, and hum. Good, now where is your anger?*

Client: Well, it's the same.

Therapist: *Still a 5?*

Client: Yes.

Therapist: *Okay, let's correct your mini-psychological reversal.* [See below.] *Tap the side of your hand, on that fleshy part, where you would do a karate chop. While you tap that spot, say three times, "I accept myself, even though I still have some of this anger."*

[Client taps and says affirmation.]

Therapist: *Okay, repeat the nine gamuts.*

Client: I can do them this time.

Therapist: *Good. Now where is your anger?*

Client: 3.

Therapist: *Great, now let's repeat the sequence. Tap the inner tip of your little finger and say, three times, "I accept and forgive them." Where is your anger now?*

Client [complying]: Well, right now it's a 1.

Therapist: *Wonderful. You reported that you were having frequent nightmares about being molested. I want you to think of the worst situation or the nightmare that stands out in your memory the most. When you think of that incident or nightmare, how much upset do you feel right now, at this moment?*

Client: Oh, at least a 10.

Therapist: *Think of that incident and tap the beginning of your eyebrow, under your eye, under your arm, collarbone, inner tip of the little finger, and collarbone* [said slowly enough to allow the client to do them]. *All right, now where is that upset when you think of that incident?*

Client: *About a 7.*

Therapist: *Now, go ahead and do the nine gamut treatments. Do you need help with them?*

Client [complying]: *No, I remember them.*

Therapist: *Where is the upset now when you focus on that incident?*

Client: *Maybe a 5.*

Therapist: *Good. Now let's repeat the beginning sequence. Tap the beginning of the eyebrow, under the eye, under the arm, collarbone spot, inner tip of the little finger, collarbone. Now, is there any remaining upset when you think of the worst incident?*

Client: *Not right now!*

Therapist: *Great. When you go home, if any of the upset returns about any of these issues, go ahead and do the last sequence [algorithm] we just did. If it doesn't remove all traces of upset right away, please call us immediately. All relationship issues are multifaceted, so there could be more that needs to be addressed. How do you feel right now?*

Client: *I feel very calm and relaxed right now.*

Therapist: *Good. Is there anything else you would like to work on right now?*

Client: *I can't think of anything.*

Therapist: *Okay. I would like to work with you in 3 days. But, remember if the upset or pain returns or you have any flashbacks or nightmares before then, try the sequence you know, and if that doesn't bring you to a 1, call us right away.*

Three days later, Linda reported that the flashbacks had stopped completely and she hadn't had any nightmares or anger episodes either. She had used the sequence only twice, when she had to deal with her siblings regarding her father's estate (she was executor), and it had quickly relieved the distress each time.

Pleased with the progress thus far, she asked if she could work on some other problems regarding her daughter and stepdaughter. She responded well on all issues. After a year, the severe grief reactions had not returned and she continued to use the sequences she was given for stress and anger relative to her daughter and stepdaughter as needed.

Treatment for Anxiety Complicated with Bereavement

The previous case study showed the use of the relatively simple algorithm for traumatic loss. The following example demonstrates the use of the somewhat more complex, but still quick and efficacious, treatment for difficulties with chronic anxiety.

Margaret, a married woman in her late 20s, contacted a therapist for help with severe and chronic anxiety. She had young children, and the anxiety was seriously interfering with her life. It was becoming impossible for her to take the children anywhere by herself. She stipulated that she wanted help with the anxiety but could not and would not discuss the death of her mother 7 years previously, which was the most shattering experience she had ever had.

Previous therapy had told her that the death of her mother was the cause of her anxiety problems and put her through many months of "inner child" emoting work and reliving the traumatic experience. She nonetheless continued to have regular nightmares of her mother dying, and they had increased recently. She believed that the past therapy had only made her anxiety worse and made the new therapist promise not to bring up that issue; she simply could not take any more suffering.

TFT is quite effective in the treatment of anxiety and past trauma without the need for talking or painful emoting and reliving, so the therapist thought Margaret could be helped in spite of the restriction she had placed on her therapy.

Several sessions produced a significant decrease in her overall and chronic anxiety level. The procedures used in these sequences were not algorithms but precise sequences determined by individual diagnosis; anxiety disorder treatments are more complex than the algorithm for phobias.

After her chronic anxiety had been lessened, work could begin on the specific phobias relative to her daily life with the children and their needs. Most of these problems responded quickly to the common algorithm for phobias. The positive results and ease with which they were attained prompted Margaret to reconsider her initial concerns and ask if it were possible to help her with the past trauma of her mother's death also, without her having to talk about it. The therapist told her that it was possible without her having to suffer unduly.

The therapist began the session by asking Margaret to focus on her mother's death in general without having to talk about it or think of anything specific. She immediately went to a 10, so the therapist asked her to tap the beginning of her eyebrow five solid taps. She was then told her to tap under her eye, under her arm, and the collarbone spot. She did so, and in less than a minute the pain was reduced to a 7. The therapist asked her to do the nine gamut treatments and repeat the sequence (eyebrow, eye, arm, collarbone), and she did. In another minute, these procedures had brought her pain to a 4. Because there was still some upset remaining, the therapist checked for a mini-psychological reversal; there was none.

Previous sessions had revealed some anger and guilt associated with Margaret's past, so the therapist led her through the algorithms for anger and guilt while thinking of her mother's death. First focusing on the anger, the therapist told her to tap the inner tip of her little finger, then the collarbone spot. Next, focusing on the guilt, the therapist asked Margaret to tap the thumb side of her index finger tip and then the collarbone spot. After doing the nine gamut treatments, she reported that she was now at a 2 in her upset. She was asked to repeat the beginning sequence— inner tip of the little finger, collarbone, index finger, collarbone—and then to rate her upset. She said she was at a 1 and began to laugh, saying "I don't believe it. To think of all that suffering I went through!"

At that point, the therapist suggested that they stop and perhaps address more aspects of the problem during the next session. The therapist explained that relationships are multifaceted and that there might be more pain associated with the trauma—but that they should be able to eliminate all of it without any emoting or reliving.

During the next several sessions, as they continued work on her anxiety, Margaret was able to bring up certain past traumatic events associated with her mother and her mother's death. Each traumatic memory responded quickly to the algorithms given above. More than 2 years after she initially addressed her mother's death, none of Margaret's symptoms or pain had recurred. Her nightmares had not returned.

Treatment of PTSD and Intense Regret

The following case illustrates how TFT can treat the extreme emotional symptoms of guilt and rational regret without removing the cognitions associated with those feelings.

A 35-year-old single woman, a journalist, Nancy, was referred to a therapist by another client of the therapist because she was suffering from overwhelming guilt, regret, depression, anger, and sleeplessness after an abortion 6 months previously and had not been able to "move past" the event. She loved her career, but her posttraumatic stress reactions were seriously affecting her performance on the job.

Nancy had been seeing a therapist for 5 months but was still experiencing overwhelming emotions and sleeplessness. She would suddenly just break down in tears at work, and was worried that these emotional outbursts would jeopardize her career. When the therapist's other client suggested that she try TFT to help eliminate the negative emotions, she felt very skeptical but agreed to give it a try.

She had been raised Catholic and had considered keeping the baby; but, after weighing all of the pros and cons, including the fact that the father of the baby did not want her to keep it, she had finally decided to have an abortion. The abortion procedure had been uneventful and not itself a trauma, but aggravated by her upbringing, the guilt of taking a life, and the regret of not having the baby at her age, her distress was overwhelming.

Regret as well as rational guilt can remain intact without the obsessive and disruptive emotional qualities present in cases such as Nancy's. The intrusive emotions can be lessened without harm to their rational bases in a client's thoughts.

Nancy was asked to think about the abortion and to rate her upset on a scale of 1 to 10. Sobbing, she said that she felt extreme regret and was concerned that maybe she had done the wrong thing. She said she was at a 10.

She was told her to tap the beginning of her eyebrow, under her eye, under her arm, and the collarbone. When asked her to rate her upset again, she said that she felt better, at a 7. She was then led through the nine gamut treatments and asked her to rate her regret at this point. (Regret itself is not an emotion but was the term by which Nancy understood her intense emotional upset.) She said she was at a 5, so the sequence was repeated: eyebrow, under eye, under arm, and collarbone. Nancy was again told to focus on the abortion and her regret, and state where she was now. She said that it was hard to tell, maybe a 2. She was led through a floor-to-ceiling eye roll while tapping the gamut spot, then asked to focus on the abortion and see if there was any regret left. She said no, no regret but maybe a little bit of guilt.

When asked to rate her guilt, she said it was probably at a 4. She was led through the algorithm for guilt—index finger, collarbone, nine gamut treatments, index finger, collarbone—after which she said her guilt was gone.

She said that sometimes she felt really depressed and angry about the abortion, but did not feel any guilt right then. It was explained that often the gains made in this therapy hold up forever, but if the depression, anger, guilt, or regret returned, she should call for an appointment right away.

In her next session, a week later, she reported that the overwhelming emotions associated with "regret" and guilt had not returned and that neither depression nor anger had come up, either. She then wanted help with general stress at work. She was under a deadline and thought that if she could eliminate her stressed feelings it would be healthier for her. She thought that she got sick more than normal and had a fear of getting of ill. The phobia algorithm was used for her fear of getting sick, and she was given a general sequence to use at work for the stress. She was told to call the therapist immediately if at any time these sequences did not work for her right away.

After a year of follow-up, the post-traumatic stress reactions had not returned, and Nancy was having success in reducing and eliminating work-related stress. She reported having fewer colds that year than she could remember in any previous year.

Treatment for Recent Bereavement

The following example shows how TFT can be effective for intense bereavement, even as soon as a few days after the loss.

A single woman in her 30s, Jenny originally contacted a therapist because she was having sleeping problems. She would wake up in the middle of the night and not be able to go back to sleep. As was standard practice, the therapist sent her a client information package that included a description of TFT, drawings, explanations of some of the more common complex procedures, and an introductory video tape. In turn, she sent a written client history.

At the time of her first appointment she called to ask if she could reschedule for another day. She did not sound good, so the therapist asked her if there was something wrong. She burst into tears and said that her best friend had been killed in an automobile accident the day before and she did not feel able to do anything. The therapist agreed to reschedule an appointment for her sleep problem but stated that it might be beneficial to try TFT to help her with her pain and sadness at losing her friend. She agreed.

Jenny had spent much time with her close friend, both at work and at leisure. The impact of the loss was so intense that she could not go to work and even was unable to leave her house.

As the therapist had suggested, TFT was used to deal with Jenny's overwhelming pain and grief before it was applied to her sleep disturbances.

When, at her first session, Jenny was asked her to quantify her grief on a scale of 1 to 10, she said she was at an 11, sobbing that the dead woman had been her closest friend for the past 15 years. She was asked to tap the beginning of her eyebrow, solidly, about five good taps, and then tap the collarbone spot about five good taps. She used her drawing and the verbal directions to locate each spot correctly. When then asked for her level of pain she said that it had eased somewhat and was at a 9. The therapist led her through the nine gamut treatments while she tapped her gamut spot. She then said that her pain had lessened even more and was probably at a 7 now.

Because she had progressed steadily after each step, indicating that there was no psychological reversal, the therapist asked Jenny to tap the beginning of her eyebrow again, five solid taps, then tap the collarbone spot five times. At this point she rated her pain and grief at about 4. This level represented a significant decrease in her pain, but the therapist thought she could perhaps be helped even more and therefore checked for the possibility of a mini-psychological reversal.

There had indeed been a mini-psychological reversal, so the therapist led her through the correction and repeated the original algorithm. Jenny now rated her pain at a 2 and mentioned that she felt sad but stronger in the face of this terrible loss. She felt as if she would be able to go to work the following day. A floor-to-ceiling eye roll treatment brought her to a 1.

Three days later, Jenny called because she was going to the funeral and the pain and anxiety level was at a 4. Also, she was feeling angry when she thought of the senseless automobile accident and the drunk driver who had caused it. Jenny was going to be delivering the eulogy and was afraid that she would not be able to complete it. Crying, of course, would be appropriate but she feared that she would not be able to continue. She rated her anger at a 6 to 7. The therapist led her through the algorithm for anger, which they were able to reduce to a 1. Then they began working on the pain and were able to reduce it to a 2. They then focused on the anxiety of delivering the eulogy; they reduced this anxiety to a 1, and Jenny said she now felt honored to be able to speak about her beloved friend.

The very next day she called, ready to begin working on her sleeping problem. This problem was easily corrected with two sessions and 8 months later had not returned. Jenny used the algorithm for trauma three or four times over the 8 months following treatment. There were a few special occasions that she and her friend had always celebrated together, and the loss was much stronger at those times.

WHY DOES IT WORK?

The precise explanation for why TFT works is still under development. However, it is clearly linked to the body's energy (acupuncture meridian) systems. Many scientists are beginning to become aware of the little known and important body energy system (Becker & Selden, 1987; Burr, 1972; Burr & Northrup, 1935; Callahan & Perry, 1991; Fischer, 1989; Ingvar, 1920; Liboff & Rinaldi, 1974; Nordenstrom, 1983; Popp, Warnke, & Koenig, 1989; Zimmerman & Roger, 1989). LEET consists of the intrabuccal emission of low levels of amplitude-modulated electromagnetic fields and constitutes a promising new therapeutic modality for central nervous system disorders.

Full explanations of how and why LEET and TFT methods work are only at the empirical level at present. However, the process is believed to be mediated by slight modifications of neurotransmitter and ion release by neurons. This speculation is supported in part by the series of studies involving the modulation of calcium and GABA release in isolated chick cerebral cortex as well as in awake, intact cat cerebral cortex by extremely low intensity and frequency amplitude-modulated radio frequency electromagnetic fields that induce tissue gradients of approximately the same amplitude as LEET in fluid around neurons (1–10 V/m) (Adey, 1989; Adey, Bawin, & Lawrence, 1982; Bawin, Kaczmarek, & Adey, 1975; Blackman et al., 1979).

LIFE AND ENERGY

When modern scientists speak of body energy, they are referring to ordinary physical or electric energy, which is a concomitant of life (see, e.g., Adey, 1989; Adey et al., 1982). TFT treatment uses the little known but quite real energy systems of the body and mind. In fact, the high efficacy of the treatment itself may be seen as a demonstration of the reality and power of these natural systems.

Humans live in a virtual sea of electric and other energy. Like fish who live in the actual sea, we are usually unaware of the constant milieu of energy. The earth itself is polarized; the commonplace pervasive electricity is evident during a violent thunderstorm. Modern physics has revealed that even in the vacuum there remains an almost incredible amount of what is called *zero-point energy*. Eminent theoretical physicist David Bohm (author of standard textbooks on relativity and quantum theory) has estimated that there is more energy in a cubic centimeter of empty space than in all the known matter in the universe (Bohm & Hiley, 1993, p. 191).

The EKG and MRI tests in medicine use the energy systems for diagnosis. Energy systems are used for diagnosis and rapid, effective treatment of psychological problems. It may be helpful to recall that the Italian Galvani discovered electricity in the leg of a frog.

Dr. Bjorn Nordenstrom (1983), a creative and well-known radiologist at the Karolinska Institute in Sweden, has written an exquisitely detailed book about his scientific investigations into the electric energy systems of the body: *Biologically Closed Electric Circuits: Clinical, Experimental, and Theoretical Evidence for an Additional Circulatory System,* published by Nordic Press.

Another good introduction of body energy is *The Body Electric: Electromagnetism and the Foundation of Life* by Robert O. Becker and Gary Selden. Dr. Becker is an orthopedic surgeon who has pioneered the scientific investigation of the body's energy system. Orthopedic surgeons are aware that broken bones do not always knit; it is a tragedy that can cause an otherwise healthy young person to lose a limb. Sometimes the placement of a battery or electric device at the site of the fracture can cause a bone to knit. It is believed that this electric stimulation may somehow regenerate or redirect the the body's natural system of healing and growth.

TFT ALGORITHMS

An algorithm is a recipe that usually works. The dictionary definition of *algorithm* is "a set of rules for solving a problem in a finite number of steps, as for finding the greatest common divisor." The TFT algorithm is an effective procedure for eliminating the perturbations or causes of the disturbing emotions. There are different algorithms for different problems. These algorithms have a high success rate (from 80% to 90%) and should reduce discomfort in clients significantly.

General Trauma Algorithm

In the case of Margaret, the TFT algorithm for treating the trauma of losing her mother was as follows:

Step 1: Determine and focus the perturbation(s) in the thought field by asking the client to think about the death and specify the SUD rating.

Step 2: Ask the client to use two fingers to tap the beginning of the eyebrow (Figure 12.1) five good taps, firm enough to put energy into the system but not hard enough to hurt or bruise.

Step 3: Ask the client to tap under the eye (Figure 12.1) about an inch below the bottom of the eyeball. Tap solidly, but not nearly enough to hurt. About five solid taps will do.

Step 4: Ask the client to tap solidly under the arm, about 4 inches directly below the armpit (Figure 12.1), five times.

Step 5: Ask the client to tap solidly on the collar bone point (Figure 12.1) five times.

Step 6: At this time, ask for a second SUD rating. If the decrease is 2 or more points, continue with step 7. If there is no change or it is only one point, correct mini-psychological reversal (see below), and repeat steps 1 through 6.

Step 7: Have the client tap the spot on the top back of the hand (Figure 12.1) or gamut spot and continue to tap while going through the nine procedures as follows (tapping about five or six times for each of the nine gamut positions):

1   Open eyes;
2   Close eyes;
3   Open eyes and point them down and to the left;
4   Point eyes down and to the right;
5   Whirl eyes around in a circle in one direction;
6   Whirl eyes around in opposite direction;
7   Hum any tune (more than one note), a few bars;
8   Count to five;
9   Hum a few bars again.

Step 8: Repeat steps 2 through 6. At this point the presenting problem typically does not bring up any trace of an upset and therefore rates a 1 on the distress scale. If this is the case, proceed to another problem, such as anger, guilt, or a phobia, or end the session. If the SUD rating has decreased but is not yet a 1, then have the client correct the mini-psychological reversal (see below) and repeat steps 1 through 8.

Floor-to-Ceiling Eye Roll

The floor-to-ceiling eye roll is typically given at the end of a successful series of treatments. The client usually reports a 1 or a 2 on the scale; this treatment serves to solidify a 1 and to bring a 2 to a 1.

Have the client tap the gamut spot on the back of the hand while the head is held rather level. (Many people want to move their head rather than their eyes.) Some deviation from the level is acceptable. Have the client turn the eyes down and rather steadily raise them all the way up. Have the client tap the gamut spot during the movement of the eyes.

Psychological Reversal Correction

Have the client tap the PR spot on the side of the hand (Figure 12.1) about midway between the wrist and the base of the little finger, on the fleshy part. Have the client say, three times, "I accept myself even though I have this problem" while tapping (and thinking of whatever the presenting problem or distress is).

Mini-Psychological Reversal Correction

Have the client tap the PR spot, as described above, and say three times, "I accept myself even though I still have some of this problem."

Anger at Death Algorithm

Step 1: Take a SUD rating.

Step 2: Have the client tap the inner tip of the little finger.

Step 3: Have the client tap the collarbone spot.

Step 4: Take a SUD rating, then either proceed with step 5 or correct psychological reversal, as in previous algorithm.

Step 5: Have the client do nine gamut treatments.

Step 6: Repeat steps 2 through 5. As in above example, SUD level should reach 1; otherwise, have the client do a mini-psychological reversal correction and repeat steps 1 through 6.

Guilt Associated with Death

For guilt associated with death, in step 2 above have the client tap the index finger (see Figure 12.1) on the tip next to the nail on the side near the thumb of the same hand. Then have the client tap the collar bone point five times, perform the nine gamut treatments, and then repeat the index finger and collar bone. If no significant changes occur, have the client correct psychological reversal or mini-psychological reversal and repeat the guilt treatment.

Effectiveness

The Florida State University Psychosocial Stress Research Program conducted a series of experiments to determine how and why TFT and three other therapies worked so well with clients complaining of symptoms of phobia and traumatic stress, including those associated with grief. The design of the study conformed to the Systematic Clinical Demonstration methodology perfected by the investigators (Figley & Carbonell, 1994).

Twelve clinical research clients agreed to participate in the TFT study, signed various release forms, and completed a series of paper-and-pencil measures (Figley & Carbonell, 1994) and a battery of biophysiological tests (heart, respiration rates, blood pressure, skin conductance, skin condition measured at baseline, following a sustained period of thinking about their presenting clinical problems) prior to and immediately following treatment. All sessions were videotaped. The clinical team for TFT was composed of the present authors.

Members of the research team debriefed the clients immediately following their treatment program. The clients were asked if the treatment had helped. If it had helped, they were asked to explain why it worked for them. All clients kept daily journals of their SUD ratings for 6 months following treatment and were called by one of the research staff each week reminding them to keep up the journals and to take a SUD rating at the time of the call. All clients returned to the clinic 6 months after treatment to be retested by means of the entire battery of paper-and-pencil and biophysiological instruments.

A detailed description of the research clients (demographic profile, presenting problems), presentation, and analysis of pre- and posttest scores on the various measures, as well as a discussion of the implications of the results for clinical practice and a new theory of traumatic stress and phobia, may be found elsewhere (Figley & Carbonell, 1995). In brief, the researchers found that clients responded quickly to the treatment with extraordinary reductions in SUD scores. Equally important, these scores appeared to remain low; there was evidence that, indeed, the presenting problems were eliminated completely.

CONCLUSION

TFT follows a methodical protocol for each specific problem. However, to determine the problem (e.g., a trauma rather than or in addition to a phobia), the therapist must follow a highly interactive procedure individualized for each client. This procedure involves a rather complex protocol of rather simple algorithms developed from a careful diagnostic procedure (Callahan & Callahan, 1996).

TFT has only recently become known as a clinically significant approach that can be incorporated in clinical practice. However, discoveries of the algorithms, the psychological reversal procedures, and the diagnostic protocol began in 1979 (Callahan, 1985).

The impressive initial findings of the Figley and Carbonell (1994, 1995) study are consistent with other less rigorous investigations and more than 10 years of clinical experience. There are, however, fundamental questions that remain in accounting for TFT's effectiveness in treating grief, anxiety, and traumatic stress associated with the death of a loved one or any source of stress: What happens in the treatment?

The senior author of the present chapter has been carrying out these types of treatments for a decade and a half, for all kinds of psychological problems in addition to grief, such as depression, phobias, addictions, chronic anger, and the like. A theory is being developed based on these experiences. The first requirement of TFT is that the client think about the problem to be treated. When a person is asked to tune in to a thought field that represents an intense problem, he or she typically becomes quite disturbed. Because the person can tune in to the same thought field after therapy and show no trace of disturbance, it seems that something is altered in the thought field during treatment.

The term for the significant and relevant entity in the thought field that creates the upset and whose absence, or more precisely subsumption, allows the reduction in negative emotion, is perturbation. Perturbation is known through its effects. It is proposed that any clinically significant therapy has its effect through the diminishing or subsumation of perturbation. It is to be hoped that this notion will be given some attention from both the positive and negative views.

TFT treatments are significant not only for their usefulness in helping clients in pain; it must be acknowledged that the treatments could not have been predicted, nor can the results be explained, by conventional psychological theories. As these treatments become more well known and their results replicated, an entirely new look at the cause and proper treatment of psychological problems will be required.

The speed and completeness of the treatments offer a new perspective on the workings of the mind and will no doubt yield new information about psychological problems. The fact that an intense psychological problem can be completely eliminated in minutes allows the study of elements of the problem and its cure as has never before been possible. Today's research has merely scratched the surface of the field of possibilities offered by these new procedures. Many new and exciting discoveries lie ahead.

REFERENCES

Adey, W. R. (1989). Electromagnetic fields, cell membrane amplification, and cancer promotion. In B. Wilson, R. Stevens, & L. Anderson (Eds.), *Extremely low frequency electromagnetic fields: The question of cancer* (pp. 211–249). Columbus, OH: Battelle Laboratories.

Adey, W. R., Bawin, S. M., & Lawrence, A. F. (1982). Effects of weak amplitude modulated microwave fields on calcium effect from awake cat cerebral cortex. *Bioelectromagnetics, 3,* 295–307.

Bawin, S. M., Kaczmarek, L. K., & Adey, W. R. (1975). Effects of modulated VHF fields on the central nervous system. *Annals of the New York Academy of Science, 247,* 74–91.

Becker, R. O., & Selden, G. (1987). *The body electric: Electromagnetism and the foundation of life.* New York: Morrow.

Blackman, C. F., Elder, J. A., Weil, C. M., Benane, S. G., Eichinger, D. C., & House, D. E. (1979). Induction of calcium ion efflux from brain tissue by radiofrequency radiation. *Radio Science, 14,* 93–98.

Bohm, D., & Hiley, B. J. (1993). *The undivided universe: An ontological interpretation of quantum theory.* New York: Routledge.

Burr, H. S. (1972). *Blueprint for immortality: The electric patterns of life.* London: Neville Spearman.

Burr, H. S., & Northrop, F. S. C. (1935). The electro-dynamic theory of life. *Quarterly Review of Biology, 10,* 322.

Callahan, R. (1985). *Five minute phobia cure.* Wilmington, DE: Enterprise.

Callahan, R., & Perry, P. (1991). *Why do I eat when I'm not hungry?* New York: Doubleday.

Callahan, R., & Callahan, J. (1996). Thought Field Therapy (TFT) and trauma: Treatment and theory. Indian Wells, CA: TFT Training Center.

Figley, C. R., & Carbonell, J. L. (1994, September). *The "Active Ingredient" project: A systematic clinical demonstration study. Toward a clinically informed methodology for investigating clinical significance.* Paper presented at the Active Ingredient Symposium, Tallahassee Memorial Regional Medical Center Psychiatric Center, Tallahassee, FL.

Figley, C. R., & Carbonell, J. L. (1995, March). *Treating PTSD: What approaches work best?* Symposium presented at the Family Therapy Networker Conference, Washington, DC.

Fischer, H. A. (1989). Photons as transmitters for intra- and inter-cellular biological and biochemical communication—The construction of a hypothesis. In F. A. Popp, U. Warnke, & H. L. Koenig (Eds.), *Electromagnetic bioinformation.* Baltimore: Urban and Schwarzenburg.

Gazzaniga, M. (1985). *Social brain.* New York: Basic Books.

Ingvar, S. (1920). Reaction of cells to galvanic current in tissue cultures. *Proceedings of the Society for Experimental Biology and Medicine, 17,* 198.

Koenig, H. L. (1989). Bioinformation—Electrophysical Aspects. In F. A. Popp, U. Warnke, & H. L. Koenig (Eds.), *Electromagnetic bioinformation.* Baltimore: Urban and Schwarzenburg.

Liboff, A. R., & Rinaldi, R. A. (Eds.). (1974). Electrically mediated mechanisms in living systems. *Annals of the New York Academy of Science, 238,* 1.

Marshall, N. (1960). ESP and memory: A physical theory. *British Journal for the Philosophy of Science, 10,* 265–286.

Nordenstrom, B. (1983). *Biologically closed electric circuits: Clinical, experimental, and theoretical evidence for an additional circulatory system.* Stockholm: Nordic.

Popp, F. A., Warnke, U., & Koenig, H. L. (Eds.). (1989). *Electromagnetic bioinformation.* Baltimore: Urban and Schwarzenburg.

Rutter, V. (1994, March/April). Oops! A very embarrassing story. *Psychology Today.*

Shapiro, F. (1993). Commentary: The status of EMDR in 1992. *Journal of Traumatic Stress, 6,* 417–421.

Shapiro, F. (in press). *Eye Movement Desensitization and Reprocessing: Basic principles, protocols and procedures.* New York: Guilford Press.

Sheldrake, R. (1989). *The presence of the past.* New York: Vintage.

Snygg, D., & Combs, A. W. (1949). *Individual behavior: A new frame of reference for psychology.* New York: Harper.

Zimmerman, J. T., & Roger, V. J. (1989). Biomagnetic fields as external evidence of electromagnetic bioinformation. In F. A. Popp, U. Warnke, & H. L. Koenig (Eds.), *Electromagnetic bioinformation.* Baltimore: Urban and Schwarzenburg.

Index

Abortion
  attachment and, 75
  survivor's guilt and, 92
  as a traumatic death event, 68, 96–97
  women traumatized by, 79
Abuse, child, 76, 173
Accelerated Information Processing Model, 235–237
Anger, 29
Anxiety, treatment by TFT, 257–258
Apex problem, 252
Arousal symptoms, 27
Assessment
  child interviews as, 145
  EMDR and, 233–234
  family interviews as, 145
  parent interviews as, 144–145
  specialized trauma interview as, 184
  Thought Field Therapy and, 226–227
  Transitional Family Therapy and, 216–217
Attachment
  behaviors in pregnancy, 71–72, 76
  to fetal child, 78–79
  grieving process and, 81–82
  psychological process of parental, 74
  role reversal in process of, 76–77
  search process and disruption in, 83–85
  timing of, 75
Avoidance, 24–27

Bereavement
  definition, 51
  family therapy and, 143–144
  process and effect of trauma and grief, 18–19

process and pregnancy loss, 81–82
psychotherapy treatment of, 202–204
symptoms in children, 19–20
traumatic death and, xvi
traumatic reexperiencing *vs.* normal
  children, 21
treatment by Thought Field Therapy, 253–254, 260–261
as a type of PTSD, 249

Children
  assessment of traumatized bereaved, 127–128
  assistance for traumatized, 164–165
  caretaker's understanding of traumatized bereaved, 128–131
  countertransference feelings, 130–131
  fantasies during traumatic event, 168
  grief groups and support system for injured school, 187–188
  grieving parent and surviving, 86–87, 115
  impact of parental grief on, 140–141
  marriage reassessment and death of, 103–104
  ongoing and long-standing trauma and, 172–177
  parent loss and bereavement symptoms in, 19–20
  parents and death of, 101
  parents' feelings *vs.,* 150
  parents' understanding of, 147
  prior life experience and traumatic response, 169–170
  reactions to death, 140, 147
  reenactment of traumatic event, 169, 171